Violence:
Diverse Populations
and Communities

Violence: Diverse Populations and Communities has been co-published simultaneously as *Journal of Multicultural Social Work*, Volume 8, Numbers 1/2 and 3/4 2000.

Violence: Diverse Populations and Communities

Diane de Anda
Rosina M. Becerra
Editors

Violence: Diverse Populations and Communities has been co-published simultaneously as *Journal of Multicultural Social Work*, Volume 8, Numbers 1/2 and 3/4 2000.

The Haworth Press, Inc.
New York • London • Oxford

Violence: Diverse Populations and Communities has been co-published simultaneously as *Journal of Multicultural Social Work*™, Volume 8, Numbers 1/2 and 3/4 2000.

The development, preparation, and publication of this work has been undertaken with great care. However, the publisher, employees, editors, and agents of The Haworth Press and all imprints of The Haworth Press, Inc., including The Haworth Medical Press® and Pharmaceutical Products Press®, are not responsible for any errors contained herein or for consequences that may ensue from use of materials or information contained in this work. Opinions expressed by the author(s) are not necessarily those of The Haworth Press, Inc.

The Haworth Press, Inc., 10 Alice Street, Binghamton, NY 13904-1580 USA

Cover design by Thomas J. Mayshock Jr.

Library of Congress Cataloging-in-Publication Data

De Anda, Diane.
    Violence: diverse populations and communities/Diane de Anda, Rosina M. Becerra, editors.
      p. cm.
    Includes bibliographical references and index.
    ISBN 0-7890-1162-X (alk. paper)–ISBN 0-7890-1163-8 (alk. paper)
    1. Violence–Cross-cultural studies. 2. Family violence–Cross-cultural studies. 3. Juvenile delinquency–Cross-cultural studies. I. Becerra, Rosina M.

HM886.D4 2000
303.6–dc21
                                                         00-044872

INDEXING & ABSTRACTING

Contributions to this publication are selectively indexed or abstracted in print, electronic, online, or CD-ROM version(s) of the reference tools and information services listed below. This list is current as of the copyright date of this publication. See the end of this section for additional notes.

- *Academic Abstracts/CD-ROM*
- *Academic Search: database of 2,000 selected academic serials, updated monthly: EBSCO Publishing*
- *Book Review Index*
- *BUBL Information Service: an Internet-based Information Service for the UK higher education community <URL:http://bubl.ac.uk/>*
- *caredata CD: the social and community care database*
- *Chicano Studies Collections*
- *CNPIEC Reference Guide: Chinese National Directory of Foreign Periodicals*
- *Criminal Justice Abstracts*
- *ERIC Clearinghouse on Rural Education & Small Schools*
- *Family Studies Database (online and CD/ROM)*
- *Family Violence & Sexual Assault Institute*
- *FINDEX www.publist.com*
- *IBZ International Bibliography of Periodical Literature*
- *Index to Periodical Articles Related to Law*
- *International Bulletin of Bibliography on Education*
- *MasterFILE: updated database from EBSCO Publishing*
- *Multicultural Education Abstracts*
- *National Clearinghouse for Bilingual Education*
- *Public Library FULLTEXT: new EBSCO product to be released*
- *Referativnyi Zhurnal (Abstracts Journal of the All-Russian Institute of Scientific and Technical Information)*

(continued)

- *Sage Public Administration Abstracts (SPAA)*

- *Social Science Source: coverage of 400 journals in the social sciences area; updated monthly; EBSCO Publishing*

- *Social Sciences Index*

- *Social Work Abstracts*

- *Sociological Abstracts (SA) www.csa.com*

- *Studies on Women Abstracts*

- *Violence and Abuse Abstracts: A Review of Current Literature on Interpersonal Violence (VAA)*

- *Vocational Search: keyword access covering 400 trade related periodicals; monthly updates; EBSCO Publishing*

Special Bibliographic Notes related to special journal issues (separates) and indexing/abstracting:

- indexing/abstracting services in this list will also cover material in any "separate" that is co-published simultaneously with Haworth's special thematic journal issue or DocuSerial. Indexing/abstracting usually covers material at the article/chapter level.
- monographic co-editions are intended for either non-subscribers or libraries which intend to purchase a second copy for their circulating collections.
- monographic co-editions are reported to all jobbers/wholesalers/approval plans. The source journal is listed as the "series" to assist the prevention of duplicate purchasing in the same manner utilized for books-in-series.
- to facilitate user/access services all indexing/abstracting services are encouraged to utilize the co-indexing entry note indicated at the bottom of the first page of each article/chapter/contribution.
- this is intended to assist a library user of any reference tool (whether print, electronic, online, or CD-ROM) to locate the monographic version if the library has purchased this version but not a subscription to the source journal.
- individual articles/chapters in any Haworth publication are also available through the Haworth Document Delivery Service (HDDS).

Violence:
Diverse Populations and Communities

CONTENTS

An Overview of *Violence: Diverse Populations
and Communities*   1

ADOLESCENTS AND VIOLENCE

War Traumas and Community Violence:
Psychological, Behavioral, and Academic Outcomes
Among Khmer Refugee Adolescents   15
S. Megan Berthold

Adolescent Violent Behavior: An Analysis Across
and Within Racial/Ethnic Groups   47
Todd Michael Franke

Gangs as Alternative Transitional Structures:
Adaptations to Racial and Social Marginality
in Los Angeles and London   71
Jewelle Taylor Gibbs

DATING VIOLENCE AND SEXUAL ASSAULT

Dating Violence Among Chinese American
and White Students: A Sociocultural Context   101
Alice G. Yick
Pauline Agbayani-Siewert

Latinas and Sexual Assault: Towards Culturally Sensitive
Assessment and Intervention   131
Georgiana Low
Kurt C. Organista

CHILD ABUSE

Exploring Child Abuse Among Vietnamese Refugees   159
Uma A. Segal

Psychological Symptoms in a Sample
   of Latino Abused Children   193
      Ferol E. Mennen

SPOUSE/PARTNER ABUSE

Understanding Chinese Battered Women in North America:
   A Review of the Literature and Practice Implications   215
      Mo-Yee Lee

Battered Immigrant Mexican Women's Perspectives
   Regarding Abuse and Help-Seeking   243
      Martina J. Acevedo

ELDER ABUSE

Tolerance of Elder Abuse and Attitudes
   Toward Third-Party Intervention
   Among African American, Korean American,
   and White Elderly   283
      Ailee Moon
      Donna Benton

Elder Mistreatment: Practice Modifications
   to Accomodate Cultural Differences   305
      Susan K. Tomita

Index   327

ABOUT THE EDITORS

Diane de Anda, PhD, is Associate Professor in the Department of Social Welfare at the UCLA School of Public Policy and Social Research. She is editor of the *Journal of Multicultural Social Work* (soon to be retitled *Journal of Ethnic and Cultural Diversity in Social Work*) as well as on the editorial boards of other scholarly journals. Dr. de Anda is the editor of *Controversial Issues in Multiculturalism* and has published numerous articles in scholarly journals on issues related to adolescent development and special problems of adolescent populations (e.g., stress and coping, violence prevention, adolescent pregnancy), particularly with Latino and multicultural youth. She has been active in community agencies and foundations focused on service to youth, is the author of a violence prevention program (*Project Peace*) in which over 10,000 youth in several school districts have participated, and the author of two books for young readers featuring Latino families: *The Ice Dove and Other Stories* and *The Immortal Rooster and Other Stories*. She received her BA in history and Secondary Teaching Credential from Mount St. Mary's College, Masters in Social Welfare (MSW) and Pupil Personnel Services Credential from the University of California at Berkeley, and PhD in Education from the University of California at Los Angeles.

Rosina M. Becerra, PhD, is Professor of Social Welfare and Policy Studies at the UCLA School of Public Policy and Social Research. Dr. Becerra has published widely on policy issues with respect to children, the elderly, and issues affecting the ethnic-minority community. She is the co-author of several books, including *Defining Child Abuse* (Free Press, 1979); *Hispanic Mental Health: Clinical Perspectives* (Grune & Stratton, 1982), and *Social Services in the Ethnic Community* (Allyn and Bacon, 1995). She has authored over 60 articles in leading professional journals. Her recent publications have focused on welfare issues addressing children, families, and immigrants. She is also a member of the editorial boards of several leading professional journals. She has a Master of Social Work (MSW) and BA in mathematics degrees. She completed her PhD at Brandeis University in Public Policy Research and has an MBA from Pepperdine University.

An Overview of *Violence: Diverse Populations and Communities*

Crosscultural comparisons of prevalence rates for various types of violence have appeared increasingly in the research literature. This narrow and limited focus, however, adds little to the understanding of similarities and differences between ethnic/cultural groups. In fact, rates alone may contribute to stereotypic and counterproductive generalizations. For research to inform policy and practice, exploration is needed of the manifestations of violence within and across different communities and populations, uncovering not only similarities and differences, but revealing within-culture perspectives regarding violent behavior that allow it to be understood within its cultural context. Moreover, the literature needs to examine the differential impact of violence across ethnic/cultural groups. The articles in this volume offer a beginning in this respect. These articles present quantitative and qualitative research and propose practice models with regard to a broad range of manifestations of violence across ethnically diverse populations. The contents of the volume are divided into two sections, those that address violence in the broader community and those that pertain to violence in the family.

Two main areas are examined with regard to *violence in the community*: (1) violence among adolescent populations, and (2) dating violence and sexual assault.

A series of recent incidents has brought adolescent violence to the forefront as an issue of concern for the general public and policymak-

[Haworth co-indexing entry note]: "An Overview of *Violence: Diverse Populations and Communities*." de Anda, Diane, and Rosina M. Becerra. Co-published simultaneously in *Journal of Multicultural Social Work* (The Haworth Press, Inc.) Vol. 8, No. 1/2, 2000, pp. 1-14; and: *Violence: Diverse Populations and Communities* (ed: Diane de Anda, and Rosina M. Becerra) The Haworth Press, Inc., 2000, pp. 1-14. Single or multiple copies of this article are available for a fee from The Haworth Document Delivery Service [1-800-342-9678, 9:00 a.m. - 5:00 p.m. (EST). E-mail address: getinfo@haworthpressinc.com].

ers alike. However, rates of adolescent violence, both in terms of perpetration and victimization, testify that it is a significant social problem beyond the occurrence of single dramatic events. Adolescents and young adults are more likely to become victims of violent crime than older persons. In 1998, about one-third of all victims of violent crime were ages 12-19 and almost half of all victims of violence were under age 25 (NCVS, 1998). Moreover, violence appears to figure differentially in the lives of adolescents across racial/ethnic groups. For example, the homicide rates for African American males are 134.6 per 100,000 and 15.6 for African American females compared to 14.4 and 5.5 per 100,000 for White males and females respectively (National Center for Health Statistics, 1992). The deaths by homicide and legal intervention for 15 to 24 year olds in 1993 were 5052 for African American youth, 1456 for White youth, and 1672 for Latino youth (despite the fact that Latino youth were one-sixth the size of the White youth population) (Monthly Vital Statistics Report, 1996).

Official rates of both violence perpetration and victimization do not capture the actual extent of adolescents' experiences with violence in the community. The data only account for perpetrators who have been apprehended and victims who have come to the attention of the authorities. Moreover, rates distinguished merely by demographic categories such as age, gender, and ethnicity contribute nothing to understanding the factors contributing to differential experiences with violence and, therefore, are relatively useless for informing decisions regarding prevention and intervention. Ethnicity, in particular, has been subject to misinterpretation as a causal factor when it has simply served as a demographic descriptor.

Self-report surveys have been employed to attempt to acquire such information from within adolescent populations themselves. For example, a study by Malik, Sorenson, and Anashensel (1997) obtained self-report information from a convenience sample of 719 adolescents representing four ethnic groups (African American, Asian American, Latino, and White) and employed three regression models to determine predictors of adolescent violence (both perpetration and victimization) beyond mere demographic variables, including ethnicity. The series of analyses demonstrated that ethnic differences in violence experiences that had indicated African American youth to have a significantly higher frequency, both as perpetrators and victims, were eliminated once extent of exposure to violence in the community and mediating factors such as substance use and personal norms were included in the model. The researchers concluded that ". . . demographic variation in perpetration and victimization are largely due to corresponding differences in exposure [to violence]" (p. 300), with African American youth experiencing the highest exposure in the study.

Although this research effort offers an important contribution to understanding the complexities that underlie ethnic differences with regard to violence in different adolescent populations, its limitations also call attention to the need for expansion of research foci and methodology to further understand the phenomenon of violence across various adolescent populations, including different ethnic groups. Expansion of this knowledge base requires both broad-based and specific population-focused research. For example, it is necessary to move beyond analyses of convenience samples to conducting large-scale surveys with representative samples across ethnic groups. At the same time, however, it is important to obtain in-depth information on adolescent populations that may form a small portion of any national sample, but demonstrate a significant at-risk profile. Finally, qualitative research also needs to be undertaken to obtain the emic perspective, allowing clearer understanding of adolescent cultures that appear from an etic perspective to be organized around violent lifestyles. These varied approaches to research are demonstrated in the first three articles.

In the concern over adolescent violence, there is a danger that in the rush to implement violence prevention programs, the complexity of the issue will not be addressed. That is, as the first three articles demonstrate, the violence experiences of adolescents are not uniform, nor are the risk factors and the motivations that drive violent behavior.

In the first article, "War Traumas and Community Violence: Psychological, Behavioral, and Academic Outcomes Among Khmer Refugee Adolescents," 144 Khmer refugee adolescents were surveyed to determine the impact of exposure to violence in their country of origin and in the United States. A high frequency of symptoms of Post-Traumatic Stress Disorder (PTSD) and clinical depression was found within this sample. Most striking, however, was the finding that these and other negative effects of exposure to violence were the result of exposure to community violence within the United States rather than their earlier war-related experiences.

In the second article, "Adolescent Violent Behavior: An Analysis Across and Within Racial/Ethnic Groups," responses from a representative sample of 6504 adolescents from the National Study of Adolescent Health provide cross-cultural data on violent behavior among youths in grades 7 through 12. Differences between youths who engaged in violent behavior and those who did not were found with respect to race/ethnicity, family cohesion, family structure, and gender. Simple causal relationships were rejected in favor of an ecological model that incorporates the interaction of familial, peer, school, and neighborhood/community factors.

The last article focused on adolescents, "Gangs as Alternative Transitional Structures: Adaptations to Racial and Social Marginality in Los Angeles and London," employs quantitative and qualitative data to demonstrate that, contrary to commonly held assumptions, violence serves a secondary and purely instrumental function in the Black youth gangs studied in both Los Angeles and London. Gangs are conceptualized as alternative social structures providing the youth with benefits that counterbalance their marginality within the society at large, including social support, increased self-esteem, and a redirection of anger and aggression.

The second area examined with respect to violence in the community involves aggression between males and females, either in a dating situation or as a victim of sexual assault. Over the past two decades, a growing body of literature has developed regarding violence in dating or during courtship among young adult and adolescent populations. Due to variations in samples, sampling procedures, methodology, and definitions of violence in the dating context, there has been wide divergence in findings, particularly with regard to prevalence rates, with some estimations over 60% (White & Koss, 1991). For example, White and Koss (1991) demonstrated in their analysis of a nationally representative sample of 4700 college students that rates varied when the type of violence was specified: 81-88% for symbolic (mainly verbal) violence versus 32-39% for physical violence. In any case, the research findings indicated that dating violence appears to be a social problem for a considerable percentage of the youth population.

Gender differences in dating violence have been examined regularly in the literature. Males and females generally demonstrate equal participation in dating violence, and in some studies females are shown to have higher frequencies of physical aggression in dating situations (Arias, Samois, & O'Leary, 1987; Malik, Sorenson, & Ana-shensel, 1997; Makepeace, 1986; White & Koss, 1991). Malik, Soren-son, and Anashensel (1997) caution, however, that higher rates among females may indicate attempts to resist sexual aggression on the part of the male. At the same time, ethnicity has received little attention in the research literature, particularly the examination of dating violence in a cultural context. Moreover, the existing research on ethnic differ-ences, including some of the research indicating lack of ethnic differ-ences, has considerable limitations. For example, Malik, Sorenson, and Anashensel's (1997) study found that ethnic differences, specifi-cally African American respondents' significantly higher rates of in-volvement in dating violence, both as a perpetrator and victim, disap-peared when exposure to violence and other mediating variables were introduced into the analysis. Use of a non-representative sample, how-ever, makes the extent to which one can generalize their findings unclear. White and Koss (1991) employed a large national sample to arrive at the same conclusion, that no differences existed among the various ethnic groups with regard to prevalence of dating violence. However, the extremely low percentages of ethnic groups (other than White) included in the analyses bring their conclusions into question as well: 86% White, 7% African American, 3% Hispanic, 3% Asian, 1% American Indian.

Parameters with regard to appropriate and acceptable behavior among dating partners, including physical and sexual aggression, are embedded in gender role expectations that are culturally bound, and, as a result, may vary across culturally diverse populations. Therefore, more important than comparative rates is research that assists in un-derstanding the cultural context, including beliefs regarding normative behavior in courtship situations and gender roles, for various ethnic populations. Little in the literature addresses the issue of dating vio-lence in this manner. This is particularly the case with respect to Asian American populations for which a few isolated studies exist (see Foo & Margolin, 1995; Tang, Critelli, & Parker, 1995). The first article in this section, "Dating Violence Among Chinese American and White Stu-dents: A Sociocultural Context," addresses this gap in the literature by examining differences in perceptions of and attitudes towards physical and sexual aggression in dating relationships between Chinese Ameri-can and White college students. A number of similarities emerged between the two samples, such as the prevalence of dating violence.

Although the majority of both White and Chinese American students did not feel that circumstances justified dating violence, Chinese American students were more likely to justify the violence in certain contexts. Moreover, for the Chinese American students, this justification appeared to be related to victimization and perpetration experiences.

Although rape is recognized as a violent act, the sexual nature of the violence continues to make it a crime that is significantly underreported and shrouded in secrecy and shame, limiting information that would be useful to rape survivors and their service providers. Estimations regarding the actual incidence of rape, therefore, have varied widely. Law enforcement agencies have estimated rates to be ten times the reported incidence (Mantak, 1995), but research using random samples has reported as high as 44% for rape and attempted rape with only an 8% reporting rate (Russell, 1982). Contributing to the reporting issue is the consistent finding that over fifty percent (53%) of rapes are committed by an acquaintance or friend and 26% by an intimate (spouse/ex-spouse or boyfriend/ex-boyfriend) with only 18% constituting rape by a stranger (Bureau of Justice, 1995). Particularly limited is information with regard to sexual assault across ethnically diverse populations, especially beyond prevalence rates to perceptions regarding sexual assault and the rape victim, the impact of the sexual assault on the rape survivor, and culturally appropriate interventions for rape survivors and their significant others. For example, Finklehor and Yllo's (1985) discussion of rape in marriage does not even address the issue of cultural differences. The few studies that have focused on crosscultural comparisons offer important, but limited, information, particularly for use by the practitioner and service provider. In Wyatt's (1985) retrospective study of a random sample of 248 women, 40% of the African American women and 51% of the White women in the sample reported sexual abuse as a child. Although the above difference did not reach statistical significance, the African American women were significantly more likely than the White women in the sample to have experienced more than one incidence of sexual abuse. Sorenson and Siegel (1992) found Hispanic respondents in their two stage cluster sample of 3000 men and women in Los Angeles to have significantly lower rates of sexual assault than their non-Hispanic White cohorts (8.1% versus 19.9%), whose lifetime prevalence rate was 2.5 times that of the Hispanic sample. No ethnic differences were found in reporting rates, which were a low of approximately 10% in each group, and in incidence of mental disorders related to the sexual assault. Although White respondents used mental health and medical services at a higher rate than the Hispanic respondents, sexually assaulted Hispanic respondents had higher utilization rates than non-assaulted Hispanic respondents, rates that approached those of the White cohort. Another finding was the within-Hispanic group difference in the rate of sexual assault, which was significantly higher for American born versus Mexican born respondents. This led the researchers to suggest that "the cultural milieu plays some role in the probability of sexual assault" (p. 100) in terms of offering protective factors that reduce risk for the immigrant group. These and other issues pertaining to sexual assault need to be further examined in a cultural context. The last article in the section on violence in the community, "Latinas and Sexual Assault: Towards Culturally Sensitive Assessment and Intervention," addresses such issues in its discussion of the impact of sexual assault on the Latina rape survivor in terms of the effects of Latino cultural values and perceptions and the dual influence of Latino and mainstream U.S. definitions of gender roles. The complex nature of the bicultural influences in the Latina's environment is recognized as contributing both positively and negatively to the rape survivor's situation, and a series of interventions and intervention guidelines are proposed that take this complexity into account.

The articles on *violence in the family* found in Volume 8(3/4) deal with issues of physical aggression among family members, specifically in reference to child abuse, spouse/partner abuse, and elder abuse.

The two child abuse articles present exploratory studies that examine the issues of accurate assessment of physical abuse and the effects of the abuse on the child's psychological functioning. Two under-researched ethnic groups are examined in these studies. A key concern whenever one examines child abuse in different cultures is the understanding of their cultural values and norms and how it may affect definitions of what constitutes abuse in the cultural context. Giovannoni and Becerra (1979), in their now classic work, show that there are differences across income groups and racial/ethnic groups in how they define child abuse. For example, there is great divergence among groups in what is defined as physical abuse and what is defined as corporal punishment. Their study suggests that differences in child-rearing practices in various cultures may affect how one determines the parameters of child abuse. The findings in the first article, "Exploring Child Abuse Among Vietnamese Refugees," also suggests that standard methods for identifying and assessing child abuse may not be valid with Vietnamese refugee populations. Inconsistencies in the parents' reports and, in particular, between parent and child appear repeatedly throughout the study. Based on these discrepancies, adaptations of methods employed by both the practitioner and the researcher exploring child abuse with this population are suggested.

Little has been written on mental health treatment of Latino children. Canino (1982) stands as one of the few authors who has specifically addressed the mental health treatment of the Latino child. In his work, he notes the importance of examining multiple levels of interaction–environmental, educational, and familial experiences–of Latino children. In the second article, "Psychological Symptoms in a Sample of Latino Abused Children," the mental health of abused Latino children is examined in contrast to a comparison group of non-abused Latino children. The analysis takes into account family and measures reflective of environment and education. The sample of abused Latino children was found to have significantly higher scores on scales measuring depression, anxiety, and dissociation, and on the total score and all subscales of the Child Behavior Checklist. However, the number of abused children whose scores indicated symptoms sufficiently deviating from the norms to identify a clinical problem varied considerably within the sample. Both the differences between the abused and non-abused samples and the variation within the abused group point to a need for further research with larger, representative samples to develop a more detailed and differentiated profile of the mental health needs of abused Latino children.

Although it is commonly recognized that differences exist among ethnically diverse populations with regard to what is and is not considered spouse/partner abuse, the comparative prevalence of this abuse, the degree of tolerance of the abuse expected of the victim, and the acceptability of intervention, the research literature documenting these differences, particularly as a basis for culturally sensitive practice, is relatively new and sparse. Moreover, the literature contains conflicting findings regarding ethnic differences and similarities in spouse/partner abuse. Several studies, including analyses of data from the National Survey of Families and Households (Sorenson, Upchurch, & Shen, 1996), indicate higher rates among non-White, especially African American samples, in contrast to White samples (Schulman, 1979; Straus & Gelles, 1986). Other studies, however, have reported similar rates for African American and White females (Wyatt, 1992) and similar rates for White and immigrant Mexican American samples, but higher rates for American born Mexican American respondents (Sorenson & Telles, 1991). In direct contrast, Straus and Smith's (1990) comparative analyses of 721 Hispanic families and 4052 non-Hispanic White families from the 1985 National Family Violence Resurvey found the rate of violence between Hispanic couples to be 54% higher than that of White couples in the survey, a rate of 23.1 per 100 couples versus 15.0, respectively. Although these rates included less severe incidents such as "pushing, slapping, shoving, or throwing things" (p. 350), the significant difference remained with regard to "severe violence" as well, 11.0 per 100 versus 5.4 per 100 couples. However, further analyses indicated that structural factors, namely "urbanicity of residence, [low] family income, and age of respondent" (p. 358) accounted for the ethnic difference that disappeared when these variables were held constant.

The one consistent finding across the literature is that male intimates are responsible for the majority of violence against women (Sorenson & Saftlas, 1994). The articles in this section seek to expand this literature by providing reviews of the literature related to specific populations (Chinese and Latina battered women), qualitative data from the women or their service providers regarding their unique experiences and the cultural factors impinging upon them, and models for culturally sensitive intervention.

The fairly recent discrediting of the myth of the model minority has resulted in scant literature on domestic problems among various Asian populations in the United States, particularly with regard to domestic violence. Prevalence rates are difficult to ascertain as many sources do not use ethnic categories that identify Asian groups. Available sources serve to indicate, however, that spousal violence may be a substantial problem in some Asian populations. For example, in Santa Clara County, California, one third of the reports of domestic violence were among Asian residents despite the fact that they comprise only 14% of the county's population (Wong, 1999).

Equally important in understanding spousal abuse in Asian communities is the need to address the diversity within the Asian population. Focus group research with women from four different Southeast Asian populations (Laotian, Khmer, Vietnamese, and Southeast Asian Chinese) found substantial differences in attitudes toward physical violence of husbands against wives, with Chinese women voicing unwillingness to tolerate physical abuse in contrast to its tolerance and acceptance as more normative by Vietnamese, Khmer, and Laotian women (Ho, 1990). In Los Angeles County, the Korean population, especially among immigrants, has the highest rate of spousal abuse among the city's Asian residents (Rhee, 1997).

An Us-Them perspective has led to a perceptual homogenizing of diverse cultural groups under the general descriptor, Asian. To develop the knowledge base with regard to spousal violence in Asian populations, research focusing on specific Asian populations must be conducted. Spousal abuse can only be understood within the specific cultural context that shapes beliefs and criteria for normative behavior. Service providers must understand this cultural context in order to design prevention, support and intervention services appropriate for each population. To this end, the article, "Understanding Chinese Battered Women in North America: A Review of the Literature and Practice Implications," offers a comprehensive review of the literature on Chinese battered women integrated with interview data from service providers in ethnic-specific programs for this population. Cultural and contextual (e.g., immigrant status) factors are noted in the detailed, three-tier model of intervention that addresses the individual, the family system, and the community. The research literature supporting the model, as well as examples of agency programs that have implemented various elements of the model, are detailed.

A broad range of theories have been employed to attempt to explain the psychological, interpersonal, and socio-cultural factors that cause, or at least foster, the occurrence of spousal/partner abuse, wife battering in particular. These most recently have included social learning theory, exchange theory, systems theory, resource theory, feminist theory, and patriarchy theory, among others (Campbell, 1992; Loue & Faust, 1998). Campbell's (1992) critical analysis of the fit and lack of fit of the various theories across a variety of world cultures very effectively demonstrates the limitations of theoretical principles to explain behavior outside of its cultural context. This is particularly important in attempting to understand the battering experiences of immigrant women whose lives are impacted by factors both in the host society and the culture of origin. One particularly under-researched group is battered Latina immigrant women, with only two published studies addressing this specific population (Kantor, Jasinski, & Aldarondo, 1994; Sorenson & Telles, 1991). These studies have provided important information on comparative prevalence rates and predictors of spousal abuse and, to some extent, attitudes and cultural beliefs regarding partner abuse. The second article in this section, "Battered Immigrant Mexican Women's Perspectives Regarding Abuse and Help-Seeking," serves to further address this gap in the literature by using data from extensive ethnographic interviews with abused Latina immigrant women to present an in-depth description of their experiences from their own perspectives and to examine the factors and dynamics they indicate through the design of a conceptual model based on social learning principles. The role of cultural factors and psychosocial stressors on the women's attitudes toward abuse and help-seeking are explored, with maternal responsibility for the welfare of the children emerging as the dominant factor determining decisions with regard to both remaining in the situation and leaving. The use of various sources of help is documented along with the women's evaluation of their effectiveness and reasons for hesitancy or non-use. Agreement and divergence from the limited research literature are noted and a theoretical model employed to explain tolerance of abuse and help-seeking behavior and to guide intervention with the population.

Attention to the vulnerability of the elderly to various forms of abuse (physical, emotional, and financial) began to be recognized in the professional literature during the 1970s (Baker, 1975; Callahan, 1988). Pillemer and Finklehor's (1988) groundbreaking study employed a stratified random sample to arrive at a prevalence rate of 32 (between 24 and 39) per 1000. Although the rate was low compared to other types of domestic abuse (e.g., child abuse), they were quick to point out that the translation of this figure into 700,000 to over 1,000,000 cases per year nationally indicated it was an important social problem to address. Beyond passing elder abuse laws and setting up protective service mechanisms, a host of issues remain regarding definitions of elder abuse, understanding factors contributing to risk for elder abuse, and prevention and intervention strategies. While academic discourse regarding definitions of elder abuse (Hugman, 1995) has been conducted and offers important clarification, obtaining information regarding definitions and perceptions of elder abuse across diverse populations is needed to inform professionals who must deal with clients rather than conceptualizations.

While integration of research on risk factors by Kosberg (1988) produced a list of factors that did not take ethnicity into account, a nine year longitudinal cohort study identified "minority" status, that is, being a member of a non-White population, as a risk factor for elder abuse, despite the acknowledgment that the finding was probably confounded with poverty (Lachs, Williams, O'Brien, Hurst, & Horwitz, 1997). Identifying race/ethnicity as a risk factor, whether accurate or not, is minimally useful in terms of social work practice. Instead, it points to the need for research that provides information regarding factors that might explain differential risk across racial/ethnic groups as well as varying manifestations of elder abuse.

Movement in this direction is provided by the article, "Tolerance of Elder Abuse and Attitudes Toward Third-Party Intervention Among African American, Korean American, and White Elderly." Cross-cultural comparisons of the views of African American, Korean, and White elderly are presented with regard to their perceptions of and attitudes towards various types of elder abuse, the causes of elder abuse, and their willingness to utilize the aid of social service agencies or the police in actual or suspected abuse. Striking differences are noted in the perceptions of the Korean elderly in contrast to those of the African American and White elderly. All three samples agreed in disapproving of blatant physical abuse; however, the Korean elderly were less likely to view other types of potential mistreatment (e.g., in regard to possible financial exploitation) as abusive and to justify the abuse under certain circumstances. The cultural differences that underlie these varied perceptions offer important implications for different models and methods of prevention and intervention.

This concept of adapting and restructuring practice models to achieve greater compatibility with the cultural context of the elderly client is the focus of the final article, "Elder Mistreatment: Practice Modifications to Accommodate Cultural Differences." The article enjoins practitioners to make major modifications in their perceptions of their roles, their objectives, and in the interventions they use, based on the cultural norms of the client. Examples include the replacement of a focus on "resolution" with an opportunity for catharsis or the creation of a power balance in the family and the employment of a variety of non-confrontational conflict management processes. The article demonstrates how the individual, family, and community can be mobilized to increase the safety of victims of elder abuse if culturally syntonic interventions are employed.

The articles in the volume offer new findings, models, and a collection and integration of the research literature available regarding various forms of violence experienced by ethnically diverse populations. However, they also serve to point out significant limitations in the literature across issues and populations. It is hoped that the issues raised in this volume will stimulate further research and systematic exploration of the impact of violence in culturally diverse communities.

REFERENCES

Arias, I., Samois, M., & O'Leary, K. D. (1987). Prevalence and correlates of physical aggression during courtship. *Journal of Interpersonal Violence, 2*, 82-90.

Baker, A. A. (1975). Granny bashing. *Modern Geriatrics, 5*(8), 20-24.

Callahan, J. J. (1988). Elder abuse: Some questions for policymakers. *The Forum, 28*(4), 453-507.

Campbell, J. C. (1992). Wife battering: Cultural contexts versus Western social sciences. In D. Ayers Counts and J. K. Brown (Eds.), *Sanctions and sanctuary: Cultural perspectives on the beating of wives* (pp. 229-249). Boulder, CO: Westview Press.

Canino, I. (1982). The Hispanic child: Treatment considerations. In R. M. Becerra, M. Karno, J. I. Escobar (Eds.), *Mental Health and Hispanic Americans: Clinical Perspectives*, New York: Grune & Stratton (Harcourt Brace Jovanovich), pp. 157-168.

Finklehor, D., and Yllo, K. (1985). *License to Rape: Sexual Abuse of Wives.* New York: Holt, Rinehart & Winston.

Giovannoni, J. E., and Becerra, R. M. (1979). *Defining Child Abuse.* New York: The Free Press.

Ho, C. K. (1990). An analysis of domestic violence in Asian American communities: A multicultural approach to counseling. *Women & Therapy, 9*(1), 129-150.

Hugman, R. (1995). The implications of the term "elder abuse" for problem definition and response in health and social welfare. *Journal of Social Policy, 24*(4), 493-507.

Kantor, G. K., Jasinski, J. L., & Aldarondo, E. (1994). Sociocultural status and incidence of marital violence in Hispanic families. *Violence and Victims, 9*(3), 207-222.

Kosberg, J. I. (1988). Preventing elder abuse: Identification of high risk factors prior to placement decisions. *The Gerontologist, 28*(1), 43-50.

Lachs, M.S., Williams, C., O'Brien, S., Hurst, L., & Horwitz, R. (1997). Risk factors for reported elder abuse and neglect: A nine-year observational cohort study. *The Gerontologist, 37*(4), 469-474.

Loue, S., & Faust, M. (1998). Intimate partner violence among immigrants. In S.

Loue (Ed.), *Handbook of Immigrant Health* (pp. 521-544). New York: Plenum Press.

Makepeace, M. (1986). Gender differences in courtship violence victimization. *Family Relations Journal of Applied Family and Child Studies, 35*, 383-388.

Malik, S., Sorenson, S., & Anashensel, C. (1997). Community and dating violence among adolescents: Perpetration and victimization. *Journal of Adolescent Health, 21*, 291-302.

Mantak, F. J. (1995). Creating an alternative framework for preventing rape: Applying Haddon's injury prevention strategies. *Journal of Public Health Policy, 16*(6), 13-28.

National Center for Health Statistics. (1996, February 29). *Monthly Vital Statistics Report, 44*(7) (Suppl.).

National Crime Victimization Survey. (1998). *Criminal Victimization in the U.S.* Washington, DC: Congressional Information Service.

Pillemer, K., & Finklehor, D. (1988). The prevalence of elder abuse: The random sample survey. *The Gerontologist, 28*(1), 51-57.

Rhee, S. (1997). Domestic violence in the Korean immigrant family. *Journal of Sociology and Social Welfare, XXIV*(1), 63-77.

Russell, D. E. (1982). The prevalence and incidence of forcible rape and attempted rape of females. *Victimology, 7*, 81-93.

Schulman, M. (1979). *A survey of spousal violence against women in Kentucky.* Washington, DC: U.S. Department of Justice, Law Enforcement Assistance Administration.

Sedlak, A. J., and Broadhurst, D. D. (1996). National incidence study of child abuse and neglect. National Center on Child Abuse and Neglect, National Clearinghouse on Child Abuse and Neglect, Washington, DC.

Sorenson, S., & Siegel, J. M. (1992). Gender, ethnicity, and sexual assault: Findings from a Los Angeles study. *Journal of Social Issues, 48*(1), 93-104.

Sorenson, S. B., & Softlas, A. F. (1994). Violence and women's health: The role of epidemiology. *Annals of Epidemiology, 126*, 1154-1164.

Sorenson, S., & Telles, C. (1991). Self-reports of spousal violence in a Mexican-American and non-Hispanic White population. *Violence and Victims, 6*(1), 3-15.

Sorenson, S., Upchurch, D. M., & Shen, H. (1996). Violence and injury in marital arguments: Risk patterns and gender differences. *American Journal of Public Health, 86*(1), 35-40.

Straus, M. A., & Gelles, R. J. (1986). Societal change and change in family violence from 1975 to 1985 as revealed by two national surveys. *Journal of Marriage and the Family, 48*, 465-479.

Straus, M. A., & Smith, C. (1990). Violence in Hispanic families in the United States: Incidence rates and structural interpretations. In M.A. Straus and R. J. Gelles (Eds.), *Physical Violence in American Families: Risk Factors and Adaptations to Violence in 8, 145 Families*, (pp. 341-367). New Brunswick, NJ: Transaction Publishers.

White, J. W., & Koss, M. P. (1991). Courtship violence: Incidence in a national sample of higher education students. *Violence and Victims, 6*(4), 247-256.

Wong, B. K. (1999). Domestic violence and Asian families. Family culture.com.

Wyatt, G. E. (1985). The sexual abuse of Afro-American and White-American women in childhood. *Child Abuse and Neglect 9*, 507-519.

War Traumas and Community Violence: Psychological, Behavioral, and Academic Outcomes Among Khmer Refugee Adolescents

S. Megan Berthold

SUMMARY. This cross-sectional survey study examined the relationship between exposure to war traumas and community violence and academic, behavioral, and psychological well-being among Khmer refugee adolescents. The 144 adolescents studied were exposed to high rates of violence. One third had symptoms indicative of PTSD and two thirds had symptoms indicative of clinical depression. The number of

S. Megan Berthold, PhD, is Senior Partner of Research Insights, Altadena, CA, 91001.

The author wishes to acknowledge the Andrew W. Mellon Foundation's Program in Immigrant Education and UCLA's Dissertation Year Fellowship for providing funding for this project. Special thanks to the Center for Language Minority Education and Research (CLMER) at California State University, Long Beach and to Drs. J. David Ramirez and Mitchell T. Maki.

[Haworth co-indexing entry note]: "War Traumas and Community Violence: Psychological, Behavioral, and Academic Outcomes Among Khmer Refugee Adolescents." Berthold, S. Megan. Co-published simultaneously in *Journal of Multicultural Social Work* (The Haworth Press, Inc.) Vol. 8, No. 1/2, 2000, pp. 15-46; and: *Violence: Diverse Populations and Communities* (ed: Diane de Anda, and Rosina M. Becerra) The Haworth Press, Inc., 2000, pp. 15-46. Single or multiple copies of this article are available for a fee from The Haworth Document Delivery Service [1-800-342-9678, 9:00 a.m. - 5:00 p.m. (EST). E-mail address: getinfo@haworthpressinc.com].

violent events they were exposed to significantly predicted their level of PTSD, personal risk behaviors, and GPA, but not their level of depression or behavior problems reported at school. Perceived social support made a difference in the lives of these youth and predicted better outcomes. The implications for research and practice are discussed. *[Article copies available for a fee from The Haworth Document Delivery Service: 1-800-342-9678. E-mail address: <getinfo@haworthpressinc.com> Website: <http://www.haworthpressinc.com>]*

KEYWORDS. Violence, Khmer, refugee, adolescents, trauma

INTRODUCTION

Since the fall of Saigon and the start of the brutal Khmer Rouge reign of Cambodia in 1975, an estimated one third of a million Khmer refugees have been resettled in the United States (U.S. Bureau of the Census, 1990). The mass violence of Pol Pot and his Khmer Rouge regime in Cambodia resulted in 1.5 to 3 million deaths or 20% to 40% of the entire population of Cambodia (Hannum, 1989; Kiljunen, 1985). Those who escaped to become refugees were often the survivors of multiple traumatic experiences, including slave labor, starvation, brainwashing, physical beatings, threatened asphyxiation, and other kinds of torture (Mollica & Jalbert, 1989). Unfortunately, the trauma did not end with the invasion of the Vietnamese in December, 1978, nor with their defeat of the Khmer Rouge. Hundreds of thousands of Khmer were forced to flee to the Thai-Cambodian border. During their escape, they faced further traumatic experiences (e.g., rapes, deaths or injury from stepping on land mines, imprisonment and torture in Thailand). While living in refugee camps, shelling, grenade and bandit attacks continued. After relocating to a new country, many faced separation from family, isolation, discrimination, stressors related to adjusting to a new country, and community violence (Berthold, 1998; Mollica et al., 1991).

The situation of Khmer refugees in the United States is but one example of refugees who have been forced to flee from war torn regions and who continue to experience ongoing violence. By the early 1990s, community violence was declared a serious public health problem (Koop & Lundberg, 1992) and an epidemic (Fitzpatrick & Boldizar, 1993) in the United States. Adolescents are one group who continue to be routinely exposed to violence and who have been exposed from a young age, making them vulnerable to developing mental health problems. Large numbers of Khmer refugee adolescents in the United States have been diagnosed as suffering from posttraumatic stress disorder (PTSD) and major depression (Berthold, 1999; Sack et al., 1994).

The purpose of this study was to explore the psychological, behavioral, and academic outcomes of exposure to war traumas and community violence among Khmer refugee adolescents. Three research questions were examined: (1) What is the level of Khmer refugee adolescents' exposure to violence and war traumas overseas and community violence in the U.S.? (2) Is lifetime exposure to violence associated with psychological, behavioral, and academic problems among Khmer refugee adolescents? and (3) Over and above the effect of exposure to violence, does the amount of social support that Khmer refugee adolescents perceive from family and friends significantly predict their level of psychological, behavioral, and academic problems?

LITERATURE REVIEW

Rates of Exposure to Violence Among Youth

Children and adolescents living in war zones have been exposed to considerable levels of violence and war traumas (Garbarino & Kostelny, 1996; Macksoud & Aber, 1996; Punamaki, 1987, cited in Garbarino & Kostelny, 1996). One study, conducted in a refugee camp (Site 2) at the Thai-Cambodian border, found that more than half of the 182 Khmer youth (aged 12-13 years old) surveyed experienced shelling or bombing, 18% stated they were close to death, 15% reported severe beatings, and 11% saw family members killed or injured (Mollica et al., 1991). Approximately one quarter of the 76 adolescents studied by Sack and his colleagues (1993) were tortured by the Khmer Rouge; one half saw others killed; one third were threatened to be killed; and two thirds had parents killed or reported missing during the Khmer Rouge regime. Among 76 Khmer middle and senior high school refugee students surveyed in the United States, half had survived violence directed at them, two thirds had witnessed violence, and half had been exposed to at least 10 different acts of violence in their lifetimes (Berthold, 1999).

Khmer refugee youth have high rates of exposure to violence, not only in their pre-immigration experiences, but through their participation in the youth culture of the United States. Layne (1996) estimates that 3.7 million adolescents in the U.S. have been seriously physically assaulted and 1.6 million adolescents have been sexually assaulted sometime in their life. In fact, many poor inner city neighborhoods in the United States resemble urban war zones and have the greatest rates of violent crime (Garbarino, Dubrow, Kostelny, & Pardo, 1992). Higher rates of violence exposure among youth in the United States have been found to be disproportionately correlated with certain characteristics such as ethnic minority background, low socioeconomic status, and residence in an inner city (Bureau of Justice Statistics, 1990, 1991; Christofel, 1990; Cooley, Turner & Beidel, 1995; Horowitz, Weine & Jekel, 1995; Jenkins & Bell, 1994; O'Carroll, 1988), characteristics descriptive of Khmer youth.

Psychosocial Sequelae Associated with Exposure to Violence

The literature suggests that adolescents exposed to community violence and war traumas frequently experience such outcomes as PTSD, depression, and risky behaviors. Children and adolescents exposed to community violence have been found to be more psychologically distressed than not-exposed youth (Fletcher, 1995; Foy, Madvig, Pynoos, & Camilleri, in press cited in Layne, 1996). Exposure to community violence is strongly associated with depressive symptoms (Freeman, Mokros, & Poznanski, 1993) and PTSD (Fitzpatrick & Boldizar, 1993).

Studies have reported a wide range of PTSD rates, from 27% to 100%, in children and adolescents exposed to community violence (McNally, 1993). In a national survey, Boney-McCoy and Finkelhor (1995) found a strong association between victimization by violence (e.g., physical assaults, parental violence, attempted and completed sexual assaults, and attempted kidnapings) and an increase in problems with a teacher at school and symptoms of PTSD.

Children and adolescents with PTSD are at risk for developing a wide range of comorbid psychiatric disorders and symptoms (Hubbard, Realmuto, Northwood, & Masten, 1995). These symptoms include, but are not limited to: dysthymia or depression, eating disorders, drug and/or alcohol abuse, complicated bereavement or grief, suicidality, difficulties with memory and concentration, reduced academic achievement, truancy, delinquent behavior, anxiety disorders, dissociation disorder, reduced impulse control, impeded or truncated moral development, aggressiveness and/or conduct disorder, and disturbed family and/or peer relationships (Amaya-Jackson & March, 1995; Atlas, Di Scipio, Schwartz & Sessoms, 1991; Eth & Pynoos, 1985a, 1985b; Freeman, Mokros, & Poznanski, 1993; Keane & Wolfe, 1990; Layne, 1996). Having at least one comorbid disorder puts adolescents at heightened risk for developing detrimental outcomes such as impaired global role functioning, conflicts with parents, academic problems, and suicide (Layne, 1996). When adolescents have more than two comorbid disorders, their risk is even greater (Lewinsohn, Rohde, & Seeley, 1995). Adolescents who fail academically (which is not uncommon for those with PTSD) are at risk for becoming unemployed, abusing drugs, engaging in criminal behavior, and becoming dependent on welfare (Hawkins, Catalano, & Miller, 1992; Neisser, 1986).

In addition to being associated with PTSD and depression, exposure to community violence has also been found to be associated with violent actions by adolescents and other risk behaviors (Raia, 1995; Saltzman, 1995; Singer, 1986). High levels of exposure to community violence have been found to be associated with a variety of high-risk behaviors by inner city junior and senior high school students in the United States such as alcohol and drug use, difficulties in school, the carrying of knives and guns, offensive and defensive fighting, and other types of violent or aggressive behavior (Attar & Guerra, 1994, cited in Cooley-Quille et al., 1995; Bell & Jenkins, 1991, 1993; DuRant, Cadenhead, Pendergrast, Slavens, & Linder, 1994; Jenkins & Bell, 1994; Saltzman, 1995). An increase in aggressive behavior in children was one of the most frequent correlates of living in communities around the world with high rates of violence (Chimienti, Nasr, & Khalifeh, 1989; Cummings, Iannotti, & Zahn-Waxler, 1985; Fry, 1988; Liddell, Kvalsvig, Qotyana, & Shabalala, 1994).

Children typically find it easier to assimilate a traumatic incident into their world view if it was an acute stressor (Garbarino & Kostelny, 1996). According to Garbarino, Kostelny, and Dubrow (1991), they do this through the use of rationalization, viewing the incident as an accident or aberration, and telling themselves that now everything has returned to normal. However, in situations of chronic, repeated traumas and stresses the consequences may be more far reaching. Horowitz and her colleagues (1995) have proposed the concept of "compounded community trauma" to reflect the pattern of repeated and prolonged exposure to multiple kinds of community and domestic violence experienced by people who live in communities where violence is endogenous. Youth living in urban cities in America or civilians in war zones frequently experience such compounded community trauma.

Chronic exposure to violence and other traumas in the United States and overseas often has been found to result in a wide range of psychological, developmental, and behavioral problems in addition to PTSD (Garbarino, Dubrow, Kostelny, & Pardo, 1992; Nader, 1989, cited in Garbarino & Kostelny, 1996; Terr, 1990; van der Veer, 1992). Children in war zones have been found to exhibit a range of symptoms including: anxiety, problems concentrating, helplessness, a sense of "futurelessness," numbness, being desensitized to threat, and high degrees of risk taking and involvement in dangerous activities (Garbarino et al., 1992; Lorion & Saltzman, 1993). Psychological, social, and behavioral problems have been found to be greater for children living in war zones who experience war traumas (Boothby, 1992; Macksoud & Aber, 1996; Rosenblatt, 1983). High rates of depressive symptoms were found in a study of 480 youth in Croatia during the war in Bosnia-Herzegovina, especially among those who fled as refugees from the war zones (Zivcic, 1993). Palestinian children exposed to political violence were found to have considerable psychological problems (Baker, 1991; Khamis, 1993; Mahjoub, Leyens, Yzerby, & Di Giacomo, 1989; Punamaki, 1989). Macksoud (1992) found that the effect of repetitive exposure to violence on children in Beirut was additive in nature in terms of the probability of their being traumatized. While Rutter (1987) suggests that the chances of experiencing developmental problems is no greater for youth with only one risk factor compared to those with no risk factors, the level of harm increases with each additional risk factor. He holds that youth with four or more risk factors have ten times the risk of experiencing developmental damage.

In their study of youth aged 10 to 16 in Lebanon during the war, Macksoud and Aber (1996) found that 16% of the variance in PTSD symptoms was accounted for by the number of war traumas experienced by the youth. The youth who were significantly most likely to exhibit PTSD symptoms were those who were bereaved, were exposed to multiple war traumas, were victims of or witnessed violent acts, and/or were exposed to combat or shelling. Youth who experienced separation from parents were significantly more likely to report depressive symptoms compared to children who experienced other war traumas.

Many Khmer adolescents have experienced compounded community trauma as defined by Horowitz and her colleagues (1995) in their work with non-Khmer youth, and exhibit high rates of emotional distress. Thirty-nine percent of the 182 children (aged 12-13) surveyed in a camp on the Thai-Cambodian border reported feeling depressed while 46% of their parents saw them as depressed (Mollica et al., 1991). The children also reported poor sleep patterns (53%), and anxiety (56%), symptoms associated with PTSD. Fifty-nine percent of the parents felt that their children had poor concentration and 66% reported rapid mood changes in their children. Not all of the findings were negative, however. Mollica and his colleagues (1991) identified a number of positive behaviors and feelings among the Khmer youth in Site 2 that were suggestive of their resilience in the midst of a very stressful situation (e.g., being willing to help others in need, treating others fairly, standing up for their rights, and enjoying jokes and being with others).

One-quarter of the 76 Khmer refugee youth aged 11 to 19 surveyed partially or fully met the PTSD criteria in one community based study in the Western United States (Berthold, 1999). Another study of Khmer high school students in the United States, who had lived in the Khmer concentration camps when they were between 8 and 12 years old, found that 50% suffered from PTSD six years after leaving the camp (Kinzie, Sack, Angell, Manson, & Rath, 1986). Three years later, a follow-up study of the same sample revealed that 48% could still be classified as suffering from PTSD while 41% had depressive disorders (Kinzie, Sack, Angell, Clarke, & Rath, 1989). In a community-based sample of 209 randomly selected Khmer adolescent refugees in the United States, Sack et al. (1994) found a prevalence rate of 22% for PTSD and 13% for major depressive disorder. The depression rates in these Cambodian adolescents were four times greater than the prevalence rate of nearly 3% reported in a study of 1,710 randomly selected high school students in Oregon (Lewinsohn, Hops, Roberts, Seeley, & Andrews, 1993).

Social Support

The literature suggests that the perception of social support may be associated with psychological well-being in youth. In Raia's (1995) study of 182 mostly African American and Latino urban sixth to tenth grade students (aged 11-15) in Los Angeles, a significant negative correlation ($r = -.33$, $p < .05$) was found between perceived social support from a parent and PTSD symptoms in the youth. Those with lower perceived support from parents reported greater PTSD and over-all symptomatology. Perceived parental social support was also signif-icantly negatively correlated with total violence exposure ($r = -.24$, $p < .01$), direct violence exposure ($r = -.25$, $p < .01$), vicarious exposure to violence ($r = -.24$, $p < .01$), and life-threatening violence ($r = -.22$, $p < .01$). Older youth perceived support from their peers significantly more often than parental support ($t = -3.02$, $p < .01$) compared to younger children. Compared to those youth who per-ceived support only from parents, youth who reported support only from peers had significantly greater total exposure to community vio-lence ($t = -2.37$, $p < .05$) and PTSD symptomatology ($t = -2.40$, $p < .05$). Greater perceptions of peer support were associated with fewer depressive symptoms, but with a mixed pattern of delinquent behavior in another study (Licitra-Kleckler & Waas, 1993). The child and ado-lescent trauma literature suggests that lack of social support is one factor that may make it hard for youth to recover from trauma and may heighten their risk of developing co-morbid psychiatric problems (Pynoos, Steinberg, & Wraith, 1995; Rutter, 1985, 1990).

METHODS

Sampling

The sample was drawn from a city in the Western United States with an estimated 40,000 Khmer, the largest community of Khmer refugees outside of Cambodia. Five criteria were used to determine who was eligible to participate in the study. Respondents were: (a) currently enrolled in one of three participating high schools with the highest numbers of Khmer adolescents in the school district, (b) self-identified as Khmer, (c) born outside of the U.S., (d) at least five years old when they resettled in the U.S., and (e) able to respond to the questionnaire in English. The school district's list of all currently enrolled high school students born outside of the United States was used to recruit respondents. In cases in which a family had more than one child or twins who met the eligibility criteria, only one child per family was selected randomly to participate.

The researchers sent an introductory letter in Khmer and English on school district letterhead co-signed by a representative of the school district to each potentially eligible adolescent and their parents/guardians. The parent instruments, introductory letter, and consent and assent forms were translated and back-translated. Telephone contact was made with each parent/guardian by one of three bilingual bicultural Khmer interviewers. Parents were first invited to participate in the study; the adolescent children of those parents who agreed to participate were then invited to respond to the survey. The response rate was high (82% for the parents and 99% for the adolescents). A total of 144 sets of parent/adolescent interviews were completed.

Instrumentation

Part I of the Harvard Trauma Questionnaire (HTQ) was used to measure the adolescents' level of exposure to violence and war traumas overseas. The HTQ is a 17-item instrument developed to assess trauma and torture related to mass violence in Southeast Asian refugees, with four response categories: "experienced," "witnessed," "heard about it," or "no" (Mollica, Caspi-Yavin et al., 1993). The HTQ has high inter-rater reliability ($r = .93$), 1-week test-retest reliability ($r = .89$, $p < .0001$), and internal consistency (Cronbach's alpha of .90) (Mollica, Caspi-Yavin et al., 1993). In this study, the Cronbach's alpha was .93.

A modified 28-item version of the original 54-item true-false Survey of Children's Exposure to Community Violence (SCECV) was used to assess the extent the adolescents either directly experienced, witnessed, or heard about specific types of violent events happening while they were in the U.S. (Richters & Saltzman, 1990). Each of the 28 items were summed across degree of exposure and across all types of violence to obtain a continuous total violence exposure score that measured the respondent's cumulative level of exposure to community violence in the U.S. Possible scores ranged from 0 to 79. The 2-week test-retest reliability with young children was .81 (Richters & Martinez, 1993). A full-scale Cronbach's alpha of .92 was obtained in a study of 1,176 junior and senior high school students (Gaba, 1995, cited in Layne, 1996). The Cronbach's alpha was .93 in this study.

The Los Angeles Posttraumatic Stress Index (LA PTSD Index), a 17-item subscale of the 43-item Los Angeles Symptom Checklist, was used to assess the extent of PTSD symptoms the adolescents experienced (King, King, Leskin, & Foy, 1995). The LA PTSD Index uses a 5-point Likert-type scale, with 0 indicating "no problem" and 4 "extreme" problem, and yields a continuous score ranging from 0 to 68. A score of 20 or higher is the diagnostic cutoff point for PTSD (Layne, 1996). The measure has strong concurrent and convergent validity, high sensitivity and specificity, a test-retest reliability of .94, and a Cronbach's alpha of .88 for adolescents (Foy, Wood, King, King, & Resnick, 1997). The Cronbach's alpha was .90 in this study.

The level of depressive symptoms of the adolescents was measured by the Center for Epidemiologic Studies Depression Scale for Children (CES-DC) (Faulstich, Carey, Ruggiero, Enyart, & Gresham, 1986). The CES-DC is a 20-item self-report depression measure with a 4-point Likert-type scale, with 0 indicating "not at all" and 3 "a lot." It yields a continuous score ranging from 0 to 60, with scores of 16 or higher indicative of major depressive disorder (Fendrich, Weissman, & Warner, 1990). The CES-DC has adequate internal consistency, test-retest reliability, and concurrent validity, with a Cronbach's alpha of .89 (Faulstich et al., 1986; Fendrich et al., 1990). The Cronbach's alpha was .86 in this study.

The extent that the adolescents in this study engaged in risky behaviors was measured by the 17-item Personal Risk Behaviors Scale (PRBS) which has been used in several studies with Khmer and other Asian adolescents (Aoki, Zane, Jang, & Ho, 1995; Zane, 1996; Zane, Park, & Aoki, in press). The responses are scored on a 4-point Likert-type scale, from "never" (1) to "a lot" (4). The instrument yields a continuous score ranging from 17 to 68, with higher scores indicating a greater level of high-risk behavior. In studies with Asian youth, the mean Cronbach's alpha was .90 with a range from .87 to .93 (Zane, Jang, Ho, & Seeberg, 1995). In this study, the Cronbach's alpha was

.72. The Khmer adolescents in this study were also asked a series of questions about their own relationship with gangs.

The Perceived Social Support from Family (PSS-Fa) and from Friends (PSS-Fr) scales were used to measure the extent that the adolescents felt that their family and friends were providing them with needed support, information, and feedback (Procidano & Heller, 1983). These scales consist of 20 agree-disagree items, and each yields a continuous score ranging from 0 to 20. A meta-analysis of all existing studies using the PSS-Fa and PSS-Fr found strong psychometric properties (Procidano, 1992). The 1-month test-retest reliabilities averaged .82 for the PSS-Fa and .79 for the PSS-Fr. No testing effects were found and the Cronbach's alphas ranged from .84 to .91. In the current study, the Cronbach's alphas were .85 for the PSS-Fa and .82 for the PSS-Fr measures.

The 6-item Orthogonal Cultural Identification Scale (OCIS) was used to ask adolescents and their parents about their own and their family's identification with Khmer and White American cultures, perceived and expressed success in those cultures, and involvement in cultural activities and traditions (Oetting & Beauvais, 1990-91). Each item has a 4-point Likert-type scale ranging from 1 "not at all" to 4 "a lot" yielding a continuous score. The difference between adolescents' and their parents' raw summed scores for Khmer orientation and for Anglo American orientation was computed. The psychometric properties of the adolescent version are strong and the properties of the more recently developed parent version are currently being evaluated (Oetting & Swaim, 1996). The reliabilities of the mean difference in the adolescent and parent scores on cultural identification with White American culture (Cronbach's alpha of .79) and Khmer culture (Cronbach's alpha of .89) were adequate in this study.

Data Collection

Employing a cross-sectional survey approach, face to face interviews were conducted with 144 Khmer refugee adolescents and their parents or guardians. The Khmer interviewers conducted in-person interviews individually with parents in their homes. Parent interviews focused on collecting basic background information and obtaining the parent's report of his/her adolescent child's level of exposure to violence and war traumas overseas. Written parental consent was obtained for the participation of each adolescent before they were interviewed. The author conducted interviews in English with each of the adolescents at their school sites after obtaining their written informed assent. Gift certificates worth $15 at a local Khmer grocery store were given to all families who participated in the study.

Data Analysis

SPSS was employed to conduct the statistical analyses. With the exception of some basic background information and the parents' reports of their adolescent children's exposure to violence and war traumas overseas, this article includes findings only from the adolescent interviews. Previous exposure to war trauma overseas, exposure to community violence in the United States, PTSD symptomatology, depressive symptomatology, personal risk behaviors, behavioral problems at school, GPA, perceived social support, cultural identification, and demographic characteristics of the adolescent respondents were examined with basic descriptive analyses. Zero-order bivariate correlations were conducted to examine the association between all of the predictor and outcome variables. Simultaneous logistic regression and hierarchical multiple regression analyses were conducted to examine the final research question. The following control variables were included in all regression analyses: gender, age, number of years in the U.S., public assistance status, and the differences between parental and adolescent cultural identification with Khmer and White American cultures.

FINDINGS

Description of the Sample

Males and females were equally represented among the adolescents. No significant gender differences were found on any of the demographic variables using Chi-square and independent-samples t-tests. The adolescents all identified as Khmer, although one fifth reported that they were of mixed ethnic heritage (i.e., 13% were Chinese Cambodian and 6% were Khmer Krom). The mean age of the adolescents was 16.35 (SD = 1.31), with an age range of 14 to 20. They were born between 1977 and 1982, almost two years after the Khmer Rouge came to power and up to nearly four years after the Khmer Rouge were overthrown by Vietnamese troops and a new government was installed. Sixty-three percent were born in Cambodia, 32% in a refugee camp in Asia, and 5% in Vietnam. Although most were born in Cambodia, they were born after the Khmer Rouge fell from power and spent at least half of their lives (9.11 years, $SD = 2.81$) in the United States. They were 7.25 ($SD = 2.46$) years old, on average, when they arrived in the United States. More than half (56%) were classified by their schools as having limited English proficiency, and females were significantly more likely to be classified as being fluent in English, $X^2(1, N = 144) = 4.67, p < .05$. More than half (54%) of the parental respondents were females: 49% were the mothers of the adolescents, 44% were the fathers, and the remaining 7% were extended family members who were the legal guardians of the adolescents. Ninety-seven percent of the respondents' families received public assistance and struggled to support an average of 6 family members in their household ($SD = 2.15$). A greater percentage of the Khmer respondents in this study lived below the poverty line and were female compared to all Khmer aged 14 to 20 in their city (U.S. Department of Commerce, 1992).

Violence Exposure of the Adolescents

The adolescent respondents were exposed to very high rates of violence during their lifetimes (see Tables 1 and 2). Virtually all of the adolescent respondents reported that they had survived violence directed at them (98%), had witnessed violence (99%), and had heard about violence happening to someone in their lifetime (99%). The adolescents experienced an average of 44 different types of violence in their lifetimes ($SD = 16.39$; see Table 3). The number of different types of violence is the summation of the number of types of violence the adolescents survived that were directed at them, witnessed, and heard about happening to others overseas and in the U.S. This figure does not take into account that some of the youth were exposed multiple times to certain types of violence.

Male adolescents had a significantly higher rate of overall lifetime exposure to violence than females, $t(142) = 2.55, p < .05$. In their lifetimes, males were significantly more likely to survive violence directed at them, $t(142) = 3.13, p < .01$, and to witness violence than female adolescents, $t(142) = 2.47, p < .05$. When the exposure was

TABLE 1. Percentage Exposed to Specific Types of Violent Events Overseas by Mode of Exposure

Type of Violence	Direct %	Witness %	Heard %
Lack food & water	29	40	96
No medical care	22	33	89
Murder of family/friends	76	16	85
Lack of shelter	32	51	95
Unnatural death family/friends	72	17	85
Combat situation	24	37	81
Close to death	16	22	51
Brain washing	1	8	57
Family separation	11	17	68
Forced isolation	3	15	58
Serious injury	9	29	62
Imprisonment	5	22	63
Torture	0	13	61
Lost or kidnapped	2	11	46
Murder of stranger(s)	2	16	79
Rape	0	14	44
Other	17	12	17

broken down by location, a greater percentage of the respondents reported being exposed to violence in the United States compared to overseas. While there were no gender differences in rates of exposure to violence overseas, males were exposed to violence significantly more often in the U.S. compared to female adolescents, $t(142) = 3.46$, $p < .01$.

Approximately three quarters of the adolescents had family members or friends who were murdered or died an unnatural death overseas (see Table 1). Nearly one quarter of the adolescents were directly exposed to combat situations, 16% were close to death themselves overseas, and 16% had witnessed the murder of family or friends prior to coming to the U.S. Approximately one third had been chased by gangs and been threatened with a weapon in the U.S. More than 80% of the adolescents had seen or heard gunfire while they were in their home, 22% had witnessed at least one drive-by shooting, and 15% had seen at least one person murdered (see Table 2). Many of the adolescents experienced chronic exposure to violence. Half were exposed to 43 or more different types of violence in their lifetime.

Using their median age as the cut point, adolescent respondents were categorized into older (age 17 to 20) and younger (age 14 to 16)

TABLE 2. Percentage Exposed to Specific Types of Violent Events in the U.S. by Mode of Exposure

Type of Violence	Direct %	Witness %	Heard %
Gunfire (while in home)	n/a	85	85
Someone with gun or knife	n/a	60	40
Chased by gangs	38	56	85
Object thrown at	33	38	50
Threatened w/ weapon	30	24	60
Hit by family member	28	34	50
Verbally threatened	27	35	70
Hit by non-family	26	34	63
Dead person	n/a	22	59
Mugged/jacked	21	22	64
Jumped/beaten up	20	47	76
Someone murdered	n/a	15	44
Attempted suicide	n/a	19	36
Serious accident	15	37	76
Arrested by police	15	51	69
House broken into	7[a] 15[b]	39	70
Asked use/sell drugs	14	22	45
Vehicular violence	14	14	41
Hit w/ blunt object	13	18	37
Seriously wounded	8	26	56
Stabbed	7	13	51
Shot/shot at by gun	6	20	79
Raped	6	8	55
Tortured	6	8	46
Choked/strangled	4	8	33
Completed suicide	n/a	4	10
Drive-by shooting	4	22	n/a
Kidnapping	3	4	30

a = house broken into while respondent was at home
b = house broken into while respondent not at home (these "a" and "b" categories are not mutually exclusive)

groups. There were no significant differences in the rates of lifetime or overseas exposure to violence between the older and younger respondents using chi-square and independent-sample t-tests. Older adolescents were significantly more likely to be exposed to violence in the U.S., $t(142) = 2.40$, $p < .05$ and to witness violence in their lifetime, $t(142) = 2.10$, $p < .05$, and in the U.S., $t(142) = 3.04$, $p < .01$.

TABLE 3. Means, (Standard Deviations), and Percentages of Violence Exposure and Related Outcomes

Variable	Final Study N = 144
Number of violent events exposed to	
Lifetime	43.8 (16.39)*
Overseas	18.3 (9.14)
In the U.S.	25.5 (13.0)**
PTSD	
Mean symptom score (0-68)	15.87 (10.87)
% with PTSD (20+)	33%
Depression	
Mean symptom score (0-60)	19.89 (10.19)
% Depressed (16+)	63%+
Personal Risk Behavior	
Mean behavior score (17-68)	21.85 (3.88)
Behavior Problems at School	
% reported at school	30%**
Perception of Social Support	
From family (0-20)	13.38 (4.69)
From friends (0-20)	15.03 (3.98)
Grade Point Average	(n = 141)
Mean GPA	2.77 (.86)++
% 1.0 and below	3.5%
% 1.1-2.0	18.4%
% 2.1-3.0	35.5%
% 3.1-4.0	42.6%

*$p < .05$. **$p < .01$. (Males significantly higher than females)
+$p < .05$. ++$p < .01$. (Females significantly higher than males)

PTSD and Depression

The adolescents experienced relatively high rates of emotional distress. One third met the cut-off criteria for PTSD (see Table 3). A Pearson's correlation analysis found that the adolescents' length of stay in the U.S. was significantly positively associated with their level of PTSD, $r = .190$, $p < .05$. Nearly two-thirds (63%) of the adolescents had symptoms indicative of major depression (see Table 3). When asked whether they thought they would be alive when they were 25 years old, only slightly more than half (54%) of the adolescents re-ported being sure that they would be.

Using the median level of exposure to violent events in their life-time as the cut point, adolescent respondents were categorized into highest exposure (43 or more types of violence) and lower exposure (42 or less types of violence) groups. No statistically significant differences in the rates of those reaching the PTSD diagnostic cut-off score were found between older and younger adolescents, males and females, or between those most highly exposed to violence versus the adolescents who were less highly exposed. Adolescent symptoms of PTSD and depression were significantly positively correlated, $r = .651, p < .001$. There were no significant differences in rates of depression between those exposed to high versus low rates of violence or between the older versus younger respondents. Female adolescents, however, were significantly more likely to be depressed than males, $X^2(1, N = 144) = 6.72, p < .05$. Adolescents who were exposed to higher rates of violence had significantly more PTSD symptoms, $t(142) = 2.93, p < .01$, and depression symptoms, $t(142) = 1.98, p < .05$, than those in the less exposed group. No significant age or gender differences existed in terms of the adolescents' level of PTSD symptoms. Although there were no significant age differences in levels of depressive symptoms, female adolescents had significantly more symptoms of depression than males, $t(142) = -3.10, p < .01$.

Academic and Behavioral Well-Being

The academic and behavioral well-being of the adolescents were also measured. In addition to self-report of their level of personal risk behaviors, data on GPA and the types and numbers of referrals for behavior problems were obtained from school records for the respondents. The adolescents reported that they had not engaged in many personal risk behaviors during the past three months (see Table 3). Fifty-nine percent, however, had felt so angry at another person that they wanted to hurt them, 26% had bullied someone younger than themselves, 17% had beaten up another person, 11% had carried weapons, 10% had stolen things belonging to someone else, and 2% had threatened to hurt someone with a weapon. There were no significant gender or age differences in terms of the level of high risk behaviors reported by the adolescents. Those exposed to higher amounts of violence, however, were significantly more likely to report engaging in personal risk behaviors than those in the less exposed group, $t(142) = 3.31, p < .01$.

Thirty percent (30%) had been reported for behavioral problems at their high school during that academic year such as: breaking rules (e.g., dress code violations, smoking, swearing, racist remarks, graffiti, lying, stealing), disruptive or defiant behavior in class, lewd behavior (e.g., "mooning" the entire class), truancy, carrying a concealed weapon, threatening others with a weapon, and incidents of violence (e.g., fighting, kicking another student in the head, gang related activities/fights). Males were reported for behavior problems at school significantly more often than females, $X^2(1, N = 144) = 9.58, p < .01$. Older adolescents and those in the high exposure group were no more likely to be reported for behavior problems at school than the younger adolescents or those exposed to fewer violent events.

While only 4% of the adolescents reported that they were currently in a gang, an additional 21% were involved in one or more gang-like activities such as being in a "kickback" (hanging out with a group loosely associated with a gang), "tagging" (graffiti), or "tagbanging" (graffiti and group deviant behaviors such as fighting, vandalism, etc.) "crew" (group). Of the total sample of adolescents, 6% were former members of a gang, and 15% had at least one family member in a gang. While over half reported that they did not have any friends in a gang, 47% had at least a few friends in a gang, and 8% reported that most or all of their friends were in a gang.

Academic achievement data were available for all but three of the adolescents. Their mean GPA was 2.77 (see Table 3 for the spread of the scores). Females had significantly higher GPAs than males, $t(139) = -2.97, p < .01$. Those adolescents in the lower exposure to violence group had higher GPAs, $t(139) = -2.88, p < .01$. Those adolescents reported for behavior problems at school had significantly lower GPAs than those not reported for school behavior problems, $t(139) = -4.80, p < .001$. There were no significant age differences in GPA. The adolescents' length of stay in the United States, however, was significantly negatively associated with their GPA, $r = -.202, p < .05$. Only 5% did not expect to graduate from high school.

Level of Perceived Social Support

Most of the adolescents reported feeling a great deal of social support from their friends and from their families (see Table 3). There were no statistically significant differences in perceptions of support from friends versus from family. There were no significant gender differences in terms of the level of social support that adolescents perceived from family and friends. Those adolescents who were in the group most highly exposed to violence perceived significantly less social support from family than those in the less highly exposed group, $t(142) = -2.05, p < .05$, but there were no differences in their perception of social support from their friends. Older and younger adolescents did not differ significantly in terms of their perceptions of social support.

The adolescents' perception of social support from family was significantly negatively correlated with their level of PTSD, $r = -.318$, $p < .001$, level of depression, $r = -.417, p < .001$, lifetime exposure to violence, $r = -.165, p < .05$, and personal risk behavior problems, $r = -.265, p < .01$. The adolescents' perception of social support from friends was significantly negatively correlated with their level of PTSD, $r = -.204, p < .05$, and level of depression, $r = -.164, p < .05$. Those adolescents, however, who perceived their friends as supportive were equally as likely to report engaging in personal risk behavior or being exposed to more violence than those who did not perceive their friends as supportive.

Predictors of Psychological, Behavioral, and Academic Outcomes

A Pearson's correlation analysis found that the adolescents' lifetime exposure to violence was positively associated with their PTSD scores, $r = .283, p < .01$, personal risk behavior problems, $r = .351, p < .001$, and negatively associated with their GPA, $r = -.248, p < .01$. Lifetime exposure to violence was a significant negative predictor of GPA even after controlling for the adolescents' level of fluency in English, $F(2, 140) = 8.31, p < .001$. Adolescent lifetime exposure to violence, however, was not significantly associated with their level of depression, $r = .133, p = .113$, and there were no significant differences in levels of lifetime exposure to violence between those adolescents who were and were not reported for behavior problems at school, $t(142) = .514, p = .608$.

The descriptive findings indicated that the majority of the adolescent respondents were exposed to greater amounts of violence in the U.S. compared to overseas. Therefore, two additional correlational analyses were conducted: the correlation of the outcome variables with exposure to violence overseas and with exposure to violence in the U.S. Adolescent exposure to war traumas overseas was not significantly associated with any of the outcomes. In contrast, the adolescents' exposure to violence in the U.S. was significantly correlated with their PTSD scores, $r = .241$, $p < .01$, personal risk behavior problems, $r = .371$, $p < .001$, and GPA, $r = -.275$, $p < .01$. Their exposure to violence in the U.S. was a significant predictor of their GPAs even after controlling for their proficiency in English, $F (2, 140) = 9.42$, $p < .001$. Adolescent exposure to violence in the U.S., however, was not significantly associated with their level of depression, $r = .159$, $p = .056$, or school behavior problems, $t(142) = 1.442$, $p = .152$.

Given that the adolescents' exposure to violence in the U.S. was significantly associated with three of the five outcomes, while their exposure to violence overseas was not associated with any of the outcomes, the remaining analyses will include lifetime and U.S. exposure to violence only. Simultaneous logistic regression and hierarchical regression analyses were conducted to examine whether perceived social support from family and friends significantly contributed to the ability to predict psychological, behavioral, and academic problems in Khmer refugee adolescents over and above the effect of exposure to violence. Each of the analyses was conducted twice. Initially, lifetime exposure to violence was included in the model. Next, the analyses were conducted again using exposure to violence in the U.S. rather than lifetime exposure to violence. A simultaneous logistic regression analysis found that perceived social support from family and friends did not significantly predict school behavior problems in the adolescents.

The remaining analyses all used the same basic hierarchical regression model that included a series of steps. The first two steps in the model did not vary throughout the rest of the study. In the first step, the six control variables were entered into the model as a block. In the second step, the adolescent's lifetime exposure to violence was entered into the model. The adolescents' perceived social support from family and their perceived social support from friends were entered into the model in the final step. This social support main effects model was conducted both for lifetime exposure to violence and exposure to violence only in the U.S. for each of the dependent variables.

When the adolescents' lifetime exposure to violence was used as a predictor, the social support main effects model explained 26% of the variance in the adolescents' level of PTSD, 30% of the variance in the adolescents' level of depression, 28% of the variance in the adolescents' level of personal risk behavior, and 16% of the variance in the adolescents' GPA. When the adolescents' exposure to violence in the United States was used as a predictor instead, the social support main effects model explained 25% of the variance in the adolescents' level of PTSD, 32% of the variance in the adolescents' level of depression, 31% of the variance in the adolescents' level of personal risk behavior, and 17% of the variance in the adolescents' GPA.

Over and above the effects of the control variables and exposure to violence, the more social support the adolescents perceived from family and friends, the less PTSD and depression they experienced. This finding, as well as those below, were true both when lifetime exposure to violence was in the model or when only U.S. exposure to violence was in the model. In the social support main effects model, females were significantly more depressed and had more PTSD symptoms. Similarly, greater social support from family (but not friends) significantly contributed to a lower level of personal risk behaviors in this sample of Khmer refugee adolescents taking into account the control variables and levels of exposure to violence. The younger adolescents, those who had lived longer in the U.S., or received public assistance were significantly more likely to have personal risk behavior problems in the social support main effects model. The Khmer refugee adolescents' perception of social support from family and friends, however, did not predict their GPA. Although social support had a significant main effect on predicting PTSD, depression, and personal risk behavior problems in these adolescents, social support did not significantly moderate the relationship between lifetime or U.S. exposure to violence and any of the outcomes.

DISCUSSION

The Khmer refugee adolescents in this study witnessed and survived violence directed at them at alarmingly high rates, particularly in the United States. They reported high rates of psychological distress, especially depression. This sample of Khmer adolescents had higher rates of depressive symptomatology than those in previous studies with Khmer youth (Kinzie et al., 1989; Sack et al., 1994) and in a random sample of high school students in Oregon (Lewinsohn et al., 1993). The percentage of Khmer adolescents in this study who were symptomatic for PTSD were comparable to rates found by Sack et al. (1996) in an older group of Khmer refugee adolescents. A higher percentage (33%) of respondents in the current study suffered from PTSD than in a previous study with middle and high school Khmer refugee adolescents from the same community (Berthold, 1999). In addition, the rate was higher than that found among U.S. combat veterans (Buydens-Branchey, Noumair, & Branchuy, 1990; Kulka et al., 1990; Saigh, 1992), of whom 20% had PTSD. The fact that the respondents were a community based sample of adolescents, rather than those seeking mental health services, makes this finding particularly striking.

Moderate levels of behavior problems were found among the respondents; a majority were not fluent in English, and they had low academic achievement on average. Those with greater lifetime exposure to violence had significantly higher PTSD scores, reported significantly more personal risk behavior problems, and had lower GPAs. This is consistent with findings from numerous studies that exposure to traumatic events or disasters has a direct effect on mental health outcomes (Fitzpatrick & Boldizar, 1993; Freedy, Kilpatrick, & Resnick, 1993; Green & Solomon, 1995; Richters & Martinez, 1993; Singer et al., 1995). Although their high rate of exposure to violence was associated with lower GPAs, it did not lead to greater behavior problems at school for the adolescents. Therefore, many of these youth who were highly traumatized and psychologically distressed may have suffered in silence. It may be that silence was rewarded in their classrooms and, therefore, seen as desired behavior by some of the Khmer students. They may have learned to adapt by remaining silent. Their teachers and others they came in frequent contact with may not have been aware of their level of distress; in fact, teachers, counselors, and school administrators at the study schools with whom these findings were shared confirmed this impression. In an earlier study by Sack and his colleagues (1986), Khmer adolescents were rated as good students by their teachers, although withdrawn and subject to daydreaming. Unfortunately, because of such high functioning or resilience exhibited by some Khmer adolescents with PTSD, their distress may not be properly identified or treated.

Contrary to expectations and findings in studies with other urban students (Freeman, Mokros, & Poznanski, 1993), those Khmer adolescents in this study who had more exposure to violence in their lifetimes did not have significantly higher rates of depression. While exposure to violence by itself was not associated with a higher level of depression in this sample of Khmer refugee adolescents, their exposure to violence in the U.S. was associated with depression once gender, age, number of years in the U.S., public assistance status, and the difference between the adolescents' and parents' identification with Khmer and White American cultures were controlled. In addition, those adolescents who perceived less social support from their family and friends were significantly more depressed. This is consistent with findings in other studies (Licitra-Kleckler & Waas, 1993; Pynoos et al., 1995; Rutter, 1985).

There may also be a cultural explanation for why the Khmer adolescents who experienced less social support from their families and friends were more depressed. Traditionally, in times of stress, Khmer individuals rely on their extended families for support, advice, and help in solving problems rather than seeking to solve their problems on their own or turning to outside individuals or agencies (Frye & D'Avanzo, 1994; Morris & Silove, 1992). Many Khmer adolescents consider their friends as part of their "extended family." Those Khmer adolescents who did not have strong support from family or friends may have felt isolated, rejected, misunderstood, not cared for, and/or overwhelmed in having to solve their problems without their traditional support system. These feelings could have contributed to their feeling depressed. Alternatively, a pre-existing depression in these Khmer adolescents could shape their perceptions of lack of social support.

While the original research questions examined the effects of exposure to lifetime violence, the findings suggested that it was the community violence they were exposed to in the United States rather than their overseas exposure to war traumas that accounted for their rates of PTSD, personal risk behavior problems, and GPAs. The youth in this study were very young, on average 7 years old, when they came to the United States, and the majority were born after the Khmer Rouge period. Unlike adults and youth who were older and lived through more extreme war traumas of the Khmer Rouge regime, the youth in this sample were generally exposed to less severe trauma overseas. It is, therefore, not surprising that their exposure overseas had less of an impact on their PTSD status than the high rates of community violence they experienced in the U.S. This finding is supported by a previous study with Khmer youth (Berthold, 1999). Although Sack and his colleagues (W. Sack, personal communication, November 3, 1997) did not measure or assess exposure to violence in the United States, they also found that those Khmer youth who were less than six years old during the Khmer Rouge regime had lower rates of PTSD. This is not to say, however, that there was no impact from violence experienced overseas. The effects of exposure to violence overseas may have been compounded by current exposure to violence in the U.S. leading to higher rates of psychological, behavioral, and academic problems. This may be particularly true for Khmer refugee youth who were chronically exposed to violence and who spent the majority of their lives living in the United States, as was the case for this sample. Additional studies are needed to examine these possibilities as well as examining possible confounding factors such as the location where the violence took place and the length of time since exposure to particular acts of violence.

Consistent with findings in the disaster literature (Kaniasty & Norris, in press) and other traumatic stress literature (Licitra-Kleckler & Waas, 1993; Procidano, 1992; Raia, 1995) that found that the perception of available support has a direct effect on mental health outcomes, social support had a main effect on the adolescents' level of PTSD, depression and personal risk behavior in this study. Better outcomes were associated with greater perceived support. It is plausible that in addition to exposure to violence, the lack of strong social support systems contribute to a greater increase in overall psychological distress which is reflected in higher rates of PTSD, depression, and personal risk behavior. One notable exception to this was that the adolescents' perceived social support from friends did not significantly contribute to their personal risk behavior problems. A number of studies found that the association with deviant peers (peers whose behavior is antisocial or delinquent) was the best single predictor of antisocial behavior in adolescents (Dishion, 1990a, 1990b; Dishion et al., 1991; Saltzman, 1995). If the peer group that some of the Khmer adolescents turned to for support was involved in personal risk behavior, these peers might have encouraged or influenced the adolescents to engage in more risky behavior. Other adolescents in the sample might have associated with pro-social peers, resulting in a mixed overall effect of perceived social support from friends on adolescent behavior.

IMPLICATIONS FOR RESEARCH AND PRACTICE

The generalizability of the findings would be enhanced in future studies by drawing a random sample and expanding the eligibility criteria to include a more diverse range of adolescents. In part because this study was designed to be exploratory in nature, there was no comparison sample. Khmer refugee adolescents living outside of the city where the previous studies were conducted could be included in the sample, and comparisons of U.S.-born versus overseas-born Khmer adolescents would help to broaden the understanding of the unique contributions of exposure to war traumas overseas versus the effects of exposure to community violence in the U.S. Studies that include other refugee groups in addition to Khmer would help to identify if there are commonalities or differences between the experiences of refugee adolescents across groups (e.g., the nature and degree of the traumatic experience, cultural differences in coping).

There is a gap in the understanding of what leads to adaptive functioning and resiliency in youth who are chronically exposed to community violence and other traumas, including war traumas. Cross-sectional studies such as this one are limited in their ability to explore complex developmental processes and cannot examine the causal relationship between the various variables. A longitudinal study that incorporates a strong qualitative component could help to trace the patterns of adaptive strategies used over time by these adolescents along with their outcomes, which might contribute to an understanding of the conditions that lead to resilience in highly traumatized refugee adolescents. An evaluation of the social support system of the youth, including both received and perceived support, should be included. This information could be useful in designing interventions to mobilize inactive or existing support figures as well as identify new support systems to help the youth cope with the violence and other stresses in their lives, and strengthen their academic, behavioral, and psychological well-being. Although the social support main effects model explained between 25% to 35% of the variance in the psychological and behavioral well-being of Khmer refugee adolescents in this study, it failed to explain a large portion of the variance. Future studies should measure other relevant variables (e.g., family violence, received social support, resettlement stress, current life stress).

The findings of this study have implications for educators and clinicians working with Khmer refugee adolescents and families and for policy makers seeking to shape the policy agenda and the delivery of effective services in an environment of increasingly limited resources. Schools, in collaboration with community based agencies, can play a meaningful role in alleviating these problems. Although the primary mission of schools is to provide their students with an education, youth who are traumatized and affected by violence frequently have difficulty concentrating and develop other symptoms that can significantly interfere with their ability to learn. The development of effective early identification, referral, and counseling services at schools and in the community would enable Khmer refugee and other students to take better advantage of the educational opportunities provided them. Services, however, need to be culturally and linguistically relevant and welcoming to Khmer and other ethnic minority students.

The Khmer refugee adolescents and their families interviewed for this study fled from war torn Cambodia and struggled to leave oftentimes violent refugee camps in Asia in order to resettle in the United States. Having escaped from violence, the parents brought their families to the U.S. hoping to find peace and a safe environment in which to raise their children. Instead, they found themselves surrounded by violence again. The adolescents in this study have been exposed to very high rates of violence in their lifetimes, such that they have been repeatedly and chronically traumatized. Although this study has important implications for the treatment of those psychologically affected by violence, ideally the results can also be useful to increase efforts in violence prevention, especially among youth. These efforts need to pay attention to refugee youth, the youth culture they enter in the United States, and their role as survivors of violence and potential perpetrators of violence.

REFERENCES

Amaya-Jackson, L., & March, J. S. (1995). Posttraumatic stress disorder. In J. S. March (Ed.), *Anxiety disorders in children and adolescents* (pp. 276-300). New York: Guilford.
Aoki, B., Zane, N., Jang, M., & Ho, T. (1995, March). *Competence Through Transitions (CTT): A culturally responsive Asian model to prevent substance abuse.* Grant No. 1H86-SPO4968-03. Paper presented at 1995 National High Risk Youth Learning Community Workshop, Center for Substance Abuse Prevention, Denver, Colorado.

Atlas, J. A., Di Scipio, W. J., Schwartz, R., & Sessoms, L. (1991). Symptom correlated among adolescents showing posttraumatic stress disorder versus conduct disorder. *Psychological Reports, 69,* 920-922.

Baker, A. (1991). The psychological impact of the Intifada on Palestinian children in the occupied West Bank and Gaza: An exploratory story. *American Journal of Orthopsychiatry, 60,* 496-504.

Bell, C. C., & Jenkins, E. J. (1991). Traumatic stress and children. *Journal of Health Care for the Poor and Underserved, 2,* 175-188.

Bell, C. C. & Jenkins, E. J. (1993). Community violence and children on Chicago's southside. *Psychiatry, 56,* 46-54.

Berthold, S. M. (1999). The effects of exposure to community violence on Khmer refugee adolescents. *Journal of Traumatic Stress, 12,* 455-471.

Berthold, S. M. (1998). The effects of exposure to violence and social support on psychological and behavioral outcomes among Khmer refugee adolescents. Unpublished doctoral dissertation, University of California, Los Angeles.

Boney-McCoy, S., & Finkelhor, D. (1995). Psychosocial sequelae of violent victimization in a national youth sample. *Journal of Consulting and Clinical Psychology, 63,* 726-736.

Boothby, N. (1992). Displaced children: Psychological theory and practice from the field. *Journal of Refugee Studies, 5,* 10-15.

Bureau of Justice Statistics (1990). *Black victims.* Washington, D.C.: U. S. Department of Justice.

Bureau of Justice Statistics (1991). *Criminal victimization in the United States, 1989.* Washington, DC: U. S. Department of Justice.

Buydens-Branchey, L., Noumair, D., & Branchuy, M. (1990). Duration and intensity of combat exposure and posttraumatic stress disorder in Vietnam veterans. *Journal of Nervous and Mental Disease, 178,* 582-587.

Chimienti, G., Nasr, J. A., & Khalifeh, I. (1989). Children's reactions to war-related stress: Affective symptoms and behavior problems. *Social Psychiatry and Psychiatric Epidemiology, 24,* 282-287.

Christofel, K. K. (1990). Violent death and injury in U. S. children and adolescents. *American Journal of Disease Control, 144,* 697-706.

Cooley, M. R., Turner, S. M., & Beidel, D. C. (1995, February). Assessing community violence: The children's report of exposure to violence. *Journal of the American Academy of Child & Adolescent Psychiatry, 34,* 201-208.

Cooley-Quille, M. R., Turner, S. M., & Beidel, D. C. (1995, October). Emotional impact of children's exposure to community violence: A preliminary study. *Journal of American Academy of Child and Adolescent Psychiatry, 34,* 1362-1368.

Cummings, E. M., Iannotti, R. J., & Zahn-Waxler, C. (1985). Influence of conflict between adults on the emotions and aggression of young children. *Developmental Psychology, 21,* 495-507.

Dishion, T. J. (1990a). The peer context of troublesome child and adolescent behavior. In P.E. Leone (Ed.), *Understanding troubled and troubling youth: Multidisciplinary perspective* (pp. 128-153). Newbury, CA: Sage.

Dishion, T. J. (1990b). The family ecology of boys' peer relations in middle childhood. *Child Development, 61,* 874-892.

DuRant, R. H., Cadenhead, C., Pendergrast, R. A., Slavens, G., & Linder, C. W. (1994). Factors associated with the use of violence among urban black adolescents. *American Journal of Public Health*, *84*, 612-617.

Eth, S., & Pynoos, R. S. (1985a). Children traumatized by witnessing acts of personal violence: Homicide, rape, or suicide behavior. In S. Eth & R. S. Pynoos (Eds.), *Post-traumatic stress disorder in children* (pp. 19-43). Washington, DC: American Psychiatric Press.

Eth, S., & Pynoos, R. S. (1985b). Developmental perspective on psychic trauma in childhood. In C. R. Figley (Ed.), *Trauma and its wake* (pp. 36-52). New York: Brunner/Mazel.

Faulstich, M., Carey, M., Ruggiero, M., Enyart, P., & Gresham, F. (1986). Assessment of depression in childhood and adolescence: An evaluation of the Center for Epidemiological Studies Depression Scale for Children (CES-DC). *American Journal of Psychiatry*, *143*(8), 1024-1027.

Fendrich, M., Weissman, M. M., & Warner, V. (1990). Screening for depressive disorder in children and adolescents: Validating the center for epidemiologic studies depression scale for children. *American Journal of Epidemiology*, *131*, 538-550.

Fitzpatrick, K M. & Boldizar, J. P. (1993). The prevalence and consequences of exposure to violence among African American youth. *Journal of American Academy of Child and Adolescent Psychiatry*, *32*, 424-430.

Fletcher, K. E. (1995). *What we know about children's post-traumatic stress responses: A meta-analysis of the empirical literature*. Unpublished manuscript.

Foy, D. W., Wood, J. L., King, D. W., King, L. A., & Resnick, H. S. (1997). Los Angeles symptom checklist: Psychometric evidence with an adolescent sample. *Assessment*, *4*, 377-383.

Freedy, J., Kilpatrick, D., & Resnick, H. (1993). Natural disasters and mental health. *Journal of Social Behavior and Personality*, *8*(5), 49-104.

Freeman, L, Mokros, H., & Poznanski, E. (1993). Violent events reported by normal urban school-aged children: Characteristics and depression correlates. *Journal of American Academy of Child and Adolescent Psychiatry*, *32*, 419-423.

Frye, B. A., & D'Avanzo, C. D. (1994). Cultural themes in family stress and violence among Cambodian refugee women in the inner city. *Advances in Nursing Science*, *16*(3), 64-77.

Fry, D. (1988). Intercommunity differences in aggression among Zapotec children. *Child Development*, *59*, 1008-1019.

Garbarino, J., Kostelny, K. & Dubrow, N. (1991). What children can tell us about living in danger. *American Psychologist*, *46*, 376-383.

Garbarino, J., Dubrow, N., Kostelny, K., & Pardo, C. (1992). *Children in danger: Coping with the consequences of community violence*. San Francisco: Jossey-Bass.

Garbarino, J., & Kostelny, K. (1996). The effects of political violence on Palestinian children's behavior problems: A risk accumulation model. *Child Development*, *67*, 33-45.

Green, B. & Solomon, S. (1995). The mental health impact of natural and technological disasters. In J. R. Freedy & S. E. Hobfoll (Eds.), *Traumatic Stress: From Theory to Practice* (pp. 163-180). New York: Plenum Press.

Hannum, H. (1989). International law and Cambodian genocide: The sounds of silence. *Human Rights Quarterly, 11*, 82-138.

Hawkins, J. D., Catalano, R. F., & Miller, J. Y. (1992). Risk and protective factors for alcohol and other drug problems in adolescence and early adulthood: Implications for substance abuse prevention. *Psychological Bulletin, 112*, 64-105.

Horowitz, K, Weine, S., & Jekel, J. (1995, October). PTSD symptoms in urban adolescent girls: Compounded community trauma. *Journal of American Academy of Child and Adolescent Psychiatry, 34*, 1353-1361.

Hubbard, J., Realmuto, G. M., Northwood, A. K, & Masten, A. S. (1995, September). Comorbidity of psychiatric diagnoses with posttraumatic stress disorder in survivors of childhood trauma. *Journal of the American Academy of Child and Adolescent Psychiatry, 34*, 1167.

Jenkins, E. J., & Bell, C. C. (1994). Violence among inner city high school students and post-traumatic stress disorder. In S. Friedman (Ed.), *Anxiety disorders in African Americans* (pp. 76-88). New York: Springer.

Kaniasty, K. & Norris, F. H. (in press). Social support dynamics in adjustment to disasters. In S. Duck (Ed.), *Handbook of Personal Relationships* (2nd ed.).

Keane, T. M., & Wolfe, J. (1990). Comorbidity in post-traumatic stress disorder: An analysis of community and clinical studies. *Journal of Applied Social Psychology, 20*, 1776-1788.

Khamis, V. (1993). Post-traumatic stress disorder among the injured of the Intifada. *Journal of Traumatic Stress, 6*, 555-560.

Kiljunen, K. (1985). Power politics and the tragedy of Kampuchea during the seventies. *Bulletin of Concerned Asian Scholars, 17*, 1749-1764.

King, L. A., King., D. W., Leskin, G., & Foy, D. W. (1995). The Los Angeles Symptom Checklist: A self-report measure of posttraumatic stress disorder. *Assessment, 2*, 1-17.

Kinzie, J. D., Leung, P. K., & Boehnlein, J. K. (1997). Treatment of depressive disorders in refugees. In E. Lee (Ed.), *Working with Asian Americans: A Guide for Clinicians* (pp. 265-274), New York: Guilford Press.

Kinzie, J. D., Sack W. H., Angell, R. H., Clarke, G., & Rath, B. (1989). A three-year follow-up of Cambodian young people traumatized as children. *Journal of the American Academy of Child and Adolescent Psychiatry, 28*, 501-504.

Kinzie, J. D., Sack, W. H., Angell, R. H., Manson, S., & Rath, B. (1986). The psychiatric effects of massive trauma on Cambodian children: I. The children. *Journal of the American Academy of Child and Adolescent Psychiatry, 25*, 370-376.

Koop, C. E., & Lundberg, G. D. (1992). Violence in America: A public health emergency. *Journal of the American Medical Association, 267*, 3075-3076.

Kulka, R. A., Schlenger, W. E., Fairbanks, J. A., Hough, R. L, Jordan, B. K, Marmar, C. R. & Weiss (1990). *Trauma and the Vietnam war generation: Report of findings from the national Vietnam veterans readjustment study.* New York: Brunner/ Mazel.

Layne, C. M. (1996). *Effects of community violence on minority high school students.* Unpublished doctoral dissertation, University of California, Los Angeles.

Lewinsohn, P. M., Hops, H., Roberts, R. E., Seeley, J., & Andrews, J. (1993). Adolescent psychopathology: I. Prevalence and incidence of depression and other DSM-III-R disorders in high school students. *Journal of Abnormal Psychology, 102,* 133-144.

Lewinsohn, P. M., Rohde, P., & Seeley, J. R. (1995). Adolescent psychopathology: III. The clinical consequences of comorbidity. *Journal of the American Academy of Child and Adolescent Psychiatry, 34,* 510-519.

Licitra-Kleckler, D. M., & Waas, G. A. (1993). Perceived social support among high-stress adolescents: The role of peers and family. *Journal of Adolescent Research, 8*(4), 381-402.

Liddell, C., Kvalsvig, J., Qotyana, P., & Shabalala, A. (1994). Community violence and youth South African children's involvement in aggression. *International Journal of Behavioral Development, 17,* 613-628.

Lorion, R. P., & Saltzman, W. (1993). Children's exposure to community violence: Following a path from concern to research to action. *Psychiatry, 56,* 55-65.

Macksoud, M. (1992). Assessing war trauma in children: A case study of Lebanese children. *Journal of Refugee Studies, 5,* 1-15.

Macksoud, M., & Aber, L. (1996). The war experiences and psychosocial development of children in Lebanon. *Child Development, 67,* 70-88.

Mahjoub, A., Leyens, J., Yzerby, V., & Di Giacomo, J. (1989). War stress and coping modes: Representations of self-identity and time perspective among Palestinian children. *International Journal of Mental Health, 18,* 44-62.

McNally, R. J. (1993). Stressors that produce posttraumatic stress disorder in children. In J. R. T. Davidson & E. B. Foa (Eds.), *Post-traumatic stress disorder: DSM-IV and beyond* (pp. 57-74). Washington, DC: American Psychiatric Press.

Mollica, R. F., Caspi-Yavin, Y., Lavelle, J., Tor, S., Yang, T., Chan, S., Pham, T., Ryan, A., & de Marneffe, D. (1993). *The Harvard trauma questionnaire (HTQ): Manual.* Unpublished manuscript, Harvard School of Public Health, Harvard Program in Refugee Trauma, Cambridge, MA.

Mollica, R. F., Fish-Murray, C., Donelan, K, Dunn-Strohecker, M., Tor, S., Lavelle, J., & Blendon, R. J. (1991). *Repatriation and disability: A community study of health, mental health, and social functioning of the Khmer residents of Site Two. Vol. 2: Khmer children (12-13 Years of Age).* Working Document, Harvard Program in Refugee Trauma: Harvard School of Public Health and the World Federation for Mental Health. Unpublished report.

Mollica, R. F. & Jalbert, R. R. (1989, February). *Community of confinement: The mental health crisis in Site Two (displaced persons camps on the Thai-Kampuchean border).* Alexandria, VA: World Federation for Mental Health.

Morris, P., & Silove, D. (1992, August). Cultural influences in psychotherapy with refugee survivors of torture and trauma. *Hospital and Community Psychiatry, 43*(8), 820-824.

Neisser, U. (Ed.). (1986). *The school achievement of minority children: New perspectives.* Hillsdale, NJ: Lawrence Erlbaum.

O'Carroll, C. W. (1988). Homicides among black males 15-24 years of age, 1970-1980. *Morbidity and Mortality Weekly Report, 37*, 543-545.

Oetting, E. R., & Beauvais, F. (1990-91). Orthogonal cultural identification theory: The cultural identification of minority adolescents. *The International Journal of the Addictions, 25(5A & 6A)*, 655-685.

Oetting, E. R. & Swaim, R. C. (1996). *Factor structure and invariance of the orthogonal cultural identification scale among American Indian and Mexican American Youth.* Unpublished paper.

Procidano, M. E. (1992). The nature of perceived social support: Findings of meta-analytic studies. In C. D. Spielberger & J. N. Butcher (Eds.), *Advances in personality assessment*, (Vol. 9, pp. 1-26), Hillsdale, NJ: Lawrence Erlbaum Associates.

Procidano, M. E., & Heller, K. (1983). Measures of perceived social support from friends and from family: Three validation studies. *American Journal of Community Psychology, 11*, 1-24.

Punamaki, R. (1989). Factors affecting the mental health of Palestinian children exposed to political violence. *International Journal of Mental Health, 18*, 63-79.

Pynoos, R. S., Steinberg, A. M., and Wraith, R. (1995). A developmental model of childhood traumatic stress. In D. Cicchetti and D. Cohen (Eds.), *Developmental psychology Vol. 2: Risk, disorder, and adaptation* (pp. 72-95). New York: John Wiley & Sons.

Raia, J. A. (1995). *Perceived social support and coping as moderators of effects of children's exposure to community violence.* Unpublished doctoral dissertation, University of California, Los Angeles.

Richters, J. E., and Martinez, P. (February, 1993). The NIMH community violence project: I. Children as victims of and witnesses to violence. *Psychiatry, 56*, 7-21.

Richters, J. E., & Saltzman, W. R. (1990). *Survey of children's exposure to community violence.* Rockville, MD: National Institute of Mental Health.

Rosenblatt, R. (1983). *Children of war.* Garden City, NY: Anchor Press.

Rutter, M. (1985). Resilience in the face of adversity: Protective factors and resistance to psychiatric disorder. *British Journal of Psychiatry, 147*, 598-611.

Rutter, M. (1987). Continuities and discontinuities from infancy. In J. Osofsky (Ed.), *Handbook of infant development* (2nd ed.). New York: Wiley.

Rutter, M. (1990). Psychosocial resilience and protective mechanisms. In J. Rolf, A. S. Masten, D. Chicchetti, K. H. Neuchterlein, & S. Weintraub (Eds.), *Risk and protective factors in the development of psychopathology* (pp. 181-214). New York: Cambridge University Press.

Sack, W. H., Angell, R. H., Kinzie, J. D., & Rath, B. (1986). The psychiatric effects of massive trauma on Cambodian children: II. The family, the home, and the school. *Journal of the American Academy of Child Psychiatry, 25*, 377-383.

Sack, W. H., Clarke, G., Him, C., Dickason, D., Goff, B., Lanham, K, & Kinzie, J. D. (1993, March). A 6-year follow-up study of Cambodian refugee adolescents traumatized as children. *Journal of American Academy of Child and Adolescent Psychiatry, 32*(2), 431-437.

Sack, W. H., Clarke, G. N., & Seeley, J. (1996). Multiple forms of stress in Cambodian adolescent refugees. *Child Development, 67*(1), 107-116.

Sack, W. H., McSharry S., Clarke G. N., Kinney R., Seeley, J., & Lewinsohn, P.

(1994). The Khmer adolescent project I. Epidemiologic findings in two genera-tions of Cambodian refugees. *Journal of Nervous and Mental Disease, 182,* 387-395.

Saigh, P. A. (1992). *History, current nosology, and epidemiology in posttraumatic stress disorder: A behavioral approach to assessment and treatment.* New York: Macmillan.

Saltzman, W. R. (1995). Exposure to community violence and the prediction of violent antisocial behavior in a multi-ethnic sample of adolescents. (Doctoral dissertation, University of Maryland, 1995). *Dissertation Abstracts International.*

Singer, S. I. (1986). Victims of serious violence and their criminal behavior: Subcul-tural theory and beyond. *Victims and Violence, 1*(2), 61-69.

Singer, M. I., Anglin, T. M., Song, L., & Lunghofer, L. (1995). Adolescents' expo-sure to violence and associated symptoms of psychological trauma. *Journal of the American Medical Association, 273,* 477-482.

Terr, L. (1990). *Too scared to cry.* New York: Harper Collins.

U.S. Bureau of the Census. (1990). *1990 census of population.* Washington, DC: U.S. Government Printing Office.

U.S. Department of Commerce. (1992, July). *1990 Census of population. General population characteristics. California.* (1990 CP-1-6; Section 1 of 3). Washing-ton, DC: author.

van der Veer, G. (1992). *Counseling and therapy with refugees.* New York: Wiley.

Zane, N. (1996, February). *Evaluation status report of the UCC Youth Scope Project* (Technical Report). Long Beach, CA: UCC Youth Scope Project.

Zane, N. Jang, M., Ho, T., & Seeberg, D. (1995). *Competence through transitions (CTT).* Grant No.: 1H86-SPO4968-04. Biannual Evaluation Report (March 1, 1995-August 31, 1995). San Francisco, CA: Four Winds Research Corporation.

Zane, N., Park, S., & Aoki, B. (in press). The development of culturally valid measures for assessing prevention impact in Asian communities. *Drugs and Soci-ety.*

Zivcic, I. (1993). Emotional reactions of children to war stress in Croatia. *Journal of American Academy of Child and Adolescent Psychiatry, 32,* 709-713.

Adolescent Violent Behavior:
An Analysis Across
and Within Racial/Ethnic Groups

Todd Michael Franke

SUMMARY. The focus of this study was on the association between family characteristics (e.g., family structure, family cohesion), race/ethnicity and their relationship to violent behaviors in adolescents. Family characteristics represent one piece of a larger ecological model that includes individual, peer, school, and neighborhood/community factors. The current study uses data from the National Study of Adolescent Health (Wave 1). Add Health was a longitudinal study of adolescents in grades 7 through 12. The survey gathered information about the respondent's health and health-related behaviors, emotional well being, and family and school environment. The variables of interest in this study are all self-reported measures of violent behavior: (1) being in a serious physical fight, (2) seriously injuring someone, (3) pulling a knife or gun on someone, and (4) shooting or stabbing someone. Differences between those who reported being involved in violent behaviors are related, at least in part, to family cohesion, family structure, gender, and race/ethnicity. Family cohesion served as a protective factor in all four models of violent behavior regardless of racial/ethnic group. Attention needs to be focused not only on the other domains involved in this ecological model (e.g., individual, family, peer, school, and neighborhood/community) but also on the possible interactive effects of variables both within and across these domains. Future interventions need to focus their efforts on the multiple dimensions of youth violence as

Todd Michael Franke, PhD, is Assistant Professor in the Department of Social Welfare, School of Public Policy and Social Research at the University of California, Los Angeles.

[Haworth co-indexing entry note]: "Adolescent Violent Behavior: An Analysis Across and Within Racial/Ethnic Groups." Franke, Todd Michael. Co-published simultaneously in *Journal of Multicultural Social Work* (The Haworth Press, Inc.) Vol. 8, No. 1/2, 2000, pp. 47-70; and: *Violence: Diverse Populations and Communities* (ed: Diane de Anda, and Rosina M. Becerra) The Haworth Press, Inc., 2000, pp. 47-70. Single or multiple copies of this article are available for a fee from The Haworth Document Delivery Service [1-800-342-9678, 9:00 a.m. - 5:00 p.m. (EST). E-mail address: getinfo@haworthpressinc.com].

well as give consideration to a multi-pronged approach in addressing the needs of youth at risk for violent behaviors. *[Article copies available for a fee from The Haworth Document Delivery Service: 1-800-342-9678. E-mail address: <getinfo@haworthpressinc.com> Website: <http://www.haworthpressinc.com>]*

KEYWORDS. Violence, adolescence, ethnicity, family, transactional model

INTRODUCTION

A great deal of national attention is focused on juvenile crime, especially violent crime. This is particularly true in light of the recent events in Colorado and Arkansas. An examination of current criminal justice statistics indicates that arrests of persons under age 18 for index offenses[1] has gone down over the past 25 years. Although this is more noticeable in the case of property crimes, it is also true for violent crimes. In 1971 persons under the age of 18 accounted for 45% of all arrests, 23% of violent crime arrests and 51% of the property crime arrests. In 1996, persons under 18 accounted for 31% of all arrests, 19% for violent crimes and 35% for property crimes. While this snapshot indicates that juveniles' proportional involvement in crime, as measured by arrest activity, has decreased, the 19% represents approximately 102,231 arrests of persons under 18 for violent crimes. Moreover, a different picture emerges if you examine the severity of the offenses committed by juveniles. Over the same 25-year period there has been an increase in the severity level of the crimes committed. In 1971, 51% of persons under 18 were referred to juvenile court and 45% were handled in police custody and released. In 1996, 69% were referred to juvenile court, and police handled only 23% (Maguire & Pastore, 1998). The lack of any substantial impact on the proportion of youth involved in violent crime and the increase in the severity of offenses has intensified the search for predictors and interventions for violent behavior among adolescents.

Violence among American youth is a significant societal problem, and one which disproportionately affects minority youth (Prothrow-Stith & Weissman, 1991). The focus of previous research has been on youth violence as it is embedded in larger contexts or problems (i.e., antisocial behavior, conduct disorders, drugs) with scant attention paid

to the correlates or predictors of youth violence (Gorman-Smith, Tolan, Zelli, & Huesmann, 1996). Many previous studies highlight the
disproportionate participation of minority youth in these acts of violence. However, often the researchers investigating the relationship
between ethnicity and violence focus on comparisons between African
American or Hispanic youth or between these racial/ethnic groups and
White youth (Cotten et al., 1994; DuRant, Cadenhead, Pendergrast,
Slavens, & Linder, 1994; Gorman-Smith et al., 1996). This paper
focuses on identifying predictors across and within racial/ethnic
groups. Specially, this paper examines one piece of an ecological
model, the relationship between family factors and race/ethnicity and
how these relationships influence the likelihood of youth violence.
The identification of protective and risk factors related to youth violence will assist in the development of more effective prevention
programs for youth exposed to social conditions that place them at risk
for engaging in violent behavior.

LITERATURE REVIEW

Explanations for violent behavior run the gamut from the biological
makeup of human beings to various learning theories, but do not
individually address all the dynamics involved in the use of violence
(Sigler, 1995). Biological theories are usually linked to some form of
biological dysfunction (Siann, 1985). The sociobiologists (Lorenz,
1971; Wilson, 1975) and those individuals using a psychoanalytic
approach (Storr, 1970) explain aggression in terms of a survival in-
stinct. The social learning theorists (Bandura, 1973; Baron, 1977)
think about violence and aggression in terms of learning by observing
or modeling others' behaviors.

The theoretical framework this study uses to understand youth violence is based on a transactional and multilevel conception of the
development of such behavior. From this perspective, violent behavior
is neither the function of the individual alone nor the experiential
context alone. Behaviors are the product of the combination of an
individual and the social systems or contextual characteristics in
which youth are embedded (i.e., individual, family, peer, school,
neighborhood) (Bronfenbrenner, 1979; Bronfenbrenner, 1986; Sameroff, 1983; Sameroff, 1987).

On the basis of the conclusions drawn from several reviews, Henggeler (1996) found that a number of correlates consistently emerge: individual, family, peer, school, and neighborhood/community. The focus of this study is on the family, as it is most proximal and often the most influential of these systems. Evidence accumulated across a number of different disorders and problems indicates that the family is an important predictor of the presence, severity, and maintenance of youth violence, drug use, and conduct disorders (Block, Block, & Keys, 1988; Patterson, 1986).

The impact of family begins very early in a child's life and is very subtle. A child's early positive interaction with family members and others provides the opportunities, skills, and recognition for appropriate social development (Catalano & Hawkins, 1996). McCord (1979; 1991) found that home atmosphere and childrearing variables are both strong predictors of juvenile and adult criminality. She reports that home atmosphere may actually be a better predictor of adult criminality than an individual's juvenile record. Wadsworth (1980) using data from the British National Survey of Health and Development found that boys whose parents had gone through a separation or divorce were more likely to commit violent crimes. Farrington (1991) showed that violent offenders were more likely to have been exposed to harsh parental discipline and parental conflict than nonoffenders. Family relationship characteristics such as low levels of parental acceptance and affection, low family cohesion and high conflict and hostility have been associated with delinquent and antisocial behavior in numerous other studies (Henggeler, 1989; Tolan & Lorion, 1988; West & Farrington, 1973).

Gorman-Smith et al. (1996) studied the relationship between family influences and participation in violent and nonviolent delinquent behaviors among a group of 362 African American and Latino male adolescents living in the inner city. Participants were classified into three groups, violent, nonviolent and nonoffenders. They found that the differences between the groups could at least in part be attributed to differences in parenting and family relationship characteristics. Mothers and boys in the violent group reported poorer discipline, less cohesion, and less involvement than mothers and boys in the other two groups.

Using an ecological-developmental model, Fraser (1996) reviewed the current research and discussed implications for preventing youth violence. His focus was primarily on childhood and early adolescence.

Fraser asserts that conditions, processes, and experiences in the family shape the behavior of children. He draws distinctions between "early" starter and "late" starter youth with respect to their aggressive behavior. Family, home life, school and peers are the primary influences in the early starter model. In contrast, the late starter model is influenced more by systemic and contextual factors outside the family.

Not all the studies find support for the effect of family factors on violent or delinquent behavior. Cotton (1994) examined the extent to which family and individual factors are associated with aggression and fighting behavior in 744 African American middle school students. Cotton found that individual characteristics, gender, age, and attitudes towards violence were associated with adolescent's reports of violence and fighting behavior. Family characteristics were associated with school suspension but not fighting behavior.

PURPOSE

The purpose of this article is to provide a closer look at a piece of a highly complex, multisystemic model of adolescent behavior using a nationally representative sample of adolescents across four different racial/ethnic groups. The study focuses on family characteristics and how they impact the association between race/ethnicity and types of violent behavior. This study is designed to answer four primary questions regarding race/ethnicity, family characteristics, and violent behavior.

1. Does race/ethnicity significantly predict involvement in four types of youth violent behavior?
2. Are there differences in the likelihood of participation in violent behaviors of youth from different race/ethnic groups?
3. What role do family characteristics play in understanding youth involvement in violent behaviors?
4. What effect do family characteristics have on the association between race/ethnicity and youth involvement in violent behaviors?

METHOD

Sample

The current study uses data from the National Study of Adolescent Health (Wave 1). Add Health is a longitudinal study of adolescents in grades 7 through 12. The primary sampling frame included all high schools in the United States that had an 11th grade and at least 30 students in the school. From this, a systematic random sample of 80 high schools was selected proportional to enrollment size and stratified by region, urbanicity, school type and percentage White. The largest feeder school was recruited when available. The final sample was 134 schools. Schools provided a roster of all enrolled students and from those rosters a random sample of 15,243 adolescents stratified by gender and grade were selected for the in-home interview. Seventy-nine percent (12,118) completed the 90-minute interviews. The participants included in this study are a representative sample of 6,504 adolescents included in the public domain dataset.

Procedure

The Add Health survey consisted of two components, an in-home component and an in-school component. The in-home component was comprised of an adolescent interview, parent questionnaire, and a picture vocabulary test. The data used in this study primarily draws from the adolescent interview. Two items were taken from the parental questionnaire. The questionnaire gathered information about the respondent's health and health-related behaviors, emotional well-being, and family and school environment. Not all sections were administered to all respondents; adolescents were screened based on their age, gender, and past experiences so that only appropriate questions were asked. The interview was administered using both CAPI (Computer-assisted Personal Interview) and audio CASI (Computer-assisted Self-Interview) techniques. The more sensitive questions were administered using audio CASI.

Measures

Dependent

The variables of interest in this study are all self-reported measures of violent behavior: "In the past 12 months, how often have each of the following things happened," (1) in a serious physical fight, (2) seriously injured someone, (3) pulled a knife or gun on someone, and (4) shot or stabbed someone. All items were dichotomized for this analysis to never (0) and once or more (1).

Independent

The analysis included socio-demographic and family characteristics. The item responses for the variables in the analysis are based on the self-report of the adolescent unless otherwise noted. The socio-demographic variables included gender, grade (7th-12th), age, parents' educational level (high school or less, some post high school education, and college graduate), whether there is enough money to pay the monthly bills (No, Yes), and total household income. Parental education and total household income are drawn from the parental questionnaire. Total household income is included as a descriptive statistic. It is missing in more than 25% of the parental questionnaires.

The family characteristics included in the analysis are family structure, family cohesion, level of parental control, and activities with parents. All of these are constructed variables. A household roster and each household member's relationship to the adolescent determined family structure. When one or both biological parents were not in the home, the adolescent was asked if any other adult in the home filled the role of mother or father for them. An intact household indicates the presence of both biological parents in the home. A reconstituted household is one in which there is one biological parent and one other adult who is viewed by the adolescent as either a mother or father. A single parent household is one in which there is one biological parent but no other adult in the role of either mother or father. A kinship household is one in which there are no biological parents, but where the adolescent is living with adult relatives who are viewed by the adolescent as mother and father figures. Kinship in this study does not imply to a formal foster care arrangement. Less than 1% of the adolescents were in adoptive homes, and they were dropped from the analysis.

Family cohesion is a constructed measure of the relationship between the adolescent and the family. Family cohesion is the sum of three items: family understands you, family has fun together, and family pays attention to you. Each of these items are on a Likert scale from 1 to 5. The possible range of scores is from 3 to 15 with higher scores indicating greater family cohesion. The internal consistency for the scale achieved a Cronbach's alpha of .79 (Cronbach, 1951).

Level of parental control is a measure of the adolescents' feelings of how much control their parents' exercise over their lives. This measure may be more accurately thought of as a measure of the adolescents' perception of parental control. It is comprised of 7 dichotomous items (No, Yes) including: "Do you make your own decisions about," friends, clothing, amount of television, and diet. Possible scores ranged from 0 to 7. The internal consistency for the scale is .63 (Cronbach's alpha). Activity with parents, a dichotomous measure (No, Yes) assesses parent involvement with the adolescent in other activities such as sports, shopping or going to the movies.

Analysis

Descriptive statistics are presented for all variables. For categorical variables, percentages are reported, and for continuous variables means and standard errors are reported. The inferential procedures used include t-tests and analysis of variance for continuous outcomes and chi-square and logistic regression for the categorical variables (Fisher, 1938; Gosset, 1908; Pearson, 1900). For the logistic regression analyses, odds ratios (unadjusted and adjusted) and 95% confidence intervals are presented. Odds ratios greater than 1.0 indicate increased likelihood of the event (e.g., serious physical fight, shooting or stabbing) occurring, while odds ratios less than 1.0 indicate a decreased likelihood. For a given variable, the unadjusted odds ratio (OR) represents the odds associated with the outcome when only one variable is in the model. When two or more variables are present in the model, each variable is simultaneously adjusted for the presence of all other variables. An adjusted odds ratio (aOR) represents the odds when other variables have been entered to the model.

All estimates were calculated using the sampling weights to represent adolescents in the 7th-12th grade in the United States. The sampling weights and design effects were used to adjust for unequal probabilities of selection and to account for non-response. Statistical analyses were performed using SUDAAN, a program that adjusts for complex sample designs when calculating variance estimates (Shah, Barnell, & Bieler, 1997). Failure to incorporate the appropriate sampling weights and design effects leads to an increased probability of type I errors.

RESULTS

Socio-Demographic Characteristics

This nationally representative sample of middle and high schools students represents approximately 22 million adolescents (Table 1).

TABLE 1. Demographic Characteristics by Race/Ethnicity

		Hispanic	African American	Asian	White	Total
	Actual Sample Size	743	1557	226	3836	6362
	Weighted Sample Size	2,712,411	3,513,159	710,833	14,879,348	21,815,752
	Percent	12.4	16.1	3.3	68.2	
		%	%	%	%	%
Gender	Male	49.9	49.8	58.8	51.0	50.8
	Female	50.1	50.2	46.2	49.0	49.2
Last or current grade	Seventh grade	17.5	16.4	13.5	17.9	17.5
	Eighth grade	15.9	16.8	16.1	16.5	16.5
	Ninth grade	20.9	17.6	13.8	17.4	17.9
	Tenth grade	19.1	17.8	17.3	16.0	16.7
	Eleventh grade	13.4	15.4	17.2	15.5	15.3
	Twelfth grade	13.2	16.0	22.1	16.7	16.1
Parental Education*	High school diploma or less	68.4	56.1	34.6	43.7	48.3
	Some post high school education	21.1	28.4	18.8	31.9	29.7
	College graduate/post college education	10.5	15.5	46.6	24.4	22.0
Usually have enough money to pay bills*	No	29.5	27.4	15.6	12.7	17.0
	Yes	70.5	72.6	84.4	87.3	83.0
		Mean (s.e.)	Mean (s.e.)	Mean (s.e.)	Mean (s.e.)	Mean (s.e.)
Total household income* (in thousands) Range (0-999)		33.0 (2.4)	32.0 (3.2)	49.0 (4.5)	51.3 (2.5)	46.4 (2.2)
Adolescent Age Range (12-20)		15.9 (.11)	16.1 (.14)	16.2 (.2)	15.9 (.05)	16.0 (.05)

* p < 0.5

Overall, adolescents are distributed evenly across gender and grade with an average age of 16.0. Adolescents are predominately White (68.2%), followed by African American (16.1%), Hispanic (12.4%) and Asian (3.3%). These percentages closely match those available from the National Center for Educational Statistics (NCES) for the racial breakdown of elementary and high school students in the United States which are 64.8%, 16.8%, 13.5% and 3.7%, respectively (Snyder, Hoffman, & Geddes, 1997). Gender and adolescent age are almost identical across the ethnic groups with the exception of Asians' gender. Although not statistically significant, this survey found males represented in a greater proportion within the Asian groups than within other racial/ethnic groups. The proportion of the four groups across grades is reasonably stable with two exceptions. The proportion of Hispanics drops in the 11th and 12th grades, and Asians tend to be over represented in the 12th grade. Neither of these represents a statistically significant difference.

The largest proportion of parents (51.7%) has more than a high school education. The average household income is just over $46,400 (parent report), and 83% of the adolescents feel that there is usually enough money to pay monthly bills in their family. Statistically significant differences are found between the racial/ethnic groups on parental education, having enough money to pay bills, and total household income. The majority of Asian (65.8%) and White (56.3%) parents have some education past high school. More than 84% of the Asian and White students report that their families have enough money to pay the monthly bills compared to approximately 71% of the African American and Hispanic families. The average total household income for the Hispanic and African American students is approximately $17,000 less per year than for the Asian and White students.

Family Characteristics

Table 2 presents the family characteristics used in this study. The majority of adolescents in school live in intact families and are in-

TABLE 2. Family Characteristics by Race/Ethnicity

		Race/Ethnicity				
		Hispanic	African American	Asian	White	Total
		%	%	%	%	%
Family Structure*	Intact	53.0	30.8	77.5	62.2	56.6
	Reconstituted	10.6	8.9	7.8	12.3	11.4
	Single	34.1	54.3	13.1	24.1	29.8
	Kinship	2.3	6.0	1.6	1.4	2.2
Activities with Parents*	No	22.7	26.3	24.9	19.3	21.0
	Yes	77.3	73.7	75.1	80.7	79.0
		Mean (s.e.)	Mean (s.e.)	Mean (s.e.)	Mean (s.e.)	Mean (s.e.)
Level of Parental Control* **Range (0-7)**		4.8 (.07)	5.0 (.09)	5.0 (.17)	5.2 (.04)	5.1 (.04)
Family Cohesion* **Range (3-15)**		11.4 (.12)	11.4 (.09)	10.9 (0.2)	11.3 (.05)	11.3 (.04)

* p < 0.5

volved in some activities with their parents. The adolescents report feeling that their parents exercise a fair amount of control ($\bar{x} = 5.1$, out of 7) and the overall level of family cohesion is high ($\bar{x} = 11.3$, out of 15). Statistically significant differences were found between racial/ ethnic groups on measures of family structure, activities with parents, and parental control. For all other student groups except African Americans, intact families represent the primary family structure. For African Americans, over 54% of the adolescents report living in a single family home. Not surprisingly, given the data on family structure, African Americans adolescents report the lowest proportion of activities with their parents followed by Asian adolescents. Although there are differences between levels of parental control, the observed difference is only .4 on a scale that ranges from 0 to 7. Whites ($\bar{x} = 5.0$) feel their parents exercise the most control and Hispanics ($\bar{x} = 4.8$) the least.

Violent Behavior

Four different measures of violence are presented in Table 3. The measures represent increased severity levels (ranging from being involved in a serious fight to shooting or stabbing someone) and decreased proportions of occurrence. Based on data drawn from these measures of violence, it is estimated that over 7 million (32.8%) adolescents report being involved in a serious fight and over 400,000 (1.9%) adolescents report stabbing or shooting someone in the past year. Generally across all of the measures, Asian and White youth tend to participate in lower proportions than either African American or Hispanic youth.

Table 4 presents the odds ratios based on a logistic regression analysis for each of the four outcome measures with race/ethnicity as the

TABLE 3. Proportion of Violent Behaviors by Race/Ethnicity

	Race/Ethnicity				
	Hispanic	African American	Asian	White	Total
	%	%	%	%	%
Serious physical fight*	40.2	42.4	30.3	29.3	32.8
Seriously injure someone*	20.3	23.9	14.5	16.9	18.4
Pulled knife or gun*	6.7	8.8	4.5	3.0	4.5
Shot or stabbed someone*	3.4	2.5	1.4	1.5	1.9

* $p < 0.5$

TABLE 4. Odds Ratio for Measures of Violent Behavior

	Race/Ethnicity	Odds ratio	95% C.I.
Serious physical fight*	White		
	Hispanic	1.6*	1.3-2.1
	African American	1.8*	1.5-2.2
	Asian	1.0	0.8-1.4
Seriously injure someone*	White		
	Hispanic	1.3	.99-1.6
	African American	1.5*	1.2-2.0
	Asian	.8	.52-1.3
Pulled knife or gun*	White		
	Hispanic	2.3*	1.6-3.2
	African American	3.1*	2.3-4.2
	Asian	1.5	.73-3.1
Shot or stabbed someone*	White		
	Hispanic	2.3*	1.4-3.8
	African American	1.7*	1.1-2.6
	Asian	.93	0.3-3.3

* p < 0.5   OR–Odds Ratio

sole predictor. The reference group is White across all four measures. The initial question for all the measures began "In the past 12 months, how often have each of the following things happened." For the question concerning serious physical fights, Hispanic and African American youth are significantly more likely than White youth to be involved in a serious physical fight. African American adolescents are 1.8 times and Hispanic adolescents are 1.6 times more likely that White adolescents to have been involved in a serious physical fight in the past year. Although not shown in the table, additional analyses indicated that the African American and Hispanic adolescents are 1.7 and 1.5 times more likely to be involved in a serious fight than Asians. No other significant differences were found. For the second outcome, Hispanic adolescents were 1.5 times more likely than White adolescents to respond that they had seriously injured someone in the past year. There are no other significant differences between the groups.

In regard to pulling a knife or gun on someone in the past year, Hispanic and African American samples were significantly different from the White sample. African American adolescents are 3.1 times and Hispanic adolescents are 2.3 times more likely than White adolescents to have pulled a gun or knife on someone in the past year. There are no other significant differences between the groups. Based on the last questions, Hispanic youth are 2.3 times and African American youth are 1.7 times more likely to have shot or stabbed someone in the past year compared to their Whites counterparts. There are no other significant differences between racial/ethnic groups. All of these results mirror the percentages found in Table 3.

Unlike Table 4, Table 5 presents the results of a logistic regression analysis, which incorporates socio-demographic and family characteristics into the model with race/ethnicity. The reference group for each categorical variable is the one with no parameter estimates (odds ratios or confidence intervals). Since all these variables are entered simultaneously, all of the odds ratios presented in Table 5 are adjusted for the presence of all the other variables in the model.

Serious Physical Fight

After controlling for several socio-demographic and family variables, Hispanics and African American youth remain significantly more likely to be in a serious physical fight than White youth. The odds ratios remain fairly stable after the incorporation of the other variables at 1.57 for Hispanic and 1.71 for African American students. The Asian students are no longer significantly different from the Hispanic or African American cohorts as was the case in the initial model.

Several other family characteristics are significantly related to being in a serious fight. Adolescents in single parent (aOR = 1.57) and kinship (aOR = 1.6) families are significantly more like than adolescents in intact families to be in a serious physical fight after controlling for all the variables in the model. Family cohesion has a positive effect on the incidence of fighting. Increases in family cohesion reduce (aOR = .88) the likelihood of being involved in a serious physical fight. Adolescent age and parental education (some post high school and college compared to high school or less) are associated with lower probability of being involved in a serious fight. Being male, compared to female, is associated with a greater likelihood (aOR = 2.81) of being in a fight.

Seriously Injure Someone

The odds of seriously injuring someone are 1.47 times greater for African American than for White adolescents. No other significant

TABLE 5. Adjusted Odds Ratio for Measures of Violent Behavior

		Serious physical fight		Seriously injure someone		Pulled knife or gun		Shot or stabbed someone	
		aOR	95% CI	aOR	95% CI	aOR	95% CI	aOR	95% CI
Race	White								
	Hispanic	1.57*	1.18-2.09	1.33	0.99-1.77	2.26*	1.61-3.19	2.99*	1.68-5.32
	African American	1.71*	1.40-2.08	1.47*	1.13-1.91	2.71*	1.90-3.87	1.94*	1.18-3.17
	Asian	1.16	0.77-1.73	0.77	0.38-1.57	2.17	0.82-5.73	1.07	0.19-6.05
Gender	Female								
	Male	2.81*	2.42-3.26	3.24*	2.71-3.87	3.37*	2.37-4.77	4.8*	2.71-8.48
Parental Education	High school diploma or less								
	Some post high school education	0.82*	0.67-0.98	0.89	0.74-1.07	0.84	0.60-1.19	0.59	0.34-1.01
	College graduate/post college education	0.55*	0.43-0.68	0.62*	0.46-0.83	0.53*	0.30-0.96	0.72	0.36-1.46
Usually have enough money to pay bills	No								
	Yes	1.05	0.81-1.36	0.97	0.80-1.18	0.93	0.65-1.34	1.08	0.60-1.92
Adolescent Age		0.86*	0.82-0.90	0.90*	0.86-0.95	0.10	0.91-1.10	0.95	0.82-1.12
Family Structure	Intact								
	Reconstituted	1.17	0.94-1.47	1.10	0.80-1.51	1.42	0.80-2.54	1.54	0.73-3.25
	Single	1.57*	1.30-1.89	1.34*	1.14-1.58	1.90*	1.29-2.81	1.90*	1.06-3.39
	Kinship	1.60*	1.04-2.48	1.86*	1.25-2.76	2.73*	1.12-6.66	3.51*	1.16-10.62
Activities with Parents	No								
	Yes	1.15	0.92-1.44	1.13	0.92-1.40	0.91	0.63-1.31	0.79	0.46-1.35
Level of Parental Control		0.96	0.91-1.01	1.00	0.92-1.08	1.08	0.98-1.18	1.13	0.95-1.35
Family Cohesion		0.88*	0.86-0.91	0.88*	0.85-0.91	0.83	0.79-.087	0.80*	0.73-0.87

* p < 0.05   aOR–Adjusted Odds Ratio

differences were found. Similar to the family characteristics for physical fights, adolescents in single parent (aOR = 1.34) and kinship (aOR = 1.86) families are much more likely than intact families to have seriously injured someone in the past year. Family cohesion again has a positive effect; increasing family cohesion is associated with a decreasing likelihood of seriously injuring someone. Having a parent who is a college graduate compared to one who has only a high school education reduces the likelihood of being involved in a fight that seriously injures someone (aOR = .62). Increasing age of the child is associated with a decreased likelihood (aOR = .90). This means that as these adolescents get older, they are significantly less likely to seriously injure someone. Males are 3.2 times more like to be involved in a fight that seriously injures someone than females.

Pulled Knife or Gun

Similar to the previous results, race/ethnicity remains as a significant predictor of the outcome. African American and Hispanic adolescents are 2.71 and 2.26 times more likely to have reported that they pulled a knife or a gun in the past year, compared to White adolescents. These differences are consistent with the unadjusted differences (see Table 3) even after controlling for socio-demographic and family characteristics. There are no other significant differences between race/ethnicity. Adolescents who come from single parent and kinship families are almost 2 and 3 times more likely to have pulled a knife or a gun on someone in the past year (aOR = 1.90, aOR = 2.73). Family cohesion is associated with a decreasing likelihood of pulling a gun or knife. Having a parent who is a college graduate compared to one who has only a high school education reduces the chances by almost a half (aOR = .53). Males are 3.37 times more likely than females to have pulled a knife or gun.

Shot or Stabbed Someone

Hispanic adolescents are almost 3 times (aOR = 2.99) and African Americans adolescents are almost 2 times (aOR = 1.94) more likely to have reported that they shot or stabbed someone in the past year, compared to White adolescents. No other significant differences were found. Family structure and family cohesion continue to perform as they have in the previous outcomes. Adolescents in single parent (aOR = 1.90) and kinship (aOR = 3.5) families are significantly more likely to have reported shooting or stabbing someone in the past year. Increasing levels of family cohesion continue to be associated with a decreased likelihood of involvement. Parental education and age no longer have a significant effect, and males are almost 5 times more likely (aOR = 4.8) than females to have reported that they shot or stabbed someone.

DISCUSSION

As Reiss (1993) notes, the increasing concern about high rates of violence in and among adolescents has made the identification of contributing factors a priority. This study investigated one piece of a larger ecological model that includes individual, family, peer, school, and neighborhood/community factors. The focus of this study was on the association between family characteristics (e.g., family structure, family cohesion), race/ethnicity and their relationship to violent be-haviors in adolescents. The racial/ethnic groups were compared across several demographic and family characteristics as well as across the four outcomes measuring self-reported violent behavior.

Some of these results may not be surprising to researchers who have worked in the area of youth violence. However, few recently pub-lished studies have been conducted on a nationally representative sample such as this one. One of the strengths of this study lies in its ability to provide researchers and clinicians with a snapshot of middle and high school adolescents' involvement in different types of violent behaviors and the relationship of these acts of violence to family characteristics.

Several patterns become apparent in examining the data across the four violence measures. Differences between those who reported be-ing involved in violent behaviors and those who did not report engag-ing in violent behaviors, at least in part, are related to race/ethnicity, family cohesion, family structure and gender. Some of these differ-ences can be explained to a lesser extent by parental education and the child's age. Each of these is addressed separately.

Family Variables

Evidence accumulated across domains indicates that the family is an important predictor of the presence, severity, and maintenance of youth violence, drug use, and conduct disorders (Block et al., 1988; Patterson, 1986). In these analyses, family cohesion serves as a protective factor in all four models of violent behavior. An examination of the odds ratios indicates that as type of violent behavior becomes more severe, the positive effect of cohesion becomes stronger. This is particularly true as you cross over from the first two measures involving physical violence to the last two measures, which involve weapons. One interpretation of this result is that when working with adolescents and families involved in violent behaviors, increases in cohesion might potentially lead to a decreased level of involvement in these risk behaviors. These results are consistent with previous research (Gorman-Smith et al., 1996; Henggeler, 1989; Tolan, 1987). This clearly demonstrates the importance of family cohesion as one avenue to address this problem. However, increases in family cohesion may provide their most substantial benefit when used as a preventative measure after early identification of a potential problem rather than as a treatment approach later on. McCord (1996), using data from the Cambridge-Somerville Youth Study, cautions that interventions designed to undo the effects of deficits in backgrounds may not work. The success of family based interventions is likely to be a function of the onset of aggressive behavior (Fraser, 1996). That is, family cohesion will work best as a form of primary prevention by identifying individuals and families who are at risk for violent behavior and intervening at that point. Intervening in a family prior to the child/adolescent engaging in serious violence maximizes the probability of any increases in family cohesion impacting the adolescent or child. Moreover, working with adolescents and their families who are identified as being at risk may be more effective as a method of prevention than as a form of remediation. Finally, if family cohesion is to be effective as a prevention approach, it will need to take into account the multisystemic nature of the problem, including the cultural context in which the violence occurs.

Growing up in a single parent family is commonly believed to contribute to the increasing incidence of violent behavior by African American and White adolescents. While some studies have found no effect for family structure (Cernkovich & Giordano, 1987), family structure in this study was found to be significantly and consistently associated with all four measures of violent behavior. As the measures increase in severity, there is a notable increase in the likelihood of adolescents in single and kinship families, compared to intact families, becoming involved. This is most evident in kinship families. However, it is unlikely that family structure in and of itself is causally related to violent behavior. It is much more plausible that numerous social-environmental factors (e.g., poverty, neighborhood context) exist that would help explicate this relationship. For example, in this study, over 20% of the single parent and kinship families report not having enough money to pay monthly bills compared to only 13% of the intact families. What needs further study are the factors related to family structures (single parent and kinship families) that directly impact the incidence of violent behaviors. For example, multiple factors in the neighborhood environment may differ between intact versus single parent and kinship families offering children and adolescents very different socialization experiences and models with respect to violent behavior. Unfortunately, these variables were not measured in the present data set.

The lack of significant findings for the other two family characteristics, activities with parents and level of parental control, is somewhat surprising. Several other studies (Gorman-Smith et al., 1996; McCord, 1996) have found discipline and mother's level of control as significant predictors of violent behavior. The difference may be one of perception. In previous studies, measures like these have been taken from the mother or parents, while in this study the level of parental control was assessed from the point of view of the adolescent. The parent may be the first to recognize that they are losing some of their control or influence over the adolescent prior to that realization setting in for the adolescent.

Socio-Demographic Characteristics

Several of the other social-demographic variables acted as protective factors. Age was a significant predictor for the first two measures, physical fight and injuring someone. With increasing age, the probability of being involved in fighting or injuring someone is reduced. An examination of the percentage of adolescents involved in each of these behaviors indicates that although a linear relationship has captured this phenomenon, the relationship may more accurately be viewed as curvilinear (quadratic). The percentage of adolescents involved in these types of violent behaviors tends to peak at around 14 or 15 and then gradually declines. Elliot (1989) using data from the National Youth

Survey reported that the peak age of involvement was 17. This has a direct bearing on the starting points for prevention efforts and goes hand in hand with the discussion of increases in family cohesion as a means of prevention. Aggressive behavior is mediated by factors such as frustration, emotional arousal and pressures towards conformity. In conjunction with efforts at increasing family cohesion, efforts need to be targeted at increasing social skills for children and early adolescents who are deemed as being at risk. Depending on the age of the child, this could include mentoring, peer mediation and training in conflict resolution as part of the range of intervention approaches. The earlier this identification occurs, the more likely a multisystemic approach will be effective.

Gender is a significant predictor across all four models. Adolescent boys are more likely than girls to engage in these types of violent behaviors. Forty-one percent of the boys report that they have engaged in a serious physical fight in the past year compared to 23% of the girls. Ten percent of the girls report being involved in a serious physical injury compared to 25% of the boys. These percentages drop off quickly for both boys and girls. What is evident is that although boys are involved in these behaviors at a higher percentage than girls, girls are clearly involved in violent behaviors as well.

Race/Ethnicity

With one exception (seriously injure someone), Hispanic and African American adolescents are significantly more likely to be involved in violent behaviors than White adolescents. The odds ratios gradually increase as the type of behavior becomes more severe, implying greater differences between racial/ethnic groups the more severe the measures of violence. Across all four measures, the consistency of the odds ratios in the full model (Table 5) compared to the model containing only race/ethnicity (Table 4) supports the conclusion that race is having an effect independent of the socio-demographic and family characteristics (Baron & Kenny, 1986).

Given this pattern of results the temptation is to conclude that reported participation in violent behavior is a function of race/ethnicity. However, these results must be interpreted with caution since it is very unlikely that race/ethnicity, in and of itself, is a causal factor for violent behavior. Violence is not a uniquely racial problem (Fingerhut & Klienman, 1990; Rosenberg, 1996). Previous studies would suggest that youth violence could in large part be accounted for by economic and social factors associated with poverty and unemployment (Rosenberg, Carroll, & Powell, 1992; Runyan & Gerkin, 1989). This paper and the data reported here also suggest the need to more closely examine other correlates that have consistently emerged: individual, family, peer, school, and neighborhood/community. Our understanding of the role of race/ethnicity in youth violence is dependent on a clearer picture of these correlates and their relationship to the economic and social causes of violence.

In this study, comparisons of socio-demographic and family characteristics indicated that compared to White and Asian youth, African American and Hispanic youth come from families in which a smaller proportion of adults have a college degree, there is a lower household income, and a lower proportion report that there is adequate money to pay monthly bills. As a percentage, far fewer Hispanic and African American adolescents come from intact homes. The final model took these factors into account but the effect of race/ethnicity remained. Thus this analysis suggests that although family and socio-demographic characteristics are related to youth violence, race/ethnicity should not be ignored. This does not mean that race/ethnicity itself determines participation in violent acts, but as posited in the ecological model, behaviors can be thought of as the product of the combination of an individual and the social systems in which they are involved. Many variables possibly related to race/ethnicity were not measured. For example, differences in various opportunities for youth (e.g., recreational, occupational) as well as neighborhood living conditions. There are many structural variables that may be important as well as differences in perceptions (e.g., of potential for success). In the area of youth violence, we cannot continue to rely on indicators like race or ethnicity. Research questions need to be fashioned that provide a richer understanding of the relationship between race/ethnicity and the other mediating/moderating variables that are encompassed in an ecological/transactional view of youth violence. From an ecological/transactional perspective, an individuals' behavior is not the result of the individual factors or environment factors in isolation from each other. Violent behaviors on the part of children and adolescents represent the complex and reciprocal interactions between the individual and their environmental systems. Research questions need to address the interactions that occur between possible combinations of factors including the individual (e.g., drug use, low verbal skills, access to firearms), family (e.g., lack of parental monitoring, intergenerational communication), peers (e.g., association with deviant peers, poor social skills), school (e.g., dropout, academic performance) and neighborhood/community (e.g., poverty, lack of employment opportunities).

IMPLICATIONS

There are no immediate cures or vaccines for the problem of violence among youth, but there are steps that can be taken in the areas of research and practice. With the exception of family cohesion, the other significant variables in this model represent immutable characteristics of individuals or families (e.g., race, gender, family structure) not amenable to change. What needs to be done from a research perspective is to continue efforts at understanding the process through which these variables are predictive. Race and ethnicity should not continue to be used as a poor proxy for the various economic and social causes of violence. In part, researchers collect data on race and ethnicity because it is easy. It is not nearly as easy to collect data on the social and economic determinants of violence. But this is where researchers need to concentrate their efforts. Future research needs to tackle questions like "Will providing good housing, quality education and reducing poverty reduce violence?" Attention needs to be focused not only on the other domains involved in this transactional/ecological model (e.g., individual, family, peer, school, and neighborhood/community), but also on examining the possible interactive effects of variables both within and across these domains. This is extremely important since not all adolescents, subject to similar economic, social, and cultural contexts, engage in violent behaviors. Although this study focused on a constellation of family characteristics, multiple risks and resiliencies are apparent. These multiple risk factors, including drug and alcohol abuse, are at least associated with violence. In fact, many antecedents of drug abuse are similar to those of violence (Johnson & Belfer, 1995).

Future interventions need to focus their efforts on the multiple dimensions of youth violence as well as give consideration to a multipronged approach in addressing the needs of youth. These approaches need to acknowledge the violence, racism, and classism that adolescents experience at the hands of adults and peers (Prothrow-Stith &

Weissman, 1991). However, better treatment alone will not reduce the rates of violence seen among adolescents. In addition, efforts need to be focused on intervention with youth when they first initiate violence and prevention for at risk youth. Approaches that combine strategies across the variety of settings are necessary in order to make headway against youth violence. These approaches must have the flexibility and comprehensiveness to address the youth's needs across the systems in which the youth is experiencing difficulty (e.g., individual, neighborhood/community, etc.) and yet have the capacity to be individualized to fit the specific strengths and needs of the adolescent and family. For some, the approach might consist of strengthening relations within the family and providing the adolescent with a closer connection to school, while for others it might be training in conflict resolution, helping the family to understand the danger of keeping unlocked firearms in the home, and making sufficient changes in the community in order to ensure that the adolescents feel safe as they move around the neighborhood.

NOTE

1. An index offense is an offense that the Federal Bureau of Investigation tracts as part of the Uniform Crime Reporting Program.

REFERENCES

Bandura, A. (1973). *Aggression: A social learning analysis.* Englewood Cliffs, NJ: Prentice-Hall.

Baron, R. A. (1977). *Human aggression.* New York: Plenum.

Baron, R. M., & Kenny, D. A. (1986). The moderator-mediator variable distinction in social psychological research: Conceptual, strategic and statistical considerations. *Journal of Personality and Social Psychology, 51*(1173-1182).

Block, J., Block, J., & Keys, S. (1988). Longitudinal foretelling drug usage in adolescence: Early childhood personality and environmental precursors. *Child Development, 59,* 336-355.

Bronfenbrenner, U. (1979). *The ecology of human development: Experiments by nature and design.* Cambridge, MA: Harvard University Press.

Bronfenbrenner, U. (1986). Ecology of the family as a context for human development. *Developmental Psychology, 22,* 723-742.

Catalano, R. F., & Hawkins, J. D. (1996). The social development model: A theory of antisocial behavior. In J. D. Hawkins (Ed.), *Delinquency and crime: Current theories* (pp. 149-197). New York: Cambridge University Press.

Cernkovich, S. A., & Giordano, P. C. (1987). Family relationships and delinquency. *Criminology, 25*, 295-321.

Cotten, N., Resnick, J., Browne, D., Martin, S., McCarracher, D., & Woods, J. (1994). Aggression and fighting behavior among African-American adolescents: Individual and family factors. *American Journal of Public Health, 84*(4), 618-622.

Cronbach, L. J. (1951). Coefficient alpha and the internal structure of tests. *Psychometrika, 16*, 297-334.

DuRant, R. H., Cadenhead, C., Pendergrast, R. A., Slavens, G., & Linder, C. W. (1994). Factors associated with the use of violence among urban black adolescents. *American Journal of Public Health, 84*(1), 612-617.

Elliot, D. S., Huizinga, D., & Menard, S. (1989). *Multiple problem youth: Delinquency, substance use and mental health problems*. New York: Springer-Verlag.

Farrington, D. (1991). Childhood aggression and adult violence: Early precursors and later life outcomes. In D. J. Pepper & K. H. Rubin (Eds.), *The development and treatment of childhood aggression* (pp. 5-29). Hillsdale, NJ: Erlbaum.

Fingerhut, L. A., & Klienman, J. C. (1990). International and interstate comparisons of homicide among young males. *Journal of the American Medical Association, 263*, 3292-3295.

Fisher, R. A. (1938). *Statistical methods for research workers*. Edinburgh: Oliver and Boyd.

Fraser, M. W. (1996). Aggressive behavior in childhood and early adolescence: An ecological-developmental perspective on youth violence. *Social Work, 41*(4), 347-361.

Gorman-Smith, D., Tolan, P., Zelli, A., & Huesmann, L. (1996). The relation of family functioning to violence among inner-city minority youths. *Journal of Family Psychology, 10*(2), 115-129.

Gosset, W. S. (1908). The probably error of the mean. *Biometrika, 6*, 1-25.

Henggeler, S. (1989). *Delinquency in adolescence*. New York: Sage.

Henggeler, S. (1996). Treatment of violent juvenile offenders-We have the knowledge: Comment on Gorman-Smith et al. (1996). *Journal of Family Psychology, 10*(2), 137-141.

Johnson, E. M., & Belfer, M. L. (1995). Substance abuse and violence: Cause and consequence. *Journal of Health Care for the Poor and Underserved, 6*(2), 113-121.

Lorenz, K. (1971). *On aggression*. New York: Bantam Books.

Maguire, K., & Pastore, A. (1998). *Sourcebook of Criminal Justice Statistics*, (Online). http://www.albany.edu/sourcebook (July, 1999).

McCord, J. (1979). Some child-rearing antecedents of criminal behavior in adult men. *Journal of Personality and Social Psychology, 37*, 1477-1486.

McCord, J. (1991). Family relationships, juvenile delinquency, and adult criminality. *Criminology, 29*, 397-417.

McCord, J. (1996). Family as crucible for violence: Comment on Gorman-Smith et al. (1996). *Journal of Family Psychology, 10*(2), 147-152.

Patterson, G. R. (1986). Performance models for antisocial boys. *American Psychologist, 41*, 432-444.

Pearson, K. (1900). On a criterion that a given system of deviations from the probable in the case of correlated system of variables is such that it can be reasonably supposed to have risen from random sampling. *Philos. Mag., 50*, 157-175.

Prothrow-Stith, D., & Weissman, M. (1991). *Deadly consequences*. New York: Harper-Collins.

Reiss, A. J., & Roth, J. A. (1993). *Understanding and preventing violence*. Washington D.C.: National Academy Press.

Rosenberg, M. L. (1996). Violence in America: An integrated approach to understanding and prevention. *Journal of Health Care for the Poor and Underserved, 6*(2), 102-112.

Rosenberg, M. L., Carroll, P. W., & Powell, K. E. (1992). Let's be clear: Violence in America is a public health problem. *Journal of the American Medical Association, 267*, 3076-3077.

Runyan, C. W., & Gerkin, E. A. (1989). Epidemiology and prevention of adolescent injury, a review and research agenda. *Journal of the American Medical Association, 262*, 2273-2279.

Sameroff, A. J. (1983). Developmental systems: Contexts and evolution. In W. Kessen (Ed.), *Handbook of child psychology: Vol. 1. History, theories, and methods* (pp. 238-294). New York: Wiley.

Sameroff, A. J. (1987). The social context of development. In N. Eisenberg (Ed.), *Contemporary topics in developmental psychology* (pp. 273-291). New York: Wiley.

Shah, B. V., Barnell, B. G., & Bieler, G. S. (1997). *SUDAAN User's Manual, Release 7.5*. Research Triangle Park:NC: Research Triangle Institute.

Siann, G. (1985). *Accounting for aggression and violence*. London: Allen and Unwin.

Sigler, R. T. (1995). The cost of tolerance for violence. *Journal of Health Care for the Poor and Underserved, 6*(2), 124-134.

Snyder, T. D., Hoffman, C. M., & Geddes, C. M. (1997). *Digest of Educational Statistics 1997*. Washington D. C.: U.S. Department of Education. National Center for Educational Statistics.

Storr, A. (1970). *Human aggression*. Harmondsworth, England: Penguin.

Tolan, P., & Lorion, R. (1988). Multivariate approaches to the identification of delinquency-proneness in males. *American Journal of Community Psychology, 16*, 547-561.

Tolan, P. H. (1987). Implications of age of onset for delinquency risk identification. *American Journal of Community Psychology, 15*, 47-65.

Wadsworth, M. E. (1980). Early life events and later behavioral outcomes in a British longitudinal study. In S. Sells, R. Crandall, M. Roff, J. Strauss, & W. Pollin (Eds.), *Human functioning in longitudinal perspective: Studies of normal and psychopathological populations* (pp. 168-177). Baltimore: Williams & Watkins.

West, D., & Farrington, D. (1973). *Who becomes delinquent?* London: Heinemann.

Wilson, E. O. (1975). *Sociobiology: The new synthesis*. Cambridge, MA: Belknap Press of Harvard University.

Gangs as Alternative Transitional Structures: Adaptations to Racial and Social Marginality in Los Angeles and London

Jewelle Taylor Gibbs

SUMMARY. This paper reports the results of a comparative study of youth gangs in minority communities in Los Angeles and London, England. A combined qualitative-quantitative research design was used to obtain information on the experiences, attitudes and behaviors of Black youth who were involved with or influenced by gangs.

Measures included two semi-structured interview schedules for focus groups and individual youth, respectively. Demographic data and statistics on social indicators were obtained for this population in both cities from government and social agency reports on rates of school drop-outs, youth unemployment, involvement in the juvenile/criminal justice system, and health/mental health utilization.

The sample included a total of 144 African-American youth, ages 15-30, in 17 focus groups and 32 for individual interviews in Los Angeles, and a total of 86 Afro-Caribbean youth, ages 15-24, in ten

Jewelle Taylor Gibbs, PhD, is the Zellerbach Family Fund Professor in Social Policy, Community Change and Practice at the School of Social Welfare, University of California at Berkeley, Berkeley, CA 94720-7400.

This paper was originally presented at the annual meeting of the American Orthopsychiatric Association, Chicago, IL, April 1995. The author gratefully acknowledges the support of The Joint Center for Political and Economic Studies, Washington, DC in 1991-92 (in London) and the Zellerbach Family Fund, San Francisco, CA for their generous funding of this research in 1993-94 (London and Los Angeles).

[Haworth co-indexing entry note]: "Gangs as Alternative Transitional Structures: Adaptations to Racial and Social Marginality in Los Angeles and London." Gibbs, Jewelle Taylor. Co-published simultaneously in *Journal of Multicultural Social Work* (The Haworth Press, Inc.) Vol. 8, No. 1/2, 2000, pp. 71-99; and: *Violence: Diverse Populations and Communities* (ed: Diane de Anda, and Rosina M. Becerra) The Haworth Press, Inc., 2000, pp. 71-99. Single or multiple copies of this article are available for a fee from The Haworth Document Delivery Service [1-800-342-9678, 9:00 a.m. - 5:00 p.m. (EST). E-mail address: getinfo@haworthpressinc.com].

focus groups and 66 for individual interviews in London. Results suggest that gangs provide minority youth with an alternative transitional structure for achieving social and economic mobility. *[Article copies available for a fee from The Haworth Document Delivery Service: 1-800-342-9678. E-mail address: <getinfo@haworthpressinc.com> Website: <http://www.haworthpressinc.com>]*

KEYWORDS. African American youth, Afro-Caribbean/West Indian youth, racial and social marginality, urban gangs, youth violence

INTRODUCTION

During the past 25 years American society has witnessed a steady increase in gangs and gang-related activities (Covey, Menard, & Franzese, 1992; Huff, 1990; Sanders, 1994). These gangs are extremely diverse in ethnicity, age, and activities, ranging from Blacks and Latinos in the inner cities, to recent Asian and Russian immigrants, to White bikers and "skinheads" (Chin & Fagan, 1995; Huff, 1990; Sanchez-Jankowski, 1991; Joe & Robinson, 1980; Shelden, Tracy, & Brown, 1997; Vigil, 1988a).

Since Thrasher's (1927) early studies of gangs in Chicago, American social scientists have analyzed the structure, functions, activities, and underlying causes of gangs (Cloward, 1960; Cohen, 1955; Krisberg, 1974; Miller, 1976; Short, 1968). These earlier studies focused primarily on socioeconomic factors such as poverty and low-income neighborhoods, lack of economic opportunities, peer group sub-cultures, and social isolation. More recent studies of the gang phenomenon have adopted a socio-cultural or transactional perspective, focusing on the symbolic meaning of gangs in specific community contexts and the perceived benefits and opportunities of the gang for its members (Bing, 1991; Decker & Van Winkle, 1997; Huff, 1990; Klein, 1995; Sanchez-Jankowski, 1991; Sanders, 1994; Spergel, 1986; Vigil, 1988). As the focus of researchers has shifted from a deviance paradigm to a comparative cultural perspective on gangs, the findings have been enriched by qualitative approaches that provide a more nuanced and multidimensional portrait of the facilitating social conditions of gang formation, the motivations of youth to join gangs, the cultural variations in the structure and characteristics of gangs, and the multiple and diverse functions gangs serve for their members (Fagan, 1989; Maxson, Whitlock, & Klein, 1998; Molidor, 1996; Spergel, 1995;

Wang, 1994). A major conclusion that can be drawn from these studies of male and female juvenile gangs is that, while many gangs are involved in anti-social activities, violence for its own sake is not a universal feature of gang life but is associated with certain types of gangs who usually engage in violent behaviors that occur in circumscribed settings in relatively ritualized situations (Bing, 1991; Evans & Taylor, 1995; Joe & Robinson, 1980; Klein, Maxson, & Cunningham, 1991; Molidor, 1996; Sanchez-Jankowski, 1991; Sanders, 1994; Spergel, 1986; Tolleson, 1997).

In Western industrialized societies, the normative view of gangs is that they are outlaw organizations steeped in a culture of deviance that both condones and promotes anti-social activities and violent behaviors. However, from the perspective of the gang members as insiders, the organization has its own norms and internal structures, and primarily serves other significant functions that transcend the deviant behaviors and instrumental violence.

In her study of Mexican-American urban gangs, Moore (1978) proposed a useful interactive model of three central factors that create favorable conditions for gang formation, e.g., the ethnic minority context, the economic system, and the system of institutions and government. Moore's model, informed by her extensive ethnographic research on Chicano gangs in East Los Angeles, provides a systemic perspective on the social, cultural, economic, and political factors that foster the development of gangs, facilitate their formation, and reinforce their legitimacy. Moreover, this model views gangs as a response to a set of historical and socio-cultural conditions that have created barriers to mobility for youth in disadvantaged and disempowered communities. In the following section, the youth gang phenomenon in Los Angeles and London will be analyzed in terms of Moore's (1978) model in order to gain a more comprehensive understanding of the factors contributing to the proliferation of Black gangs in both of these cities.

Ethnic Minority Context

In cities such as Los Angeles and London, minority families frequently live in segregated neighborhoods with high density housing, deteriorating facilities, and high crime rates (Bhat, Carr-Hill, & Ohri, 1988; Gooding-Williams, 1993). These families have histories of racial discrimination and/or exploitation and are both socially isolated and marginalized by the dominant society. Minority youth in these communities often perceive barriers to their success in schools and in jobs, and limited options for social or economic mobility (Adler, Ovando, & Hocevar, 1984; Cashmore & Troyna, 1982; Gibbs, 1992, 1993; Solomos, 1988; Taylor, 1995; Wilson, 1987, 1996). For immigrant youth there are generational conflicts with their parents and additional barriers to cultural adaptation, often exacerbated by racial and linguistic differences (Bhat, Carr-Hill, & Ohri, 1988; Gibbs & Huang, 1989; Solomos, 1989). This complex social reality provides the socio-cultural context in which gangs can become a viable alternative option for many ethnic minority youth (Sanchez-Jankowski, 1991; Klein, 1995; Smith & Krohn, 1995; Taylor, 1990; Vigil & Long, 1990).

The Economic System

The economic system in industrialized countries such as the United States and England tends to operate in ways that perpetuate low occupational stratification for minority workers, resulting in lower earnings, high rates of unemployment and high rates of poverty (Ashton, 1986; Troyna & Smith, 1983). Minority youth are more likely to experience high rates of unemployment, persistent job instability, and discrimination in the primary labor market where jobs pay higher wages, provide better benefits, and offer more mobility (Freeman & Holzer, 1986; Solomos, 1988; Warr et al., 1987). With limited incentives to succeed in the legitimate employment sector, minority youth may be easily recruited into gang activities in order to obtain illegitimate income (Fagan, 1990; Hagedorn, 1988; Taylor, 1990; Wilson, 1996).

System of Institutions and Government

The system of institutions and government in the United States and England reflect inequality for ethnic minorities in every major institution, including the systems of education, employment, criminal justice, health, and social welfare services (Farley & Allen, 1989; Small, 1994; Solomos, 1989). The cumulative impact of institutional racism is reflected in the anger, alienation, and distrust of ethnic minority youth toward the schools, the labor unions, the police, and social agencies (Cashmore & Troyna, 1982; Gibbs, 1988; Solomos, 1988;

Taylor, 1995). These anti-establishment sentiments can be tapped by gang leaders and channeled into anti-social activities that provide outlets for the frustrations of these minority youth (Davis, 1993; Solomos, 1988).

The major purpose of this paper is to apply and extend Moore's (1978) theoretical framework to a study of contemporary gangs of young Black males in two major inner cities of the United States and England. The goals of the paper are: (1) to examine the growing phenomenon of gangs among urban Black males in two major industrialized Western societies; (2) to analyze the factors that facilitate favorable conditions for the development of gangs in urban areas; and (3) to delineate and describe the multiple psychological, social and economic functions that gangs provide for their members in these urban environments.

METHODS

The data on these gangs are drawn from a comparative analysis of African-American youth, in the 15-30 year age range, in Los Angeles, California and Afro-Caribbean youth[1] in London, England. The data reported in this paper are part of a larger ongoing study of the comparative socioeconomic status of Black youth in Canada, Great Britain and the United States (Gibbs, 1993, 1994).

The study was conducted from 1992-1994 through a dual research strategy, using a qualitative approach to obtain data from a diverse sample of Black youth with a semi-structured interview instrument, and a quantitative approach to obtain information on social indicators for Black youth, 15-30, in the areas of education, employment, and involvement in the juvenile and adult criminal justice systems in London and Los Angeles. The same research strategies and measures were employed in both cities.

The research was conducted in three stages: (1) Stage I: Three focus groups of Black youth in each city were set up to discuss their concerns, identify significant social and economic issues, and target key areas for developing research questions; (2) Stage II: Focus groups were recruited to discuss the issues/concerns identified in Stage I;

---

1. Afro-Caribbean youth are those whose parents or grandparents immigrated from the British West Indies; they also identify themselves as African-Caribbeans and Blacks.

(3) Stage III: Individual youth were recruited for life history interviews, and statistics on demographic data and social indicators were collected. The study was conducted in London in the Spring of 1992 and the Summer of 1993; it was conducted in Los Angeles over a 15-month period from September, 1993 through November, 1994.

Measures

Two forms of a semi-structured interview were developed for this study.

1. *Focus group interview.* This interview explored the attitudes and experiences of young Black youth in the educational system, in the labor market, and in the juvenile/criminal justice system. This interview lasted from one and a half to two hours.
2. *Individual interview.* This interview included demographic and biographical questions and covered the same topics as in the focus group interview. The individual interview lasted 60 to 90 minutes.

Data were collected from official sources on the status of Black youth, 15-30, in education, employment, and the juvenile/criminal justice system in both cities:

1. *Educational status.* Educational status and outcomes were measured by high school completion and/or drop-out rates for the youth;
2. *Employment status.* Employment status was measured by employment and/or unemployment rates;
3. *Juvenile/criminal justice status.* Involvement in the juvenile/criminal justice system was measured by arrest rates and incarceration rates for the youth.

Sample

Youth were recruited in two phases from a range of agencies and institutions serving the Afro-Caribbean community in London and the African-American community in Los Angeles. These institutions/agencies were selected by reputation from established leaders of civil rights organizations (e.g., the Los Angeles Urban League, the Commission for Racial Equality in London), elected officials, prominent clergymen, and leaders of professional associations. Cooperating agencies included Boys/Girls Clubs, Y.M.C.A., high schools and community colleges, youth development programs, job training programs, community centers, sports and recreation programs, church youth groups, and gang prevention programs.

All focus groups and individual interviews in London were conducted by the author; in Los Angeles the author and one African-American female doctoral student conducted focus group and individual interviews. The interviews were carried out in informal settings with minimal structure to facilitate spontaneous responses and frank discussion of the concerns and problems impacting the daily lives of these youth.

In the first stage of the study, youth, 15-30, were recruited to participate in a focus group at a specific community agency or setting. Agencies obtained permission slips from parents or their surrogates for youth under 18 to participate in the focus groups. In London, 86 youth (48 males, 38 females) participated in ten focus groups and in Los Angeles, 144 youth (85 males, 59 females) participated in 17 focus groups (see Table 1). These youth represented a broad spectrum of Black youth from diverse socioeconomic backgrounds with a range of experiences. However, four (40%) of the London and six (35%) of the Los Angeles focus groups were composed primarily of former gang members, juvenile offenders, youth with behavioral problems, or youth at risk for gang involvement.

In the second phase of the study, individual youth, 15-30, were recruited from the same agencies and organizations through a "snowball" sampling technique. In London, a total of 36 youth (20 males and 16 females), 15-30, and in Los Angeles a total of 32 youth (18 males and 14 females), 15-30, participated in the individual interviews. This paper reports results only for the focus groups in the study with specific attention to their knowledge of, attitudes about, experiences with, and participation in gangs or gang-related activities in London or Los Angeles.

Data Analysis

All interviews were recorded on tape with the consent of the participants; responses were summarized directly on the interview forms for individuals and the focus group discussions were transcribed.

TABLE 1. Sample of Youth Focus Groups

Demographics	London (n = 86)		Los Angeles (n = 144)	
Gender	Number	%	Number	%
Male	48	55.8	85	59.1
Female	38	44.2	59	40.9
Age	Age Distribution	%	Age Distribution	%
	15-17:16	18.6	15-17:47	32.6
	18-21:32	37.2	18-21:63	43.8
	22-25:24	27.9	22-25:18	12.5
	26-30:14	16.3	26-30:16	11.1
Range	15.0-30.0		15.0-30.0	
Mean Age	20.8		18.9	
S.D.	4.3		4.1	
Student Status	Number	%	Number	%
Not in School	30	34.9	18	12.5
High School Student	35	40.7	80	55.5
College Student	21	24.4	46	31.9
Employment Status	Number	%	Number	%
Unemployed	30	34.9	76	52.8
Part-Time Employment	34	39.5	51	35.4
Full-Time Employment	22	25.6	17	11.8

The interviews and focus group sessions were coded for content analysis and thematic analysis (Miles & Huberman, 1988). In addition to comments on the four major institutional systems, themes were categorized according to substantive topics (e.g., health, violence, drugs, gangs, teen pregnancy, housing, family, recreation, social policies, politics, racism, etc.) and level of analysis (micro, mezzo or macro). Major and minor themes were determined by frequency ratios in the focus group discussions. The demographic data on the individual interview forms and the focus group consent forms were coded and analyzed for descriptive information.

The quantitative data obtained from official government records were analyzed for measures of educational performance, labor force activity, and delinquency/criminal offenses. These data were used as independent measures to cross-validate the qualitative responses of the participants regarding their educational level, employment status, and involvement in the juvenile or criminal justice system. Methodological issues in conducting this research and overall results of the study have been reported in previous publications (Gibbs & Bankhead-Greene, 1997; Gibbs & Bankhead, in press).

FINDINGS

Gangs as a Visible Phenomenon

First, the issue of gangs and gang-related activities was spontaneously listed as one of the five major issues impacting on the lives of Black youth by all the focus groups in both cities (see Table 2). Gang drug-dealing and violence was a major daily concern of youth in both cities, where the majority of each group (60-80%) were affected in some ways by gangs. Most of these youth (80% in Los Angeles; 55% in London) were personally acquainted with gang members, lived in neighborhoods claimed by specific gangs, or had formerly participated in a gang.

Three types of gang members were described in Los Angeles: (1) current active members, (2) original gangsters (O.G.'s), who were older and inactive, and (3) "wannabees," younger boys who associated with gang members, adopted their colors and symbols and sometimes participated in minor gang-related activities. Afro-Caribbean gangs in London were described as more loosely structured and more

TABLE 2. Major Issues for Black Youth Focus Groups in London and Los Angeles

Issues*	Los Angeles (n = 144)	London (n = 86)
Lack of jobs/employment	1	1
Poor schools/educational facilities	2	3
Lack of community activities/ recreational facilities	3	2
Gangs/neighborhood violence	4	5
Drug trade	5	4

*The rankings of the issues identified by focus groups in each city were averaged across all groups to obtain the relative rankings in the above table.

mobile, moving between cities in England and between England and the Caribbean to conduct their illegitimate activities.

Gang members in both cities reported that they had engaged in a variety of illegal activities, including drug sales, burglaries, car thefts, gambling, and "hustling." Los Angeles former gang members also reported past involvement in drive-by shootings, violent gang fights, and periods of incarceration, but these were less frequently reported by London respondents.

In Los Angeles and in London, gang rivalries over territory ("turf"), drug distribution, graffiti challenges, and women, occasionally erupted into armed confrontations between gangs. Innocent bystanders have been caught in the crossfire, prompting media attention and community outrage (Bing, 1991).

The widespread popularity of the "gangsta" image in South Central Los Angeles ("gangsta rap," baggy clothing, gold chains) (Morgenthau, 1993) and the Rastafarian identity (reggae, dreadlocks, ethnic clothing) in Afro-Caribbean neighborhoods in London (Gilroy, 1987) has resulted in inflated estimates of gang membership by the police in both communities. In 1993, the Los Angeles police claimed that there were 393 gangs with approximately 48,000 active members; in the South Central area there were 85 gangs with 25,000 active members on file (Los Angeles Police Department, 1994). The two major African-American gangs are the "Crips" and the "Bloods," concentrated primarily in the public housing developments and lower-income areas of Watts and South Central Los Angeles (Bing, 1991). In London, the Afro-Caribbean gangs are called "Yardies," are located mainly in the areas of Brixton, Notting Hill and South London, communities with large concentrations of Caribbean immigrants. Estimates of gang members in London were more difficult to obtain, but police and community leaders reported that these gangs were becoming increasingly visible and violent in the inner-cities (Klein, 1995).

Factors Fostering Gang Formation

As Moore (1978) has proposed, the interaction of racial minority status, low-socioeconomic status, and institutional racism fosters favorable conditions for the formation of gangs and the recruitment of gang members, in Los Angeles and in London as well, where young Black males are the primary targets of racial discrimination and differential treatment in the public schools, in the job market, and in the juvenile justice system (Cashmore & Troyna, 1982; Gibbs, 1988; Gooding-Williams, 1993; Solomos, 1988). Focus group members and individual respondents in both cities were nearly unanimous in identifying racism in these three institutions as their primary problems, followed by concerns over gangs, violence, drugs, and police brutality.

Education. In the area of education, there were remarkable similarities in the experiences of Black youth in elementary and secondary schools in both communities. Respondents complained about five major problems for Black students in the schools in both cities: (1) tracking or streaming of Black students in the least challenging basic or general programs; (2) disproportionate placement in special education programs; (3) differential treatment in terms of disciplinary practices, suspension and expulsion rates; (4) lack of information about Black history and culture in the standard curriculum; and (5) lack of Black role models among the faculty, administrators, and staff.

Statistics on educational outcomes lend support to these assertions. Drop-out rates for Black youth in the class of 1988 in the Los Angeles Unified School District (L.A.U.S.D.) ranged from 63%-79% for high schools in South Central Los Angeles, compared to an overall drop-out rate of 39.2% for all students in their cohort in the district (Oliver, Johnson, & Farrell, 1993). In 1990, over 40% of Black youth, 16-24, in London had dropped out of high school or failed to quality for a general certificate of secondary education (GCSE) (Jones, 1993).

Employment. In the area of employment, focus groups in both cities described discriminatory practices in all phases of employment from job-seeking to job termination. Respondents reported that White employers frequently discouraged Black job applicants, challenged their qualifications, paid them lower salaries, treated them unfairly on the job, and terminated them without sufficient cause.

In 1990, Black youth had high rates of unemployment in Los Angeles, where over 40% of 15-24-year-old African American youth were out of work (Oliver, Johnson, & Farrell, 1993) and in London, where the rate of unemployment for Afro-Caribbean youth, 15-24 years, was over 25% in 1990 (Jones, 1993). In both cities, the unemployment rate for Black youth was twice the rate for White youth, and Black males had higher rates of unemployment than Black females.

Criminal justice system. Black youth in both cities viewed the juvenile and adult criminal justice system with anger and hostility, reporting frequent police harassment of Black males, unwarranted arrests, physical assaults, and a general lack of respect and due process for their rights. Judges, lawyers and probation officers were all viewed as participants in a legal system that systematically discriminates against Black males at every stage of the criminal justice process, and serves as an instrument of social control to maintain Black males at the bottom rung of these societies (Baker, 1994; Carr-Hill & Drew, 1988; Davis, 1993; Krisberg et al., 1986; Solomos, 1988).

Statistics indicate that young Black men are also over-represented in the criminal and juvenile justice systems in both cities (Gooding-Williams, 1993; Carr-Hill & Drew, 1988). In 1990, African-American males, 12-18, in Los Angeles County constituted 40% of all cases adjudicated in the juvenile courts, while older African-American youth, 20-30, also represented over 25% of those involved in the criminal justice system (Los Angeles Police Department, 1993).

Thus, these findings suggest that the intersection of marginal racial minority status, low-socioeconomic status, and discriminatory experiences in education, employment and the juvenile/criminal justice system contributes to a social context that fosters the development of gangs among Black youth in Los Angeles and London.

MULTIPLE FUNCTIONS OF GANGS

Current and former gang members offered a number of reasons for joining a gang, such as: friendship, surrogate family, safety, social activities, social status, respect, excitement, income, power, and just to have "something to do." Although the gang members in this study acknowledged that they sometimes engaged in violent behaviors, they viewed the violence as instrumental in achieving many of these other goals rather than as an end in itself. In their world view, violence was the ultimate strategy to use to obtain the resources and the rewards that were otherwise unattainable through legitimate channels (Bing, 1981; Vigil, 1988a; Evans & Taylor, 1995; Sanders, 1994). While the Black youth in both cities reported very similar motivations for joining gangs, Afro-Caribbean youth in London were more likely than African-American youth in Los Angeles to emphasize joining a gang as an affirmation of one's cultural identity and solidarity. However, groups in both cities viewed the gang as a vehicle for social identity and a form of social protest against the dominant White society. The responses of the focus group members and the individual youth were grouped into ten major functions served by membership in a gang: source of group identity, surrogate family, social status, self-esteem, social structure, social activities, security, social support, source of income, and redirection of anger and aggression.

1. *Source of group identity.* Many of these youth view the gang as a source of a group social identity, transcending ethnicity and social class.

> D.W., an older gang member in Los Angeles, recalls his interest in joining the Crips: "Being a home boy, you know, I wanted to be cool, hip-slicking cool. If you put a crowd of gang bangers across the street every day for ten days, and if I go over and stand with them every day, then I'm one of them now. It's just the environment you're brought up in. It's like a community of people who get together against the oppressor. It's like a tribe."

> B.K., the 19-year-old son of Jamaican immigrants in London, revealed: "Sometimes I feel like an outsider in Britain the way people look at me and treat me like I don't belong here. When I'm with my Jamaican mates, I feel at home, you know, we all come from the islands, and we got the same roots."

2. *Surrogate family.* The gang as a substitute family is a recurrent theme in both cities where respondents compared the gang to a family in terms of its roles, its stability, its rules, and its values. Former gang members were more likely than other respondents to describe their families of origin as dysfunctional, disorganized, or non-supportive.

> R.J., a former gang leader of the Bloods in Los Angeles, describes his close ties to the gang members: "It was like a family I could do things with that I couldn't do with my normal family. These people were tighter with me than my real family–they were people who were moving around with me, they were going to help me survive, they were going to be down with me."

> M.T., a 24-year-old Trinidadian immigrant in London, explained his attraction to the gang: "When I was younger, both my parents worked all the time. They never had time to take me to a soccer game or to a park on Sunday. That's how I got involved with a

rough crowd in my neighborhood. They became like my family–people who showed some interest in me; people I could count on when I got into trouble."

3. *Social status.* Gang members said they derived greater social status from their gang than from their family, particularly when the gang was successful in generating income for consumer goods such as cars, jewelry, stereos, and clothes.

L.D., a second-generation Jamaican immigrant in London, says: "What you see is what you get. A Black man can't make it here without a little business on the side. You got to join up with the right group to get some respect, to find your niche."

C.R., a 19-year-old high school dropout in Los Angeles, commented: "No way you can score with the chicks if you don't belong to a posse. You ain't nothing around here if you don't hang with the right gang because these chicks are looking for a dude who can show them a good time and get the goods for them."

4. *Self-esteem.* Gang members also view the gang as a source of an enhanced sense of self-esteem and being identified as a gang member earned one a degree of respect, envy, and fear from one's peers, enhancing one's reputation in the community and reinforcing one's sense of importance.

B.J., who has been in and out of juvenile hall in Los Angeles, says: "A lot of young brothers out there join gangs to try to get a name for themselves in the street. If you make a name in the street, you get respect in your neighborhood. People don't mess with you wherever you go. You got 'juice' and nobody tries to challenge you."

A.N., a 22-year-old Jamaican-born immigrant reported: "They keep the Black man down in this country and don't give you any respect. If you're in a gang, at least you get some attention and people watch their backs when you're around. Even the police show you some respect."

5. *Social structure*. Members agreed that the gang provided a more stable *social structure* with clear rules, discipline and norms in contrast to their home environments that were often disorganized and chaotic.

> K.C., living in a group home in London says: "I used to tell my Mum to buzz off when she started on me about things, but you don't challenge the gang leader. The cardinal rules are discipline and allegiance to the leader, so when he says you play by the rules and you have to put the group before yourself, then you don't ask any more questions."

> E.T., a 17-year-old probationer in Los Angeles, commented: "My mother is a junkie and my father is in prison, so I never had no decent home life. Ever since I joined the gang, I know I can count on a place to stay, food to eat, and clothes to wear. It's a relief to have some kind of schedule in my life."

6. *Social activities*. One of the major inducements of gang membership for many Black youth is organized social activity. With few public recreational facilities, movies or parks in their neighborhoods, "hanging out with the homeboys" in Los Angeles or "checking out the action" in London were popular forms of socializing, as well as sports, parties, entertainment and athletic events.

> P.D., a school drop-out in Los Angeles says: "A gang is like a club. We get together to form a posse because there's nothing to do in the 'hood.' So we have our own social activities–just chilling-out, you know."

> O.F., an 18-year-old son of a single Jamaican mother in London, complained: "If we stand around on the street corners or in front of clubs, the police arrest us for disturbing the peace. But in the gang we can drive around to parties and take trips out of the estates (projects) where we can just relax."

7. *Social support*. From these social activities and interactions, they gained a feeling of social support which they perceived as unavailable or inadequate from their own families. In fact, many respondents who were involved with gangs described their families as non-supportive,

highly critical, abusive and/or neglectful, behaviors which had alienated them from their families by early adolescence.

> G.N., a recent immigrant to London from Jamaica, comments: "My Dad works two jobs and my mom is sick, always stays in her room. If I didn't take up with the gang, I wouldn't know how to survive out here. I hooked up with my island people so I could figure out how to make it, you know, as a West Indian in this White country."

> H.W., a 24-year-old former gang leader in Los Angeles, said: "I always got a lot of support from my homeboys in the gang. Whenever I had an idea or made a suggestion, people listened. They didn't tear me down or tell me I was stupid like my family always did."

8. *Security.* The constant need for a feeling of security is linked to social support as a major incentive for joining a gang, particularly in neighborhoods with a history of internecine gang violence. Respondents reported that the gang provided safety in numbers and security from attacks by other gangs or battles over "turf" issues.

> M.C., an "O.G." from South Central asserts: "You don't feel safe if you don't belong to a gang. You got to watch your back all the time 'cause you never know when someone's gonna jump you just for no reason. If they see you're with your homies, they leave you alone."

> G.P., a second-generation unemployed Trinidadian, points out: "My mates are looking out for me when we're out in the street. It's dog-eat-dog out there and every person is out to take advantage of the situation. If you try to go it alone, you become a target, so you best find some mates to protect your interests."

9. *Source of income.* Gang activities are not only social or recreational, but primarily for the purpose of generating income for its members through the sale of drugs, stolen property, gambling or "street hustling." Respondents reported spending much time and energy in discussing, planning, and implementing illegal activities to generate income. As most gang members are not regularly employed

and have few sources of legitimate income, these activities assure their economic self-sufficiency.

> F.P., incarcerated in a Los Angeles juvenile camp, complains: "The O.G.'s recruit the young brothers into the gangs–they promise them money and clothes and stuff. Then they get them to sell drugs or steal things to make a profit for the gang."

> R.S., an 18-year-old Jamaican drop-out, comments: "The Brits don't want to hire us and you can't survive on the dole (welfare), so how's a man to make it without some little business on the side? If I didn't sell ganja (marijuana), I wouldn't be able to maintain myself."

10. *Redirection of anger and aggression.* Several former gang members described themselves as being "really wild," undisciplined, and indiscriminately hostile before joining a gang, but feeling more in control of themselves after joining a gang which ironically provided a greater rationale for their antisocial activities and focused their feelings of anger and aggression on more specific targets. Some viewed gang activities as a way to direct their aggression more appropriately. For example, gang members in London usually attack members of rival gangs and rarely attack innocent bystanders, according to several respondents.

> E.J., an O.G. now working as a gang counselor in Los Angeles, recalls: "Before I joined the gang, I was always angry, always fighting. Got myself into lots of trouble. After I joined the gang, I learned how to channel that anger, to use force only when necessary, not to waste my time and energy on stupid stuff."

> L.B., a 24-year-old Jamaican former gang leader, says: "I got out of the gang because the battle over drugs was out of control. When I started in the gang, I was an angry youth, but we fought with our fists and clubs. Now they fight with guns over a few pounds of heroin. I got out to learn a trade. I'd rather be poor than dead or crippled."

According to these respondents, gang members use violence as an instrumental means to achieve many of the other goals they seek in the group, such as a sense of security, a source of income, and social status.

Finally, "gangs" are synonymous with "youth" in these communities where most members become inactive in their late 20's or early 30's. To cite one former gang leader in Los Angeles: "You get out of the gang by the time you're 30 years old because by that age you're either in jail, crippled, or dead." In Brixton (a London suburb), a recently "retired" gang member concurs: "I just got tired of duckin' and dodgin' the police all the time. I'm thinking of settling down, maybe getting married, so now I'm looking for a real job, you know, something respectable." Although respondents reported that one rarely resigns from the gang without fear of retaliation, members are allowed to "retire" and become inactive, at which time they assume the status of "original gangsters" (O.G.'s) and become advisers or mentors to younger active gang members.

DISCUSSION

The results of this study indicate: (1) that gangs are a visible and significant phenomenon among Black youth both in Los Angeles and London; (2) that the interaction of racial minority status, low socio-economic status, and institutional racism fosters favorable conditions for recruitment of gang members in both cities; and (3) that gangs do, in fact, fulfill a number of important psychological, social and economic functions for their members beyond engaging in anti-social and violent activities (Decker & Van Winkle, 1997; Goldstein, 1991; Shelden, Tracy, & Brown, 1997; Vigil, 1988b) although the latter may be vehicles for fulfilling these functions.

A content analysis of these focus group discussions elicited ten major themes delineating the central functions fulfilled by gangs in their lives and daily functioning. In order of their relative frequency in group discussions, these ten themes are: social identity, surrogate family, social status, self-esteem/self-image, social structure, social activities, social support, security, source of income, and redirection of anger and aggression. Each theme is described briefly in terms of its functional role in the psychosocial adaptation of these youth.

1. *Social identity.* Gang membership provides these marginal, alienated youth with a sense of group belongingness and a positive social identity that is an alternative to the devalued and demeaned identity

frequently projected on to them by the dominant White society. Through the use of dress, symbols and language, the gang also allows them to incorporate aspects of their ethnic minority culture into an alternative identity that promotes cultural uniqueness and solidarity in response to social exclusion from mainstream society in the United States and England. For example, African-American gang members in Los Angeles have developed a distinctive form of dress including brightly-colored head ties ("do-rags"), club jackets, and baggy pants that reflect inner-city "hip-hop" styles, as well as a lexicon of slang associated with "black English" and urban rap music (cf. Bing, 1991; Gibbs, 1996). Similarly, gang members in London have developed a social identity based on "roots," a derivative of Afro-Caribbean culture that includes speaking a patois, wearing dreadlocks, and espousing Rastafarian ideology. This alternate social identity also incorporates the use of violence as a legitimate means to achieve the goals of the gang.

2. *Surrogate family.* Gang membership offers these youth a substitute quasi-family unit with its age-graded and hierarchical structure and its socialization to specific norms and values, an alternative to their own non-supportive or dysfunctional families. In Los Angeles, the majority of the gang members were alienated from their families and describe them in hostile and negative terms. Many complained of abusive, drug-addicted and anti-social parents who had frequently neglected, assaulted or abandoned them. In London, several of the respondents had joined their immigrant parents as adolescents and often felt excluded from the family unit and estranged from an unfamiliar culture. Their involvement in anti-social activities and their casual acceptance of violence might reflect the displacement of their anger at their parents onto more acceptable social targets.

3. *Social status.* Gang membership offers these youth enhanced social status in inner city neighborhoods where material possessions are often valued and admired as alternative symbols of success, irrespective of their origin or legitimacy. For these alienated youth, the usual channels of social mobility are blocked, especially for those who had dropped out of high school, were unemployed, and disconnected from traditional sources of social or economic achievement.

4. *Self-esteem/self-image.* Gang membership fosters a sense of self-esteem and a positive self-image in these youth by providing a sense of meaning, importance, and direction as an alternative to an otherwise

meaningless, purposeless, and unfocused life; albeit the value of gang membership is antithetical to mainstream social values. Within the context of their very constricted environments, these gang members have developed their own set of values that provide an alternative framework for evaluating their behaviors and goals, i.e., the ends are justified by the means, no matter how antisocial or violent.

5. *Social structure.* Gang membership provides these youth with a sense of order, greater discipline and goal-directed activity that is an alternative to an unstructured and undisciplined lifestyle, although the disciplined activities are frequently directed toward illegal and antisocial goals. Many of these youth grew up in fatherless homes or homes where both parents were unable to provide much supervision, regular meals, or appropriate discipline. They sometimes expressed a sense of relief that the gang had a strong leader and older members who established rules, enforced discipline, and rewarded conformity to the gang's norms, thus alleviating their anxiety about unclear expectations and the lack of structure in their lives.

6. *Social activities.* Gang membership offers opportunities for social and recreational activities through parties, sports, entertainment, and travel. These activities are organized by and for gang members, their partners and family members, affording them the semblance of "normal" leisure-time pursuits and a tenuous link to the wider community of participants and spectators. Since gang members are usually shunned by law-abiding youth and their families, they form social bonds within their groups to fulfill their needs for organized social and recreational activities.

7. *Social support.* Gang membership provides these youth with social support and mutual reinforcement that is an alternative to their perceived lack of parental support or alienation from community social institutions. In Los Angeles, the gangs are organized into "sets," smaller groups from a specific neighborhood, which function as cohesive units within the larger gang organization. In London, the gang members are linked by their Caribbean island origin, so they share a common heritage and reaffirm their cultural roots through external signs and symbolic behaviors.

8. *Security.* Gang membership provides its members with a sense of safety and security from the external threats of other gangs, their vulnerability to attack outside their own "turf," and their confrontations with the police. Gang members both in Los Angeles and London

expressed the need to be hypervigilant against the real possibility of attack from rival gang members, on whom they projected all their fears and insecurities.

9. *Source of income.* Gang membership provides a regular source of illegitimate income derived from the sale of drugs, burglaries, street hustling or other illegitimate activities. Although the income is illegitimate, it may be channeled into legitimate businesses and assets to avoid police scrutiny. In Los Angeles, gang members rationalized that the income gained from their illegal activities was a form of reparations from the dominant society that had oppressed them. Similarly, gang members in London justified their drug dealing operations as a response to a government that had colonized and exploited them.

10. *Redirection of anger and aggression.* Gang membership affords a vehicle for these youth to redirect some of their feelings of anger and aggression into prescribed anti-social activities with fairly predictable parameters, as an alternative to random violence directed against the general community. These youth often perceive that retaliatory violence or the threat of preemptive violence against their designated enemies is a strategy of self-preservation and personal safety in an unpredictable environment (Copeland, 1974; Decker & Van Winkle, 1997; Molidor, 1996; Sanders, 1994 Tolleson, 1997). At the same time, they may rarely display aggressive behaviors in the security of their own neighborhoods or in areas designated as outside of their enemies' territory. Thus, much of the violence initiated and carried out by the gang members could be characterized as instrumental, i.e., directed toward achieving a particular goal, rather than interpersonal or random.

This analysis of the major functions of gang membership for Black youth in Los Angeles and London supports the hypothesis that the gang itself becomes an alternative structure through which these marginalized minority youth can achieve certain basic psychological needs (social identity, self-esteem/self-image, sense of security, and redirection of anger and aggression), basic social needs (surrogate family, social structure, social support and social activities), and basic socioeconomic needs (source of income, social status) (Covey, Menard, & Franzese, 1992; Decker & Van Winkle, 1997; Hagedorn, 1988; Goldstein, 1991; Sanchez-Jankowski, 1991; Vigil, 1988).

In conjunction with this analysis of gang activities, it is also possible to view the gang as an *alternative structure* for the training of alienated inner city youth in leadership skills, entrepreneurial skills, and political skills (Bing, 1991; Moore, 1978; Taylor, 1990). The recent emergence of gangs in political activities in cities such as Los Angeles and Chicago lends credence to this hypothesis and suggests the potential power of gangs to influence urban political developments (*New York Times*, March 1995).

Since Black youth presumably age out of these gangs by their early 30's, active membership in the gang is time-limited and often results in serious injury, imprisonment or death at the hands of a rival gang or, less frequently, from a fellow gang member. In Los Angeles, many of the former gang members reported that they had witnessed drive-by shootings, had attended numerous funerals of fellow gang members and had themselves been victims of gunshot wounds. In London, former gang members reported fewer incidents of violence in the past, but they expressed concern over the recent escalation of gun battles in the 1990's between rival gangs in competition over the lucrative drug trade.

As they approach the age of 30, many of the older gang members apparently tire of the risk-taking behavior, the fear of retaliation, and the threat of arrest and imprisonment (Bing, 1991; Moore, 1991; Vigil & Long, 1990). Entering Erikson's (1968) stage of intimacy versus isolation, these young men seem to take stock of their lives and many eschew violence and begin to seek legitimate jobs, to establish families, and to develop a productive adult role in their communities.

Despite this "aging out" phenomenon, gang members have very few options for legitimate jobs due to the stigma of incarceration or a poor employment history (Covey, Menard, & Franzese, 1992; Shelden, Tracy, & Brown, 1997). In both cities, former gang members reported that they could find jobs primarily in gang intervention services or youth community programs. A minority had really transformed their lives by their late 20's through higher education, civic involvement, the helping professions (teaching, social work), working in the skilled trades, or setting up small businesses. Two well-known former leaders of the "Crips" and the "Bloods" in Los Angeles have been honored by President Clinton for their leadership in promoting the gang truce after the 1992 civil disturbances following the acquittals of the White police officers who assaulted Rodney King. In fact, President Clinton honored them at a luncheon during his first inauguration in January 1993 as part of his platform to rehabilitate the inner cities of America by reducing violence and providing employment opportunities to unemployed minority youth.

Given that the gang may provide an *alternative* structure for Black youth to adapt to their racial and social marginality in two predominantly White societies, gang membership is typically a *transitional* phase for these youth. It is a transitional phase which is particularly appealing to minority youth who feel excluded from mainstream society because of discrimination against them in schools, jobs, and the criminal justice system, all of which reaches its zenith for young Black males in late adolescence and early adulthood (Cashmore & Troyna, 1982; Gibbs, 1988; 1994; Solomos, 1988). Thus, for low-income Black youth in the inner cities in the United States and England, where the traditional avenues of mobility are blocked or perceived as unavailable, the gang also serves as an important *transitional structure* through which they can meet a number of their basic psychological, social and economic needs.

In London, where many Afro-Caribbean youth are the first-generation born and reared in England, the gang may function as a bridge between the West Indian culture of their parents, from which they are alienated, and the British culture of their host country, from which they are excluded (Gilroy, 1987; Small, 1983; Solomos, 1988). Caught between the norms and values of West Indian Caribbean culture and the institutional barriers of British society, these Afro-Caribbean youth reported feeling extremely self-conscious about being "marginal men" and viewed the gang as the source of an alternative social identity which supersedes race, class and nationality (Baker, 1994; Gilroy, 1987; Institute of Race Relations, 1987; Stonequist, 1935).

As is the case with the Afro-Caribbean youth in London, many African-American youth in Los Angeles are first-or second-generation Californians whose parents migrated from the South during and after World War II for better economic opportunities (Glasgow, 1981; Gooding-Williams, 1993; Horne, 1995). They have had to negotiate constantly between the southern folkways and expectations of their parents and the realistic barriers in the local schools and the labor market for Black youth. Consequently, both of these groups of Black youth have experienced frequent generational and cultural conflicts with their parents, who have sometimes responded by expelling them from the household and inadvertently pushing them toward the gang as a strategy for survival (Fagan, 1989; Krisberg, 1974; Sanchez-Jankowski, 1991). The gang then has become a *de facto* family for these youth, the crucible in which they have attempted to resolve their conflicted identity, their cultural confusion, and their need for social and emotional support.

IMPLICATIONS

Most traditional approaches for preventing, reforming or suppressing gangs have not proven to be either effective or long-lasting (Goldstein & Huff, 1993; Klein, 1995). In his critique of these approaches, Klein (1995) aptly notes: "Gangs are by-products of their communities: they cannot long be controlled by attacks on symptoms alone; community structure and capacity must also be targeted" (p. 147). Klein and other experts advocate community prevention and early intervention strategies which target at-risk youth as pre-teens and early adolescents with comprehensive programs of community outreach, parental involvement, youth development and recreation activities, development of school alternatives-to-violence curricula, job training and placement, and policy-community collaborative projects to reduce gang violence (Covey, Menard, & Franzese, 1992; Fox, 1985; Goldstein & Huff, 1993; Sanders, 1994; Spergel & Grossman, 1997). These authors also advocate conflict resolution strategies and violence prevention curricula as primary prevention approaches in elementary and secondary schools.

Increasingly, social workers and other helping professionals recognize the need for community-based youth intervention programs that involve mentoring, tutoring, substance abuse education, and conflict resolution workshops in small-group formats with intensive one-to-one relationships in order to provide personal support, skill building, and individualized counseling to youth at risk for gang participation (Freedman, 1993; Marshall, 1996; Mincy, 1994). Community practice also involves working to improve macro-economic forces as well as the functioning of community institutions (Weil, 1996).

If urban politicians and policy makers are seriously concerned about preventing the spread of gangs, they must develop viable solutions for these youth by strengthening their vulnerable families, improving their schools, developing violence prevention programs in schools and local communities, and increasing their employment opportunities (Gibbs, 1988; Solomos, 1988; Wilson, 1996). Without such realistic options in the 21st century, inner-city minority youth may continue to view gangs as an alternative vehicle for social identity and social mobility in urban industrialized societies that have consistently denied them access to full participation as valued and productive citizens.

REFERENCES

Adler, P., Ovando, C., & Hocevar, D. (1984). Familiar correlates of gang membership: An exploratory study of Mexican-American youth. *Hispanic Journal of Behavioral Sciences, 6*(1), 65-76.

Ashton, D. N. (1986). *Unemployment under capitalism: The sociology of British and American labor markets.* Brighton, England: Wheatsheaf.

Baker, D. (1994). *Reading racism and the criminal justice system.* Toronto: Canadian Scholar's Press, Inc.

Bandura, A. & Walters, R. H. (1959). *Adolescent aggression.* New York: Ronald Press.

Benyon, J. & Solomos, J. (Eds.) (1987). *The roots of urban unrest.* Oxford: Pergamon Press.

Ben-Tovim, G., Gabriel, J., Lew, I., & Stredder, K. (1986). *The local politics of race.* London: Macmillan.

Bhat, A., Carr-Hill, R., & Ohri, S. (Eds.). *Britain's Black population* (2nd Ed.). Aldershoot, England: Gower.

Bing, L. (1991). *Do or die.* New York: Harper Collins.

Brown, C. (1984). *Black and White Britain.* London: Heinemann.

Carr-Hill, R. & Drew, P. (1988). Blacks, police and crime. In A. Bhat, R. Carr-Hill, & S. Ohri (Eds.), *op.cit.*, pp. 29-60.

Cashmore, E. & Troyna, B. (Eds.). (1982). *Black youth in crisis.* London: George Allen and Unwin.

Chin, R. & Fagan, J. (1995). Social order and gang formation in Chinatown. In F. Adler & W. Laufer (Eds.), *The legacy of anomie theory: Advances in criminology theory,* Vol. 6. New Brunswick: Transaction Publishers.

Cloward, R. (1960). *Delinquency and opportunity: A theory of delinquent gangs.* Glencoe, IL: Free Press.

Cohen, A. (1955). *Delinquent boys: The culture of the gang.* New York: Free Press.

Commission for Racial Equality. (1984). *Racial equality and the youth training scheme.* London: Commission for Racial Equality.

Commission for Racial Equality. (1992). *Annual report.* London: Commission for Racial Equality.

Copeland, A. D. (1974). Violent Black gangs: Psycho and psychodynamics. *Adolescent Psychiatry, 3, 340-353.*

Covey, H., Menard, S., & Franzese, R. (1992). *Juvenile gangs.* Chicago, IL: Charles C. Thomas Publishers.

Davis, M. (1993). Uprising and repression in L.A. In Gooding-Williams (Ed.), *Reading Rodney King, reading urban uprising* (pp. 142-154). New York: Routledge.

Decker, S. H., & Van Winkle, B. (1996). *Life in the gang: Family, friends and violence*. Cambridge, England: Cambridge University Press.

Eggleston, J., Anjali, M., Dunn, D., & Wright, C. (1986). *Education for some: The educational and vocational experiences of 15-18 year old members of minority ethnic groups*. Stoke: Trentham Books.

Erikson, E. (1968). *Identity: Youth and crisis*. New York: W. W. Norton & Company, Inc.

Evans, J. P. & Taylor, J. (1995). Understanding violence in contemporary and earlier gangs: An exploratory application of the theory of reasoned action. *Journal of Black Psychology, 21*(1), 71-81.

Fagan, J. (1989). The social organization of drug use and drug dealing among urban gangs. *Criminology, 27*(5), 633-669.

Fagan, J. (1990). Social processes of delinquency and drug use among urban gangs. In C. R. Huff (Ed.), *Gangs in America* (pp. 183-221). Newbury Park, CA: Sage Publications.

Farley, R. & Allen, W. R. (1989). *The color line and the quality of life in America*. New York: Oxford University Press.

Fox, J. R. (1985). Mission impossible? Social work practice with Black urban youth gangs. *Social Work, 30*(1), 25-31.

Freedman, M. (1993). *The kindness of strangers: Adult mentors, urban youth, and the new volunteerism*. Cambridge, England: Cambridge University Press.

Freeman, R. & Holzer, H. (Eds.) (1986). *The Black youth employment crisis*. Chicago, IL: The University of Chicago Press.

Gibbs, J. T. (1996). *Race and justice; Rodney King and O. J. Simpson in a house divided*. San Francisco: Jossey-Bass Publishers, Inc.

Gibbs, J. T. (1994). Marginality and mobility: Afro-Caribbean youth in London and Toronto. Paper presented at Department of Social Work, McGill University, Montreal, Canada.

Gibbs, J. T. (1993). British, Black and blue. *Focus*. (April, 3-8), Washington, D.C.: Joint Center for Political and Economic Studies.

Gibbs, J. T. (1992). *After the L.A. riots: Social work's role in healing the cities*. San Francisco: Many Cultures Publishing.

Gibbs, J. T. (Ed.). (1988). *Young, Black and male in America: An endangered species*. Westport, CT: Greenwood Press.

Gibbs, J. T. & Bankhead, T. (in press). Joblessness and hopelessness: The case of African American youth in South Central Los Angeles. *Journal of Multicultural Social Work*.

Gibbs, J. T. & Bankhead-Greene, T. (1997). Issues of conducting qualitative research in an inner-city community: A case study of Black youth in post-Rodney King Los Angeles. *Journal of Multicultural Social Work, 6*(1/2), 41-57.

Gibbs, J. T. & Huang, L. N. (Eds.). (1989). *Children of color: Psychological interventions with minority youth*. San Francisco: Jossey-Bass, Inc.

Gilroy, P. (1987). *There ain't no Black in the Union Jack*. London: Hutchinson.

Glasgow, D. (1981). *The Black underclass*. New York: Vintage Books.

Goldstein, A. (1991). *Delinquent gangs: A psychological perspective*. Illinois: Research Press.

Goldstein, A. P. & Huff, C. R. (Eds.) (1993). *The gang intervention handbook.* Chicago, IL: Research Press.

Gooding-Williams, R. (Ed.) (1993). *Reading Rodney King: Reading urban uprising.* New York: Routledge.

Hacker, A. (1992). *Two nations: Black and White: Separate, hostile, unequal.* New York: Charles Scribner's Sons.

Hagedorn, J. (1988). *People and folks: Gangs, crime, and the underclass in a rustbelt city.* Chicago: Lake View Press.

Horne, G. (1995). *Fire this time: The Watts uprising and the 1960's.* Charlottesville, VA: University Press of Virginia.

Huff, C. R. (Ed.) (1990). *Gangs in America.* Newbury Park, CA: Sage Publications.

Institute of Race Relations. (1987). *Policing against Black people.* London: Institute of Race Relations.

Joe, D. & Robinson, N. (1980). Chinatown's immigrant gangs: The new young warrior class. *Criminology, 18*(3), 337-345.

Jones, R. L. (Ed.) (1989). *Black adolescents.* Berkeley, CA: Cobb & Henry.

Jones, T. (1993). *Britain's ethnic minorities.* London: Policy Studies Institute.

Klein, M. W., Maxson, C. L., & Cunningham M. (1991). "Crack," street gangs and violence. *Criminology, 29*(4), 623-650.

Krisberg, B. (1974). Gang youth and hustling: The psychology of survival. *Issues in Criminology, 9*(1), 115-131.

Krisberg, B., Schwartz, I., Fishman, G., Eiskovitz, Z., & Guttman, E. (1986). *The incarceration of minority youth.* Minneapolis, MN: University of Minnesota Press..

Larson, T. E. (1988). Employment and unemployment of young Black males. In J. T. Gibbs (Ed.), *op.cit.,* pp. 97-128.

Los Angeles Police Department. (1994). Interview with Captain Norman Rouiller, Commander of South West Area Precinct, May 13, 1994.

Marshall, J., Jr., & Wheeler, L. (1996). *Street soldier.* New York: Dell Publishing.

Maxson, C., Whitlock, M., & Klein, M. (1998). Vulnerability to street gang membership: Implications for practice. *Social Service Review, 72*(1), 70-91.

Miles, M. & Huberman, A. M. (1994). *Qualitative data analysis.* Thousand Oaks, CA: Sage Publications.

Miller, W. B. (1976). Youth gangs in the urban crisis era. In J. F. Short (Ed.), *Delinquency, crime and society.* Chicago: University of Chicago Press.

Mincy, R. B. (Ed.) (1994). *Nurturing young Black males.* Washington, DC: The Urban Institute Press.

Molidor, C. (1996). Female gang members: A profile of aggression and victimization. *Social Work, 41*(3), 251-257.

Moore, J. W. (1978). *Homeboys: Gangs, drugs and prison in the barrios of Los Angeles.* Philadelphia: Temple University Press.

Moore, J. W. (1991). *Going down to the barrio: Homeboys and homegirls in change.* Philadelphia: Temple University Press.

Morgenthau, T. (1993). The new frontier for civil rights: Gang violence in the Black community. *Newsweek, 122*(22), Nov. 29), 65-6.

Newburn, T. & Stanko, C. (1994). *Just boys doing business? Men, masculinity and crime*. London: Routledge Press.

Oliver, M. L., Johnson, J. H., & Farrell, W. C. (1993). Anatomy of a rebellion: A political-economic analysis. In R. Gooding-Williams (Ed.), *Reading Rodney King, reading urban uprising* (pp. 117-141). New York: Routledge.

Perkins, U. E. (1987). *Explosion of Chicago's Black street gangs: 1900 to present*. Chicago: Third World Press.

Robins, L. N. (1966). *Deviant children grow up*. Baltimore: Williams & Wilkins Co.

Sanchez-Jankowski, M. S. (1991). *Islands in the street: Gangs and American urban society*. Berkeley, CA: University of California Press.

Sanders, W. B. (1994). *Gangbangs and drive-bys: Grounded culture and juvenile gang violence*. New York: Aldine de Gruyter.

Shelden, R. G., Tracy, S. K., Brown, W. B. (Eds.) (1997). *Youth gangs in American society*. Belmont, CA: Wadsworth.

Short, J. (1968). *Gang delinquency and delinquent subcultures*. Chicago: University of Chicago Press.

Small, S. (1994). *Racialized barriers: The Black experience in the United States and England in the 1980's*. New York: Routledge.

Smith, C. & Krohn, M. D. (1995). Delinquency and family life among male adolescents: The role of ethnicity. *Journal of Youth and Adolescence, 24*(1), 69-93.

Smith, D. J. & Gray, J. (1983). *Police and people in London. Vol. IV: The police in action*. London: Policy Studies Institute.

Solomos, J. (1988). *Black youth, racism, and the state: The politics of ideology and policy*. Cambridge: Cambridge University Press.

Solomos, J. (1989). *Race and racism in contemporary Britain*. London: Macmillan.

Spergel, I. A. (1986). The violent gang problem in Chicago: A local community approach. *Social Service Review, 60*(1), 94-131.

Spergel, I. A. & Grossman, S. (1997). The little village project: A community approach to the gang problem. *Social Work, 42*(5), 456-470.

Stonequist, E. V. (1935). The problem of the marginal man. *American Journal of Sociology, 41*, 1-12.

Taylor, C. S. (1990). Gang imperialism. In C. R. Huff (Ed.), *op.cit.* (pp. 103-115).

Taylor, R. L. (Ed.) (1995). *African-American youth: Their social and economic status in the United States*. Westport, CT: Praeger.

Thrasher, F. M. (1927). *The gang: A study of 1,313 gangs in Chicago*. Chicago: University of Chicago Press.

Tolleson, J. (1997). Death and transformation: The reparative power of violence in the lives of young, Black, inner-city gang members. *Smith College Studies in Social Work, 67*(3), 415-431.

Troyna, B. & Smith, D. I. (1983). *Racism, school and the labor market*. Leicester, England: National Youth Bureau.

Troyna, B. & Williams, J. (1986). *Racism, education and the state*. London: Croom Helm.

Vargas, L. A. & Koss-Chiono, J. D. (Eds.), *Working with culture: Psychotherapeutic interventions with ethnic minority children and adolescents*. San Francisco: Jossey-Bass Publishers.

Vigil, J. D. (1988a). *Barrio gangs: Street life and identity in Southern California.* Austin: University of Texas Press.

Vigil, J. D. (1988b). Group processes and street identity: Adolescent Chicano gang members. *Ethos, 16*(4), 421-45.

Vigil, J. D. & Long, J. M. (1990). Emic and Etic perspectives on gang culture: The Chicano case. In C. R. Huff (Ed.), *Gangs in America* (pp. 55-67). Newbury Park, CA: Sage Publications.

Wang, A. Y. (1994). Pride and prejudice in high school gang members. *Adolescence, 29*(114), 279-291.

Warr, P. et al. (1987). The experience of unemployment among Black and White urban teenagers. *British Journal of Psychology*, V. 76.

Weil, M. O. (1996). Community building: Building community practice. *Social Work, 4*(3), 481-501.

Wilson, W. J. (1987). *The truly disadvantaged.* Chicago: The University of Chicago Press.

Wilson, W. J. (1996). *When work disappears.* New York: Alfred A. Knopf.

DATING VIOLENCE
AND SEXUAL ASSAULT

Dating Violence Among Chinese American and White Students: A Sociocultural Context

Alice G. Yick
Pauline Agbayani-Siewert

SUMMARY. A sample of 289 Chinese American and 138 White students from a university campus was recruited from social science courses to complete a survey on perceptions of and experiences with dating violence and gender role beliefs. White students were more

Alice G. Yick, PhD, is a Moses Fellow at Hunter College, School of Social Work, New York, NY 10021.

Pauline Agbayani-Siewert, PhD, is Assistant Professor, University of California, Los Angeles School of Public Policy and Social Research, Department of Social Welfare, Los Angeles, CA 90095.

The authors would like to acknowledge the Institute of American Cultures at the University of California, Los Angeles (UCLA) and the Senate Faculty Grant at UCLA for their support of this research.

[Haworth co-indexing entry note]: "Dating Violence Among Chinese American and White Students: A Sociocultural Context." Yick, Alice G., and Pauline Agbayani-Siewert. Co-published simultaneously in *Journal of Multicultural Social Work* (The Haworth Press, Inc.) Vol. 8, No. 1/2, 2000, pp. 101-129; and: *Violence: Diverse Populations and Communities* (ed: Diane de Anda, and Rosina M. Becerra) The Haworth Press, Inc., 2000, pp. 101-129. Single or multiple copies of this article are available for a fee from The Haworth Document Delivery Service [1-800-342-9678, 9:00 a.m. - 5:00 p.m. (EST). E-mail address: getinfo@haworthpressinc.com].

likely to define dating violence as physical and sexual aggression compared to the Chinese American students. Although the majority of students from both ethnic groups did not agree that dating violence is justified under various circumstances, the Chinese American students were more likely to provide a contextual justification for the use of dating violence. Findings also indicated that 20% of Chinese American students and 31.3% of the White students have experienced some form of physical dating violence since they started dating. For both the Chinese American and White students, those who were more likely to agree that various acts of physical aggression are considered dating violence were less likely to perpetrate physical dating violence in the last 12 months. The sociocultural context of dating violence and implications for practice and research are discussed. *[Article copies available for a fee from The Haworth Document Delivery Service: 1-800-342-9678. E-mail address: <getinfo@haworthpressinc.com> Website: <http://www.haworthpressinc.com>]*

KEYWORDS. Dating violence, Chinese American college students, gender role beliefs, sociocultural context

INTRODUCTION

Courtship provides an opportunity for adolescents and young adults to rehearse adult roles and problem-solving skills in intimate relationships (Bernard & Bernard, 1983; Flynn, 1987; Suarez, 1994). However, in exploring their newly-founded sexuality and roles with the opposite sex, they may conform to extreme, stereotypical gender roles in which the male assumes the dominant role, and the female takes on the more submissive role (Suarez, 1994). In handling conflicts, extreme strategies such as violence may be employed.

Initial studies in the United States on dating violence indicate that physical, sexual, and psychological aggression in dating relationships are prevalent. Makepeace (1981) found that 20% of a sample of college students experienced dating violence, and 70% reported being acquainted with someone who had experienced dating violence. Other prevalence estimates of physical aggression in dating relationships range from a low of 14.3% to a high of 60% (Bernard & Bernard, 1983; Deal & Wampler, 1986; Riggs, O'Leary, & Breslin, 1990; Gray & Foshee, 1997; Neufeld, McNamara, & Ertl, 1999). The literature also shows that both males and females engage in violence (Bethke & Dejoy, 1993; Deal & Wampler, 1986; Worth, Matthews, & Coleman, 1990; Gray & Foshee, 1997).

Most of the research on dating violence has focused on White college students (Cate, 1992; Follingstad, Rutledge, Polek, & McNeill-Hawkins, 1988; Makepeace, 1986), but minimal research has been conducted with Asian Americans such as Chinese American students (Foo & Margolin, 1995). Myths of Asian Americans being "model minorities" perpetuate the misconception that Asian Americans are problem-free (Crystal, 1989). However, research has indicated that the Asian community is not immune to intimate violence. In a study on sexual aggression among college males in Hong Kong, 20% reported committing some type of sexual aggression against their partner, and 2% admitted to forced sexual intercourse with their female dates (Tang, Critelli, & Porter, 1993). In another study conducted by the same researchers (Tang, Critelli, & Porter, 1995), 20% of Chinese females in a Hong Kong sample of an undergraduate class reported unwanted sexual contact by their dating partners.

It is crucial to examine Asian dating violence in a sociocultural context for several reasons. First, the Census Bureau predicts that by the middle of the next century non-Hispanic Whites will account for only half the U.S. population (Rosenblatt, 1996). Between 1980 and 1990, the Asian American population increased by 107%, comprising 2.9% of the U.S. population (*Asian Week*, 1990). Mirroring these overall demographic trends, the number of minority students in U.S. college and university campuses grew by 9.1% during the 1990 to 1991 period (Evangelauf, 1993). In 1994, college minority enrollment continued to rise, especially among Asian American populations (Gose, 1996).

Second, the Chinese culture has often been described as patriarchal (Ho, 1987; Tseng & Wu, 1985). The distribution and maintenance of power is allocated patrimonially (Bradshaw, 1994), and gender roles in Chinese culture are based upon hierarchical relationships in which men assume the dominant role (Ho, 1987). From birth, Chinese women are under the supervision of their fathers; after marriage, they are expected to obey their husbands, and if they outlive their husbands, they are to defer to their sons (Watson & Ebrey, 1992). In has been argued that structural factors such as these are related to violence against women. Specifically, feminist theorists assert that violence against women is rooted in patriarchal ideologies which results in male domination and an imbalance of the power distribution in male and female relationships (Dobash & Dobash, 1979). Moreover, research also suggests that adherence to traditional gender role beliefs is related to perceptions of and the use of intimate violence (Bernard & Bernard, 1983; Finn, 1986; Sigelman, Berry, & Wiles, 1984). In addition, exchange and resource theorists argue that when a man perceives his status relative to his wife is inconsistent with societal norms (i.e., a move towards egalitarianism), he may use violence in order to maintain his status (Campbell, 1992).

Finally, as the cultural diversity on university campuses continues to grow, culturally appropriate and sensitive services are needed to target and meet the diverse needs of students and the general community. Due to limited cross-cultural research on intimate violence and the general adherence to Western cultural hegemony in the social sciences (Hoff, 1992), the development of effective services and policies for specific ethnic groups has been impeded. Although the terms "cultural relevance" and "ethnic-specific service" have become common truisms in the field, Western paradigms are generally adopted due to the limited knowledge base. Consequently, victims of ethnic minority groups may be reluctant to seek institutional assistance, since services are not congruent with the group's cultural values. In fact, research has consistently documented that Asian Americans tend to underutilize social mental health services (Lee, 1997; Uba, 1994; Takeuchi, Mokuau, & Chun, 1992).

Given the lack of empirical data on dating violence among Chinese American young adults, the goal of this research study was to examine the factors shaping Chinese American students' perceptions of and their experiences with dating violence. To this end, the following research questions facilitated the study: (1) What are Chinese American students' definitions and contextual justifications of and experiences with dating violence? (2) What are Chinese American students' gender role beliefs? (3) What is the relationship between Chinese American students' perceptions of dating violence, gender role beliefs, and experiences with dating violence? A sample of White students is used as a point of comparison in order to understand the cultural context of Chinese Americans' perceptions of and experiences with dating violence.

REVIEW OF THE LITERATURE

Asian Cultural Values and Violence Against Women

Dobash and Dobash's (1979) landmark study traced the historical legacy of violence against women and its link to patriarchal ideologies and societal acceptance of violence against women. In Asia, norms of patriarchy buttressed much of the social order (Wong, 1995; Bradshaw, 1994). In China, for example, patriarchal norms led to the exploitation of Chinese women (Honig and Hershatter, 1988; Gilmartin, 1990). Female infanticide, slavery, child prostitution, forced marriage, rape, and wife abuse were common forms of exploitation of women (Gilmartin, 1990; Watson and Ebrey, 1991). Violence against women was (and is) also common in other Asian countries. Throughout Korean history, for example, the battering of women has been justified by cultural mores, which is believed to be rooted in male dominance (Song, 1992). Confucian precepts teach women that obedience to their husbands and their husbands' family is vital. Men are taught that they are valued more highly than women (Ho, 1990; Song, 1992). From birth, little boys are socialized to believe that sons are more valued than daughters (Ho, 1990).

Confucianism also prescribes specific rules regarding the family. A hierarchical structure defines roles of husbands and wives and parents and children (Chung, 1992). Each member has specific obligations, is bound by loyalty and filial piety, and is taught to not bring problems or disgrace on to the family. As a result, individuals' behaviors and conduct are modulated by the family and are considered a reflection of the entire family system (Ishisaka & Takagi, 1982). The concept of saving face is extremely important because the individual is heavily invested in protecting herself/himself as well as the entire family from shame. Related to this theme is the emphasis on social harmony. In contrast to Western notions of expressing individuality and maintaining a confrontational stance in order to protect one's rights, self-control, shame, and cooperation with the group are highly valued, and there is reluctance to disclose any incidents which might bring shame not only on to themselves but to the entire family system (Ho, 1987; 1990).

Perceptions of Dating Violence

The literature defines dating violence as any physical, psychological, or sexual act of aggression perpetrated against an individual in a dating context (Bernard & Bernard, 1983). Yet, how individuals define or perceive a particular social problem is influenced by sociocultural factors (Giovannoni & Becerra, 1979). Studying perceptions of dating violence can provide insight into the nature of dating violence.

Attitudes or perceptions can be viewed as underlying structures for behaviors, and as a result, understanding perceptions of dating violence can shed light on the etiology and maintenance of intimate violence (Dent & Arias, 1990). It has been speculated that there is a direct link between social attitudes and behaviors (Dent & Arias, 1990). In other words, individuals who sanction the use of interpersonal violence may be more likely to employ violence against their partners and/or possibly be victimized (Riggs & O'Leary, 1989). Tontodonato and Crew (1992) found that those who believed that violence between intimate partners is justified were three times more likely to experience intimate violence. Foo and Margolin (1995) also reported that justifying dating aggression in situations in which a partner is humiliated was a good predictor of individuals using dating violence. In examining the literature on dating and domestic violence, Carlson (1987) compares the differences and similarities of dating and domestic violence. Carlson (1987) cautions that attitudes toward violence do not consistently distinguish between violent and nonviolent individuals. Attitudes in themselves are not sufficient to suppress the occurrence of violence in dating relationships (Carlson, 1987).

Views of circumstances justifying dating violence is another element examined in the research literature. Studies generally show that American students believe that interpersonal violence is unacceptable (Henton, Cate, Koval, Lloyd, & Christopher, 1983; Smith & Williams, 1992). However, some believe that violence is justified in certain situations. Greenblat (1985) found that the majority of students did not support the use of violence toward spouses and rejected the view that husbands employ violence to demonstrate their love toward wives. However, a third considered violence warranted in situations of self-defense. Other studies have found a similar theme (Yick & Agbayani, 1997; Makepeace, 1986; Roscoe, 1985). Situations involving humiliation or jealousy are also frequently cited as being justifiable. Stereotypically, the cause of male violence is linked to cases where the male ego is attacked or in cases of public rejection and humiliation. Respondents frequently report that intimate violence is justified in cases of sexual infidelity (Arias & Johnson, 1989; Roscoe, 1985). Comparing a sample of Asian and White college students, Foo and Margolin (1995) found that the Asian students were more likely to justify dating violence in situations surrounding humiliation compared to their White counterparts. Although they did not speculate the reason for this trend, it is plausible that Asian cultural values emphasizing loss of face (Zane, 1993) may affect Asian students' perceptions. Yick and Agbay-ani-Siewert (1997) also maintained that Chinese values underscoring the importance of the family may be the reason why Chinese Americans justified domestic violence in cases of extramarital affairs.

Gender Role Beliefs and Dating Violence

Finn (1986) reported that male college students who endorsed traditional gender role beliefs were more likely to tolerate the use of violence in relationships. Similarly, other studies have demonstrated that violent men who scored higher on masculinity scales, and who endorsed more traditional attitudes toward women, were more likely to endorse violence compared to their non-violent counterparts (Bernard, Bernard, & Bernard, 1985; Thompson, 1991; Worth, Matthews, & Coleman, 1990). Thompson (1991) asserts that this trend is not limited to men; both men and women who have a history of employing physical aggression with dating partners were more likely to rate themselves as masculine. Follingstad, Rutledge, Polek, and McNeill-Hawkins (1988) found that victimization is also related to gender role beliefs. Female victims who reported earlier onset of dating victimization were more likely to endorse traditional values about gender roles.

However, the association between gender role beliefs and experiences with intimate violence is tenuous. Other studies have found no relationship between gender role perceptions and experiences with intimate violence (Bernard & Bernard, 1983; Neidig, Friedman, & Collins, 1986). In part, the ambiguity stems from the manner in which gender role beliefs are operationalized. Some researchers define gender role beliefs as attitudes toward gender roles and prescribed behaviors. Traditional expectations about women include obedience, deference, and loyalty regarding various issues in all spheres of their lives (Sugarman & Frankel, 1996). On the other hand, other researchers define gender role beliefs as gender role orientations or schema. This definition refers to the extent an individual's self-description embodies cultural definitions of gender appropriate attributes (Bem, 1993; Sugarman & Frankel, 1996). This research study focuses on gender role beliefs; that is, beliefs about women's rights and roles in various social domains in society. This conceptual definition of gender role beliefs was selected because of Asian cultural belief systems regarding patriarchal roles between men and women.

METHODOLOGY

Sample

This study is a subset of a larger cross-cultural sample on dating violence conducted at University of California, Los Angeles. A total of 289 Chinese American undergraduate students and 138 White students were recruited from Asian American Studies, social welfare, and other social sciences classes during one complete academic year. These classes were targeted because of the high enrollment of Asian students. Graduate students entered classrooms to distribute self-administered questionnaires and informed students of the voluntary nature of the study. Students took approximately 15-20 minutes to complete the surveys in the classroom.

Measures

The Perceptions of and Attitudes Toward Dating Violence Questionnaire was originally developed to measure attitudes towards domestic violence in the Chinese American community (Yick & Agbayani-Siewert, 1997). It was modified to include dating violence and contained two scales: Definitions of Dating Violence Scale and Contextual Justification of Dating Violence Scale. The Definition of Dating Violence Scale is comprised of nine closed-ended items that measure the extent to which respondents agree or disagree whether physical (e.g., punching one's date/partner in the face), psychological (e.g., criticizing one's date/partner in front of others) and sexual acts of aggression (e.g., forcing one's date/partner to have sex) are dating violence. A Cronbach's alpha of .80 demonstrated the internal consistency of the measure. The Contextual Justification of Dating Violence Scale is comprised of nine closed-ended questions that assess the extent to which respondents agree or disagree whether certain situations justify the use of dating violence. Examples of question items include having an affair, flirting, and disobeying one's date/partner. A Cronbach's alpha of .89 was obtained. Both scales employed a six-point Likert-type scale on which 1 indicated "Strongly Disagree" and 6 "Strongly Agree," with no neutral anchor point.

The Conflict Tactics Scale (CTS) (Straus, 1979) was used to measure students' perpetration and victimization experiences with dating violence. The CTS is a 14-item scale that measures the strategies individuals employ in handling conflict in a relationship (Straus, 1979). This 14-item version is used primarily in paper-pen administration, and it includes three subscales: Reasoning, Verbal Aggression, and Physical Violence. Respondents were asked how often they have used a particular behavior with or against a partner, as well as how often their partners have used that behavior with or against them in the *past 12 months*. Respondents were asked to select from six closed-ended responses ranging from never to three or more times. The instrument has tested high in reliability and construct validity (Straus, 1979). Cronbach's alpha was .89 for the Reasoning Subscale, .94 for the Verbal Aggression Subscale, and .99 for the Physical Violence Subscale. Although a newer version of the CTS (Straus, Hamby, Boney-McCoy and Sugarman, 1996) has been developed which includes sexual abuse and extent of injury experienced by the victim, it was decided that the new instrument was too long given the limited time constraints class instructors had given to the researchers. Respondents were also asked if they have ever experienced any physical violence (i.e., hitting, pushing) by a dating partner *since they started dating*.

The 15-item Attitude Toward Women Scale developed by Spence, Helmreich, and Stapp (1973) was used to measure gender role beliefs, which entail beliefs about the rights and roles of women in vocational, educational, intellectual, marital, and sexual domains. The measure uses a four-point Likert-type scale response format. Scores range from 1 to 4, with higher scores indicating egalitarian attitudes towards women. Cronbach's alpha of .80 with this sample is comparable to the original Cronbach's alpha of .85 with White female college students (Daugherty & Dambrot, 1986).

Demographic questions included students' current age, gender, ethnicity, class standing, place of birth, length of residency in the U.S., affiliation with fraternity/sorority, and when they first started dating.

Data Analysis

Measures of central tendencies and univariate analyses were used to describe demographic variables, perceptions of and experiences with dating violence, and gender role beliefs. Chi-squares, two-tailed t-tests, and analysis of variances were performed to examine ethnic and gender differences. Zero and first order correlations were employed to determine relationships between selected variables.

FINDINGS

Refer to Table 1 for the demographic profile of the sample. In general, more Chinese American and White females participated in the study. The sample was comprised of more upperclassmen (juniors and seniors) for both the Chinese American and White samples. The Chinese American students, however, were younger and started dating later than the White students. More (61.5%) of the Chinese American students were foreign-born compared to the White students (10.1%). Chinese American and White students who were born outside the United States have resided in the United States slightly over a decade.

Chinese American Students' Perceptions of Dating Violence

Table 2 shows the general factorial analysis of variance (ANOVA) that was conducted in comparing the definitions of dating violence among Chinese American and White students. Both ethnic groups were equally likely to define dating violence in physical and sexual terms. However, ANOVA findings demonstrated ethnic differences in definitions of dating violence. White students were significantly more likely to define dating violence in physical and sexual terms than the Chinese American students. Although the Chinese American students

TABLE 1. Demographic Profile of the Chinese American and White Sample[1]

	Chinese American	Whites
Gender (Females)	59.5	68.1
Age (Mean)	20.1	21.98[a]
Class Standing		
Freshman	13.1	2.9
Sophomore	23.9	10.2
Junior	29.8	33.6
Senior	33.2	53.3
U.S. Born (No)	61.5	10.1[b]
Years in U.S. (Mean)	12.9	11.1
Fraternity/Sorority (Yes)	6.2	4.5[c]
Age first started dating (Mean)	16.39	15.51[d]

[1] All values are in percentages unless otherwise indicated.
[a] $t = -4.96$, df = 153.358, $p \leq .001$
[b] $X^2 = 99.32$, df = 1, $p \leq .001$
[c] $X^2 = 7.93$, df = 1, $p \leq .01$
[d] $t = 4.49$, df = 349.61, $p \leq .001$

were less likely to define dating violence in terms of psychological aggression, the ANOVA findings did not reveal any statistically significant ethnic differences. In both groups, females were likely to define psychological and sexual acts of violence as dating violence significantly more often than males.

Table 3 presents the general factorial analysis of variance (ANOVA) findings for mean scores for contextual justifications by gender and ethnicity. In general, students from both ethnic groups indicated that they did not agree that certain situations warranted the use of violence. However, the ANOVA findings indicated that Chinese American students were more likely to provide a contextual justification for the use of dating violence compared to their White student counterparts ($F = 21.5$, $p \leq .001$). In addition, in both ethnic groups, males were significantly more likely to agree that dating violence is justified under certain circumstances ($F = 15.9$, $p \leq .001$).

Table 4 shows the mean scores for Chinese American and White

TABLE 2. Definitions of Dating Violence

| | Chinese | | | | White | | | | | Gender Effect[1] | Ethnicity Effect[1] |
| | Female | | Male | | Female | | Male | | df | F | F |
	M	SD	M	SD	M	SD	M	SD			
Physical											
Psychological Definition	4.00	.89	3.62	.81	4.26	1.07	3.72	1.06	1,350	17.44***	2.5
Sexual Definition	5.79	.70	5.53	.94	5.98	.11	5.73	1.00	1,354	5.1*	9.3**

* $p < .05$; ** $p < .01$; *** $p < .001$
[1] Main effects of gender and race were tested by using general factorial analysis of variance. None of interaction terms were significant.

TABLE 3. Contextual Justifications

| | Chinese | | | | White | | | | | Gender Effect[1] | Ethnicity Effect[1] |
| | Female | | Male | | Female | | Male | | df | F | F |
	M	SD	M	SD	M	SD	M	SD			
Contextual Justifications	1.93	.92	.234	.94	1.46	.63	1.87	.96	1,342	15.9***	21.5***

* $p < .05$; ** $p < .01$; *** $p < .001$
[1] Main effects of gender and race were tested by using general factorial analysis of variance. None of interaction terms were significant.

TABLE 4. Chinese American and White Students' Contextual Justifications of Dating Violence

	Mean	S.D.	df	t
She is caught having an affair				
Chinese	2.56	1.54		
Whites	1.61	1.06	367.723	7.380***
She is drunk				
Chinese	1.91	1.11		
Whites	1.34	.94	309.739	5.442***
He acted in self-defense				
Chinese	3.64	1.51		
Whites	3.75	1.54	418	-.687
She is screaming hysterically				
Chinese	2.10	1.21		
Whites	1.43	.91	343.286	6.345***
She's unwilling to have sex				
Chinese	1.55	1.22		
Whites	1.19	.90	353.418	3.430***
She is nagging				
Chinese	1.67	1.02		
Whites	1.25	.82	321.439	4.553***
He's in a bad mood				
Chinese	1.51	.97		
Whites	1.20	.82	310.399	3.453***
She's flirting				
Chinese	1.93	1.20		
Whites	1.34	.96	327.919	5.515***
She disobeyed				
Chinese	1.55	1.06		
Whites	1.20	.82	337.198	3.725***

***$p \leq .001$

students for each contextual justification situation and the results of the t-tests on ethnic differences. Overall, with the exception of situations of self-defense, Chinese American students were significantly more likely to agree that dating violence is warranted if a woman is caught having an affair, is drunk, screaming hysterically, unwilling to have sex, nagging, flirting, disobeying her partner, and if he is in a bad mood.

Chinese American and White Students' Experiences with Dating Violence

Table 5 compares students' experiences with physical dating violence by ethnicity and gender. Students were asked if they had ever experienced any physical violence in a dating relationship since they

TABLE 5. Comparison of Chinese American and White Students' Experiences with Physical Dating Violence

| | Chinese American | | | White | | |
	Total	Males	Females	Total	Males	Females
	%	%	%	%	%	%
Victim of physical dating violence since started dating	21.4	25.2	18.8	31.3	36.6	28.9
Victim of physical dating violence in the last 12 months	13.5	18.6	9.8	12.7	19.4	9.5
Perpetrated physical dating violence in the last 12 months	23.2	17.0	27.6	14.9	13.2	15.8

started dating. Slightly more than 20% of the Chinese American students reported being victims compared to 31.3% of the White students. However, chi-square analyses did not reveal any ethnic differences. Students were also asked if they had been victims and perpetrators of physical violence in a dating relationship in the last 12 months. Slightly more (13.5%) Chinese American students disclosed to being a victim than their White counterparts (12.7%), although this is not statistically significant. Almost a quarter (23.2%) of the Chinese American and 14.9% of the White students admitted to using some type of physical aggression against a date or partner in the last 12 months. However, chi-square analyses did not show any differences between the two ethnic groups.

Chi-square analyses did not reveal any gender differences within the two groups. Although not statistically significant, more Chinese American and White males reported to being victims of physical dating violence in the last 12 months and since they started dating. (Refer to Table 5).

Relationship Between Chinese American and White Students' Perception of and Experiences with Dating Violence

Tables 6a and 6b display the Pearson and partial correlations between definitions of and contextual justifications of dating violence with experiences with physical dating violence. For both the Chinese

TABLE 6a. Relationship Between Chinese American Students' Perceptions of Dating Violence and Experiences with Physical Dating Violence

	Perpetrating (Last 12 mos.)		Victim (Last 12 mos.)	
	r	Control for gender	r	Control for gender
Definitions				
Physical	−.18**	−.20**	−.16*	−.16**
Psychological	−.11	−.13*	−.07	−.04
Sexual	−.11	−.14*	−.10	−.08
Contextual Justifications	.18**	.21***	.19**	−.16*

*p ≤ .05 **p ≤ .01 ***p ≤ .001

TABLE 6b. Relationship Between White Students' Perceptions of Dating Violence and Experiences with Physical Dating Violence

	Perpetrating (Last 12 mos.)		Victim (Last 12 mos.)	
	r	Control for gender	r	Control for gender
Definitions				
Physical	−.19*	−.20*	−.05	−.07
Psychological	−.20*	−.23*	−.06	−.02
Sexual	−.037	−.08	.06	.08
Contextual Justifications	.17	.16	.05	.01

*p ≤ .05

American and White students, those who were more likely to agree that various acts of physical aggression are considered dating violence were less likely to perpetrate physical dating violence in the last 12 months. Although the correlations were weak, after controlling for gender, Chinese Americans students who tended to define psychological and sexual acts of violence as dating violence were less likely to perpetrate dating violence. In addition, for Chinese American students, those who were more likely to agree that certain situations justify the use of dating violence were more likely to perpetrate physical dating violence in the last 12 months. However, this was not true for the White students.

Although the correlations were weak, Chinese American students who were more likely to define physical acts of aggression as dating violence were less likely to be victims of physical dating violence, and this was true after controlling for gender (r = −.16, p ≤ .01). In addition, Chinese students who agreed that certain situations justified the use of violence were also more likely to have been a victim of physical dating violence in the last 12 months. However, this was not the case for the White students. Definitions of and contextual justifications were not significantly related to White students' victimization experiences with physical dating violence in the last 12 months.

Relationship Between Gender Role Beliefs and Perceptions of and Experiences with Dating Violence

The Attitude Toward Women Scale indicated that these Chinese American students had somewhat egalitarian gender role beliefs (M = 3.31). However, White students were more egalitarian (M = 3.53) than the Chinese American students, although this was not statistically significant. There were statistically significant gender differences in the two ethnic groups. Chinese American females were more egalitarian (M = 3.47) compared to Chinese American males (M = 3.05) (t = −8.76, df = 203.11, p ≤ .001). Similarly, White females were more egalitarian (M = 3.67) compared to their White male counterparts (M = 3.19) (t = −4.95, df = 42.29, p ≤ .01).

Table 7 summarizes the correlations between gender role beliefs and definitions and contextual justifications of dating violence. Although the relationships between gender role beliefs and definitions of dating violence were weak, they demonstrate that both Chinese American and White students who adhered to more egalitarian beliefs about gender roles were more likely to define various types of aggression, such as physical, psychological, and sexual acts of aggression against dates/partners as dating violence. Even after controlling for gender, there are statistically significant, albeit weak, relationships between

TABLE 7. Correlations Between Gender Role Beliefs and Definitions of and Contextual Justifications of Dating Violence for Chinese and White Students

	Chinese Gender Role Beliefs		White Gender Role Beliefs	
	r	Control for Gender	r	Control for Gender
Definitions				
Physical Violence	.36***	.35***	.21***	.27***
Psychological Violence	.21***	.13***	.30***	.18***
Sexual Violence	.26***	.22***	.30***	.27***
Contextual Justifications	− .33***	− .26***	− .44***	− .37***

*** p ≤ .001

gender role beliefs and definitions of various types of aggression as dating violence (see Table 7).

Chinese American and White students who were more traditional in their gender role beliefs were more likely to agree that dating violence is justified under certain types of situations. After controlling for gender, there is still a statistically significant negative relationship between gender role beliefs and contextual justifications of dating violence.

Pearson correlations were also conducted for both the Chinese American and White students to examine the relationship between gender role beliefs and physical victimization in the last 12 months and since students started dating. In addition, correlations examined gender role beliefs and perpetration experiences with dating violence in the last 12 months. However, findings did not indicate any statistically significant relationships.

DISCUSSION

Definitions of Dating Violence

Generally, intimate violence is defined in physical terms. Sigler (1989) noted that, historically, physical abuse generally receives greater public scrutiny and outcry, whereas neglect, psychological, and emotional abuse are more difficult to document. As a result, there is a general proclivity among researchers and the general public to associate abuse with physical violence. Although the findings were not statistically significant, the Chinese American students were less likely to define dating violence in psychological terms compared to their White student counterparts. Understanding the Chinese cultural context can assist in explaining this trend. Western orientations tend to focus on a dichotomy between the mind and the body, whereas the Chinese emphasize a holistic view (Kleinman, 1986). Consequently, for the Chinese, there is less attention to intrapsychic concerns (Hsu, 1985). This is notably reflected in the expression of psychological distress through physical symptoms. Empirical findings have consistently shown that the Chinese tend to somatize their distress (Leung, 1996; Kuo & Kavanaugh, 1994, Tseng, 1975).

Both Chinese American and White females were more likely to

define psychological and sexual acts of aggression as dating violence. This may be related to the general finding that men are more tolerant of aggression. For example, in the arena of domestic violence, males tend to be more tolerant of family violence and are less likely to view it as a serious problem compared to their female counterparts who are more likely to be the recipients of that violence (Koski & Mangold, 1988). In addition, the literature on rape indicates that men are more likely to endorse rape-tolerant attitudes (Holcomb, Holcomb, Sondag, & Williams, 1991; Muehlenhard & Linton, 1987). In two studies on rape attitudes with Asian American students, Asian males endorsed rape myths and held more negative attitudes toward rape victims compared to Asian females (Lee & Cheung, 1991; Mori, Bernat, Glenn, Selle, & Zarate, 1995).

Contextual Justifications of Dating Violence

Overall, both the Chinese American and White students did not believe that certain circumstances justified dating violence. However, compared to the White students, the Chinese American students were more likely to provide a contextual justification for the violence. Sigler (1989) argued that justifications of force are embedded in a culture that states that violence is acceptable if the reasons are appropriate. These cultural norms also tend to prescribe rules of retributive justice; consequently, if there is sufficient provocation for violence, then these rules can be invoked (Greenblat, 1985). For the Chinese, notions of retributive justice may be tied to Chinese cultural values emphasizing "loss of face" (Zane, 1993). King and Bond (1985) noted that concern with face is not unique to the Chinese; however, for the Chinese, loss of face involves not only shame experienced by an individual member, but the collective unit (i.e., family).

Compared to the White students, the Chinese American students were also more likely to agree that dating violence is justified if a woman is caught having an affair, is drunk, screaming hysterically, unwilling to have sex, nagging, flirting, disobeying her partner, and if he is in a bad mood. These situations deviate from Chinese prescriptions of the family and women's roles. Extramarital affairs and flirtations, for example, defy the centrality of the family. The family in Chinese culture is regarded as a fundamental unit of the society (Wu & Tseng, 1985). The heart of Confucianism also emphasizes harmony in family relationships, which indicates well-being, economic prosperity, and a flourishing society (Szalay, Strohl, Fu & Lao, 1994). A woman disobeying, inebriated, or nagging may be regarded as digressing from Chinese standards of women's roles. Traditional Chinese families are arranged in a specific hierarchal order based upon age and gender (King & Bond, 1985). Women have specific roles within the family as caretakers and nurturers and are to be supportive, obedient, and virtuous (Uba, 1994). Chinese males are socialized to preserve these roles and maintain the prescribed social order.

Experiences with Dating Violence

Myths of Chinese Americans being "model minorities," unassertive, and passive perpetuate the belief that intimate violence such as dating violence is uncommon in the Chinese American community. However, findings from this study show that there were no ethnic differences in rates of dating violence. Slightly more than a fifth of the Chinese American students reported experiencing physical violence in a dating relationship since they started dating, and more than 10% experienced physical violence *in the last 12 months*. Of concern is that Chinese American students in this sample started dating at about 16 years of age, and are currently about 20 years of age. Within a period of four years, a fifth have been victims of physical violence.

The dating violence literature has indicated that the rates of dating violence are similar across gender (Arias, Samios & O'Leary, 1987; LeJeune & Follette, 1994; White & Koss, 1991). Both men and women employ physical aggression in dating relationships. This study found a similar trend. In fact, more females reported committing physical violence compared to males in the last 12 months. Unfortunately, the social context in which the violence was employed is not explicated. It may be that females are using physical aggression in self-defense. Females may also be more likely to use minor forms of violence due to the power dynamics and then view these behaviors as dating violence. In fact, this is one of the criticisms of the Conflict Tactics Scale–its unidimensionality; that is, it focuses on the violent behavior while ignoring the context and the consequences of the violent behavior (Smith, 1994). Many feminist critics assert that the instrument fails to take into account the power dynamics involved. A man striking a woman has different consequences and meanings than a woman striking a man (Brush, 1990). A man hitting a woman with his fist, for example, will result in greater injury.

Relationship Between Perceptions of and Experiences with Dating Violence

The findings did indicate that definitions of and contextual justifications of dating violence were related to Chinese American students' victimization and perpetration experiences with dating violence. For this sample of students, it appears that individuals who believe that dating violence is warranted under certain situations are at greater risk of either being victimized or committing physical violence against a date or partner. Other empirical studies have demonstrated similar trends (Foo & Margolin, 1995; Tontodonato & Crew, 1992). This suggests that attitudes tolerating aggression may translate into actual behaviors. It also suggests that there is an underlying belief that aggression is an acceptable response. Possessing an attitude that it is acceptable to physically abuse someone because they are having an affair may then be translated into aggressive behavior. Similarly, a victim who endorses a similar attitude may not seek assistance for the abuse, thinking that the violence is deserved.

Relationship Between Gender Role Beliefs and Perceptions of and Experiences with Dating Violence

Findings from this study showed that the Chinese American students from this sample held egalitarian views about gender roles. Their egalitarian views may be a function of their education and their level of acculturation. However, the White students were more egalitarian than the Chinese American students. However, in both ethnic groups, the males were more traditional. These gender differences across ethnic groups may be explained by social exchange theory, which examines social behaviors as processes of exchange. The premise underlying social exchange theory is that individuals seek social relationships and interactions in which they can acquire the greatest reward for the least cost (Emerson, 1981; Leonard, 1996). Thus, it may be in the best interest for Chinese and White men to endorse traditional values since they have more to gain with the status quo than Chinese or White females.

In this study, gender role beliefs were correlated with both perceptions of and experiences with dating violence. These findings are consistent with studies on domestic violence and rape attitudes. For example, Hillier and Foddy (1993) found that individuals with traditional attitudes toward women assigned greater blame to domestic violence victims compared to their egalitarian counterparts. Similarly, Costin and Schwartz (1987) reported that those who held more traditional and restrictive beliefs about the social roles of women were more likely to hold negative attitudes toward rape victims.

LIMITATIONS OF STUDY AND DIRECTIONS FOR FUTURE RESEARCH

One of the major issues of the study is its generalizability to the Chinese American student population. Because social science and Asian American Studies classes were targeted due to the high enrollment of ethnic minority students, the concern is whether students who tend to enroll or major in social science disciplines are qualitatively different in their views about social issues compared to students from other fields. However, a random sample of all courses offered at the university would yield a sample with a substantially lower ethnic minority composition. Future university sampling designs would need to include a random sampling of all courses representing the various disciplines without compromising the ethnic make-up of the sample. In addition, the sample is comprised of undergraduate students at a major university, hence they were likely to be more liberal than others from their respective ethnic groups in the community. Spence and Helmreich (1978) found that while in college, individuals tend to be more liberal in their attitudes toward women. Moreover, as individuals move upward in social class, they tend to become more homogeneous (Zeff, 1982). For example, Agbayani-Siewert (Under Review) found that despite differences in family income, gender, and racial or ethnic background, Chinese and Filipino American university students who strive to middle class tended to comprise a homogeneous group. She found no practical differences in attitudes toward women between the two ethnic/racial groups. Future studies should focus on community samples, which might uncover more gender variations within Chinese American groups. The finding that more Chinese American female students perpetrated physical dating violence compared to their male counterparts warrants further examination. This finding is supported by previous empirical findings on intimate violence, indicating that women are as likely to assault their partners as males (Straus, Gelles, & Steinmetz, 1980). However, data from service providers reveal the opposite: Females are more likely to be victims of partner assault. Moreover, due to the physical disparity between males and females, women are more likely to sustain more serious injuries than a male victim (Brush, 1990). The issue partially stems from the closed-ended format of the Conflict Tactics Scale. As with all survey designs, qualitative and contextual nuances of meaning could not be captured. One of the major criticisms of the Conflict Tactics Scale is that it fails to explore issues of power, the causes and contexts of intimate violence, and the extent of injuries sustained (Brush, 1990; Yllo, 1988). As a result, future empirical investigations would require a qualitative research design to examine the reasons why Chinese females employed physical aggression, the degree or severity of the force, and the context in which the violence occurred. Recently, the authors have completed focus groups with Chinese and Filipino American students to explore these issues. In addition, a study examining the contexts in which dating violence occurs needs to be conducted. Although a new version of the CTS (Straus, Hamby, Boney-McCoy, and Sugarman, 1996) has been developed that takes into account context and injury, due to restriction of classroom time imposed by instructors, this new lengthier version could not be employed.

The trend that females perpetrated violence more often than males may also be a reflection of how Chinese Americans define violence. How a group defines violence may have an impact on reports of experiences with violence. Focus groups findings on female Filipino university students found that physical acts of aggression, such as slapping with an open hand by a male partner, is sometimes interpreted as warranted discipline and/or demonstrations of caring (Buenjemia, 1998). For example, one female focus group participant stated that she deserved to be hit by her partner, because she was flirting with other males at a party. She stated that her behavior provoked him, and his hitting was an indication of his love for her. The same study found that Filipino males defined nagging as abusive.

Finally, it is crucial to recognize the immense diversity of the Asian American population. This study's sample was not large enough to examine within-group differences such as Chinese students from Hong Kong, China, Taiwan, and other parts of Asia. There are tremendous within group differences that are brought about by immigration forces, political and economic backgrounds, country of origin, and the acculturation process that impact perceptions and behaviors. Although this study has inherent limitations, it offers new insights into Chinese Americans' attitudes and experiences with dating violence.

PRACTICE IMPLICATIONS

During adolescence and young adulthood, social and gender role identities are being challenged and formed. All this transpires when students are making developmental and cognitive transitions. During this phase, the task is to shift from concreteness and absolutism to relativism and ambiguity (Chickering, 1984). For example, the early phase of gender role and sexual identity formation is confined to concrete prescriptions of gender role expectations and stereotypes (Gilligan, 1982). Having been socialized in traditional patriarchal households, some Chinese American students who encounter new ideas about masculinity and femininity may experience dissonance. During periods of gender role confusion, young adults frequently adopt rigid forms of sexist behaviors (Gilligan, 1982). When conflicts ensue, and the individuals lack fully mature negotiating and conflict resolution skills, the use of violence may be employed. Working with dating violence victims and perpetrators, particularly from different cultural groups, is a challenge for service providers. Green (1982) noted that culturally-competent service delivery involves the use of ethnographic information in the planning and implementation of interventions. Service providers need to recognize value differences in perceptions of violence and that they may be rooted in the group's cultural norms. For example, the Chinese may be more likely to provide a contextual justification for dating violence because of the emphasis of Asian cultural norms in "saving face." Similarly, the concept of victimization may be colored by cultural norms about authority, hierarchy, and gender role beliefs.

Consideration of cultural differences in styles of communication patterns will also impact planning of interventions. Service providers, for example, will need to consider the basic differences in styles of communication between Western and traditional Chinese cultures when planning conflict resolution and management workshops. Minimization of conflict in interpersonal relationships is emphasized in Chinese cultures (Yick, Shibusawa, & Agbayani-Siewert, Under Review). Sustaining harmony in relationships is valued, and direct confrontation is avoided (Sue, 1981). Therefore, Western models of interventions in negotiating conflict might include indirect communication patterns. For example, the workshop can include vignettes that portray a violent situation between a Chinese male and female dating partner. The workshop facilitator can ask the participants to brainstorm ways for the couple in the vignette to resolve the conflict instead of asking them directly how they would deal with the situation. A discussion could follow with the facilitator suggesting alternative pro-social behaviors that may have not been identified by the students.

The use of student services, counseling, campus hot-lines, residential counselors, and support groups are important during a time when gender role and sexual identity confusion are engendered. Yet, the literature has consistently reported the underutilization of mental health services by Asian Americans (Kitano, 1969; Sue & Sue, 1974). Consequently, many students are left not knowing where to turn for help. As a result, the role of peer and residential counselors can play an important role. Asian American students are more likely to seek help from peers. Japanese American students, for example, stated they were less likely to seek the help of professional counselors, but preferred the help of friends, compared to their White counterparts (Suan & Tyler, 1990). As a part of their training, peer and residential counselors can be educated on conflict management skills, negotiation skills, and anger and stress management. In addition, they can be informed how cultural norms can influence views about conflict and violence. This is particularly important because residential counselors may be called upon by immigrant students who lack social supports or who may not know where to seek assistance.

The provision of culturally sensitive services may be one of the most crucial elements for utilization and retention. Flaskerud (1986) identified culture compatibility, ethnic match, and language match of the therapist and client as being important predictors to utilization and retention. Therefore, staffing of campuses' psychological services needs to include professionals and peer counselors who match the ethnic make-up of the student population and/or are culturally knowledgeable and sensitive. Such an approach must recognize the range of diversity among the Chinese student population. Issues of immigration, generational level, acculturation, and socioeconomic status contribute to the heterogeneity of the Chinese American population.

Campus and community education are also vital. General topics can include information about what comprises dating violence, the risk factors associated with victimization and violent behavior, and the link between attitudes toward violence, gender role stereotypes, and actual violence. Yet, the contents of educational workshops need to be culturally-specific. Understanding that the Chinese culture does not focus on psychological or intrapsychic concerns (Hsu, 1985), it would be important to focus on recognizing psychological abuse. Education can be targeted at student organizations, where the topic of dating violence can be introduced in student meetings or their assistance elicited for campus-wide awareness campaigns. Ethnic-specific organizations may provide a particularly effective vehicle for examining date rape issues within the context of cultural values and norms. This within-group setting may allow for both critical evaluation of values and norms which are used to justify violent behavior in dating situations and the evoking of counterposing cultural values which militate against such behaviors and foster interpersonal harmony and respect.

REFERENCES

Agbayani-Siewert, P. (Under Review). Testing the assumption of cultural similarity: The case of Chinese and Filipino Americans. *Social Work*.

Arias, I., & Johnson, P. (1989). Evaluations of physical aggression among intimate dyads. *Journal of Interpersonal Violence, 4*, 298-307.

Arias, I., Samios, M., & O'Leary, K. D. (1987). Prevalence and correlates of physical aggression during courtship. *Journal of Interpersonal Violence, 2*, 82-90.

Asian Week (1991). *Asians in America*. San Francisco: Author.

Bem, S.L. (1993). *The lenses of gender: Transforming the debate on sexual inequality*. New Haven, CT: Yale University Press.

Bernard, J. L., Bernard, S. L., & Bernard, M. L. (1985). Courtship violence and sex-typing. *Family Relations: Journal of Applied Family & Child Studies, 34*, 573-576.

Bernard, M. L., & Bernard, J. L. (1983). Violent intimacy: The family as a model for love relationships. *Family Relations: Journal of Applied Family & Child Studies, 32*, 283-286.

Bethke, T.M, & DeJoy, D.M. (1993). An experimental study of factors influencing the acceptability of dating violence. *Journal of Interpersonal Violence, 8*, 36-51.

Bradshaw, C.K. (1994). Asian and Asian American women: Historical and political considerations in psychotherapy. In Lillian Comas-Diaz and Beverly Greene (Eds.), *Women of color: Integrating ethnic and gender identities in psychotherapy* (pp. 72-113). New York, NY: Guilford Press.

Brush, L.D. (1990). Violent acts and injurious outcomes in married couples: Methodological issues in the National Survey of Families and Households. *Gender and Society, 4*, 56-67.

Buenjemia, J. (1998). Dating violence within the Filipino college community: Problem or preoccupation? UCLA, Asian American Studies Center, Unpublished research paper.

Campbell, J.C. (1992). Prevention of wife battering: Insights from cultural analysis. *Victimology, 10*, 174-185.

Campbell, A., Muncer, S., & Coyle, E. (1992). Social representation of aggression as an explanation of gender differences: A preliminary study. *Aggressive Behavior, 18*, 95-108.

Carlson, B.E. (1987). Dating violence: A research review and comparison with spouse abuse. *Social Casework, 68*, 16-23.

Chickering, A. (1984). *Education and Identity*. San Francisco, CA: Jossey-Bass.

Chin, K. (1994). Out-of-town brides: International marriage and wife abuse among Chinese immigrants. *Journal of Comparative Family Studies, 25*, 53-69.

Choi, A., & Edleson, J.L. (1996). Social disapproval of wife assaults: A national survey of Singapore. *Journal of Comparative Family Studies, 27*, 73-88.

Chung, D.K. (1992). Asian cultural commonalities: A comparison with mainstream American culture. In Sharlene Furuto, Renauka Biswas, Douglas K. Chung, Kenji Murase, and Fariyal Ross-Sheriff (Eds.), *Social Work Practice with Asian-Americans* (pp. 27-44). Newbury Park, CA: Sage Publications.

Costin, F., & Schwartz, N. (1987). Beliefs about rape and women's social roles: A four-nation study. *Journal of Interpersonal Violence, 2*, 46-56.

Crystal, D. (1989). Asian Americans and the myth of the model minority. *Social Casework, 70*, 405-413.

Daugherty, C.G., & Dambrot, F. H. (1986). Reliability of the Attitudes Toward Women Scale. *Educational & Psychological Measurement, 46*, 449-453.

Deal, J.E., & Wampler, K. (1986). Dating violence: The primacy of previous experience. *Journal of Social and Personal Relationships, 3*, 457-471.

Dent, D.Z., & Arias, I. (1990). Effects of alcohol, gender, and role of spouses on attributions and evaluations of marital violence scenarios. *Violence and Victims, 5*, 185-193.

Dobash, R.E., & Dobash, R.P. (1979). *Violence against wives: A case against patriarchy*. New York, NY: Free Press.

Eagly, A.H., & Steffen,V.J. (1986). Gender and aggressive behavior: A meta-analytic review of the social psychological literature. *Psychological Bulletin, 100*, 309-330.

EDK Associates (1993). *Men beating women: Ending domestic violence. A qualitative and quantitative study of public attitudes on violence against women*. San Francisco, CA: Family Violence Prevention Fund.

Emerson, R.M. (1981). Social exchange theory. In M. Rosenberg & R.H. Turner (Eds.), *Social psychology: Sociological perspectives* (pp. 30-65). New York: Basic Books.

Evangelauf, J. (1993). Number of minority students in colleges rose by 9% from 1990 to 1991, U.S. reports. *Chronicle of Higher Education, 39*, No. 20, A30.

Finn, J. (1986). The relationship between sex role attitudes and attitudes supporting marital violence. *Sex Roles, 14*, 235-244.

Flaskerud, J.H. (1986). The effects of culture-compatible intervention on the utilization of mental health services by minority clients. *Community Mental Health Journal, 22*, 127-141.

Flynn, C.P. (1987). Relationship violence: A model for family professionals. *Family Relations, 36*, 295-299.

Follingstad, D.R., Rutledge, L.L., Polek, D.S., & McNeill-Hawkins, K. (1988). Factors associated with patterns of dating violence toward college women. *Journal of Family Violence, 3*, 169-182.

Foo, L., & Margolin, G. (1995). A multivariate investigation of dating aggression. *Journal of Family Violence, 10*, 351-377.

Gilligan, C. (1982). *In a different voice.* Cambridge, CA: Harvard University Press.

Gilmartin, C. (1990). Violence against women in contemporary China. In Jonathan N. Lipman and Stevan Harrell (Eds.), *Violence in China: Essays in culture and counterculture* (pp. 203-225). New York: State University of New York Press.

Giovannoni, J.M., & Becerra, R.M. (1979). *Defining child abuse.* New York: Free Press.

Gose, B. (1996). Minority students were 24% of college enrollment in 1994. (More Asian-Americans and Hispanic-Americans attend college). *Chronicle of Higher Education, 42*, No. 37, A32.

Gray, H.M. & Foshee, V. (1997). Adolescent dating violence: Differences between one-sided and mutually violent profiles. *Journal of Interpersonal Violence*, Vol. 12, No. 1, 126-141.

Green, J.W. (1982). *Cultural awareness in the human services.* Englewood Cliffs, NJ: Prentice Hall.

Greenblat, C.S. (1985). "Don't hit your wife . . . unless . . . ": Preliminary findings on normative support for the use of physical force by husbands. *Victimology, 10*, 221-241.

Henton, J.M., Cate, R., Koval, J., Lloyd, S., & Christopher, S. (1983). Romance and violence in dating relationships. *Journal of Family Issues, 4*, 467-482.

Hillier, L., & Foddy, M. (1993). The role of observer attitudes in judgments of blame in cases of wife assault. *Sex Roles, 29*, 629-644.

Ho, C. (1990). An analysis of domestic violence in Asian American communities: A multicultural approach to counseling. *Women & Therapy, 9*, 129-150.

Ho, M. (1987). *Family therapy with ethnic minorities.* Newbury Park, CA: Sage Publications.

Ho, M. (1989). Applying family therapy theories to Asian/Pacific Americans. *Contemporary Family Therapy, 11*, 61-70.

Hoff, L.A. (1992). Review essay: Wife beating in Micronesia. *Journal of Micronesian Studies, 1*, 199-221.

Holcomb, D.R., Holcomb, L.C., Sondag, K. A., & Williams, N. (1991). Attitudes about date rape: Gender differences among college students. *College Student Journal, 25*, 434-439.

Honig, E. and Hershatter, G. (1988). Violence against women. In Emily Honig & Gail Hershatter, *Personal voices: Chinese women in the 1980's* (pp. 273-307). Stanford, CA: Stanford University Press.

Hsu, J. (1985). The Chinese family: Relations, problems, and therapy. In W.S. Tseng and D.Y.H. Wu (Eds.), *Chinese culture and mental health* (pp. 95-112). Orlando, FL: Academic Press.

Ishisaka, H.A. and Takagi, C.Y. (1982). Social work with Asian-and Pacific Americans. In James Green (Ed.), *Cultural awareness in the human services* (pp. 122-156). Englewood Cliffs, NJ: Prentice-Hall, Inc.

King, A.Y.C., & Bond, M.H. (1985). The Confucian paradigm of man: A sociological view. In Wen-Shing Tseng and David Y.H. Wu (Eds.), *Chinese culture and mental health* (pp. 29-45). Orlando, FL: Academic Press, Inc.

Kitano, H.H. (1969). Japanese-American mental illness. In S. C. Plog & R.B. Edgerton (Eds.), *Changing perspectives in mental illness* (pp. 256-284). New York: Holt, Rinehart & Winston.

Kleinman, A. (1986). Illness meanings and illness behavior. In S. McHugh and M. Vallis (Eds.), *Illness behavior: A multidisciplinary model* (pp. 149-160). New York, NY: Plenum Press.

Koski, P.R., & Mangold, W.D. (1988). Gender effects in attitudes about family violence. *Journal of Family Violence, 3,* 225-237.

Kuo, C.L., & Kavanaugh, K.H. (1994). Chinese perspectives on culture and mental health. *Issues in Mental Health Nursing, 15,* 551-567.

Lee, E. (1997). Overview: The assessment and treatment of Asian American families. In Evelyn Lee (Ed.), *Working with Asian Americans: A guide for clinicians* (pp. 3-36). New York, NY: The Guilford Press.

Lee, M.Y.H. (1993). A life preserver for battered immigrant women: The 1990 Amendments to the Immigration Fraud Amendments. *Buffalo Law Review, 41,* 779-805.

Lee, H., & Cheung, F.M. (1991). The Attitudes Toward Rape Victims Scale: Reliability and validity in a Chinese context. *Sex Roles, 24,* 599-603.

LeJeune, C., & Follette, V. (1994). Taking responsibility: Sex differences in reporting dating violence. *Journal of Interpersonal Violence, 9,* 133-140.

Leonard, E.D. (1996). A social exchange explanation for the Child Sexual Abuse Accommodation Syndrome. *Journal of Interpersonal Violence, 11,* 107-117.

Leong, F.T.L. (1986). Counseling and psychotherapy with Asian Americans. *Journal of Counseling Psychology, 33,* 196-206.

Leung, K. (1996). The role of beliefs in Chinese culture. In M.H. Bond (Ed.), *The handbook of Chinese psychology* (pp. 247-262). Hong Kong, Oxford University Press.

Makepeace, J.M. (1981). Courtship violence among college students. *Family Relations, 30,* 97-102.

Makepeace, J.M. (1986). Gender differences in courtship violence victimization. *Family Relations: Journal of Applied Family & Child Studies, 35,* 383-388.

Mori, L., Bernat, J.A., Glenn, P.A., Selle, L.L., & Zarate, M.G. (1995). Attitudes toward rape: Gender and ethnic differences across Asian and Caucasian college students. *Sex Roles, 32,* 457-467.

Muehlenhard, C.L., & Linton, M.A. (1987). Date rape and sexual aggression in dating situations: Incidence and risk factors. *Journal of Counseling Psychology, 34,* 186-196.

Neufeld, J., McNamara, J.R., and Ertl, M. (1999). Incidence and prevalence of dating partner abuse and its relationship to dating practices. *Journal of Interpersonal Violence, 14*, 125-136.

Riggs, D. S., O'Leary, K. D., & Breslin, F. C. (1990). Multiple correlates of physical aggression in dating couples. *Journal of Interpersonal Violence, 5*, 61-73.

Riggs, D.S., & O'Leary, K. D. (1989). A theoretical model of courtship aggression. In M.A. Pirog-Good and J. E. Stets (Eds.), *Violence in dating relationships: Emerging social issues* (pp. 53-71). New York, NY: Praeger Publishers.

Roscoe, B. (1985). Courtship violence: Acceptable forms and situations. *College Student Journal, 19*, 389-393.

Rosenblatt, R.A. (1996, March 14). Latinos, Asians to lead rise in U.S. population. (Census Bureau report). *Los Angeles Times.* p. A1.

Sigelman, C.K., Berry, C.J., and Wiles, K.A. (1984). Violence in college students' dating relationships. *Journal of Applied Social Psychology, 14*, 530-548.

Sigler, R.T. (1989). *Domestic violence in context: An assessment of community attitudes.* Lexington, MA: D.C. Heath & Company.

Smith, M. D. (1994). Enhancing the quality on violence against women: A feminist approach. *Gender and Society, 8*, 109-127.

Smith, J.P., & Williams, J.G. (1992). From abusive household to dating violence. *Journal of Family Violence, 7*, 153-165.

Song-Kim, Y.I. (1992). Battered Korean women in urban United States. In Sharlene Furuto, Renauka Biswas, Douglas K. Chung, Kenji Murase, and Fariyal Ross-Sheriff (Eds.), *Social Work Practice with Asian-Americans* (pp. 213-226). Newbury Park, CA: Sage Publications.

Spence, J. & Helmreich, R. (1978). *Masculinity and femininity: Their psychological dimensions, correlates and antecedents.* Austin, TX: University of Texas Press.

Spence, J.T., Helmreich, R., & Stapp, J. (1972). A short version of the Attitudes Toward Women Scale (AWS). *Bulletin of Psychometric Society, 2*, 219-220.

Straus, M.A., Hamby, S.L., Boney-McCoy, S., and Sugarman, D.B. (1996). The revised Conflict Tactics Scales (CTS2): Development and preliminary psychometric data. *Journal of Family Issues, 17*, 283-316.

Straus, M.A. (1979). Measuring intrafamily conflict and violence: The Conflict Tactics (CT) Scales. *Journal of Marriage & the Family, 41*, 75-88.

Straus, M.A., Gelles, R.J., & Steinmetz, S.K. (1980). *Behind closed doors: Violence in the American family.* Garden City, N.Y.: Anchor Press/Doubleday.

Suan, L.V., & Tyler, J.D. (1990). Mental health values and preferences for mental health resources of Japanese-American and Caucasian American students. *Professional Psychology: Research and Practice, 21*, 291-296.

Suarez, K.E. (1994). Teenage dating violence: The need for expanded awareness and legislation. *California Law Review, 82*, 423-471.

Sue, S., & Sue, D.W. (1974). MMPI comparisons between Asian-American and non-Asian students utilizing a student health psychiatric clinic. *Journal of Counseling Psychology, 21*, 423-427.

Sugarman, D.B., & Frankel, S.L. (1996). Patriarchal ideology and wife-assault: A meta-analytic review. *Journal of Family Violence, 11*, 13-40.

Szalay, L.B., Strohl, J.B., Fu, L., & Lao, P. (1994). *American and Chinese percep-*

tions and belief systems: A People's Republic of China-Taiwanese comparison. New York, NY: Plenum Press.

Takeuchi, D.T., Mokuau, N., & Chun, C.A. (1992). Mental health services for Asian Americans and Pacific islanders. *Journal of Mental Health Administration, 19,* 237-245.

Tang, C.S., Critelli, J.W., & Porter, J.F. (1993). Motives in sexual aggression: The Chinese context. *Journal of Interpersonal Violence, 8,* 435-445.

Tang, C.S., Critelli, J.W., & Porter, J.F. (1995). Sexual aggression and victimization in dating relationships among Chinese college students. *Archives of Sexual Behavior, 24,* 47-53.

Thompson, E.H. (1991). The maleness of violence in dating relationships: An appraisal of stereotypes. *Sex Roles, 24,* 261-278.

Tontodonato, P., & Crew, B. K. (1992). Dating violence, social learning theory, and gender: A multivariate analysis. *Violence & Victims, 7,* 3-14.

Torres, S. (1991). A comparison of wife abuse between two cultures: Perceptions, attitudes, nature, and extent. *Issues in Mental Health Nursing, 12,* 113-131.

Tseng, W.S. (1975). Nature of somatic complaints among psychiatric patients: The Chinese case. *Comprehensive Psychiatry, 16,* 237-245.

Tseng, W., & Wu, D.Y.H. (1985). *Chinese culture and mental health.* Orlando, FL: Academic Press, Inc.

Uba, L. (1994). *Asian Americans: Personality patterns, identity, and mental health.* New York, NY: Guilford Press.

Watson, R.S., & Ebrey, P.B (1992). *Marriage and inequality in Chinese society.* Berkeley, CA: University of California Press.

White, J.W., & Koss, M.P. (1991). Courtship violence: Incidence in a national sample of higher education students. *Violence & Victims, 6,* 247-256.

Wong, R.R. (1995). Divorce mediation among Asian Americans: Bargaining in the shadow of diversity. *Family and Conciliation Courts Review, 33,* 110-128.

Worth, D.M., Matthews, P.A., & Coleman, W.R. (1990). Sex role, group affiliation, family background, and courtship violence in college students. *Journal of College Student Development, 31,* 250-254.

Yick, A., Shibusawa, T. & Agbayani-Siewert, P. (Under Review). Psychological and physical aggression in Chinese American families: Mental health outcomes. *Family Relations.*

Yick, A., & Agbayani-Siewert, P. (1997). Perceptions of domestic violence in a Chinese American community. *Journal of Interpersonal Violence, 12,* 832-846.

Yllo, K. (1988). Political and methodological debates in wife abuse research. In K. Yllo and M. Bograd (Eds.), *Feminist perspectives on wife abuse* (pp. 28-50). Newbury Park, CA: Sage Publications.

Zane, N. (1993). An empirical examination of loss of face among Asian Americans. Los Angeles: UCLA, National Research Center on Asian American Mental Health.

Zeff, S. (1982). A cross-cultural study of Mexican Americans, Black Americans, and White Americans at a large urban university. *Hispanic Journal of Behavioral Sciences, 4,* 245-261.

Latinas and Sexual Assault: Towards Culturally Sensitive Assessment and Intervention

Georgiana Low
Kurt C. Organista

SUMMARY. This paper will discuss the problem of sexual assault among Latinas, an under-researched population whose social and cultural characteristics contextualize the trauma of sexual assault in ways that need to be considered by service providers striving to provide culturally syntonic interventions. The authors will present the sparse empirical data on sexual assault among Latinas, including prevalence, assault characteristics, and post-assault sequelae. Given the bicultural reality of most Latinas in the U.S., a working model of sexual assault in Latinas is presented that frames the problem as occurring within both traditional Latino and modern American gender role systems. The result is a dual dilemma for Latina victims of sexual assault with both negative and positive implications that need to be better understood by victims and service providers. *[Article copies available for a fee from The Haworth Document Delivery Service: 1-800-342-9678. E-mail address: <getinfo@haworthpressinc.com> Website: <http://www.haworthpressinc.com>]*

KEYWORDS. Latinas, sexual assault, rape, cultural competence

Georgiana Low, BA, is an MSW student at the School of Social Welfare, University of California, Berkeley, CA.

Kurt C. Organista, PhD, is Associate Professor, School of Social Welfare, University of California, Berkeley, CA.

[Haworth co-indexing entry note]: "Latinas and Sexual Assault: Towards Culturally Sensitive Assessment and Intervention." Low, Georgiana, and Kurt C. Organista. Co-published simultaneously in *Journal of Multicultural Social Work* (The Haworth Press, Inc.) Vol. 8, No. 1/2, 2000, pp. 131-157; and: *Violence: Diverse Populations and Communities* (ed: Diane de Anda, and Rosina M. Becerra) The Haworth Press, Inc., 2000, pp. 131-157. Single or multiple copies of this article are available for a fee from The Haworth Document Delivery Service [1-800-342-9678, 9:00 a.m. - 5:00 p.m. (EST). E-mail address: getinfo@ haworthpressinc.com].

INTRODUCTION

Sexual assault is a particularly devastating trauma that impacts all women to some degree. In the United States it is estimated that one in five women will be raped in their lifetime (Koss, Gidycz & Wisniewski, 1987). The United States has been described by some as a "rape culture" that seems to regulate rather than prohibit rape (Holzman, 1996; Rozee, 1993). This harsh description is consistent with pervasive national violence that leads many to conclude that the U.S. is one of the most violent nations in the world (Lore & Schultz, 1993). Yet, it is also fair to say that most, if not all, societies continue to struggle with gender role systems that underreact and regulate the sexual abuse of women (Rozee, 1993).

Fear of rape has been theorized to keep women in their place. Feminists argue that sexual assault is a societal tool that both emerges from and reinforces oppressive gender roles (Herman, 1992; Brownmiller, 1975). A feminist, socio-cultural perspective has become the dominant theoretical framework in the United States for understanding sexual victimization and its aftermath (Donat & D'Emilio, 1992). Women's actions and movements, self-expression, self-presentation, and agency within relationships are constrained by the fear of sexual assault. Thus sexual assault can be seen as an insidious trauma as described by Root (1992), eroding a woman's sense of safety and well being. For women who are directly victimized, the impact of sexual assault is acute and can result in serious psychological, social, and relational damage (Roth & Newman, 1991; Siegel, Golding, Stein, Burnam, & Sorenson, 1990; Marhoeffer-Dvorak, Resick, Hutter, & Girelli, 1988). Furthermore, the impact of sexual assault ripples out into the victim's family and community.

Theories and interventions in the rape crisis field have been shaped in response to the experiences and needs of White, middle-class women. Western middle-class values are embedded in both the research that has been conducted on sexual assault as well as in the services provided for survivors (Holzman, 1996). Thus, just as with feminist psychologies, analyses of ethnicity, class, and culture have been largely ignored (Espin, 1997; Comas-Diaz, 1994). Only within the last decade have researchers begun to develop a body of work that begins to document the experience of sexual assault among women of color (Root, 1996; McNair & Neville, 1996; Lefley, Scott, Llabre, &

Hicks, 1993; Friedman, 1992; Sorenson & Siegel, 1992). From this growing body of work, the need to view sexual assault experiences within an interlocking matrix of gender, ethnicity, and class has become more explicit. To this end, this article focuses on cultural and socioeconomic factors that inform the particular experience of Latinas with sexual assault.

It is essential to regard a rape survivor within her socio-cultural context, in order to understand her unique experience and to provide her with appropriate interventions that facilitate recovery and to build a sense of empowerment and self-worth. For example, power differences in this country are likely to render Latinas more vulnerable to sexual assault, while simultaneously creating obstacles to accessing services to deal with the aftermath. Cultural factors will also affect the meaning that a Latina will make of an assault as well as the responses of her family and community (Hough, Canino, Abueg, & Gusman, 1996; Lefley, Scott, Llabre, & Hicks; 1993). Further, her devaluation as a woman of color in this country may make her more vulnerable to negative, psychological post-rape sequelae (Root, 1996).

PREVALENCE OF SEXUAL ASSAULT

According to the U.S. Department of Justice (1988), rates of violent crime reported to the police are highest for people that live in the inner city, are of lower socioeconomic status, and are members of ethnic minority groups. Rapes reported to the police follow this pattern, with the exception that Latinas report lower rates than non-Hispanic Whites (Sorenson & Siegel, 1992). It is presently unclear whether these lower rates reflect protective mechanisms within the culture (e.g., conservative gender roles, high protection of women), a reluctance to report sexual assaults when they occur, or a different understanding of what constitutes sexual assault on the part of Latinas.

Because rape is considered to be the most underreported violent crime, however, one cannot rely solely on criminal justice statistics. For example, two large, non-criminal setting rape surveys found that only between 10% and 30% of women who had experienced rape actually reported the incident to police (Kilpatrick et al., 1985; Russell, 1982). For women of color, historical race relations in this country most likely make it even more difficult to feel safe in reporting crimes for fear of negative stereotypes of the community, abuse by authorities, and fear of not being taken seriously (Root, 1994). Women of color may also feel conflicted about turning men from their communities over to a police system with a legacy of racism and unequal protection for people of color (Comas-Diaz, 1994). For instance, rapists who are men of color are more likely to be sentenced than White men and their sentences tend to be longer (Sorenson & Siegel, 1992). Ethnic loyalty, and empathy for the situation of Latino men, may make it difficult for women to prioritize their own safety in this regard.

Most prevalence studies have focused primarily on non-minority White women or have included statistically insignificant numbers of women of color. Koss et al. (1987) are among the first to break down rape statistics by ethnic status. These researchers administered the Sexual Experiences Survey to a national sample of 6,159 male and female college students from 32 educational institutions. While findings are limited in generalizability to post-secondary students, it was found that 1 out of 4 women had experienced rape, with important numerical differences between ethnic groups: 16% of European American women (n = 2655), 10% of African American women (n = 215), 12% of Latinas (n = 106), 7% of Asian American women (n = 106), and 40% of American Indian women (n = 20). Research has documented higher prevalence in Asian American women, in contrast to the above data, depending on country of origin, immigration history and social class (Friedman, 1992; Kuoch, Miller, & Scully, 1992). Similar findings will likely emerge across different groups of Latinas in future research.

Sorenson and Siegel (1992) analyzed sexual assault data from the Los Angeles Epidemiologic Catchment Area (LA-ECA) prevalence study which included over 3000 community respondents, almost half of whom were of Mexican ancestry. These researchers found lifetime prevalence rates of sexual assault consistent with national crime data: 8.1% for Latinas as compared to a 19.9% for non-Hispanic Whites. Interestingly, it was also found that U.S. born Mexicans were three times more likely than Mexico-born Mexicans to have been sexually assaulted. This latter finding suggests that diminishing Latino culture combined with exposure to a devalued ethnic minority status, linked to high rates of poverty, may leave Latinas vulnerable to sexual assault as well as other problems. Alternatively, it could be that more acculturated Latinas have absorbed modern feminist ideas which empower them to speak about their experiences. More research is needed to investigate the complex relation between acculturation and sexual assault for Latinas in the United States.

Characteristics of the assault. Assault characteristics were similar for both Latinas and non-Latina Whites in the above LA-ECA study: The assailant was most likely to be a friend or acquaintance; use of force most often took the form of verbal pressure, and the type of sexual activity outcome was most often intercourse. Two-thirds of all abused women in the sample reported two or more assaults with an average of 3.2 assaults, underscoring the pervasiveness of repeated victimization.

Confounding variables in sexual assault research. Assessing prevalence rates for rape and sexual assault is problematic in general, although research in the last decade has become more sophisticated (Sorenson & White, 1992). Several factors complicate establishing an accurate picture of women's experiences of sexual violence. Russell's (1982) groundbreaking study in 1982 sought to confirm the suspicion that national crime statistics seriously underrepresented the actual incidence and prevalence of sexual assault. Russell (1982) surveyed 930 randomly selected adult female residents of San Francisco and found that incidence rates were 13 times higher than rates reported by the FBI.

Russell (1982) points out that women are more likely to respond positively to a multi-question assessment as opposed to a single question about sexual assault. This may be related to the sensitive nature of the topic and the need to establish a relationship between interviewer and respondent. For this reason, Sorenson and Siegel (1992) placed questions about sexual assault at the end of the interview in the aforementioned LA-ECA study. These researchers also stressed the importance of having interviewers who match the ethnic background of respondents in order to foster trust when conducting cross-cultural research. Matching of language for non-English speaking women is obviously essential.

Cultural factors can also contribute to the reluctance of women to discuss sexual assault openly. Sex and sexuality are private matters. Many Latinas, depending on their level of acculturation, will be quite modest in this arena. Although rape is generally considered a violent and not a sexual act, the assault directly impacts a woman's sense of herself as a sexual person. Latina rape victims appear to subscribe to rape myths more so than their non-Latina White and African-American counterparts (Lefley et al., 1993). Thus they are probably at higher risk for feeling responsible and despoiled by a sexual assault, thereby inhibiting needed disclosure and help-seeking. Cultural beliefs about rape and gender will also affect whether she defines an assault as rape as well as whether she feels entitled to or feels she will get some benefit from disclosure. These issues have a direct impact on the outcome of a woman's assault experience; positive support and the opportunity to process the event are both important in recovery (Roth & Newman, 1991). Thus, cultural and social variables influencing sexual assault need to be considered.

CULTURAL AND SOCIAL VARIABLES IN LATINA SEXUAL ASSAULT

Latinas are a diverse group with varying levels of acculturation, a wide range of nationalities, differing immigration histories, and varying family structures, socioeconomic levels, educational attainment, and occupational status. When working with any individual, it is fundamental to understand the potential commonalities she may have with other women in her group, while being open to her as a complex individual with a unique narrative and life story. Further, subgroups within the U.S. are obliged to understand and negotiate the dominant culture to some degree. Most people of color in this country are bicultural or multicultural (Comas-Diaz, 1994). For a Latina who has been sexually victimized, aspects of her experience may be universal, other aspects may be very specific to her ethnocultural group, while still others will be unique to her. The purpose of cultural sensitivity is to illuminate cultural themes and possibilities without becoming rigid or stereotypic. Marsella et al. (1996) has defined culture as:

> Shared learned behavior which is transmitted from one generation to another to promote individual and group adjustment and adaptation. Culture is represented externally as artifacts, roles and institutions, and is represented internally as values, beliefs, attitudes, cognitive styles, epistemologies, and consciousness patterns. (p. 117)

The Cultural Backdrop of Rape

In an ethnographic survey of 35 non-industrial societies, Rozee (1993) found that rape was present in all societies sampled, in both normative and non-normative forms. Sixty-three percent of the societies sampled had definitions of non-normative, punishable forms of rape in which genital contact occurred against the will of a victim. However, 97% of the societies had different forms of normative rape defined by Rozee as genital contact not chosen by women but occurring within condoned customs or rituals. Six categories of normative rape were described including marital rape (i.e., sex with spouse against her will), exchange rape (e.g., custom of lending wives to other men as gesture of good will between men), punitive rape (e.g., rape of enemy women during war), status rape (i.e., coercive sex between individuals of significant power differentials), ceremonial rape (i.e., including defloration rituals prior to marriage and virginity tests), and theft rape (i.e., taking sexual advantage of slaves, human spoils of war, etc.). Because of their cultural acceptability, these latter forms of rape are rarely or only minimally punished despite trauma to women. Rozee notes the analogy in current U.S. society in which semi-condoned forms of rape are similarly under-punished and thereby semi-sanctioned and regulated (i.e., marital, date, and acquaintance rape).

Rozee asserts the need to use a female experience centered definition of rape based on the absence of choice whether or not certain forms of genital contact are condoned by cultural norms. Rozee's definition expands conventional definitions of rape beyond their obviously taboo forms to include those that are minimized as normal and acceptable cultural rituals. Her study is important for illustrating the complex cultural backdrop of sexual abuse and how definitions of and responses to rape are embedded within male dominated, sexist gender role systems. Latinas in the U.S. have the added burden of experiencing sexual assault within the gender role systems of both the U.S. and the Latino culture of origin. Multicultural research is needed to better understand such overlapping cultural contexts.

Research on Latinas. Lefley et al. (1993) conducted a rare multicultural study of culture-based beliefs about rape in rape victims. A sample of 101 rape victims was selected from 881 consecutive admissions to the Rape Treatment Center of the University of Miami-Jackson Memorial Medical Center in Dade County, Florida. Given the study's focus on "ordinary" women of child bearing age, women were excluded if they had a prior history of rape and/or incest, psychiatric history, or cognitive impairment. Of the 101 rape victims studied, 37 were African American, 36 Latina, and 28 non-Hispanic

White. Latina participants were of Cuban and Central American background and, to control for "cultural homogeneity," were restricted to
those whose parents were from Spanish speaking countries, and who
were married to Latinos (if married).

Assessment of rape myths, including their internalization, was conducted by presenting nine rape scenarios to the participants. In each, it
was clear that the female was forced to have sex with the man, but the
scenarios varied in ways that the literature suggests are important to
the concept of rape, such as use of a weapon, victim-rapist relationship, social role of the victim, and the context of the rape. Results
revealed that Latinas had the highest acceptance of rape myths which
held that women contribute to rape through their dress or behavior,
and that women are responsible for controlling men's sexuality as well
as their own. Latinas also were highest in perceptions of people in
their community as subscribing to myths and as having punitive attitudes toward victims. With regard to psychological distress, Latinas
were highest, White women were lowest, and African American
women were intermediate. Furthermore, Latinas were most likely to
employ avoidance as a coping mechanism.

The above results are consistent with other studies on attitudes
towards rape which consistently reveal more traditional attitudes towards women, and greater subscription to rape myths, on the part of
Latinos as compared to White and African Americans. For example,
Williams (1985) conducted a multicultural study of both rape victims
and community residents in San Antonio, Texas, and found that Mexican American respondents (n = 340) were more likely to subscribe to
rape myths as compared to both Anglo (n = 335) and African American (n = 336) community residents (Williams and Holmes, 1981;
1982); employing the same rape scenarios used by Lefley et al., Williams and associates found that Mexican American residents and rape
victims were more victim blaming, less inclined to prosecute assailants, and more anti-feminist in judgment. The small sample of rape
victims consisted of 32 White, 11 African American, and 18 Mexican
American females. As compared to White and African American rape
victims, Mexican American rape victims had the highest mean scores
on the study's crisis scale that assessed degree of threat, inability to
respond with adequate coping mechanisms, and disruption of routine
functioning.

Consistent with the above studies, Fischer (1987) found that even among bilingual and bicultural Latino college students, their attitudes towards women and forcible date rape were more traditional than those of their White counterparts (i.e., less rejecting of date rape, less likely to blame male perpetrators). As a group, these studies imply that Latino gender role ideologies facilitate self-blame in Latina victims of sexual assault. The result can be a context of shame and blame that prohibits the Latina rape victim from talking about her experience within her family and community. Moreover, victim blaming following sexual assault has documented negative effects on a woman's healing process. For example, Ullman (1996) found that the relation between negative social reactions to rape and negative psychological outcome in victims was mediated by avoidant coping. It appears that rape culture embedded in both Latino and American gender role systems can produce a dual dilemma for Latina victims of sexual assault that needs to be critically examined.

Gender Roles

Rape myths emerge from traditional gender roles and values within a culture. The bicultural reality of Latinas in the U.S. is that of negotiating, to varying degrees, a relatively traditional Latino gender role system and a relatively modern U.S. gender role system. Comas-Diaz (1994) asserts that women of color in this country are hybrid women. White women are the generic "woman" in most texts in the U.S., while ethnic minority women require an ethnic descriptor (Mexican-American women, Puerto Rican women, etc.). The experiences of women of color are qualitatively different from those of White women, because of the intersection of their gender and ethnicity, as well as their historical experiences of colonization within the United States.

Although there is little empirical data on Latino gender roles, many authors describe a Latina's identity as a woman as integrally tied to her relationship with the collective whole of family and community (Boyd-Franklin & Garcia-Preto, 1994). Latinas usually occupy a central position within the family, often carrying the responsibility of keeping the family together by providing caretaking and nurturing. They traditionally are responsible for maintaining family relationships, mediating conflicts, and preventing confrontations. Her role will depend, however, on where she falls on the continuum of traditional to modern gender roles within the larger context of acculturation.

Regardless of acculturation, Latinas are likely to be more familistic and collectivist than their non-Latina White counterparts (Sabogal et al., 1987). The Latina's extended definition of the self, as realized through connection with family, community and universe, often protects the group by subordinating the individual's needs to those of the collective (Comas-Diaz, 1994). White feminists and mental health workers looking through the lens of the dominant culture may pathologize Latinas' subjugation of their needs to those of the family, thereby missing the ways that their role within the family contributes to both their survival and sense of security (e.g., self-esteem enhancing, central role in ministering to health and emotional problems of family members). At the same time, such Latina roles may impede them from obtaining needed help after a sexual assault, thus increasing the risk of developing long-term negative consequences. Thus, the delicate task is to affirm and maintain the survival enhancing aspects of Latino culture while simultaneously helping Latinas acknowledge and express their abuse experiences. For example, while the traditional roles of Latinas can be recognized as promoting the well being of the family, ignoring the needs of the abused Latina can also be framed as failing to attend to the needs of the entire family. Framing issues in such a manner provides an avenue for modifying or transforming traditional gender roles in a more bicultural direction.

Moreover, the traditional Latino primacy of collective family needs over the individual needs of the Latina wife/mother, can be addressed by stressing the mutual needs of the Latina and other family members, especially in challenging context of acculturation in which Latino families must often do more with fewer traditional supports (e.g., less extended family support with increasing acculturation). For example, while U.S. Latinas continue to be primarily responsible for the domain of the home, many must work outside the home out of economic necessity. If bicultural flexibility is not exercised in Latino family roles, the resulting overburden on the Latina wife/mother will eventually impact the entire family. One way of conceptualizing the adaptive expansion of the Latina gender role is to advance beyond the traditional gender role of Marianismo to the more progressive Hembrismo as discussed below.

Marianismo. The pros and cons of Latino gender roles are apparent in the value and practice of Marianismo which originally stems from worship and emulation of the Virgin Mary, connoting women's moral superiority alongside an admirable ability to endure suffering inflicted on them by men (Comas-Diaz & Duncan, 1985). According to Morales and Reyes (1998), Marianismo is connected to a conception of motherhood as sacred. In the role of mother, women gain respect and power. But Marianismo also implies sexual purity and suppression; women are responsible for keeping themselves pure before marriage and once married they should not enjoy sex too much. As in many cultures, there is a line drawn between a *dona* (lady) who deserves protection and support, and a *puta* (whore) who deserves an abusable outcast status. This traditional dichotomous definition of female sexuality has implications for the Latina survivor of sexual assault, including questionable support and even self-blame.

Hembrismo. Hembra denotes female gender and Hembrismo is now discussed as a sex positive female style of displaying strength, perseverance, flexibility, and ability to survive while continuing to maintain a feminine identity (Boyd-Franklin & Garcia-Preto, 1994). However, traditionally it has also been used pejoratively to refer to women that have become too independent, controlling, and male-like (Morales & Reyes, 1998). In the spirit of biculturation, Latina feminists have recently reclaimed the concept of Hembrismo as a progressive challenge to machismo, because of its connotations of autonomy (Morales & Reyes, 1998). This more androgenous and bicultural gender role does indeed appear to be a useful concept for beginning dialogues about increasing self-care in Latinas and challenging Marianismo.

Familism

The stresses of acculturation, poverty, and discrimination may be mediated by familism. Latinas come from a culture that places a high value on interpersonal connectedness and interdependence. One manifestation of this value that has consistently been cited in the literature is *familismo* or the primacy of the family in providing life-long and cross-generational support, structure, and purpose in life (Falicov, 1998; Sabogal et al., 1987). For Latinas who immigrate to this country, familism may be an important buffer to the stressors of adjusting to an often hostile host country.

Stressors other than migration, including the trauma of sexual victimization, can also be mediated by a strong orientation toward family.

If a woman is able to reveal her experience to the family, she may be able to tap into a nurturing natural support system and regain a sense of protection and connection with other people (e.g., family members may take a more active role in the future safety of the victim). However, she may also feel that revealing her experience will threaten the family and thus may choose to keep it secret in order to protect the stability of the family and to protect herself from censure. For instance, imagine that a sixteen-year-old Chicano is being molested by an uncle. By revealing her experience she will essentially be asking the family to choose to align itself with either her or the assailant. Given the potential for such negative scenarios such as victim-blame or violent retribution against the uncle, the victim may choose instead to deny or minimize the problem.

Rape counselors must emphasize to the families of rape victims that sexual assault harms the entire family and that time and energy need to be directed towards the recovery of the woman versus venting rage and seeking revenge in ways that can destroy a family with unnecessary lethal and legal consequences (Lefley et al., 1993). Legal measures of pressing charges must also be discussed as options that can be an adaptive part of the recovery process.

In summary, U.S. and Latino-based gender role systems present Latinas with a range of norms and values, each of which offers its own set of pros and cons to consider with regard to the problem of sexual assault. For example, while familism and traditional gender roles may promote support and valuable central roles for women, they may also inhibit the recognition of responses to sexually related matters. Similarly, while the modern U.S. gender roles system may help Latinas become more autonomous as sexual beings capable of better defining, discussing, and responding to sexual assault, such changes may dislocate her from valued family and community roles. Such conflicts also need to be addressed in connection with socioeconomic factors.

Social and Economic Status of Latinas

According to Holzman (1996), rape in the U.S. is not uniformly distributed because poverty makes it difficult for women to avoid dangerous neighborhoods, jobs, and individuals. It is estimated that very poor women are four times more likely to be raped with homeless women representing the extreme (Karmen, 1982). Given the disproportionately high poverty rates of U.S. Latinos, SES should be considered a risk factor. For example, poverty rates for Latinos are: 32.5% for Puerto Ricans, 27% for Central and South American, 26.4% for Mexican Americans, and 15.4% for Cuban Americans as compared to 7.3% for non-Hispanic Whites (Marger, 1997). Further, undocumented Latinas represent an especially vulnerable sub-group given reports of rape by those who transport them across the border, employ them, and even by corrupt immigration officials (Hamilton, 1989).

Social class is also strongly related to the availability of services needed to respond to sexual assault and post-assault recovery. To be effective, social workers must acknowledge the many threats to well being that exist in this country for those who are disenfranchised because of status dimensions such as SES, race, ethnicity, gender, and sexual orientation. Status dimensions include a group's access to political power and economic and educational resources, as well as where their ethnic and gender groups are situated in the social hierarchy of power. Latinas in this country face the double jeopardy of being women and people of color, both devalued statuses. As Root (1996) points out:

> The lower one's status, the more invisible that individual and her distress, and the more likely she is to be objectified. It is the objectification of others that allows individuals to commit atrocities against other individuals. (p. 364)

SEQUELAE OF SEXUAL ASSAULT

Symptomatic Responses

Empirical studies confirm that people who have been sexually assaulted exhibit a variety of emotional, behavioral and somatic responses (Ullman, 1996; George, Winfield & Blazer, 1992; Murphy et al., 1988; Marhoefer-Dvorak, Resick, Hutter & Girelli, 1988). Responses are strongly negative, and while they tend to diminish over time; approximately 25% of those assaulted still show significant signs of impairment one year post-assault (Siegel et al., 1990). Fear, anxiety, depression and sexual dysfunction are the most commonly noted reactions to sexual assault.

There continues to be a paucity of data on the effects of sexual assault on Latinas. The primary source of quantitative information available is from the LA-ECA study (Sorenson & Siegel, 1992). In this study, the researchers found similar assault outcomes for Latinas and non-Latina Whites. The most common reaction in this study was anger, reported by three-quarters of all violated women. Fear, anxiety, and depression were pronounced, being reported by half of the sample. Fear appeared to be particularly persistent over time. Assailant use of physical threat was associated with high fear/anxiety levels as well as high levels of depression, as were assaults that resulted in intercourse. Younger age at time of assault, use of physical threat, and greater probability of intercourse as the outcome of assault were all predictors of sexual distress.

Lefley et al.'s (1993) study contradicts the above findings to some degree. Latinas in that study had higher degrees of psychological distress than White and African American participants, especially on a measure of obsessive/compulsive symptoms. However, in both of the above studies, severity of the assault appeared to transcend ethnicity in affecting psychological response.

Trauma and Dimensions of Security

Root (1996) identifies four dimensions of security that are threatened by a sexual assault: physical, psychological, interpersonal, and spiritual. The assault itself, on a concrete level, introduces a threat to survival and imparts physical harm, sometimes resulting in permanent physical damage. Because the mind and body are inseparable, visceral memories of the assault and somatic reactions also affect the survivor's experience of herself as a physical being. Psychologically, an assault shatters one's assumptions about the perceived ordered nature of one's environment, conceptions of good and evil, and ideas about personal control and responsibility, creating a sense of dislocation and helplessness. For Latina immigrants, sexual assault can elicit excessive fear of life in the U.S. and interfere with adaptation to the U.S.

On an interpersonal level, a trauma inflicted by another human being is an experience of betrayal, violation of stolen personal space, invalidation of the self and broken attachments that damage trust in others and in the self. For Latinas whose traditional social support systems are already stretched, sexual assault especially taxes their human resources. Finally on the spiritual level, sexual assault challenges the meaning of life and diminishes the feeling of connectedness to one's god and the universe. There is anecdotal evidence that some

Latinas have viewed their sexual assault as punishment from God (Contreras & Mendez, 1978).

A sexual assault, as with other traumas, can shatter an individual's construction of reality and challenge her coping strategies. Traditional models that explore how trauma affects an individual's cognitive schema come from a White male perspective of time limited events, often singular in nature (Hough, Canino, Abueg & Gusman, 1996; Herman, 1992). These models suggest adaptive and normative pre-assault cognitive schema and post-assault maladaptive schema. Resolution, then, is seen as an integration of meanings into a new positive schema of self, others, and the world.

However, Root (1996) cautions that traditional models that explore how traumas shatter assumptions of the world may not be adequate to describe the experiences of women of color. She introduces the concept of "insidious trauma" which is characterized by repetitive and cumulative experiences perpetrated by persons who have power over one's resources and destiny and directed toward people of lower status. Considering that most of the female victims in the LA-ECA survey (Siegel et al., 1990) reported an average of 3.2 sexual assaults, the concept of insidious trauma should be considered for women in general, although poorer women are more likely to lack response resources.

Root (1996) points out that insidious trauma shapes reality and reinforces constructions of reality, rather than shattering previously held beliefs. Insidious traumas may contribute to a construction of the world as malevolent and of the self as inadequate. A new trauma, such as a sexual assault, may, therefore, reinforce this idea of a malevolent world. On the other hand, experiences with multiple traumas can sometimes promote the development of survival strategies and resiliency. Research needs to be designed around a more complex understanding of trauma, such as Root's model in order to comprehend how a life context of micro-aggressions and insidious trauma affects a woman's experience of sexual assault.

IMPLICATIONS
FOR CULTURALLY COMPETENT TREATMENT

Working Model of Sexual Assault in Latinas

Culturally competent rape services acknowledge the lived experience of the Latina victim while clarifying both the conflicts and benefits of biculturality. Such services could benefit by conceptualizing the problem of sexual assault in Latinas as occurring within the overlapping contexts of traditional Latino and modern U.S. gender role systems. While such a cultural location presents a dual dilemma for Latina victims, each of these gender role systems expose Latinas to challenging combinations of both positive and negative influences on sexual assault that need to be better understood in order to reconcile dual dilemmas as well as capitalize on bicultural advantages.

With regard to the traditional Latino gender role system, negative influences on victims of sexual assault include endorsements of victim-blaming and assailant-excusing rape myths. Such myths appear to be rooted in traditional, narrow conceptions of women as responsible for the sexual behavior of men and needing to be sexually pure (i.e., not "tainted" by rape). Such community-wide myths appear to translate to a lack of support for victims and, when internalized, excessive post-assault distress and lack of adaptive coping (Lefley et al., 1993; Williams, 1985). As compared to White and African American rape victims, Latina rape victims report more victim-blame and less post-assault social support. For example, in the study by Williams and Holmes (1981) 63% of White and 50% of African American rape victims reported that their needs had been met as much as possible. In contrast, 70% of Mexican American victims reported that their needs had only been partially met or not at all. Further, Mexican American women reported more passivity and withdrawal from normal routines and more negative feelings towards men (e.g., more mistrust).

On the positive side of Latino gender roles, natural supports for women (e.g., protection by extended family members) as well as central family roles that confer value, status, and self-esteem in women need to be used as foundations for generating greater care for victims. The prior suggestion of framing rape as harmful to the entire family and focusing attention on recovery, versus victim-blaming or revenge, exemplifies a bicultural expansion of both male and female gender roles by situating the needs of victims within the context of, and not in competition with, general family needs.

With regard to the modern U.S. gender role system, negative influences on Latina victims of sexual assault include the continuing struggle to sensitize men, the public, and social services to the problem of sexual assault against women. Residual sexism in the U.S. is exacerbated by racism towards Latinas who are disproportionately poor and at a disadvantage with regard to both gender and SES-related power. The link between rape and poverty has been documented for women in general (Holzman, 1996), and the link between sexual assault and acculturation for Latinas has also been documented (Sorenson & Siegel, 1992).

On the positive side of American gender roles is the progressive women's movement that continues to advance public understanding of sexual assault against women, and that advocates feminist-sensitive attitudes and services that promote adaptive coping. Latinas living in the U.S. are increasingly exposed to modern, feminist ideas and roles that encourage them to acknowledge and actively cope with sexual assault both within their families and communities as well as with law enforcement and social services. While cultural conflicts are inherent in such feminist development, progress in this bicultural direction can be advanced in culturally sensitive ways. For example, shifting Latinas from Marianismo-like gender roles to Hembrismo, as conceptualized by Latina and other feminists of color (Boyd-Franklin & Garcia-Preto, 1994; Morales and Reyes, 1998), represents a beginning. Well-documented obstacles to service for Latinos need to be addressed as does the need to make such services responsive to the culture and experience of Latinos.

Culture and Gender Sensitive Sexual Assault Services for Latinas

Service utilization. With regard to post-sexual assault service utilization, Sorenson and Siegel (1992) found that both Latinas and non-Latina Whites were equally likely to report to police, although the actual number are characteristically unimpressive (i.e., 9.6% and 10.8%, respectively). It was also found that Latinas were less likely than their non-Latina White counterparts to seek any health service regardless of need, the nature of the assault, age, and medical insurance. Further, Latinas were less likely than non-Latina Whites to see a psychologist, but more likely to see a member of the clergy. When compared to non-assaulted Latinas in the LA-ECA study, Latinas with a history of sexual assault were more likely to have utilized general medical services in the past six months. Thus, underutilization of needed services is a problem for sexually assaulted Latinas and outreach efforts via general medical providers and clergy would be logical starting places. For example, medical and religious service providers could be provided workshops on sexual assault in general, and on

Latinas in particular, to help them better recognize and respond to the needs of victims that are likely to seek them as services of first choice.

Accessibility and acceptability. In order for services to be effective, they need to be sensitive to the client's socio-cultural context. Services must be accessible in terms of location, language compatibility, cost, and availability of staff familiar with Latino culture and experience. Latinas tend to access medical services for emotional problems at a higher rate than mental health services (Padilla, Carlos, and Keefe, 1976). Providing rape counseling through medical clinics may be one approach to reaching Latinas who have been assaulted. Maintaining connections with community organizations in order to establish legitimacy within the community, as well as developing referral sources, may also be important for rape treatment centers.

Model program. In a National Institute of Mental Health (NIMH) funded, national, cross-site analysis of exemplary rape crisis programs, the Sexual Assault Center of San Joaquin County in Stockton, California, was chosen as one of the nine programs considered to be particularly effective in addressing the needs of victims in the community (Harvey, 1985). The term exemplary refers to model programs that have had significant impact on sexual assault treatment and prevention at local, regional, and national levels, according to national advisory panel of the National Center for the Prevention and Control of Rape (NCPCR), which was established by Public Law 94-63 and located within the NIMH. Of the 50 programs selected by the panel, 9 were chosen as exemplary based on standardized phone interviews with directors, site visits, and program case studies.

One of the unique aspects of this program is that its clientele corresponds proportionately to the racial and ethnic demographics of San Joaquin county, which has a large Latino population. Some factors that might explain the center's success in serving the local Latino population include its multi-service orientation that incorporates comprehensive advocacy, accompaniment, and counseling services to adult and child victims of sexual assault, as well as community education and prevention services. It is housed in an accessible downtown office space, in the same building as a job program for low income women and an advocacy organization for abused women. Whenever possible, Latina clients are matched with Latina staff and a concerted effort is made to maintain a representative group of bilingual and bicultural staff and volunteers. According to Harvey (1985):

At all levels of programming, The Sexual Assault Center puts a special emphasis on the importance of multicultural, bilingual services. The staff is culturally and racially diverse; volunteers are recruited and services publicized through the Spanish-speaking radio and television stations and bilingual presentations to church groups. Materials are developed in both English and Spanish and much consideration is given to issues facing minority communities. Client record keeping and program evaluation regularly examine the center's service to minority and Spanish speaking groups. (p. 73)

The agency has developed a credible reputation within the community due to its outreach efforts and high quality of services. Unfortunately, evaluative outcome research is not a part of this program as is generally the case with direct service agencies that prioritize service delivery and lack research capacity.

Specific Interventions

Rape treatment services must evaluate whether their services are appropriate to meet the particular needs of Latinas. The influence of gender roles as well as other bicultural issues is a place to start such evaluations. Holzman (1996) identifies Western values embedded in rape crisis counseling models that may conflict with the cultural values ethnic minority women may bring to the counseling relationship:

1. individualistic independence versus interdependence with family and community;
2. self-determination versus deference to authority;
3. open and direct communication versus discretion, tact, and indirect communication; and
4. emotional expressiveness versus restraint, particularly with regard to anger. (p. 54)

Counseling techniques need to be modified to match a woman's values and needs. For instance, it is important to consider the victim's family and other relationships, rather than seeing her solely as a hurt individual. Lefley et al. (1993) suggest that the family support system should be engaged as soon as possible when working with Latina clients who have been sexually assaulted. Counselors should emphasize that rape, and misconceptions about rape, harm the entire family while establishing clear boundaries between primary and secondary victimization. Counselors may find that male members of the family need to process feelings of guilt and failure for not being able to protect the victim. Therapy can help families grapple with a new awareness of their lack of control while focusing on the need to support the victim.

Should victim blaming occur in more traditional Latino families, members should be provided psychoeducation about rape and sexual assault including reflection on how such problems may be viewed differently from traditional and modern perspectives. Family therapy is a process within which to pursue such therapeutic goals beginning with crisis intervention.

Family crisis intervention. Harris (1991) outlines a pertinent family crisis intervention model for the treatment of post-traumatic stress that includes a five step problem solving approach: (1) making psychological contact with the family; (2) examining the dimensions of the problem; (3) exploring possible solutions; (4) assisting with concrete action; and (5) following up to check progress. Assuming that the family plays a critical role in the recovery process, family crisis intervention seeks to strengthen family function in the face of crisis and to facilitate family adaptation to the crisis. This may require restructuring of roles and rules within the family. For instance, male family members may need to expand their gender role prescriptions by taking on more child rearing, homemaking or nurturing tasks within the family during victim recovery and beyond. Conversely, the victim may need to develop new skills in eliciting emotional and practical support. Harris suggests that the victim seek individual treatment while her family is seen by the family therapist. In this way the family can honestly vent feelings without hurting the victim and vice-versa. Coordination between the therapists offers an avenue for the family to learn about the feelings and needs of the victim. Again, emphasis on healing the entire family should be stressed. Because sexual assault services are likely to involve asserting the rights of women not to be sexually violated, the incorporation of such feminist approaches seems inevitable but must be sensitively applied as discussed below.

Feminist and ethnic psychologies. Comas-Diaz (1994) suggests that elements of feminist and ethnic minority psychologies need to be combined in an integrative approach to counseling with ethnic minority women. Both approaches view the individual within her socio-cultural environment as well as understanding her identity development as integrally connected to her family and community relationships. Attention needs to be given to the Latina's ethnic and gender identity in the therapeutic process in order to help her reestablish a positive self-concept. Attention should also be given to the meaning that she makes of the assault in order to identify maladaptive thoughts and to clarify any conflicting cultural values. For example, traditional rape myths must be countered by defining rape as sexual, genital contact without consent even if a woman dresses in an attractive manner or expresses romantic attraction and affection to a potential assailant. Issues of marital rape must be similarly pursued. Cognitive behavioral approaches can also be helpful in confronting unhelpful, gender-role based beliefs.

Cognitive behavioral therapy. De Anda (1997) suggests that cognitive-behavioral therapy (CBT) has the potential of being relatively culture free or more open to cultural adaptation. Depending on the skills of the practitioner, she contends that CBT is a heuristic which allows for collaboration between client and therapist in defining the problem and agreeing on interventions, thus limiting the impact of the therapist's cultural judgments. With regard to sexual assault, CBT provides a helpful format for discussing competing gender role systems and the need to reach flexible, bicultural compromises (e.g., progressing from Marianismo to Hembrismo as previously discussed).

Organista and Valdes Dwyer (1996) describe ways in which CBT combined with clinical case management is an effective treatment strategy for Latinas suffering from depression and traumatic experiences. Their program has been implemented in the Division of Psychosocial Medicine at the San Francisco General Hospital, in the heart of the Latino Mission District, and is instructive in formulating treatment plans for Latina survivors of sexual assault. The program includes several important structural and therapeutic modifications of traditional services in order to accommodate the cultural and practical realities of their Latino clients. The first step was in decreasing barriers to utilization of services by making services free, hospital-based (accessible), and delivered by linguistically as well as ethnically matched therapists. Medical staff have been trained to recognize symptoms of depression and anxiety and to refer clients for psychosocial evaluation. From assessment through intervention, bilingual and bicultural Latino staff use a Latino relationship protocol to engage clients, emphasizing such culture-based values as *respeto* (showing proper respect for formal and traditional roles and relationships) and *personalismo* (formal yet warm and personalized way of speaking and relating to clients).

Treatment is delivered in a group format consisting of predominantly immigrant Latina women (Mexican and Central American) who share common problems and experiences in the U.S. Patients are taught to increase rewarding activities both with family members and alone to combat negative mood states as recommended by Lewinsohn, Muñoz, Youngren, and Zeiss (1986). Such activities interrupt the vicious cycle that occurs when depression leads to inactivity and vice versa. But while behavioral activity schedules tend to prioritize self-care above caring for others, the group emphasizes self-care as a means to more effective family care. Also, the clients state that they are motivated to engage in reinforcing activities in order to "distract" themselves from problems.

Clients are also taught to identify, challenge and change thoughts and beliefs related to negative moods and that inhibit adaptive behaviors on their part. Cognitive restructuring is based on the classic works of Beck, Rush, Shaw, and Emery (1979), as well as Ellis' rational emotive therapy (Ellis and Grieger, 1977). However, client beliefs are never referred to as irrational or as distortions of reality. Instead, they are referred to as partial or "half-truths" that need to be made into "complete-truths." Further, teaching clients how to restructure their beliefs is greatly streamlined for ease and simplicity.

For example, a severely depressed woman from Mexico disclosed how she felt permanently "stained" for having been sexually abused as an adolescent by her mother's live-in boyfriend. The problem had been exacerbated by her mother's reaction which was a mixture of disbelief, denial, and victim-blame. The group was asked if it were true that rape or other forms of sexual assault permanently "stain" a woman for life, thus initiating a dialogue about traditional Latino and more modern beliefs about sexual abuse. In order to begin shifting the client's beliefs in a healthier direction, she was asked to complete the following sentence: "Yes, it is true that I feel stained from being sexually abused, but. . . . . . ," to which the woman was able to respond "but I was the one taken advantage of." From such a beginning, work proceeded to place proper blame on the perpetrator, to redefine stained victim role to an injured survivor in need of healing via helpful beliefs, activities, social supports, and sensitive services. Even the estranged relationship with the client's mother was discussed, focusing on helping the client to better understand that such negative reactions are problems within the mother, family, culture (e.g., the role of denial, rigid gender roles, etc.), as well as the role of economic dependency.

Transcending Latino culture. Respect for the client's culture does not preclude offering another perspective. As discussed, sexual assault is promoted by beliefs about gender within the culture. Traditional gender roles put women at risk for further victimization and poor psychological outcome. Helping women assert their needs, while respecting cultural beliefs about gender, is both important and possible. For example, Comas-Diaz and Duncan (1985) describe culturally sensitive assertiveness training with Latinas in which women are taught to preface assertiveness messages with phrases such as "Con todo respeto" (with all due respect), and "Me permite decir algo?" (would you permit me to say something?). These prefaces explicitly acknowledge deference to authority and other culture and gender based power differences in relationships. At the same time, these prefaces create channels for assertive communications of pressing feelings and cognitions. Women are also prepared for negative culture-based responses in which their assertiveness may be misperceived as disrespectful. In addition to not internalizing angry responses and criticisms of others, women are taught to say that if the other person does not choose to listen to them, they will feel distant and distraught, although they would prefer to feel close.

Familism can be re-visioned in order to help the victim help herself. Distinguishing supportive aspects of familism and traditional gender roles from the dysfunction of violence and abuse is essential. Focusing on the goal of returning the whole family to health, the counselor can help the victim to re-examine her responsibilities as a woman. Because Marianismo may imply that women are responsible for the sexual transgressions of men, emphasizing the assailant's full responsibility for the sexual assault is primary (e.g., challenging rape myths), even if the perpetrator is a family member or acquaintance. Such assailants need to be described as disrespectful and harmful to the entire family as well as the individual victim. The concept of respect can also be expanded to include respecting a woman's choice in sexual matters.

The central institution of motherhood can be used to persuade Latina victims to devote needed attention to their proper recovery. The analogy of oxygen mask protocol on airplanes, in which adults are instructed to secure their own masks before those of their children, is useful for stressing the common family good of self-care. By identifying potential cultural conflicts (i.e., "I can't focus on myself when I have children to take care of") the counselor and client can discover ways that the needs of the victim and her extended network can merge rather than being at odds. Family and community members can be enlisted as allies and support in this endeavor.

CONCLUSION

Although much Latina-focused sexual assault research is needed to clarify prevalence, assault characteristics, and post-trauma sequelae, community education campaigns and outreach efforts to places like medical settings and churches are needed now to respond to the needs of affected women. To be sensitive, such efforts will need to consider a variety of cultural factors such as rape myths and beliefs, gender roles, and familism which may serve to either help or exacerbate the problem of sexual assault among Latinas. Similarly, the application of mainstream gender roles may help and hinder adjustment in various ways. Such efforts will also need to consider several negative structural factors including the different ways that the disadvantaged dual status of being female and Latina contextualizes sexual assault. The indication that sexual assault may increase with acculturation raises the question of how to provide prevention and intervention services to both immigrant and native-born Latinas in ways that reinforce protective cultural factors, but which also transcend culture to help Latinas better protect themselves and prioritize their needs in a bicultural world.

REFERENCES

Beck. A. T., Rush. J. R., Shaw, B. F., & Emery, G. (1979). *Cognitive therapy for depression*. New York: The Guilford Press.

Boyd-Franklin, N., & Garcia-Preto, N. (1994). Family therapy: A closer look at African American and Hispanic Women. In L. Comas-Diaz and B. Greene (Eds.),

Women of color: Integrating ethnic and gender identities in psychotherapy (pp. 239-264). New York: The Guilford Press.

Brownmiller, Susan (1975). *Against our will: Men, women and rape.* New York: Simon and Schuster.

Comas-Diaz, L. (1994). An integrative approach. In L. Comas-Diaz and B. Greene (Eds.), *Women of color: Integrating ethnic and gender identities in psychotherapy* (pp. 287-318). New York: The Guilford Press.

Comas-Diaz, L., & Duncan, J. W. (1985). The cultural context: A factor in assertiveness training with mainland Puerto Rican women. *Psychology of Women Quarterly, 9,* 463-476.

Contreras, T. & Mendez, I. D. (1978). Si necesita ayuda, llama. . . . . .Counseling for Latina rape survivors. In S. Davidson (Ed.), *Contemporary approaches in counseling young women* (pp. 33-44). Arizona: New Directions for Young Women.

de Anda, D. (1997). Are there theories that are sufficiently culture free to be appropriate and useful for practice with multicultural clients? In D. de Anda (Ed.), *Controversial issues in multiculturalism* (pp. 142-152). New York: Allyn & Bacon.

Donat, P., & D'Emilio, J. (1992). A feminist redefinition of rape and sexual assault: Historical foundations and change. *Journal of Social Issues, 48,* 9-22.

Ellis, A. & Grieger, R. (1977). *Handbook of Rational Emotive Therapy.* New York: Holt, Rinehart, & Winston.

Espin, O. (1997). *Latina realities: Essays on healing, migration, and sexuality.* Boulder, CO: Westview Press.

Falicov, C. J. (1998). *Latino families in therapy.* New York: The Guilford Press.

Fischer, G. J. (1987). Hispanic and majority student attitudes toward forcible date rape as a function of different attitudes towards women. *Sex Roles, 17*(1/2), 93-101.

Friedman, A. R. (1992). Rape and domestic violence: The experience of refugee women. In E. Cole, O. Espin, and E. Rothblum (Eds.), *Refugee women and their mental health* (pp. 65-78). New York/London: The Haworth Press, Inc.

George, L., Winfield, I., & Blazer, D. (1992). Socio-cultural factors in sexual assault: Comparison of two representative samples of women. *Journal of Social Issues, 48,* 105-125.

Hamilton, J. A. (1989). Emotional consequences of victimization and discrimination in "special populations" of women. *Psychiatric Clinics of North America, 12*(1), 35-51.

Harris, C. (1991). A family crisis intervention model for the treatment of post traumatic stress reaction. *Journal of Traumatic Stress, 4,* 195-207.

Harvey, M. (1985). Exemplary rape crisis programs: A cross site analysis and case studies. Bethesda, MD: National Institute of Mental Health.

Herman, Judith Lewis (1992). *Trauma and recovery.* New York: Basic Books.

Holzman, C. (1996). Counseling adult women rape survivors: Issues of race, ethnicity and class. *Women & Therapy, 19,* 47-62.

Hough, R., Canino, G., Abueg, F., & Gusman, F. (1996). PTSD and related stress disorders among Hispanics. In A. Marsella, M. Friedman, E. Gerrity and R. Scurfield (Eds.), *Ethnocultural aspects of posttraumatic stress disorder* (pp. 301-338). Washington, DC: American Psychological Association.

Karmen, A. (1982). Introduction. In B. R. Price & N. J. Sokoloff (Eds.), *The criminal justice system and women* (pp. 185-201). New York: Clark Boardman.

Kilpatrick, D. G., Best, C. L., Veronen, L. J., Amick, A. E., Villeponteaux, L. A., & Ruff, G. A. (1985). Mental health correlates of criminal victimization: A random community survey. *Journal of Consulting and Clinical Psychology, 53,* 866-873.

Koss, M. P., Gidycz, C. A., & Wisniewski, N. (1987). The scope of rape: Incidence and prevalence of sexual aggression and victimization in a national sample of higher education students. *Journal of Consulting and Clinical Psychology, 55,* 162-170.

Kuoch, T., Miller, R., & Scully, M. (1992). Healing the wounds of the Mahantdori. In E. Cole, O. Espin, and E. Rothblum (Eds.), *Refugee women and their mental health* (pp. 191-208). New York/London: The Haworth Press, Inc.

Lefley, H., Scott, C., Llabre, M., & Hicks, D. (1993) Cultural beliefs about rape and victims' response in three ethnic groups. *American Journal of Orthopsychiatry, 63,* 623-631.

Lewinsohn, P. M., Muñoz, R. F., Youngren, M. A., & Zeiss, A. M. (1986). *Control your depression* (revised edition). New York: Prentice-Hall.

Lore, R. K., & Schultz, L. A. (1993) Control of human aggression: A comparative perspective. *American Psychologist, 48,* 16-25.

Marger, M. N. (1997). Hispanic Americans. In M. N. Marger, *Race and ethnic relations: American and global perspectives* (4th ed.) (pp. 281-321). Belmont, CA: Wadsworth Publishing Co.

Marhoefer-Dvorak, S., Resick, P. A., Hutter, C. K., & Girelli, S. A. (1988). Single versus multiple incident rape victims: A comparison of psychological reactions to rape. *Journal of Interpersonal Violence, 3*(2), 145-160.

Marsella, A., Friedman, M., & Huland-Spain, E. (1996). Ethnocultural aspects of PTSD: An overview of issues and research directions. In A. Marsella, M. Friedman, E. Gerrity and R. Scurfield (Eds.), *Ethnocultural aspects of posttraumatic stress disorder* (pp. 105-129). Washington, DC: American Psychological Association.

McNair, L. D. & Neville, H. A. (1996). African-American women survivors of sexual assault: The intersection of race and class. *Women & Therapy, 18*(3/4), 107-118.

Morales, J. & Reyes, M. (1998). Cultural and political realities for community social work practice with Puerto Ricans in the United States. In F.G. Rivera & J. L. Erlich (Eds.), *Community organizing in a diverse society* (3rd ed.) (pp. 75-96). Boston: Allyn and Bacon.

Murphy, S. M., Amick-McMullan, A. E., Kilpatrick, D. G., Haskett, M. E., Veronen, L. J., Best, C. L., & Saunders, B. E. (1988). Rape victims' self esteem: A longitudinal study. *Journal of Interpersonal Violence, 3*(4), 355-370.

Organista, K. C., & Valdes Dwyer, E. (1996). Clinical case management and cognitive behavioral therapy: Integrated psychosocial services for depressed Latino primary care patients. In P. G. Manoleas (Ed.), *The cross-cultural practice of clinical case management in mental health* (pp. 119-143). New York: The Haworth Press, Inc.

Padilla, A. M., Carlos, M. L., & Keefe, S. E. (1976). Mental health service utilization by Mexican Americans. In M. R. Miranda (Ed.), *Psychotherapy with the Spanish-speaking (Monograph No. 3)*. University of California, Los Angeles: Spanish Speaking Mental Health Research Center.

Root, M. (1996). Women of color and traumatic stress in "domestic captivity": Gender and race as disempowering statuses. In A. Marsella, M. Friedman, E. Gerrity and R. Scurfield (Eds.), *Ethnocultural aspects of posttraumatic stress disorder* (pp. 363-387). Washington, DC: American Psychological Association.

Roth, S., & Newman, E. (1991). The process of coping with sexual trauma. *Journal of Traumatic Stress, 4*, 279-297.

Rozee, P. D. (1993). Forbidden or forgiven? Rape in cross-cultural perspective. *Psychology of Women Quarterly, 17*(4), 499-514.

Russell, D. E. H. (1982). The prevalence and incidence of forcible rape and attempted rape of females. *Victimology, 7*, 81-93.

Sabogal, F., Marin, G., Otero-Sabogal, R., Marin, B. V., & Perez-Stable, E. J. (1987). Hispanic familism and acculturation: What changes and what doesn't? *Hispanic Journal of Behavioral Sciences, 9*, 397-412.

Siegel, J., Golding, J., Stein, J., Burnam, M., & Sorenson, S. (1990). Reactions to sexual assault: A community study. *Journal of Interpersonal Violence, 2*, 229-246.

Sorenson, S., & Siegel, J. (1992). Gender, ethnicity and sexual assault: Findings from a Los Angeles study. *Journal of Social Issues, 48*, 93-104.

Sorenson, S., & White, J. (1992). Adult sexual assault: Overview of research. *Journal of Social Issues, 48*, 1-7.

Ullman, S. (1996). Social reactions, coping strategies, and self-blame attributions in adjustment to sexual assault. *Psychology of Women Quarterly, 20*, 505-525.

U.S. Department of Justice (1988). Criminal victimization in the United States, 1986. Washington, DC: Bureau of Justice Statistics.

Vasquez, M. (1994). Latinas. In L. Comas-Diaz and B. Greene (Eds.), *Women of color: Integrating ethnic and gender identities in psychotherapy* (pp. 114-138). New York: The Guilford Press.

Williams, J. E. (1985). Mexican American and Anglo attitudes about sex role and rape. *Free Inquiry in Creative Sociology, 13* (1), 15-20.

Williams, J. E. & Holmes, K. A. (1982). In judgement of victims: The social context of rape. *Journal of Sociology and Social Welfare, 9*, 154-169.

Williams, J. E. & Holmes, K. A. (1981). *The second assault: Rape and public attitudes*. Westport, CT: Greenwood Press.

CHILD ABUSE

Exploring Child Abuse
Among Vietnamese Refugees

Uma A. Segal

SUMMARY. This exploratory pilot project sought to determine what one group of Southeast Asian refugees, the Vietnamese, perceived were areas of difficulty in their adjustment to the United States. Furthermore, based on factors correlated with the physical abuse of children, and on literature that states that child abuse is not culture-specific, this study sought to assess whether child abuse is prevalent among this population. Findings were inconsistent and suggested that common methods of identifying the occurrence of child abuse may not be valid in its assessment among populations that may fear the repercussions of admitting to the use of corporal punishment to discipline their children. Implications for research are discussed. *[Article copies available for a fee from The Haworth Document Delivery Service: 1-800-342-9678. E-mail address: <getinfo@haworthpressinc.com> Website: <http://www.haworthpressinc.com>]*

Uma A. Segal, PhD, is Associate Professor in the Department of Social Work and a Fellow of the Public Policy Research Centers at the University of Missouri-St. Louis.

Funding for this research was provided by the University of Missouri-St. Louis' Research Award Fund and its Small Grants Fund.

[Haworth co-indexing entry note]: "Exploring Child Abuse Among Vietnamese Refugees." Segal, Uma A. Co-published simultaneously in *Journal of Multicultural Social Work* (The Haworth Press, Inc.) Vol. 8, No. 3/4, 2000, pp. 159-191; and: *Violence: Diverse Populations and Communities* (ed: Diane de Anda, and Rosina M. Becerra) The Haworth Press, Inc., 2000, pp. 159-191. Single or multiple copies of this article are available for a fee from The Haworth Document Delivery Service [1-800-342-9678, 9:00 a.m. - 5:00 p.m. (EST). E-mail address: getinfo@haworthpressinc.com].

KEYWORDS. Child abuse, Vietnamese, refugees

INTRODUCTION

As a result of the Vietnam War, several Southeast Asian refugees from Vietnam, Laos and Cambodia fled their native countries from communist regimes. Many sought refuge in the United States, and currently the total population of this refugee group numbers well over one million. The first of these refugees began arriving in 1975 after the fall of Saigon, and as with most refugee movements, the first wave was composed of highly educated, affluent and well connected individuals who rapidly adjusted into the Western society. Unlike the elite of the first cohort, the second and subsequent groups have been fisherman, farmers, peasants and laborers, and despite U.S. resettlement programs, they have experienced significant difficulties acclimatizing themselves to life in the fast-paced, computer-dominated environment of the United States (Fong, 1992; Lum, 1992). The extremely hazardous and degrading experiences of most later migrating Southeast Asian refugees increased their risk for developing major depressive and post traumatic stress disorders (Kinzie, Boehnlein, Leung, Moore, 1990; Lin & Shen, 1991) and somatic ailments such as headaches, low energy, and weakness (Foulks, Merkel & Boehnlein, 1992). In addition, a constellation of poverty, isolation, issues of acculturation, identity, and poor language proficiency increased their levels of frustration, stress, and emotional distress (Bemack, 1989; Cambon, 1989; Vega & Rumbaut, 1991) and may well have led to violence toward spouses (Norton & Manson, 1992) and children (Ima & Hohm, 1991).

Based on literature in the U.S. regarding adjustment of refugees, this exploratory pilot project conducted in the St. Louis metropolitan region sought to determine what one group of Southeast Asian refugees, the Vietnamese, perceived were areas of difficulty in their adjustment to the United States. Furthermore, based on the factors correlated with the physical abuse of children, and on literature that states that child abuse is not culture-specific, this study sought to assess whether child abuse is prevalent among this population. While there is no scholarly discussion of child abuse in Southeast Asia, themes of the prerogative of parents to discipline children as they see fit, the acceptability of corporal punishment, and the sanctity of the family abound. These may well have obscured recognition of child abuse in cultures of Southeast Asia.

BACKGROUND AND SIGNIFICANCE

Asian Americans constitute the fastest growing minority, both by birth and immigration (U.S. Bureau of Census, 1991), suggesting that this is a population that will soon warrant greater attention by legislative bodies, businesses, and human service providers. The overwhelming perception of Asian immigrants is that they constitute a "model minority," are professionally successful, and, according to their own cultural notions of health, are emotionally and mentally well-adjusted. What this label obscures is the plight of Southeast Asian refugees, the isolation of older Asian Americans, the conjugal violence, and the intergenerational turbulence experienced among Asian families (Khinduka, 1992). Furthermore, while many Asian Americans are economically successful, most Southeast Asian refugees live below the poverty line in the United States (Associated Press, February 28, 1993).

Refugee Resettlement

The U.S. Refugee Act of 1980 provides for federal programs to assist the process of resettlement through the Office of Refugee Resettlement. The programs–English language teaching, job training, medical care–are designed to promote self-subsistence skills. The primary goal of the Refugee Resettlement Program is to encourage economic self-sufficiency within the shortest possible time after a refugee enters a state. Resettlement, however, does not resolve cultural, economic, or social problems for many, but compounds them by compelling refugees to adopt the life style of a foreign culture (Mayadas & Segal, 1999). The socio-economic background of refugees varies with the economic development of their countries of origin. Foreign-born Vietnamese in the United States currently number approximately 770,000 (U.S. Census Bureau, 1997a). Most of the more recent arrivals came from rural backgrounds, and their levels of literacy, education, and skill are relatively low. Moreover, many have skills that are not directly transferable to Western industry, business, and technology. Thus, the number of Vietnamese refugees with marketable or employable skills is limited. As a result of these factors, this group of refugees has been dependent on external aid for longer than the Refugee Resettlement Program envisioned (Law & Schneiderman, 1992), and the inability to speak English has been a major deterrent to finding and retaining jobs (Silver, 1998).

Psycho-Social Adjustment of Vietnamese Refugees

Adjustment to resettlement is a lengthy process. Not only must refugees become acculturated to a foreign culture, they must also come to terms with the phenomena that forced them from their homes and the ensuing separations from family and support systems. Vietnamese refugees may experience stress associated with loss and grief for loved ones, social isolation and strained family relationships, change in social status, culture shock, and conflicts in acculturation. A recent report by the United Nations indicates that well over 40 million of the world's refugees run a high risk of depression, anxiety, and post traumatic stress disorder (Mitra, 1995) that may further lower their capacity to adjust to a new country. Studies suggest that lack of economic resources, minority status, lack of social support and loss of native language and culture are associated with greater psychological distress (Hurh & Kim, 1988; Rumbaut, 1991). In the US, even for those who are successful eventually, the struggle is usually long and arduous and " . . . its impact is felt for a lifetime . . . " (Nguyen, 1994, p. 25).

Cultural Values and Family Structure

The traditional Asian family structure provides stability, interpersonal intimacy, social support (Segal, 1998), and a relatively stress-free environment (DeVos, 1978) for it members. However, immigrant and refugee experiences cause major disruptions in family life and create pressures that destabilize established family relationships and affect role performance. In the traditional Asian patriarchal joint family, age, gender, and generational status of individuals serve as the primary determinants of behavior and role relationships (Jung, 1998). Interdependence is fostered, self-identity is inhibited (Segal, 1998), and a conservative orientation, resistive to change, is rewarded. Children are valued for their economic ability to contribute to the survival of the family and to provide security for parents in their old age (Tanwar, 1988).

Throughout their lives, children are expected to be docile, obedient, and a source of pride for their families. The Western concept of adolescence and the establishment of one's psychosocial identity (Erikson, 1963) is absent in the Asian/Vietnamese culture as one moves directly from childhood into adulthood (Mydans, 1994). Children are believed to be the property of their parents, and they continue to be perceived as extensions of their parents throughout the lifetime of the latter.

Child Abuse Among Vietnamese Refugees

A major issue in resettlement is the disruption of the extended family structure. Refugee communities, in many cases, serve as surrogate families, meeting the needs for both emotional and material support; however, these pseudo-familial structures do not totally substitute for the natural family (Lum, 1992). Furthermore, because children and youth rapidly become more fluent in English, they frequently act as the English language negotiators, undermining the authority of elders (Furuto & Murase, 1992) and threatening the Asian value of "filial piety," which is the honor, reverence, obedience, loyalty, and love owed those who are in positions of power relative to oneself (Chao, 1992; Lum, 1992). Socioeconomic and socio-cultural changes have been found to be correlated with increases in child maltreatment, but most often the increases in child maltreatment appear to be attributed to breakdowns in traditional values and practices (Korbin, 1991). Refugee families face unique problems that have a potential effect upon parent-child relationships. With the movement from Third World and agrarian communities, refugee children are no longer producers, but consumers, no longer assets, but liabilities (LeVine & LeVine, 1985; Logan, 1979).

As the acculturation process proceeds, there is an increase in intergenerational tension and alienation between parents and children, with internal conflicts becoming manifested in gang membership, drug abuse, juvenile delinquency, and running away (Furuto & Murase, 1992; Ingrassia et al., 1994). Parents often resort to physical discipline that is not acceptable in the United States, but which may well have been sanctioned in Vietnam (Ahn, 1994; Furuto & Murase, 1992). Child abuse among Vietnamese refugees, both in their native countries and in the United States, has received little attention. However, McKelvey and Webb's (1996) study does indicate that child abuse may be prevalent also in this population, and Ima and Hohm (1991) suggest that physical abuse may, in fact, be more common among the Asian and Pacific Islander refugees than among the general U.S. population. Furthermore, although in the U.S. child abuse is found across all economic levels of society and ethnic groups, studies suggest that the physical abuse of children may be more prevalent in conditions of poverty, as many of the environmental circumstances of potential abusers are concomitants of poverty. These circumstances may include financial stress, less opportunity to escape from child rearing, less inhibition to express and discharge aggression, and greater cultural approval for harsh discipline (Gil, 1973). A disproportionate number of Vietnamese refugees live below the poverty line. There are fewer supports to share in child rearing, and corporal punishment is viewed as an acceptable, if not preferred, means of discipline for many Vietnamese (Ahn, 1994; Ima & Hohm, 1991; Furuto & Murase, 1992), perhaps increasing the children's vulnerability to parental abuse.

While there is little empirical evidence to support, or refute, the occurrence of child maltreatment among Vietnamese refugees, practitioners involved in efforts to resettle Vietnamese refugees reveal that they strongly suspect child abuse among this population they serve, although they have no knowledge of its extent or severity (Crosslin, 1996; Leung, 1993, Silver, 1998). Despite the paucity of empirical research on child abuse among Vietnamese refugees, Ima and Hohm's (1991) study clearly indicates that this may be a problem of significant proportions. The scarcity of published material may merely indicate that few researchers are concerned or interested enough to address this issue, or that the basic survival needs of the population are so great that social service providers have focused on ensuring refugee access to resources. There may be little opportunity to devote efforts or resources into examining family relationships within a culture that is highly suspicious of outside intervention (Ho, 1992). Based on this and suggestions in the literature that child abuse may be prevalent among the Vietnamese, this exploratory project sought to identify if the physical abuse of children, as defined in the West, is evident among this group of refugees. In addition, information about factors that in the U.S. have been found to be associated with child abuse was sought to determine if similar correlations exist within this population. Furthermore, findings about support networks were expected to offer potentially untapped resources for intervention.

Children of Vietnamese Refugees

Although not suffering the extent of trauma and difficulties faced by their parents, children of refugees frequently face immense acculturative stresses as they grow up in households in the context of urban poverty. Parents, who are their primary supports, often lack the experience and material resources to help them negotiate safely through poor educational systems, street crime, lack of employment, racism and intolerance (Bean et al., 1992; Segal, 1994). Often, because of the more rapid acculturation of their children, these parents have lost the status of the "knowledgeable elder."

While all adolescents in the U.S. are faced with a certain amount of intergenerational tension, children of refugees often find themselves between the two vastly different worlds of their parents and their peers (Portes & Zhou, 1993; Segal, 1991; Suro, 1992). They often tend to emulate patterns of personal vulnerability and family disintegration that characterize other U.S. minorities (Vega & Rumbaut, 1991). It was anticipated that this pilot study would not only provide some empirical evidence of the occurrence of child abuse among Vietnamese refugees, but would also begin to empirically assess the impact of resettlement on the mental health of refugee parents and their adolescent children.

METHODS

Sampling

Based on census figures and discussions with demographers, resettlement agencies, government officials and immigrant/refugee associations, there are currently 4,705 foreign-born Vietnamese in the St. Louis Metropolitan area (Dine, 1994). Target subjects for this study were foreign-born Vietnamese who had children between the ages of 8 and 18 living at home. An even distribution of women and men were sought because literature suggests that the refugee experience affects

men and women differently and, for a number of reasons, acculturation for Southeast Asian refugee women may be somewhat easier than
it is for the men (Lum, 1992).

Letters in Vietnamese were mailed to 80 potential respondents who
were identified through the telephone directory based on their Vietnamese surnames. A week later, two trained bilingual Vietnamese
graduate research assistants (one male and one female) contacted the
recipients of the letters to determine if they were appropriate candi-
dates for the sample: (1) if they were, in fact, Vietnamese, (2) if they
were (or had been) married, (3) if they had children living at home,
and (4) if they were willing to participate in the study. If they fulfilled
each of these conditions, the research assistant further explained that
the study focused on adjustment in the US and relationships among
family members, and invited participation of the potential subjects and
one child in the family. All communications were conducted in Vietnamese.

All research instruments, letters of invitation, and consent/assent
forms were translated, and "back-translated" by different translators
to ensure that the essence of the statements was not lost in the translation. Of the 80 letters mailed, 28 resulted in responses from subjects
who met the study criteria.

Instrumentation

Demographic Questionnaire. Information was requested on the subject's age, marital status, educational level, health, occupation, family
income, number of children, length of stay in the United States and
occupation in Vietnam. Similar information was also obtained for the
subject's spouse.

The Semi-Structured Interview with Parents. The structure of the
interview was based on the research literature and understanding of the
local community gained through preliminary field work and was developed to closely approximate an informal "conversation" (McCracken,
1988; Merton et al., 1990). The interviews were used to explore subjective experiences related to resettlement and acculturation among
the refugees. This research approach is flexible and responsive to the
particular situation of each person and each refugee group (Rogler,
1989), and is particularly useful in identifying key issues in the acculturation process, understanding types of mental health problems en-
countered by the refugees, and identifying help-seeking patterns. The

semi-structured interview with subjects sought responses to issues such as the following: (1) reason for leaving country of origin/precipitating event; (2) experience between leaving country of origin and resettling in St. Louis; (3) experience since arrival in St. Louis; (4) reception by Americans; (5) perceptions of the US culture; (6) economic status and associated concerns; (7) current support systems; (8) most difficult experience since resettling in the U.S.; (9) most encouraging experience since resettling; (10) perceptions about child rearing in the U.S., and perceptions of children's adjustment to changes; (11) feelings regarding cultural continuity and change; and (12) services utilization.

The Semi-Structured Interview with Children. The semi-structured interview with the children lasted about 10-15 minutes and was designed to assess children's perceptions of their performance in school, leisure-time activities, friendships with American children, relationships with siblings, and perceptions of discipline used by their parents.

Child Abuse Potential Inventory (CAPI). The CAPI (Milner, 1986; Milner, 1990; Milner & Wimberley, 1979) is a questionnaire that assists in the screening of physical child abuse reports (Nayak & Milner, 1998). The questionnaire is self-administered and requires individuals to agree or disagree with specific statements which can then be grouped into seven sub-scales: a distress scale, a rigidity scale, an unhappiness scale, a loneliness scale, a problems with child and self scale, a problems with the family scale, and a problems with others scale. The questionnaire consists of 160 items in which are embedded 77 items that comprise the 7 sub-scales. The reliability of the scales is high as are their construct and predictive validity (Caliso & Milner, 1992, Nayak & Milner, 1998), and studies suggest that they are applicable across cultures (Bringiotti, Barbich & De Paúl, 1998; Haz, & Ramirez, 1998).

Conflict Tactics Scale (CTS). The CTS was designed to assess methods of conflict resolution used by families in the United States (Straus, 1979, 1995). Three different methods are measured: (1) reasoning, (2) verbal aggression and (3) violence. The CTS specifically involves asking respondents what they did or what their children did when there was an argument or disagreement. The list of possible actions begins with those that are of low coerciveness (discussion), but continues to become progressively coercive and violent (using a weapon). The sequence is believed to enhance the likelihood that the subject will become committed to the interview and continue to answer the questions. In their analyses of responses, Straus, Gelles and Steinmetz (1981) in the U.S. and Segal (1995) in India found that there was no noticeable drop in the completion of the list. Straus (1979) indicates that it is particularly important to distinguish between abusive violence and the milder forms of family violence and corporal punishment that are often considered acceptable in society, since they usually pose less danger to the child than do the former.

The Basic English Skills Test (BEST). The BEST tests literacy skills at a very basic level. The Literacy Skills section was selected for the project because of its high reliability in measuring the literacy competencies of low proficiency non-English speaking populations. A unique measurement tool designed for adult ESL (English as a Second Language) populations, it targets basic survival skills such as filling out simple personal data and reading calendars and telephone directories (Center for Applied Linguistics, 1986; Silver, 1998).

Operationalization of Variables. Variables were operationalized using a combination of theoretical constructs and subjects' perceptions of their life situations.

1. *Financial Problems.* Whether or not a subject had financial problems was based on household income (since resources are usually pooled even if unrelated individuals reside together [Lum, 1992]), number of people in the household, number of dependents, and whether the subjects perceived themselves as having financial difficulties.
2. *Low English Proficiency.* Subjects were determined to demonstrate low English proficiency if they scored below a level VI on the BEST.
3. *Strong Social Support Network.* The presence of extended family members, mention of strong friendships, and indication of useful social service agencies were identified as indicative of a support network.
4. *Feelings About Adaptation to the U.S.* Areas expected to be evaluated were the American lifestyle, food, climate, health, acceptance/discrimination, desires to return to country of origin, and concerns regarding raising children in the U.S. However, as the questions were open-ended, no specific direction was sought for this variable.

5. *Potential for Abusing Children.* This was based on responses on the CAPI.
6. *Use of Corporal Punishment.* Based on the results of the CTS, assessment was made of whether or not corporal punishment was used and whether it was "normal" or "abusive." A CTS was completed for the eldest child in the family between the ages of 8 and 18. If parents reported having engaged during the previous year in the behavior described, the behavior was coded as having occurred. Reasoning, verbal abuse, "normal" violence and "abusive" violence were identified to assess behaviors, as reported by the subjects.

Data Collection

The research assistants, who had been trained to administer the BEST, the semi-structured interviews and the translations of the CAPI and CTS, collected the data from 28 subjects and their children (n = 28) at the subjects' homes during a one-time visit of approximately 2 1/2 to 3 hours. Given the sensitive nature of the subject matter, it was essential that research assistants be trained to emit appropriately empathic behavior, use good interpersonal and interviewing skills to gather information, be receptive to the specific needs of the subjects, be able to identify potentially high risk clients and abusive behavior, and be cognizant of issues and methods of maintaining confidentiality. Although the questionnaires can be self-administered, responses were taken by the research assistants to minimize misunderstanding and to encourage questionnaire completion. The interviews were recorded on audio-tapes and transcribed by two other bilingual Vietnamese graduate research assistants. Participants were given a nominal payment of ten dollars for their participation in the project.

FINDINGS

The demographic characteristics of the 28 adult participants are presented in Table 1. There was a fairly equal distribution between genders; however, the majority of the subjects (71.4%) were between 41 and 65 years of age. Most were married (78%); approximately half of them had three or more children, and the majority had no other

TABLE 1. Demographic Characteristics of Respondents (n = 28)

		Frequency	%
Gender	Male	12	46.1
	Female	14	53.9
Age	26-40 years	7	25.9
	41-65 years	20	74.1
Marital Status	Married	21	77.8
	Divorced	1	3.7
	Widowed	5	18.5
# of Children	1 or 2	13	48.8
	3 or 4	12	44.4
	5 or 6	2	7.4
Educational Level	< 8 years	8	29.6
	High school	12	33.3
	Some college	5	18.5
	College	2	7.4
Spouse's Education	< 8 years	9	40.9
	High school	8	36.4
	Some college	3	13.6
	College	2	9.1
Monthly Family Income	< $500	4	14.8
	$501-1,000	12	44.4
	$1,001-2,000	7	25.9
	$2,001-3,000	4	14.8
Occupation	unemployed	4	14.8
	unskilled	23	85.2
Spouse's Occupation	unemployed	4	18.2
	unskilled	15	68.2
	skilled	3	13.6
Health	excellent	8	29.6
	good	10	37
	satisfactory	3	11.1
	poor	6	22.2
Spouse's Health	excellent	7	13.8
	good	8	36.4
	satisfactory	2	9.1
	poor	5	22.7
Length of Stay in U.S.	< 2 years	5	18.5
	2 to 5 years	15	55.6
	6 to 10 years	4	14.8
	11 to 15 years	2	7.4
	> 15 years	1	3.7
Other Relatives in St. Louis	none	21	80.1
	parents	2	7.7
	siblings	2	7.7
	aunts/uncles	1	3.8

relatives living locally (80.8%). Most had a high school education or less (74.1%), an annual family income of less than $12,000 (59.3%), and had been in the U.S. for five years or less (71.4%).

Income Level

According to the poverty thresholds of the U.S. Census Bureau (1997), taking into account the upper level of the family income range reported by the subject and the lower range of the family size, 59.3% of the subjects were living below the poverty line. However, in the interviews, only one subject indicated a concern over his financial condition, and most subjects (39.9%) perceived that life in the US was materially better than in Vietnam (see Table 2). Only 7.4% indicated difficulty associated with a low level (poor) job. Given reported income levels, one would expect these subjects to have financial difficulties; this was not supported by their perceptions.

English Proficiency

Of the 28 adult subjects, 8 could not complete any portion of the BEST. More subjects attempted the writing portion of the test (71.4%) than the reading section (64.3%), and only 7.1% performed at level VI on the test. Thus, 92.9% were of low English proficiency.

Support Network

While most subjects indicated that they had friends, none explored the extent of the relationships. The majority of the subjects 21 (75%) had no relatives in the St. Louis area; 2 (7.1%) had parents; 2 (7.1%)

TABLE 2. Perceptions About Living in the United States (n = 28)

Perception		Frequency	%
Easier than Vietnam	Materially	11	39.9
	Greater freedom	6	21.4
	More physical security	1	3.6
More uncomfortable	Miss home/family	3	10.7
	Lack of English skills	1	3.6
Happiness	Satisfactory	4	14.3
	Happier	2	7.1

had siblings, and 1 (3.6%) had aunts/uncles (see Table 1). Most of the subjects had received some help from U.S. social service agencies–the International Institute (44.4%), churches (14.8%), and USCC/Government (11.1%). While 11.1% had received no assistance in adjusting to the U.S., 11.1% had received help from the Vietnamese community. Based on the CAPI, which has a "Loneliness Scale" that is embedded in the 160-item questionnaire, the loneliness level for all subjects was normal (see Table 2).

Reasons for Leaving Vietnam and Feelings About Adaptation to the United States

Primary reasons for leaving Vietnam appeared to be political (60.7%) or related to family (Table 3). Overall, most respondents indicated that it was easier living in the U.S. than in Vietnam (see Table 2). However, a number of additional feelings surrounding adaptation to life in the U.S. were revealed. Issues related to children were the primary concern of the overwhelming (75.1%) majority of the population, particularly with regard to education (53.6%). In fact, children's education tied with job security (22.2%) as the item mentioned most frequently as the "best thing that ever happened" to them (see Table 4). Obedience and discipline were the two areas of concern mentioned by the majority (73%) of the parents with respect to raising children. Major concerns and areas of difficulty revolved around the children's behavior/future and subjects' own poor English language skills. Nearly sixty percent (59.3%) identified language as a major difficulty.

TABLE 3. Reasons for Leaving Vietnam (n = 28)

	Frequency	%
Political		
Identified as dangerous	9	32.1
Imprisoned	5	17.9
Not accept communism	3	10.7
Family		
Has interracial child	5	17.9
Is interracial	3	10.7
Family reunification	1	3.6
Better life in the United States	2	7.1

TABLE 4. Major Concerns in the U.S. (n = 28)

Areas of Concern	Frequency	%
Children		
Education	15	53.6
Future	5	17.9
Behavior	1	3.6
Language	3	10.7
Personal health	3	10.7
Personal security	1	3.6

Potential for Abusing Children

The CAPI indicated that responses of subjects on the "tendency to abuse children" scale was elevated for 19 (67.9%) of the subjects (see Table 5). Embedded in the CAPI are also questions that measure a subject's tendency to falsify (fake) "good" and "bad" responses which may invalidate some answers. However, Milner (1986) indicates that if subjects' scores are elevated for "tendency to abuse" *and* if the scores on the "faking good responses" scale is either normal or elevated, it is assumed that the "tendency to abuse" is positive. Of the respondents, 16 (57.1%) falsified good responses, and 9 (32.2%) had elevated abuse scores; 12 (42.9%) did not falsify good responses, and of them 10 (35.7%) had elevated abuse scores.

Methods of Discipline

Discussion was the form of discipline reported by the greatest number of parents (96.4%). Next in frequency were more aggressive forms of discipline, shouting and screaming (71.4%) and threatening to spank or hit (64.3%). Over half of the parents (57.1%) reported actually hitting their child (on the bottom with a bare hand), but an equal number reported providing an alternative activity as a means of discipline. A few parents revealed that they used other forms of violence (see Table 6). A number of parents used other non-physical, but aggressive measures, such as calling them names (42.9%) or threatening to put them out of the house (39.3%).

TABLE 5. Child Abuse Potential Inventory

CAPI Differences		
Tendency to abuse	**Normal**	**Elevated**
Male	4	8
Female	5	9
Unknown	0	0
Strength of ego	**Normal**	**Elevated**
Male	12	0
Female	14	0
Unknown	2	0
Sense of loneliness	**Normal**	**Elevated**
Male	12	0
Female	14	0
Unknown	2	0
Rigidity level	**Normal**	**Elevated**
Male	0	12
Female	0	14
Unknown	0	2
Unhappiness level	**Normal**	**Elevated**
Male	6	6
Female	3	11
Unknown	1	1
Problems with self/child	**Normal**	**Elevated**
Male	11	1
Female	11	1
Unknown	2	0
Problems with family	**Normal**	**Elevated**
Male	12	0
Female	11	3
Unknown	0	2
Problems with others	**Normal**	**Elevated**
Male	9	3
Female	12	2
Unknown	1	1

Other Results on the CAPI

In addition to measuring subjects' potential to abuse their children, other scales on the CAPI measured subjects' (a) ego strength, (b) sense of loneliness, (c) distress level, (d) rigidity level, (e) unhappiness level and (f) problems with people level. The last scale measured (i) problems with children and self, (ii) problems with family, and (iii) problems with others (see Table 5). Most scales indicate fairly similar responses for both males and females; however, the "unhappiness"

TABLE 6. Methods Used to Discipline Child (n = 28)

Method	Frequency	%
Discussion	27	96.4
Provided alternative activity	16	57.1
Took away privileges	12	42.9
Non-physical aggression		
Shouted or screamed	20	71.4
Called child names or dumb and lazy	12	42.9
Swore or cursed	5	17.9
Threatened to put out of house	11	39.3
Put out of the house	4	14.3
Locked out of the house	0	0
Locked in dark room or closet	0	0
Physical aggression		
Shook child	5	17.9
Pinched child	3	10.7
Threatened to spank or hit child	18	64.3
Hit child on the bottom with bare hand	16	57.1
Slapped child on the hand, arm or leg	3	10.7
Slapped face, head or ears	2	7.1
Hit child on the bottom with object	6	21.4
Hit part of body, other than bottom, with object	2	7.1
Threw or knocked child down	0	0
Hit with fist or kicked the child	0	0
Hit the child over and over again	0	0
Grabbed child around the neck	0	0
Pushed head into the toilet or sink	0	0
Threatened with knife or gun	0	0
Burned or scalded child on purpose	0	0

and the "problems with family" scales indicate greater frequencies of elevation for women than for men.

Ego Strength. No subjects indicated elevated ego strengths, and, furthermore, among these, 16 (57.1%) had elevated scores on the "faking good responses" scale. Only one (3.6%) of these subjects had an elevated score on the "faking bad responses" scale suggesting that 27 (96.4%) of the subjects did not have a very high level of self-esteem.

Sense of Loneliness. The sense of loneliness score was not elevated for any subject, however, of these, 16 (57.1%) had elevated scores on the "faking good responses" scale, suggesting that this percentage (57.1%) may, in fact, have been lonely.

Distress Level. The distress level for 13 (46.4%) of the subjects was elevated, and the "faking good response" scale was elevated for 15 (53.6%) of the total sample, 5 (17.9%) of whom had elevated scores for both distress and "faking good responses."

Rigidity Level. The rigidity level was elevated for all 28 subjects; however, one (3.6%) subject had an elevated score for "faking bad responses," hence, only 27 (96.4%) are categorized as being at a high level of rigidity.

Unhappiness Level. The unhappiness level was elevated for 17 (60.7%) subjects, and of the 16 (57.1%) for whom the "faking good response was elevated," 7 (25%) had an elevated unhappiness level. One (3.6%) had an elevated score for "faking bad responses" on the "normal" level; therefore, 17 (60.7%) are identified as being unhappy.

Problems with People Level. Three sub-scales measured reported problems with people.

> *Problems with Children and Self*-Only 2 (7.1%) indicated elevated scores on this scale.
>
> *Problems with Family*-Three (11.1%) of the subjects indicated problems with the family.
>
> *Problems with Others*-Four (14.8%) subjects indicated problems with others.

Results of Interviews with Children and Comparison with Parental Responses

Although 28 children were interviewed–one for each adult respondent–a large portion of the recording for one child was inaudible, therefore, there were only 27 usable responses. Nineteen females and 8 males were interviewed. Of these, 10 (37%) were between the ages of 8 and 12 years, 15 (55.6%) were aged 13-16, and 2 (7.4%) were 17-18 years old. The largest number, 15 (55.6%), had been in the country between 2 and 5 years.

When asked how their parents disciplined them, in direct contrast to the parents report, only 1 (3.7%) stated that her parents "talked" to her. The majority (n = 14, 51.9%) indicated they were scolded or condemned. Six (22.2%) indicated that they were spanked or hit, and 4 (14.8%) said they had privileges taken away from them. Interestingly, most children (n = 17, 63.0%) stated they agreed with the punishment they received, although 4 (14.8%) said they did not agree, and one said she sometimes agreed.

Four (15.4%) parents indicated that they had shaken their children to discipline them, but of the four children who were shaken, one (3.8%) indicated only being "talked" to; two (7.7%) stated they were scolded/condemned, and one (3.8%) that privileges had been taken away.

Six (23.1%) parents indicated that they had hit their child with an object, yet of these children, none revealed being hit. Although six (23.1%) children admitted to being hit with an object by their parents, these were children whose parents stated that they had not hit their child with an object.

Fifteen (57.7%) parents indicated that they spanked their children on the bottom with their bare hands, yet only 3 (11.5%) of the children corroborated that. The others claimed that their parents "talked" to them (n = 2, 7.7%), scolded/condemned them (n = 7, 26.9%) or took away privileges (n = 3, 11.5%). Three (11.5%) children of the 11 (42.3%) parents who stated that they did not spank their children, stated that the parents did, in fact, spank them.

Two (7.7%) parents stated that they had hit their children with objects on parts of the body other than the bottom, yet their children said they either "talked" to them (n = 1, 3.8%) or scolded/condemned them (n = 1, 3.8%). Only one (3.8%) child of 3 (11.5%) parents who said they slapped their children on the hand, arm or leg indicated being hit.

The "tendency to abuse" scale on the CAPI was elevated for 19 of the 26 parents for whom there were complete interviews with children. All parental responses of the six of the children who indicated that their parents hit them were consistent in that they evidenced a tendency to abuse. However, the parents of the two children who indicated that their parents "talked" to them also indicated a tendency to abuse as did 8 of the 14 whose children said they "scolded or condemned" them. Of the four parents whose children claimed they disciplined them by taking away privileges, three displayed a tendency to abuse.

DISCUSSION

Adjustment

The demographic information revealed that the majority of the subjects were in their middle years, were married with at least 50% of them having 3 or more children. Most had no relatives living in the region, had little education, even in Vietnam, were not functionally proficient in English and, based on U.S. thresholds of poverty, were living below the poverty line. The U.S. Bureau of the Census in 1980 revealed a 35.1% poverty level for the Vietnamese, and this had dropped to 15.6% by 1990. Yet this sample indicates a poverty level of 59.3%.

These characteristics would suggest some social and financial difficulty in living in the United States; however, in the semi-structured interviews, most subjects mentioned no financial problems or concerns about the lack of a support system. The primary concern mentioned was regarding the children's future, and the area of difficulty was reported to center around poor English language skills. Furthermore, no family conflicts were mentioned. All these results are very inconsistent with earlier findings that Southeast Asian refugees suffer from adjustment difficulties (Fong, 1992; Lum, 1992), economic problems (Dunn, 1994), and a number of mental health problems (Tran & Ferullo, 1997). According to Tran (1998), those Vietnamese-Americans who have lived in the U.S. for twenty or more years have adjusted and adapted well, but such was not suggested regarding the relatively new arrivals. Therefore, based on the existing literature, it is surprising that this group of subjects, most of who had been in the United States for less than 5 years, indicated little or no adjustment difficulties during their interviews. Reasons for lack of complaint about any issues in the United States may be twofold. On one hand, this group of Vietnamese may have, in fact, greatly improved the quality of their lives from that which they had in Vietnam, and, in the larger framework, the freedom that they experience in the United States supersedes their experience of adjustment difficulty. While they may have several obstacles to overcome on a daily basis, when interviewed by a stranger, they move from mention of the mundane problems of day-to-day existence to viewing their lives more holistically. Such perspective may take into account the freedom of life in the United States, and, when pitted against the constraints, the lack of opportunity, and the economic difficulties they faced in Vietnam, the subjects may feel less need to complain to a stranger. On the other hand, since the Asian family is bound by the cultural norm of protecting its problems from the view of outsiders, it seems highly unlikely that these Vietnamese subjects would honestly discuss intra-family issues with a stranger, albeit a Vietnamese one, during a single exploratory interview. They would seek to present themselves as best as possible and second guess what the researcher might expect of the well-adjusted individual.

Child Maltreatment

The Vietnamese proverb that states "When we love our children, we give them a beating; when we hate our children, we give them sweet words" (Freeman, 1989, p. 28; Ima & Hohm, 1991) captures the essence of the importance of corporal punishment for discipline among the Vietnamese. Most of the subjects of this study, however, seemed aware that in the United States corporal punishment is not considered as acceptable as it is in Vietnam and may worry about the possibility of losing their children if corporal punishment is disclosed. Many said that the "American way" of disciplining is different from the "Vietnamese way." Some indicated that they still disciplined in the Vietnamese way, but would not elaborate. This awareness of norms regarding corporal punishment was reflected in the responses to the CTS. About half of the parents indicated that they used "acceptable" forms of corporal punishment, such as hitting the child on the bottom with a bare hand, but none indicated having engaged in any of the "abusive" forms of violence, such as hitting repeatedly. Non-aggressive forms of violence, such as shouting or calling the children names, were admitted. This was inconsistent with the findings of Ima and Hohm (1991), who found that although the Vietnamese constitute only 23% of the Asian and Pacific Islander refugee and immigrant population, they made up 36% of their sample in the study of child maltreatment. Furthermore, of Ima and Hohm's sample, 71.9% were referred for physical abuse.

The Conflict Tactics Scale (Straus, 1979) has been found to be valid in a number of international studies and continues to be used internationally as any review of the *Journal of Child Abuse and Neglect* will reveal. However, in this study of a population that is believed to favor hitting child as an intrinsic part of child rearing, most members in this group of subjects, who have not yet had a chance to become acculturated into the American culture, rarely indicated the use of corporal punishment to discipline their children. The study incorporated a number of different mechanisms that allowed some cross-checking of results, and the findings revealed several inconsistencies. Although the subjects indicated in the interviews and through CTS that they rarely used corporal punishment, the CAPI suggested a high tendency to abuse among most of the subjects. Furthermore, despite the level of satisfaction portrayed by most subjects in the interview, a large percentage of them revealed a number of stresses through the CAPI in which it is not quite as easy to camouflage feelings.

There were also a number of inconsistencies between the parental responses and those of the children. Although some of the parents admitted to using "acceptable" violence on their children, most of the children who experienced this reported that they were "scolded" and did not mention any form of corporal punishment. Perhaps this was to shield their parents, or it may have been to avoid further discipline for sharing private family matters. In any case, this glaring discrepancy warrants further examination. It is possible that some parents, more familiar with Vietnamese ways than with American ones, reported harsher punishment than that in which they engaged, believing such was warranted of good Vietnamese parenting.

Ahn (1994) suggests that, ordinarily, Americans and Vietnamese may have very basic differences regarding perceptions of the nature of children and of the parent-child relationship. This may include issues of dominance and submission between parent and child (Gray & Gosgrove, 1985). Tran (1998) states that "Changes in parenting styles and authority have created stressful consequences for many Vietnamese parents" (p. 274), but the reference is very oblique and does not identify either parenting styles or consequences. One may even be led to assume that in addition to the traditionally acceptable corporal punishment, stress will further increase the likelihood of child maltreatment in this population.

Findings of the current study also differ dramatically from those of another face-to-face interview study by the author with 313 middle class professionals (Segal, 1995) in India, an Asian nation with somewhat similar parent-child relationships as those found in Vietnam. In this study, 56.9% stated they had engaged in "acceptable" violence (Straus' 1979 definition) toward their children. However, it is interesting that 41.9% readily admitted to engaging in abusive violence, and 2.9% indicated they had engaged in "extreme" violence against their children. That this educated group of Indians so openly acknowledged what would be termed child maltreatment in Occidental countries, especially when the subjects were identifiable, suggests that these behaviors are sanctioned in India. Had these Indians been interviewed in the United States, having become familiar with child abuse reporting laws, they would less likely have made such admissions. Perhaps the Vietnamese subjects would have responded differently if they were interviewed in Vietnam.

This assessment is reinforced by the results of the CAPI with these Vietnamese subjects. Those characteristics that have repeatedly been found in the literature to be associated with the tendency to abuse, such as loneliness, high levels of rigidity, feelings of unhappiness, and feelings of distress were elevated in this population. In addition, the scale that measured the tendency to abuse was also elevated for a large number of subjects. The embeddedness of the scales among the 160 items in the CAPI helps to identify "faked" responses, hence, it may be a better measure of the likelihood of abuse than is the direct questioning of the CTS. Interestingly, the children who were interviewed tended to corroborate a low incidence of corporal punishment. Those that said they were hit, did not specify how or to what extent, and almost all the children indicated that they agreed with whatever form of punishment they received. Certainly, parental presence during the interviews may have biased the children's responses; however, the parents would not permit the researcher to interview the children privately.

Straus et al.'s (1981) and Segal's (1995) studies reveal that subjects tend to honestly respond to the CTS as one moves up the scale from low abuse behaviors to highly abusive ones. This, however, appears to be effective only if the subjects do not fear the ramifications of revelations regarding their methods of child discipline. If the subjects are of a clinical population, if they are anonymous, or if they believe their behavior is socially sanctioned, they are more likely to answer honestly. If they are afraid that their children will be taken away, if they are concerned that they will be jailed, if they are refugees and have experienced maltreatment by authorities, they may admit only to that which is safe.

In addition to being very inconsistent with other studies (Ima & Hohm, 1991; McKelvey & Webb, 1995), the results of this study are extremely inconclusive. What is apparent, however, is that the Conflict Tactics Scale might not be an appropriate tool to evaluate conflict resolution among refugees, or those people who may fear reprisals if they respond honestly. The CAPI, with its embedded scales, indicated a 57.1% frequency of "faked good responses." As people cross national boundaries and settle in different countries, they often find themselves in alien social and cultural environments in which norms of behavior and family role relationships are unfamiliar and where traditional patterns of internal family interaction are challenged (Mayadas & Segal, 1999).

IMPLICATIONS FOR SOCIAL WORK PRACTICE AND RESEARCH

Research and practice in social work are, intrinsically, fraught with a variety of difficulties. As subjects of researchers and clients of practitioners become increasingly more ethnically and culturally diverse, it becomes important to recognize that a variety of additional factors can complicate data collection and service provision. The number of publications focusing on social work practice with ethnic minorities is increasing, however, there is less attention directed toward research issues. Even less is known about research with immigrant groups, particularly with refugees.

Much of the extant study of child abuse among refugees focuses on clinical populations. This pilot project targeted a non-clinical population of Vietnamese refugees and yielded interesting, if inconsistent, results. However, all conclusions and observations must be tentative and may not be readily generalized, given the size and selectivity of the sample. Although the researcher's lack of Vietnamese language skills was a handicap, some cross-checks were undertaken: (1) All instruments were translated and "back-translated" into English. (2) The two research assistants translated and transcribed interviews with different subjects, except for 5 which both translated and transcribed resulting in very similar translated interviews. Despite limitations of the study, the project did reveal that the CAPI did not appear to be a good predictor of behavior reported by the CTS. Given the nature of the two instruments, it is easier to provide inaccurate responses in the latter, hence it appears that a tool such as the former, which seeks a range of responses to identify a behavior, may be more appropriate to tap sensitive areas of behavior. In addition, parental actions were not corroborated in all instances in children's reports.

This project revealed that not all assessment tools are appropriate across cultures and is useful as a pilot to provide guidelines for future larger scale research and for practitioners in assessing family function-ing and child maltreatment. In practice with minorities, Lum (1992) suggests that there are at least four practice issues related to the client system: resistance, communication barriers, personal and family back-ground, and ethnic community identity. While these issues may also impinge on research efforts, fear of exposure, past experience with oppression, and mistrust of authority also affect information sharing by refugees (Congress, 1997). Furthermore, directiveness and ap-propriate self-disclosure help establish credibility, roles, and authority, important ingredients in the relationship with this population. Model 1 integrates these and suggests the need for researchers, as well as practitioners, to not only be culturally sensitive, but to work to estab-lish rapport and trust with refugees either in gathering data or deliver-ing services.

As in any relationship between client and worker, a number of factors impact communication and, hence, service delivery. In work-ing with refugees, workers must be cognizant that in addition to the numerous personal and social issues that prevent any client from seek-

MODEL 1. Working with Refugee Families

ing assistance, there are several barriers between refugees and practi-tioners/researchers. Resistance to help from practitioners emerges from shame and guilt associated with the acceptance of help from strangers. Language differences, variations in non-verbal cues, and subjects that are not discussed openly result in the refugees' erection of communication barriers. The privacy of the family is paramount, so issues of family dynamics are not shared with the practitioner. Finally, because of the terrifying experiences to which most refugees have been subjected, they continue to mistrust authority and fear exposure. Practitioners, seen as figures of authority who dispense resources on behalf of organizations, are not to be trusted. Therefore, little personal information is disclosed. Practitioners and researchers must become aware of these conditions that can hinder the development of an ade-quate working relationship with refugees. In order to develop a rapport based on understanding and trust, practitioners must educate them-selves about both general and specific refugee experiences and also about the community culture. Using their awareness of services and resources and employing their professionals skills, they may need to modify their methods of intervention. Self-disclosure must be used to increase credibility and authority, while understanding must be used to develop the relationship. While refugees may fear authority, individu-als from many Eastern cultures are also taught to respect (and obey) it. Hence, directiveness, a skill often used only minimally with the major-ity U.S. population, is one that can be most effective with Vietnamese refugees. Despite American social work's emphasis on the need to be "non-judgmental and non-directive," both the Asian culture and the refugee experience suggest that once rapport and trust have been es-tablished between practitioners and clients, a clear directive is more effective in helping in the resolution of problems (Jung, 1998). Final-ly, researchers interested in exploring sensitive and personal issues may find that the culture and experience of the refugee family may prevent disclosure. Researchers, unlike practitioners, may need to avoid a direct approach. Research tools that employ embedded meth-ods (such as the use of psychological tests or instruments such as the CAPI) may yield results that more adequately reflect reality than may methods such as direct questions in interviews or questionnaires.

Furthermore, researchers must be aware that a single contact with potential subjects will rarely yield usable results. Assurance of confi-dentiality may be meaningless to individuals who have been traumatized by many horrific refugee experiences. Vietnamese refugees view researchers and service providers as figures of authority who have the recourse to cause harm. The perception is that the less information shared, the safer the refugee is. Thus, in order to gather accurate data, the researcher must establish rapport and trust with the subjects prior to attempting to gather data. Rapport may require that researchers convey that they are familiar both with the Vietnamese culture as well as with issues surrounding refugee experiences. Some professional self-disclosure can be most effective. In order to establish trust, researchers must convey that they are most concerned about the welfare of the refugee population, and the research will ultimately benefit refugee populations. Institutional Review Boards ensure that research subjects provide informed consent, however, while this alerts subjects to the liabilities associated with the research, it can raise a barrier to honesty. Therefore, it is imperative that refugee subjects recognize and accept the benefits of the research for themselves, for their families and for their communities.

The results of this study suggest that individual interviews of such a sensitive nature may not reflect reality. The use of group interviews, preferably with groups that are naturally occurring in the community or of focus groups that meet for several sessions, may be more effective in yielding accurate responses than the individual interview. Such discussions may focus on values, beliefs, and preferences rather than on their specific behaviors, as this removes focus from individual actions. In addition, the group environment disperses attention, and group support may allow more open discussion and revelation of individual perceptions and values, factors that often temper behavior. In addition, since gender and role are important factors in the Vietnamese community, these groups should be single gender and mediated by same-gender Vietnamese facilitators. There is some disagreement about the preferred ethnicity of the facilitator. Some practitioners in St. Louis have suggested that non-Vietnamese facilitators may be more effective as the Vietnamese can be hesitant to be open to someone in authority and of a similar background.

Children must be interviewed separately from the parents, either individually or in groups. Findings of this study that show inconsistencies between parental and child responses make suspect even those in which the absence of violence is reported by both parents and by children.

The inconsistencies among measurement instruments in this study suggested that self-reports may not furnish an accurate picture of refugee adjustment or family violence within refugee communities. Preferable may be inventories, such as the Child Abuse Potential Inventory, in which key questions are embedded and which look at a range of responses that provide evidence of a particular behavior or attitude.

The overall experience of most Vietnamese refugees, including the trauma of relocation, isolation from family and friends, problems in acculturation, and the economic stresses associated with the inability to find and hold a job, may increase depression, lower self-esteem, decrease psychological well-being, decrease coping skills, and increase anger and frustration. It may well be that the U.S. policy for refugees aiming for "economic self-sufficiency in as short a time as possible" may not be enough to resettle individuals. Active outreach, continuing support programs, and intervention services may need to be implemented specifically to help refugees deal with the social and emotional traumas of relocating and adjusting to an alien culture. However, to truly understand the extent of the difficulties faced, research efforts must be directed toward those who do not come to the attention of social service agencies, yet struggle with adjustment.

CONCLUSIONS

The rise in delinquency, substance abuse, and gang activity among Southeast Asian youth may be a symptom of family disintegration, as adults find their traditional methods of coping with family issues are no longer appropriate in the United States. To help prevent escalating problems in the Vietnamese community as today's young children reach adolescence and adolescents become adults, it becomes important for Vietnamese parents to regain power in their families. Given what is known about some of the precursors of child abuse and its effects, and given the plight of a large proportion of the Vietnamese, it is important that social service researchers and providers in the United States become cognizant of the potential time-bomb in this community. It is time to focus not only on the practical issues of Vietnamese resettlement, but also to become aware of family violence and dysfunction and sensitize researchers and practitioners to the needs in this community.

The Refugee Resettlement Program's goals of resettling refugees by providing them with the basic ingredients for survival are laudable. Many refugees are able to use this assistance and successfully bridge the social and cultural gap between them and the host population. However, adjustment to resettlement is a lengthy process. Not only must refugees become acculturated to a foreign culture, they must also come to terms with the phenomena that forced them from their homes and the ensuing separation from family and support systems. Difficulties posed by the inability to speak English and different cultural patterns and social norms are often exacerbated by the xenophobia of both the host and the refugee (Mayadas & Elliott, 1992). Furthermore, despite growing numbers of programs to help refugees cope with issues that cause them distress, most refugees are hesitant to seek mental health services. This reluctance may be attributed to the pervasive cultural conditioning regarding privacy, coupled with fears about reliving trauma or jeopardizing newly acquired safety. By isolating itself in the ethnic enclaves, the refugee community reinforces the mainstream perception that it is effectively resettled in the United States. Separation from daily interaction with the host society and its social services helps refugees continue to "save face" as they struggle to make their new homes. Increased sensitivity and acceptance, in association with outreach programs, may ensure that refugees receive services that will help them cope with the traumas they have experienced. The design of any such program must allow them to draw on their tremendous strengths that have permitted them to weather exploitation and danger and enabled them to maintain an attitude of perseverance and hope.

REFERENCES

Ahn, H.N. (1994). Cultural diversity and the definition of child abuse. In Barth, R.P. & Berrick, J.D. *Child welfare research review*, Vol. 1, New York, NY: Columbia University Press, 28-55.

Bean, R.D., Chapa, J., Berg, R. & Sowards, K. (1992). Educational and sociodemographic incorporation among Hispanic immigrants to the United States. In Edmonston, B. & Passel, J.S. (eds). *The integration of America's newest immigrants*.

Bemack, F. (1989). Cross-cultural family therapy with Southeast Asian (SEA) refugees. *Journal of Strategic and Systematic Therapies* 8, 22-27.

Bringiotti, M.I., Barbich, A. & De Paúl, J. (1998). Validacion de Una Version Preliminar del Child Abuse Potential Inventory para su Uso en Argentina, *Child Abuse and Neglect*, 22(9), 881-888.

Caliso, J.A. & Milner, J.S. (1992). Childhood history of abuse and child abuse screening. *Child Abuse and Neglect*, 16(5),647-659.

Center for Applied Linguistics. (1986). *Basic English Skills Test (BEST)*, Washington, DC: Office of Refugee Resettlement.

Chambon, A. (1989). Refugee families' experiences: Three family themes–family disruption, violent trauma and acculturation. *Journal of Strategic and Systematic Therapies* 8, 3-13.

Chao, C.M. (1992). The inner heart: Therapy with Southeast Asian families. In Vargas, L.A. & Koss-Chioino, J.D. (eds). *Working with culture: Psychotherapeutic interventions with ethnic minority children and adolescents*, San Francisco, CA: Jossey-Bass Publisher, 157-181.

Congress, E.P. (1997). Ethical issues and future directions. In Congress, E.P. (ed). *Multicultural perspectives in working with families*. New York: Springer, 333-338.

Crosslin, A. (1996). Interview with Crosslin, Executive Director of the International Institute of Metropolitan St. Louis, St. Louis, MO.

DeVos, G. (1978). Selective permeability and reference group sanctioning: Psychological continuities in role degradation. Paper presented at Seminar on Comparative Studies in Ethnicity and Nationality, University of Washington, Seattle.

Dine, P. (May 21, 1994). An invisible population. *St. Louis Post-Dispatch*, B1-4,5.

Dunn, A. (1994, May 19). Southeast Asians highly dependent on welfare in U.S.: 30% of families get aid. *New York Times*, A1, A13.

Erikson, E. (1963). *Childhood and society*, New York: W.W. Norton.

Fong, R. (1992). A history of Asian Americans. In Furuto, S.M., Biswas, R., Chung, D.K., Murase, K. & Ross-Sheriff, F. (eds). *Social work practice with Asian Americans*, Newbury Park, CA: Sage Publications, 3-26.

Foulks, E.F., Merkel, L. & Boehnlein, J.K. (1992). Symptoms in non-patient Southeast Asian refugees. *Journal of Nervous and Mental Disease*, 180(7), 466-468.

Freeman, J.M. (1989). *Hearts of sorrow: Vietnamese-American lives*, Stanford, CA: Stanford University Press.

Furuto, S.M. & Murase, K. (1992). Asian Americans in the future. In Furuto, S.M., Biswas, R., Chung, D.K., Murase, K. & Ross-Sheriff, F. (eds). *Social work practice with Asian Americans*, Newbury Park, CA: Sage Publications, 240-253.

Gil, D. (1973). *Violence against children*, Cambridge, MA: Harvard University Press.

Gray, E. & Gosgrove, J. (1985). Ethnocentric perception of childrearing practices in protective services, *Child Abuse and Neglect*, 9(3), 389-396.

Haz, A. M. & Ramirez, V. (1998). Preliminary validation of the Child Abuse Potential Inventory in Chile. *Child Abuse and Neglect*, 22(9), 869-880.

Ho, M. K. (1992). Differential application of treatment modalities with Asian American youth. In Vargas, L.A. & Koss-Chionino, J. D. (eds). *Working with culture*, San Francisco: Jossey-Bass, 182-203.

Hurh, W. M. & Kim, K.C. (1988). Uprooting and adjustment: A sociological study of Korean immigrants' mental health. Final report to National Institute of Mental Health, Macomb, IL: Department of Sociology and Anthropology. Western Illinois University.

Ima, K. & Hohm, C.F. (1991). Child maltreatment among Asian and Pacific Islander refugees and immigrants: The San Diego case. *Journal of Interpersonal Violence*, 6(3). 267-285.

Ingrassia, M., King, P., Tizon, A., Scigliano, E. & Annin, P. (April 4, 1994). America's new wave of runaways. *Newsweek*, 64-65.

Jung, M. (1998). *Chinese American family therapy*, San Francisco, CA: Jossey-Bass, Inc.

Khinduka, S. (1992). Foreword. In Furuto, S.M., Biswas, R., Chung, D.K., Murase, K. & Ross-Sheriff, F. (eds). *Social work practice with Asian Americans*, Newbury Park, CA: Sage Publications, vii-ix.

Kinzie, J.D; Boehlein, J.K., Leung, P.K., Moore, L.J. (1990). The prevalence of posttraumatic stress disorder and its clinical significance among Southeast Asian refugees. *American Journal of Psychiatry* 147(7). 913-917.

Korbin, J.E. (1991). Cross-cultural perspectives and research directions for the 21st century. *Child Abuse and Neglect*, 15, Sup.1, 67-77.

Law, C.K. & Schneiderman, L. (1992). Policy implications of factors associated with economic self-sufficiency of Southeast Asian Refugees. In Furuto, S.M., Biswas, R., Chung, D.K., Murase, K. & Ross-Sheriff, F. (eds). *Social work practice with Asian Americans*, Newbury Park, CA: Sage Publications, 167-183.

Leung, S. (1993). Interview with Leung, Director of Social Work at the International Institute of Metropolitan St. Louis, St. Louis, MO.

LeVine, S. & LeVine, R. (1985). Age, gender, and the demographic transition: The life course in agrarian societies. In Rossi, A. (Ed.), *Gender and the life course*, New York: Aldine, 29-42.

Lin, K. & Shen, W.W. (1991). Pharmacotherapy for Southeast Asian psychiatric patients. *Journal of Nervous and Mental Disease*, 179(6), 346-350.

Logan, R. (1979). Sociocultural change and the perception of children as burdens. *Child Abuse and Neglect*, 3, 657-662.

Lum, D. (1992). *Social work practice and people of color*, Pacific Grove, CA: Brooks/Cole Publishing Company.

Mayadas, N.S. & Elliott, D.E. (1992). Integration and xenophobia: An inherent conflict in international migration. In Ryan, A.S. (ed). *Social work with immigrants and refugees*. New York: The Haworth Press, Inc., 47-62.

Mayadas, N.S. & Segal, U.A. (1999, in press). Refugees in the 1990s: A United States' perspective. In Balgopal, P. (ed). *Immigration in the United States*, New York: Columbia University Press.

McCracken, G. (1988). *The long interview*. Newbury Park, CA: Sage.

McKelvey, R.S. & Webb, J.A. (1995). A pilot study of abuse among Vietnamese Amerasians. *Child Abuse and Neglect*, 19(5), 545-553.

Merton, R.K., Fiske, M. & Kendall, P.L. (1990). *The focused interview: A manual of problems and procedures*, 2nd ed. New York: The Free Press.

Milner, J.S. (1986). *The Child Abuse Potential Inventory: Manual* (2nd ed). Webster, NC: Psytec.

Milner, J.S. (1990). *An interpretive manual for the Child Abuse Potential Inventory*, Webster, NC: Psytec.

Milner, J.S. & Wimberley, R.C. (1979). An inventory for the identification of child abusers. *Journal of Clinical Psychology*, 35, 95-100.

Mitra, N. (May 26, 1995). Report warns of 'Unheralded Crisis.' *India Abroad*, 34.

Mydans, S. (June 21, 1994). Laotian's arrest in killing bares a generation gap. *New York Times*, A8.

Nayak, M.B. & Milner, J.S. (1998). Neuropsychological functioning: Comparison of mothers at high-and low-risk for child physical abuse. *Child Abuse and Neglect*, 22(7), 687-704.

Nguyen, N. (1994). Life's biggest lemon. *Refugees*, 95, 25.

Norton, I.M. & Manson, S.M. (1992). An association between domestic violence and depression among Southeast Asian refugee women. *Journal of Nervous and Mental Disease*, 1 80(1), 729-730.

Portes & Zhou (1993). The new second generation: Segmented assimilation and its variants. *Annals of the American Academy of Political and Social Science*, 530, 74-96.

Rogler, L. (1989). The meaning of culturally sensitive research in mental health. *American Journal of Psychiatry*, 146(3), 296-303.

Rumbaut, R.G. (1991). The agony of exile: A study of the migration and adaption of Indochinese refugee adults and children. In Ahearn, F.L. & Athey, J.L. (eds). *Refugee children: Theory, research, and services*, Baltimore, MD: Johns Hopkins Press.

Saran, P. (1985). *The Asian Indian experience in the United States*. New Delhi, India: Vikas Publishing House, PVT, Ltd.

Segal, U. A. (1991). Cultural variables in Asian Indian families. *Families in Society*, 72(4), 233-242.

Segal, U.A. (1994). Delinquency, substance abuse and gang behavior as indicators of family difficulties among Southeast Asian refugees. Presented at the 10th International Congress on Child Abuse and Neglect 1994, Kuala Lumpur, Malaysia (September, 1994).

Segal, U.A. (1995). Child abuse by the middle class? A study of professionals in India. *Child Abuse and Neglect*, 19, 213-1227.

Segal, U.A. (1998). The Asian-Indian American family. In Mindel, C.H., Habenstein, R.W. & Wright, R. Jr. (eds.). *Ethnic families in America*, 4th edition, Saddle River, NJ: Prentice-Hall, 331-360.

Silver, M. (1998, October 20). Interview with Margaret Silver, Director of Education, The International Institute of Metropolitan St. Louis, St. Louis, MO.

Silver, M. (1994). *A two-year report on the Family English Literacy Program*. International Institute of St. Louis, St. Louis, MO.

Straus, M.A. (1995). *Manual for the Conflict Tactics Scales (CTS) and test forms for the revised Conflict Tactics Scales*, Durham, NH: UNH, Family Research Laboratory.

Straus, M.A. (1979). Measuring intrafamily conflict and violence: The Conflict Tactics Scales. *Journal of Marriage and the Family*, 41(1) 75-88.

Straus, M.A., Gelles, R. & Steinmetz, S. (1981). *Behind closed doors*, New York: Anchor Books.

Suro, R. (January 20, 1992). Generational chasm leads to cultural turmoil for young Mexicans in the US, *The New York Times*, A14.

Tanwar, T. (1988). Media and child abuse. In National Institute of Public Cooperation and Child Development. *National Seminar on Child Abuse in India: 22-24 June, 1988*, New Delhi: NIPCCD, 120-136.

Tran, T.V. (1998). The Vietnamese-American family. In Mindel, C.H., Habenstein, R.W. & Wright, R. Jr. (eds.). *Ethnic families in America*, 4th edition, Saddle River, NJ: Prentice-Hall, 254-283.

Tran, T.V. & Ferullo, D.L. (1997). Indochinese mental health in North America: Measures, status and treatments. *Journal of Sociology and Social Welfare*, 24(2), 3-20.

U.S. Bureau of Census. (June 12, 1991). Census bureau releases 1990 census counts on specific racial groups (press release).

U.S. Census Bureau. (1997a). Annual Demographic Survey (March CPS Supplement) 1997 Data Table Topic List. Country of origin and year of entry into the U.S. of the Foreign born, by citizenship status: March 1997. *http://www.bls.census.gov/cps/pub/1997/for born.htm*

U.S. Census Bureau (1997b). Poverty thresholds by size of family and number of children: 1997. *http://www.census.gov/ftp/pub/hhes/poverty/threshold/thresh97.html*

Vega W.A. & Rumbaut, R.G. (1991). Ethnic minorities and mental health. *Annual Review of Sociology*, 17, 351–383.

Psychological Symptoms in a Sample of Latino Abused Children

Ferol E. Mennen

SUMMARY. This study compared Latino children who were victims of child abuse with similar children who were not abused on measures of depression, anxiety, behavior problems, and dissociation. Abused children were found to have higher levels of symptoms on the majority of symptom measures. There were differences in the evaluation of distress levels on the self report versus parent/guardian report measures. Mean scores of the abused children on the self report measures were not in the clinical range, although a substantial number of children had high levels of distress. In contrast, the results of the parent/guardian measures revealed mean scores in the clinical range of problems. Implications for research and practice are included. *[Article copies available for a fee from The Haworth Document Delivery Service: 1-800-342-9678. E-mail address: <getinfo@haworthpressinc.com> Website: <http://www.haworthpressinc.com>]*

KEYWORDS. Child maltreatment, child abuse, Latino children, abuse effects, psychological symptoms

INTRODUCTION

Child abuse continues to be one of the most serious social problems in our society with the number of victims on the rise. In 1994, there

Ferol E. Mennen, DSW, is Associate Professor in the School of Social Work, University of Southern California, Los Angeles, CA.

This research was made possible through Grant 90-CW-1039 from the Administration for Children and Families, Department of Health and Human Services.

[Haworth co-indexing entry note]: "Psychological Symptoms in a Sample of Latino Abused Children." Mennen, Ferol E. Co-published simultaneously in *Journal of Multicultural Social Work* (The Haworth Press, Inc.) Vol. 8, No. 3/4, 2000, pp. 193-213; and: *Violence: Diverse Populations and Communities* (ed: Diane de Anda, and Rosina M. Becerra) The Haworth Press, Inc., 2000, pp. 193-213. Single or multiple copies of this article are available for a fee from The Haworth Document Delivery Service [1-800-342-9678, 9:00 a.m. - 5:00 p.m. (EST). E-mail address: getinfo@haworthpressinc.com].

were 1,011,628 substantiated or indicated cases of maltreatment in the United States with 26% of that number victims of physical abuse and 14% victims of sexual abuse (National Center on Child Abuse and Neglect, 1996). The number of unreported cases, while unknown, would considerably inflate these numbers (Tower, 1993). A substantial amount of research has concluded that child abuse can cause serious psychological consequences (Flisher et al., 1993; Haviland, Sonne, & Woods, 1995; Kolko, 1996; McClellan, Adams, Douglas, McCurry, & Storck, 1995; Merry, & Andrews, 1994). While the empirical evidence has grown, the specific knowledge on the effects of abuse on minority populations has not kept pace. The purpose of this research was to address that imbalance by evaluating the effects of abuse on one particularly understudied group, Latino children.

Latinos are an increasingly large segment of the population. In 1993, the Census Bureau estimated that 22.8 million or 8.9% of the total population was of Hispanic origin and that 29.6% of these Hispanics were under 15 (U.S. Census Bureau, 1993). (Although the term Latino is currently preferred, the U.S. Government continues to use the term Hispanic to refer to those whose ancestors came from a Spanish speaking country.) Hispanic victims made up 12.2% of the victims of maltreatment in 1994 (U.S. Department of Health and Human Services, 1996). If the social work profession is to appropriately serve the needs of Latino child abuse victims, specific knowledge about their reactions to abuse is necessary.

REVIEW OF THE LITERATURE

Research has clearly established that child abuse (sexual, physical, or a combination) has the potential to lead to serious consequences for its victims. While some children have high rates of problems, others may seem to escape the most debilitating outcomes (Cohen & Mannarino, 1988; Friedrich, Urquiza, & Beilke, 1986). The greatest volume of research has developed on the effects of sexual abuse with some studies looking at adults abused as children and others focusing on child victims. In studies on children, sexual abuse has been linked to higher levels of depression (McLeer et al., 1998; Mennen & Meadow, 1994; Moran, & Eckenrode, 1992; Wozencraft, Wagner, & Pellegrin, 1991), anxiety (Johnson & Kenkel, 1991; Mennen & Meadow, 1993), low self-concept (Cavaiola & Schiff, 1989; Hotte & Rafman, 1992), and behavior problems (Cohen & Mannarino, 1988; Einbender & Friedrich, 1989). Substantial rates of post-traumatic stress disorder (McClellan et al., 1995; McLeer, Callaghan, Henry, & Wallen, 1994), and major depression (Kaufman, 1991) have also been found in samples of sexually abused children. Highlighting the potentially on-going effects of sexual abuse, a study by Merry and Andrews (1994) discovered that 63.5% of sexually abused children continued to qualify for an Axis I diagnosis one year after their abuse had ended.

Although not as extensive as the research on sexual abuse, research on the effects of physical abuse has found an association with many kinds of problems. Of particular interest is a study using a community probability sample of 665 children (Flisher et al., 1997). The researchers found that physical abuse was associated with a number of psychiatric disorders including mood disorders, anxiety disorders, and disruptive disorders, even after controlling for income, family psychiatric history, and a history of sexual abuse. This study is particularly valuable because it is drawn from the community at large. The physical abuse had not been previously disclosed to child welfare or mental health agencies; thus the effects were not compounded by the possible trauma of disclosure and action by the child welfare authorities.

In other studies, victims of physical abuse have been found to suffer from depression (Allen & Tarnowski, 1989; Kazdin, Moser, Colbus, & Bell, 1985; Livingston, Lawson, & Jones, 1993; Toth, Manly, Cicchetti, 1992), post-traumatic stress disorder (Famularo, Kinsherff, & Fenton, 1992; Haviland, Sonne, & Woods,, 1995; Livingston et al., 1993) and attention-deficit disorder (Famularo et al., 1992; Livingston et al., 1993). One study found that 79% of the children entering a treatment program for physically abused children and their families qualified for an Axis I diagnosis (Kolko, 1996). Physically abused children are most frequently found to suffer from externalizing behavior problems, including aggression, conduct disorders, and behavior problems (Famularo et al., 1992; Livingston et al., 1993; Pelcovitz et al., 1993; Prino & Peyrot, 1994; Trickett, 1993).

While there is a growing body of research outlining the effects of child abuse, little of that research looks at race and/or ethnicity and child abuse. The studies that include race/ethnicity as a study variable are more likely to include African-American and White children with little attention to Latinos. The research that addresses child abuse in minority populations has concentrated on the incidence of abuse (with studies of sexual abuse predominant) and specific characteristics of abuse. Some of the incidence studies omit Latinos in their samples (for example, Tzeng & Schwarzin, 1990), and results from the few studies that include Latinos are conflicting. Some have reported higher rates of sexual abuse within Latino samples than within White or African-American samples (Kercher & McShane, 1984; Lindholm & Willey, 1986), while others have found lower rates (Stein, Golding, Siegel, Burnam, & Sorenson, 1988). One study (Huston, Parra, Prihoda, & Foulds, 1995) reported that Mexican-American children were more likely to be sexually abused by a family member than Anglo or African-American children and had lower rates of penetration. In contrast, others have found that Latino children were more likely to experience penetration than other racial/ethnic groups (Lindholm & Willey, 1986; Rao, DiClemente, & Ponton, 1992). In reported cases of maltreatment (this includes physical abuse, sexual abuse, neglect, and emotional maltreatment) reported to authorities in 1994, Latinos represented 12.2% of the cases while their percentage of the population was 13.7% (U.S. Department of Health and Human Services, 1996).

Studies of the psychological effects of child abuse have infrequently evaluated race/ethnicity as a factor in abuse. Many studies do not note the racial/ethnic composition of their samples (for example, Finkelhor, Hotaling, Lewis, & Smith, 1990; Guzder, Paris, Zelkowitz, & Marchessault, 1996), others have only African-American and White children in their samples (for example, Kazdin, Moser, Colbus, & Bell, 1985; Scerbo, & Kolko, 1995), and others do not analyze racial/ ethnic differences (for example, Feldman et al., 1995) limiting knowledge of the effects of abuse on Latinos. The few studies that evaluate the effects of abuse on Latino children have found few differences between them and their non-Latino peers. Sexually abused girls were found to have very similar kinds of symptoms to their White and African-American peers (Mennen, 1994). While African-American sexually abused boys were found to have higher rates of anger than their Latino peers, there were no differences in levels of depression (Moisan, Sanders-Phillips, & Moisan, 1997).

PURPOSE

The purpose of this exploratory study was to begin to address the gaps in the knowledge about the psychological effects of child abuse in Latinos by evaluating the effects of abuse in a sample of Latino children using multiple measures of symptomatology. It was hoped that by replicating instruments used in previous studies of child abuse, that the study could begin to contribute to understanding whether Latino victims reacted in similar or different ways from samples of non-Latino children.

METHODS

Sample

The abused children in the study were drawn from community agencies providing services to both abused and non-abused children. Inclusion criteria were: the child (1) was a victim of child abuse, (2) between 6 and 12 years old, (3) Latino, (4) able to participate in the research process, and (5) in treatment less than two months. Comparison children were solicited through a small school in a primarily low income Latino neighborhood. Those parents who returned a solicitation form were contacted by a researcher who arranged for an interview with the parent and child to complete the research protocol. Although child abuse was not screened in the comparison group, the solicitation letters indicated that participants were being sought to serve as a comparison for abused children, thus making it unlikely that abusing families would volunteer. Families were reimbursed $25.00 for their participation.

The final sample consisted of 31 abused and 21 comparison children. The two groups were similar in age and gender. Those in the abused group more frequently requested Spanish and were somewhat more likely to be in SES 1 (refer to Demographic Information Form under Instrumentation) than the comparison children. All of the participating families were Latino with the majority identifying themselves as Mexican-American. (One family identified as Central American and two as Latino.) (See Table 1 for Demographic Information.)

In the abused group, abuse was verified by the local child protective agency and/or the therapist working with the child and family. Children were victims of sexual abuse alone (n = 11), physical abuse alone (n = 8), both physical and sexual abuse (n = 7), and confirmed physical abuse with sexual abuse suspected but not yet confirmed (n = 5).

TABLE 1. Demographic Variables

	Abused	Comparison
Age (in years)	9.2	8.8
Female	64.5%	54.5%
Socioeconomic Status*		
At Level 1	95.8%	70.6%
At Level 2	4.2%	29.2%
Children tested in English*	58.1%	95.2%

* p < .05

Information about the extent and specifics of the abuse was often incomplete, because (1) the referral information accompanying the child was inadequate, (2) foster parents frequently did not know many of the details of the abuse, and/or (3) the child had not yet discussed this information with their therapist. The primary perpetrators of the sexual abuse were all male and all known to the victim. Eleven of the perpetrators were father or father figures (father = 6, stepfather = 1, mother's boyfriend = 4); 3 were other relatives (sibling = 1, grandfather = 1, and cousin = 1), and 5 were by another known person. Four of the children were known to have multiple perpetrators. Abuse included fondling, oral sex and both vaginal and anal intercourse.

The perpetrators of physical abuse were much more likely to be female with 12 children having been abused by a female and 7 by a male (some children were abused by more than one person). The perpetrators were the father (n = 5), mother (n = 9), stepfather (n = 1), mother's boyfriend (n = 1), sibling (n = 1), cousin (n = 1), and foster parent (n = 1). Information about the physical abuse was very incomplete and should be questioned since the abusing parent was often the one informing the worker about the abuse.

Instrumentation

Instruments were administered to the parents and children separately in the agency where the child was being served or in the participating school. All instruments were available in both English and Spanish, and participants were asked which versions they preferred. Both English speaking and bilingual English/Spanish speaking researchers were available to administer the instruments and answer any questions the participants might have.

Demographic Information Form. Demographic information was

collected through forms specifically designed for the project. Socio-economic status was determined using the Hollingshead Four Factor Index of Social Status (Hollingshead, 1975). For purpose of this study, categories 1 (unskilled laborers and menial service workers) and 2 (machine operators and semiskilled workers) were combined into SES 1 and category 3 (Skilled craftsmen, clerical, sales workers) and 4 (minor professional, technical) were combined into a new SES 2. No families scored higher than SES level 4 on the Hollingshead Index.

Child Behavior Checklist (CBCL) (Achenbach, 1991). Parents or guardians completed the CBCL. This widely used self-report measure yields a Total Problem score, scores for Internalizing and Externalizing Behaviors, and nine problem syndrome scores (Withdrawn, Somatic Complaints, Anxious/Depressed, Social Problems, Thought Problems, Attention Problems, Delinquent Behavior, Aggressive Behavior, and Sex Problems). The manual reports test-retest reliability at one week of 0.95 for non-referred children on the problem scores. For referred children, the subscale average reliabilities ranged from 0.70 to 0.93. Validity is supported by numerous studies which have reported significant correlations between the CBCL and other problem measures (Achenbach, 1991). A Spanish version is available. T scores have been developed to allow comparison by gender and age. A score of 60 on the Total Problem scales is considered the clinical cut-off point with scores between 60 and 63 designated as the borderline range. A score of 67 on the syndrome scales is considered the clinical cut-off point with a score of above 70 considered definitely in the clinical range, and the scores between 67 and 70 in the borderline range (Achenbach, 1991).

Children's Depression Inventory (CDI). The CDI, a 27-item-self report measure for school age children, was the measure of depression (Kovacs, 1983; 1992). Internal consistency coefficient alphas ranged from .70 to .86 (Kovacs, 1985). Test-retest reliability has been variable with scores ranging from a high of .87 at one-week, another with a score of .84 at nine weeks, and a low of .38 at one week in another sample (Siegel, 1984). The inventory has a Total Score which represents an overall evaluation of depression and five subscales that measure different components of depression: Negative Mood, Interpersonal Problems, Ineffectiveness, Anhedonia, and Negative Self-Esteem. The scores have been normed for age levels to create standard scores with a mean of 50 and standard deviation of 10 (Kovacs, 1992). A Spanish version of the instrument available from the author underwent further translations and back translations for the purposes of this study.

Revised Children's Manifest Anxiety Scale (RCMAS) (Reynolds & Richmond, 1985). Anxiety was measured with the RCMAS, a 36-item self-report measure which yields a Total Anxiety score and 3 subdimensions of anxiety. Coefficient alpha internal consistency scores for the Total Anxiety score ranged from .79 to .85 across different aged samples. Test-retest reliability for the Total Anxiety score ranged from .97 to .98 in a 3 week retest and .68 in a 9 month retest sample (Reynolds & Richmond, 1985). The instrument has a Total Anxiety score to represent an overall evaluation of anxiety. There are three subscales, Physiological Anxiety, Worry/Oversensitivity, and Social Concerns, representing dimensions of anxiety, and a Lie scale which measures children's tendency to give socially approved or answers representing "ideal" behavior. The scores have been standardized for gender and age. The Total Anxiety score has a mean of 50 and standard deviation of 10; the subscales have a mean of 10 and standard deviation of 3 (Reynolds & Richmond, 1985). This instrument was translated into Spanish with the publisher's permission.

Child Dissociative Checklist (CDC) (Putnam, 1990). Dissociation was measured using the CDC. The scale has 20 items relating to dissociative tendencies. Scores can range from 0 to 40 with higher scores reflecting higher levels of dissociation. Sexually abused girls in the validation study had a mean score of 6 (S.D. = 6.4) and the controls had a mean of 3 (S.D = 2.7). This measure has a Cronbach alpha of .89 and a test-retest reliability at one year of .84 in abused children and .79 in matched controls. The instrument was translated into Spanish with the author's permission (Putnam, 1992, personal communication).

Data Analysis

Due to the small sample size and the exploratory nature of the research, univariate t-tests without correction for multiple comparisons and bivariate correlations were used.

FINDINGS

The abused children scored higher than the comparison children on the majority of the clinical measures (see Table 2). On the Children's

TABLE 2. Comparison of Scores on Clinical Measures by Abuse Status

Test	Abused		Non-abused		t-test	
	Mean	SD	Mean	SD	t	p value
CDI	N = 29		N = 17			
Total	53.8	13.6	46.7	7.1	2.33**	
Negative Mood	51.2	11.6	46.4	5.5	1.90	
Interpersonal Prob.	58.5	14.2	52.0	13.3	1.54	
Ineffectiveness	51.9	11.7	47.6	6.1	2.56*	
Anhedonia	53.6	13.2	48.6	8.4	1.56	
Neg. Self Esteem	51.9	11.7	47.6	6.1	1.63	
RCMAS	N = 30		N = 16			
Total	53.7	9.1	45.1	8.3	2.97**	
Worry	11.0	3.2	8.8	2.9	2.31*	
Social	10.5	2.9	8.9	2.8	1.71	
Physiological	9.7	2.6	7.7	2.4	2.44*	
Lie	10.6	2.9	9.7	3.4	1.07	
CBCL	N = 31		N = 21			
Total	64.7	11.6	46.8	8.1	6.11***	
Internalizing	63.0	11.2	46.7	7.4	5.88***	
Externalizing	62.0	12.3	45.2	9.5	5.27***	
Withdrawn	64.0	11.3	52.8	4.6	4.98***	
Somatization	58.7	8.8	53.5	5.3	2.60***	
Anxious/Dependent	62.6	10.7	51.0	2.0	5.87***	
Social Problems	61.5	9.5	53.7	4.2	4.03***	
Thought	61.4	10.6	52.5	5.2	3.99***	
Attention	62.5	11.2	53.0	5.1	4.17***	
Delinquent	63.0	9.8	53.3	4.5	4.85***	
Aggression	64.0	12.2	51.8	3.2	5.32***	
Sex Problems	59.7	11.0	52.0	5.7	3.06***	
Dissociation Scale	N = 31		N = 21			
	8.7	6.6	0.7	1.3	6.47***	

* p ≤ .05
** p ≤ .01
*** p ≤ .001

Depression Inventory the abused group scored significantly higher on the Total Score, the Ineffectiveness subscale, and approached significance (p = .065) on Negative Mood. On the Revised Children's Manifest Anxiety Scale, the abused group scored significantly higher on the Total Score, the Worry, and Physiological Anxiety subscales. There was a trend toward higher scores on the Social Anxiety subscale (p = .095). There were no differences on the Lie Scale.

The abused children scored higher on all dimensions of the Child Behavior Checklist (see Table 2) indicating that the caretakers of the abused children perceived their children as having significantly more behavior problems in each of the measured areas. The abused children had higher scores on the Dissociation Scale for Children than the non-abused children.

In order to determine whether language might influence performance on any of the symptom measures, English and Spanish speaking abused children were compared (the comparison was done only on the abused group because there was only one Spanish speaker in the comparison group.) There were no differences on any of the symptom measures by language.

Clinical Significance of Outcome Scores

The scores of the study children can be compared with published norms on the clinical measures in order to evaluate the level of distress in both groups. The mean of 53.8 for the abused group on the Total Score of the Children's Depression Inventory is within the normal range (Kovacs, 1992). However a substantial number of children scored outside the normal range. Over 27% (27.2%) of the abused children scored in the above average range (T score $\geq$ 60), and 13.8% of the children scored in the much above average range (T $\geq$ 70) or in the top 2 1/2 percent of the population (Kovacs, 1992). In contrast, none of the comparison children scored in the above average range.

Similarly, on the Revised Manifest Anxiety Scale, the mean score of 53.7 is within the normal range when compared with standardization samples. However, 26.7% of the children scored more than one standard deviation above normative samples, a level which should be given some attention in the evaluation of anxiety (Reynolds & Richmond, 1985). As on the depression measure, none of the comparison children scored in the above average range.

On the CBCL, the children can be compared with standardization samples that were used to norm the instrument (Achenbach, 1991). With a mean Total Problems Score of 64.7, 74.2% of the abused sample scored above the clinical cut-off point (T $\geq$ 60). Of that group, 41.9% of the sample were in the clinical range of behavior problems (T $\geq$ 64) and 32.3% were in the borderline clinical range. In the comparison group, only 1 child (4.8%) was in the borderline range and no one was in the clinical range. On the Internalizing Score, 58.1% of the abused children scored above the cut-off point with 41.9% in the clinical range. None of the comparison children scored in the borderline or clinical range. On the Externalizing Score 54.8% of the abused group was above the cut-off point, with 38.7% in the clinical range. Only one of the comparison children (4.8%) was in the borderline range and none in the clinical range.

The mean score on the Dissociation Scale for Children of 8.7 (SD = 6.6) is somewhat higher than that of sexually abused girls on the validation sample (Putnam, 1990). The mean in the comparison sample of 0.7 is much under that of abused children. Furthermore, 38.2% of the abused children scored above the mean of sexually abused children and 19.4% scored above the mean reported for children diagnosed with Multiple Personality Disorder or Dissociative Disorder (Putnam, 1990), while none of the comparison children had levels at or above that mean.

Correlations between the broad scales of the clinical outcome measures were performed in order to try to determine how the different measures might relate to each other. The self-report measures have a significant correlation (r = .6906, p = .000) indicating that almost half of the variance in one report measure is explained by the score on the other measure (see Table 3). The only parent report measure that significantly correlates with the CDI is the Total Problem Score on the CBCL. The Total Anxiety Score of the RCMAS is significantly correlated with the Externalizing Scale of the CBCL, and the Dissociation Measure. The parent report measures also correlate with each other with each measure significantly correlating with all others. As would be expected, the highest correlations are found on the dimensions of the CBCL-Total Score is made up of the sum of the Internalizing and Externalizing syndromes. However, the CBCL scores are also significantly related to the Dissociation Score.

TABLE 3. Correlation Matrix of Clinical Symptom Variables for Abused Children

	CDI Total	RCMAS Total	CBCL Total Problems	Internal	External	Dissociation
CDI	1.0000	.6906*	.4044*	.2196	.4636*	.3024
RCMAS		1.0000	.2738	.0855	.3723*	.3809*
CBCL			1.0000	.8041*	.8845*	.7321*
Total						
Internal				1.0000	.5098*	.5962*
External					1.0000	.6128*
Dissoc						1.0000

* p < .05

DISCUSSION

In this sample, the abused Latino children exhibit more clinical symptoms than the comparison sample. Although the abused children have significantly higher scores on the self-report measures of anxiety and depression and on a number of the subscales, these scores are not in the clinical range. These children can be said to be more distressed than their peers on all the symptom measures, but as a group, they are not reporting clinically significant symptoms. However, a number of these children reported very high levels of distress. About one quarter of the children scored more than one standard deviation above the mean on both measures, a level which indicates possible problems with depression (Kovacs, 1992) and anxiety (Reynolds & Richmond, 1985). The comparison group had no children in the distressed range. Again this highlights the differences in symptom levels between the two groups. Some of the abused children are seriously distressed, while none of the comparison children report problems.

The caretakers of the abused children present a different picture of their children's level of symptoms. They see their children as being much more problematic than comparison parents see their children. The abused children scored significantly higher on all scales of the CBCL. The group mean on each of the Total Problem Scores is in the clinically significant range and nearly three quarters of the children score above the cut-off point on Total Problems and well over half above the cut-off point on the Internalizing and Externalizing dimensions. Parents and caretakers see their children as having difficulties on all domains. Not only are they reporting acting out types of difficulties such as aggression and delinquent behavior, they are noting difficulties with anxiety, as well as withdrawn and somatic behaviors. In contrast, parents of comparison children report few problems with their children. Only one child scored in the borderline range of the broad band scales of the CBCL, indicating few behavior problems in that group.

The levels of dissociation reported by the caretakers of the abused children match sexually abused children in standardization samples for the dissociation measure. Noteworthy is that nearly a fifth of the children have scores on this measure similar to children diagnosed with a dissociative disorder. Dissociation is not a problem in comparison children. These high levels of dissociation in a subsample of abused children could indicate very serious psychopathology such as Dissociative Identity Disorder (formerly Multiple Personality Disorder), Post-traumatic Stress Disorder, or Dissociative Amnesia. This finding indicates that Latino victims of child abuse are also at risk for some of the most serious psychological outcomes found in other populations of victims (Chu & Dill, 1990).

The difference between the parents' evaluation and children's self-report is interesting. There is a high correlation between children's self-report of depression and anxiety. Most interesting is that the children's self report of depression correlates with the Externalizing scale of the CBCL, but not the Internalizing scale, the scale that is supposed to measure depressive aspects. Children who report themselves as depressed may be suffering from a masked depression and appear to their parents as a behavior problem. The anxiety measure does correlate with the Externalizing Scale and the Dissociation Scale. These correlations, though modest, are to be expected since these scales all measure dimensions of anxiety or anxiety disorders.

Parents seem to report children as troubled who do not necessarily report themselves as troubled. This lack of agreement between parents and children has been previously reported (Cohen & Mannarino, 1988); it is interesting to note that the same pattern holds true in Latino children. These differences may be caused by a number of factors. First, it may be that the scales are measuring different dimensions of problems. Another possibility is that parents, particularly foster parents, may expect higher levels of distress from children who have had these abuse experiences. However, this possibility does not seem to be supported by the data. There were no differences between children living with foster parents and those with their own parents. In fact, the only difference that approached significance had children living with parents higher on the internalizing scale of the CBCL (Mennen, 1997).

Language did not relate to any of the outcome scores in the abused group. Both English and Spanish speaking children had similar levels of distress indicating that the level of acculturation is unrelated to symptoms following child abuse.

It should be noted that because of the small sample size, all conclusions are tentative and need further study. The most important contribution of this research is the focus on Latino children, a group that despite its increasing number in child welfare populations, has been neglected. This study found that Latino children look very much like other children who have been victims of abuse. They have higher symptom rates than non-abused children, but are not uniformly symptomatic (Cohen and Mannarino, 1988; Friedrich et al., 1986). In each of these earlier studies, while a substantial number of children scored in the clinical range of problems, over half of the children scored in the normal range of behavior. Thus, for abused children, both Latino and others, the experience of abuse is not sufficient to predict a negative psychological outcome. While it has the potential to relate to serious psychological problems, it can also be incorporated by the child in ways that do not produce negative psychological consequences.

Particularly noteworthy are the high rates of dissociation among some of these abused children. Dissociation has been found to be one of the mechanisms by which individuals cope with overwhelming trauma (Briere, 1992; Herman, 1992; Putnam, 1993). The experience and memories of the trauma (abuse) are perceived as too psychologically devastating for the victim and for self-protection are walled off through the process of dissociation (Janoff-Bulman, 1992). Thus, this study supports the proposition that some Latino children process child abuse as a traumatic response and utilize dissociation to cope with the aftermath and are thus at risk for serious dissociative disorders.

Further, global symptom measures may not be the most effective way of measuring the distress of these children. While they may not exhibit classic symptoms of depression and anxiety, they may manifest symptoms in other areas. Behavior problems, attention, delinquency, withdrawal, social problems were ones that seemed notable to the caretakers of these children. Specific measures that evaluate these dimensions may be more useful than global symptom measures of anxiety and depression.

IMPLICATIONS

The study has a number of implications for both practice and research. For practice with child welfare populations, screening of all abused children is recommended. Latino children are similar to other abused children in that some are highly distressed, and others seem to have fewer problems. Screening needs to employ a number of measures including those from caretakers, the children themselves, and others who interact with the child such as teachers, and day care providers. Instruments designed to measure symptoms common to abuse should be included. While global symptoms measures such as those used in this study have value for screening children with significant levels of anxiety and depression, they may miss other more abuse specific difficulties. The Trauma Symptom Check List for Children (Briere, 1995) which was not available at the beginning of this study, is specifically designed to measure abuse specific problems and would be a valuable screening measure. The CBCL continues to be a useful screening tool because of its ease of administration and scoring, its wide acceptance, and its utility as a device to measure parents' perceptions of their children.

It is also important that social workers recognize that services to abusive families need to address the child's problems (either individually or conjointly) as well as the parents. Interventions in child abuse have sometimes focused on helping the parents learn more effective parenting skills and remediating the environmental and parental problems while neglecting the child's difficulties (Heneghan, Horwitz, & Leventhal, 1996; Schuerman, Rzepnicki, & Littell, 1994). The interactive nature of parent/child problems (Bronfenbrenner, 1979; Walsh, 1996) necessitates intervention on both levels. A seriously distressed child will make it difficult for a mother to implement new parenting strategies just as it will be difficult for a behaviorally disordered child to improve without the parent learning more effective child-rearing methods. This family focus is particularly essential with this population given the centrality of the family in Latino culture (Keefe & Padilla, 1987).

This family focus should be respected in planning interventions, and social workers must be sensitive to the concept of *familismo*, important in Latino culture (Becerra & Greenblatt, 1983; Marin & Marin, 1991). Thus a family focused intervention may need to reach beyond the nuclear family defined as relevant by Anglo social workers to incorporate extended family into the interventions. The approach of social workers must also be culturally sensitive incorporating the sincere personal demeanor of *personalismo* valued by Latino clients (Fernandez, Lui, & Bing, 1993). One model that incorporates these attitudes and offers promise for intervention in Latino families that have been identified as abusive is Multisystemic Therapy. MST is a family oriented approach that has proved effective with anti-social children and adolescents (Henggeler, Schoenwald, Borduin, Rowland, &

Cunningham, 1998). In this model, intervention is home-based, strengths-focused, takes place on multiple levels, including the family and community, and has a strong relational base between the therapist and the family, thus incorporating many of the attributes that are culturally relevant for Latino families.

Further, treatment should be targeted to the kinds of symptoms that abused children are experiencing with special attention to behavior problems, Post-traumatic Stress Disorder, and trauma-like symptoms since these seem to be common problems in abused children. There is growing research support for the effectiveness of Cognitive Behavioral interventions to treat trauma symptoms resulting from child abuse (Finkelhor & Berliner, 1996). Gradual exposure to the traumatic memory, modeling, cognitive reframing, thought stoppage, and safety education have been used successfully with both abused children and their families (Cohen & Mannarino, 1996; Deblinger, Lippmann, & Steer, 1996).

While these methods show promise, they have not yet been evaluated with Latino children to learn if the methods are directly transferable or need some adaptation because of cultural differences. For example, thought stopping is a method that can be used to help a child with the intrusive memories common in trauma reactions. In this method a child identifies the intrusive thought, is then trained to shout "stop" when the thought occurs, next speaks, then whispers "stop" and finally says "stop" internally. This may work as designed or may need to be modified. The necessity of revealing internal thoughts may be viewed as requiring too much self-disclosure and thus not culturally consistent for the Latino child (Zambrana, 1995). Safety training in which the social worker teaches children how to protect themselves from dangerous situations, may work as designed, or may need to include family members in the teaching process to avoid the social worker being perceived as interfering with the normal authority of the family (Ramirez, 1989). It will be important that social workers learn these techniques so their effectiveness can be evaluated on this population. Additionally, it is essential that bilingual social workers be trained to deliver effective interventions since a sizable number of Latino children are more comfortable in Spanish.

There are a number of implications for research. Most importantly, studies need to secure larger samples in order to be able to adequately answer complex research questions about the interaction of abuse characteristics, symptoms, and race/ethnicity. This could be done best by targeting children as they come into the child welfare system, rather than depending on agencies referring the children to a research project. In order to accomplish this, researchers must deal with the child welfare bureaucracies. These bureaucracies are often large, confusing, difficult to access, and resistant to research. In spite of these difficulties, it is only through working with these agencies that researchers will secure larger more representative samples. Such studies would be expensive because of the demands for more personnel to monitor intake, perform random sampling, and do the necessary interviews. It is essential that sufficient funds be allocated for such research.

Related is the need to secure more random samples of abused children. Sampling from the intake of child welfare agencies is a beginning step. Although that would only locate children who have been reported for abuse, it may be the only feasible solution. Sampling from other child serving agencies such as schools, medical facilities, and day care would leave researchers in the dilemma of needing to report cases not previously reported.

Research must focus on the needs of Latinos and other under-represented minorities in the child welfare system. There is a great deal of information on White and African-American children in the child welfare system, but little on Latino, Asian, and other minorities. In order to do this, research must be targeted at agencies in areas serving large numbers of these children. There will also need to be further work done on developing instrumentation that is appropriate cross culturally.

In conclusion, while this study indicates that the symptom picture of Latino child abuse victims is very similar to other abused children, it is essential that researchers continue to explore the consequences of abuse in this population. Of particular relevance is evaluating whether specific circumstances of abuse relate to differential outcomes. Concurrently, social workers must work for effective and culturally relevant interventions to deal with the negative consequences of child abuse. This would not just include translating into Spanish the treatment manuals used in many effective interventions and training social workers in effective intervention methods, but adapting effective interventions to be more culturally appropriate. Finally, social workers should be involved in evaluating the effectiveness of these methods and their adaptations. This may require not only evaluation of outcomes, but process evaluation of the intervention components to obtain qualitative information from the participants to gauge the extent to which they experience the process as culturally appropriate.

REFERENCES

Achenbach, R. M. (1991). *Manual for the Child Behavior Checklist/4-18 and 1991 profile*. Burlington, Vt.: University of Vermont Department of Psychiatry.

Becerra, R. M., & Greenblatt, M. (1983). *Hispanics seek health care: A study of 1,088 veterans of three war eras*. Latham, MD: University Press of America.

Briere, J. (1992). *Child abuse trauma: Theory and treatment of the lasting effects*. Newbury Park, CA: Sage.

Bronfenbrenner, U. (1979). *The ecology of human development: Experiments by nature and design*. Cambridge, MA: Harvard University Press.

Cavaiola, A. A. & Schiff, M. (1989). Self-esteem in abused chemically dependent adolescents. *Child Abuse & Neglect, 13*, 327-334.

Chu, J. A. & Dill, D. L. (1990). Dissociative symptoms in relation to childhood physical and sexual abuse. *American Journal of Psychiatry, 147*, 887-892.

Cohen, J. A., & Mannarino, A. P. (1988). Psychological symptoms in sexually abused girls. *Child Abuse & Neglect, 12*, 571-577.

Einbender, A. J. & Friedrich, W. N. (1989). Psychological functioning and behavior of sexually abused girls. *Journal of Consulting and Clinical Psychology, 57*, 155-157.

Famularo, R., Kinsherff, R., & Fenton, T. (1992). Psychiatric diagnosis of maltreated children: Preliminary finding. *Journal of the American Academy of Child and Adolescent Psychiatry, 31*, 863-867.

Feldman, R. S., Salzinger, S., Rosario, M., Alvarado, L. Caraballo, L., & Manner, M. (1995). Parent, teacher, and peer ratings of physically abused and nonmaltreated children's behavior. *Journal of Abnormal Child Psychology, 23*, 317-334.

Fernandez, F., Lui, P., Bing, E. (1993). AIDS among minorities in the United States: The mental health impact of AIDS on ethnic minorities. In A. Gaw (Ed). *Culture, ethnicity, and mental illness*. Washington, DC: American Psychiatric Press.

Finkelhor, D., & Berliner, L. (1995). Research on the treatment of sexually abused children: A review and recommendations. *Journal of the American Academy of Child and Adolescent Psychiatry, 34*, 1408-1423.

Finkelhor, D., Hotaling, G., Lewis, I., A., Smith, C. (1990). Sexual abuse in a national survey of adult men and women: Prevalence, characteristics, and risk factors. *Child Abuse & Neglect, 14*, 19-28.

Flisher, A. J., Kramer, R. A., Hoven, C. W., Greenwald, S., Alegria, M., Bird, H. R., Canino, G., Connell, R., & Moore, R. E. (1993). Psychosocial characteristics of physically abused children and adolescents. *Journal of the American Academy of Child and Adolescent Psychiatry, 36*, 123-131.

Friedrich, W., Urquiza, A. & Beilke, R. (1986). Behavior problems in sexually abused young children. *Journal of Pediatric Psychology. 11*, 47-57.

Guzder, J., Paris, J., Zelkowitz, P., & Marchessault, K. (1996). Risk factors for borderline pathology in children. *Journal of the American Academy of Child & Adolescent Psychiatry, 35*, 26-33.

Haviland, M. G., Sonne, J. L., & Woods, L. R. (1995). Beyond posttraumatic stress disorder: Object relations and reality testing disturbances in physically and sexually abused adolescents. *Journal of the American Academy of Child & Adolescent Psychiatry, 34*, 1054-1059.

Heneghan, A. M. Horwitz, S. M., & Leventhal, J. M. (1996). Evaluating intensive family preservation program: A methodological review. *Pediatrics, 97*, 535-542.

Henggeler, S. W. Schoenwald, S. K., Borduin, C. M., Rowland, M. D., & Cunningham, P. B. (1998). *Multisystemic treatment of antisocial behavior in children and adolescents*. New York: The Guilford Press.

Herman, J. L. (1992). *Trauma and Recovery*. New York: Basic Books.

Hotte, J. P., & Rafman, S. (1992). The specific effects of incest on prepubertal girls from dysfunctional families. *Child Abuse & Neglect, 16*, 273-283.

Huston, R. L, Parra, J. M., Prihoda, T. J., & Foulds, D. M. (1995). Characteristics of childhood sexual abuse in a predominantly Mexican-American population. *Child Abuse & Neglect, 19*, 165-176.

Janoff-Bulman, R. (1992). *Shattered assumptions: Toward a new psychology of trauma*. New York: The Free Press.

Johnson, B. K. & Kenkel, M.B. (1991). Stress, coping, and adjustment in female adolescent incest victims. *Child Abuse & Neglect, 15*, 293-305.

Kaufman, J. (1991). Depressive disorders in maltreated children. *Journal of the American Academy of Child & Adolescent Psychiatry, 30*, 257-265.

Kazdin, A. E., Moser, J., Colbus, D., & Bell, R. (1985). Depressive symptoms among physically abused and psychiatrically disturbed children. *Journal of Abnormal Psychology, 3*, 298-307.

Keefe, S. E., & Padilla, A. M. (1987). *Chicano ethnicity*. Albuquerque, NM: University of New Mexico Press.

Kercher, G. A. & McShane, M. (1984). The prevalence of child sexual abuse victimization in an adult sample of Texas residents. *Child Abuse and Neglect, 8*, 495-501.

Kolko, D. J. (1996). Clinical monitoring of treatment course in child physical abuse: Psychometric characteristics and treatment comparisons. *Child Abuse & Neglect, 20*, 23-43.

Kovacs, M. (1983). *The Children's Depression Inventory: A self-rated depression scale for school-aged children*. Unpublished manuscript.

Kovacs, M. (1985). The Children's Depression Inventory (CDI). *Psychopharmacology Bulletin, 21*, 995-998.

Kovacs, M. (1992). *Children's depression inventory manual*. North Tonawanda, NY: Multi-Health Systems.

Lindholm, K. J., & Willey, R. (1986). Ethnic differences in child abuse and sexual abuse. *Hispanic Journal of Behavioral Sciences, 8*, 111-125.

Livingston, R., Lawson, L., & Jones, J. G. (1993). Predictors of self-reported psychopathology in children abused repeatedly by a parent. *Journal of the American Academy of Child & Adolescent Psychiatry, 32*, 948-953.

Marin, G. & Marin, B. (1991). *Research with Hispanic populations.* Newbury Park, CA: Sage Publications.

McClellan, J., Adams, J., Douglas, D., McCurry, C., & Storck, M. (1995). Clinical characteristics related to severity of sexual abuse: A study of seriously mentally ill youth. *Child Abuse & Neglect, 19,* 1245-1254.

McLeer, S. V., Callaghan, M., Henry, D., & Wallen, J. (1994). Psychiatric disorders in sexually abused children. *Journal of the American Academy of Child & Adolescent Psychiatry, 33,* 313-319.

McLeer, S.V., Dixon J.F., Henry D., Ruggiero K., Escovitz K., Niedda T., Scholle R. (1998). Psychopathology in non-clinically referred sexually abused children. *Journal of the American Academy of Child & Adolescent Psychiatry.* 37:1326-33.

Mennen, F. E. (1997). Family environment, stress, and cognitive functioning in physical and sexual abuse: Final report to the administration for children and families. Department of Health and Human Services.

Mennen, F. (1994). "Sexual Abuse in Latina Girls: Their Functioning and a Comparison with White and African American Girls." Submitted to *The Hispanic Journal of Behavioral Sciences, 16,* 475-486.

Mennen, F. E. & Meadow, D. (1993). "The relationship of sexual abuse to symptom levels in emotionally disturbed girls." *Child and Adolescent Social Work Journal, 10,* 319-328.

Mennen, F. E., & Meadow, D. (1994). Depression, anxiety, and self esteem in childhood sexual abuse: A research study. *Families in Society, 75,* 74-81.

Merry, S. N. & Andrews, L. K. (1994). Psychiatric status of sexually abused children 12 months after disclosure of abuse. *Journal of the American Academy of Child & Adolescent Psychiatry, 33,* 939-944.

Moisan, P. A., Sanders-Phillips, K., & Moisan, P. A. (1997). Ethnic differences in circumstances of abuse and symptoms of depression and anger among sexually abused Black and Latino boys. *Child Abuse & Neglect, 21,* 473-488.

Moran, P. B., & Eckenrode, J., (1992). Protective personality characteristics among adolescent victims of maltreatment. *Child Abuse & Neglect, 16,* 743-754.

Pelcovitz, D., Kaplan, S., Goldenberg, B., Mandel, F., Lehane, J., Guarrera, J. (1994). Post-traumatic stress disorder in physically abused adolescents. *Journal of the American Academy of Child & Adolescent Psychiatry, 33,* 305-312.

Prino, C. T. & Peyrot, M. (1994). The effect of child physical abuse, and neglect on aggressive, withdrawn, and prosocial behavior. *Child Abuse & Neglect, 18,* 871-884.

Putnam, F. W. (1990). *Child Dissociative Checklist* (v3.0–2/90). Unpublished manuscript.

Putnam, F. W. (1993). Dissociative disorders in children: Behavioral profiles and problems. *Child Abuse & Neglect, 17,* 39-45.

Ramirez, O. (1989). Mexican American children and adolescents. In J. T. Gibbs, L. H. Huang, & Associates (eds.) *Children of color: Psychological interventions with minority youth,* pp. 224-250. San Francisco: Jossey-Bass.

Rao, K., DiClemente, R. J., & Ponton, L. E. (1992). Child sexual abuse of Asians compared with other populations. *Journal of the American Academy of Child and Adolescent Psychiatry, 31,* 880-886.

Reynolds, C. R. & Richmond, B. O. (1985). *Revised Children's Manifest Anxiety Scale (RCMAS) Manual.* Los Angeles: Western Psychological Services.

Scerbo. A. S., & Kolko, D. J. (1995). Child physical abuse and aggression: Preliminary findings on the role of internalizing problems. *Journal of the American Academy of Child and Adolescent Psychiatry, 34*, 1060-1066.

Schuerman, J. R., Rzepnicki, T. L., & Littell, J. H. (1994). *Putting families first: An experiment in family preservation.* New York: Aldine de Gruyter.

Stein, J. A., Golding, J. M., Siegel, J. M., Burnam, M. A., & Sorenson, S. B. (1988). Long-term psychological sequela of child sexual abuse: The Los Angeles epidemiologic catchment area study. In G. E. Wyatt & G. J. Powell (Eds.), *Lasting effects of child sexual abuse* (pp. 135-156). Newbury Park, CA: Sage.

Toth, S. L., Manly, J. T., Cicchetti, D. (1992). Child maltreatment and vulnerability to depression. *Developmental Psychology, 27*, 148-158.

Tower, C. C. (1993). *Understanding child abuse and neglect.* (2nd ed.). Boston: Allyn & Bacon.

Trickett, P. K. (1993). Maladaptive development of school-aged, physically abused children: Relations with the child rearing context. *Journal of Family Psychology, 7*, 134-147.

Tzeng, O. C. S., & Schwarzin, H. J. (1990). Gender and race differences in child sexual abuse correlates *International Journal of Intercultural Relations, 14*, 135-161.

U.S Census Bureau (1993). Current Population Reports, Series P20-475, *The Hispanic population in the United States.* Washington, D.C.: Author.

U. S. Department of Health and Human Services, National Center on Child Abuse and Neglect. (1996). *Child maltreatment 1994; Reports from the states to the National Center on Child Abuse and Neglect.* Washington, DC: U.S. Government Printing Office.

Walsh, F. (1996). The concept of family resilience: Crisis and challenge. *Family Process, 35*, 261-281.

Wozencraft, T., Wagner, W., & Pellegrin, A. (1991). Depression and suicidal ideation in sexually abused children. *Child Abuse & Neglect, 15*, 505-511.

Zambrana, R. E. (1995). *Understanding Latino families: Scholarship, policy, and practice.* Newbury Park, CA: Sage.

Understanding Chinese Battered Women in North America: A Review of the Literature and Practice Implications

Mo-Yee Lee

SUMMARY. Spouse abuse is an ignored, invisible, but significant problem in the Chinese community. This paper describes the experience of Chinese battered women in North America and provides suggestions for culturally sensitive and competent interventions for them. The discussion is based on an extensive review of the literature regarding Chinese battered women. In understanding the experience of Chinese battered women and their strategic responses to the abuse, helping professionals are urged to consider cultural, contextual, as well as individual factors including family dynamics. A three-tier model of intervention for treatment of spouse abuse in the Chinese community is

Mo-Yee Lee, PhD, is Assistant Professor, College of Social Work, The Ohio State University, Columbus, OH 43210.

[Haworth co-indexing entry note]: "Understanding Chinese Battered Women in North America: A Review of the Literature and Practice Implications." Lee, Mo-Yee. Co-published simultaneously in *Journal of Multicultural Social Work* (The Haworth Press, Inc.) Vol. 8, No. 3/4, 2000, pp. 215-241; and: *Violence: Diverse Populations and Communities* (ed: Diane de Anda, and Rosina M. Becerra) The Haworth Press, Inc., 2000, pp. 215-241. Single or multiple copies of this article are available for a fee from The Haworth Document Delivery Service [1-800-342-9678, 9:00 a.m. - 5:00 p.m. (EST). E-mail address: getinfo@ haworthpressinc.com].

proposed that targets the individual battered women, the family system, and the larger community. *[Article copies available for a fee from The Haworth Document Delivery Service: 1-800-342-9678. E-mail address: <getinfo@haworthpressinc.com> Website: <http://www.haworthpressinc.com>]*

KEYWORDS. Spouse abuse, Chinese battered women, multicultural social work, cultural competence

INTRODUCTION

After more than 25 years of work by feminist activists, scholars, and practitioners who have been the force behind the Battered Women's Movement, the issue of domestic violence has gained enough public prominence that it now can be considered mainstream in North America (Schechter, 1996). The proliferation of our collective knowledge and understanding of violence against women and its treatment in North America has, however, largely neglected the experience of women from diverse ethnoracial backgrounds. The impact of culture and ethnicity upon one's experience of battering has been poorly documented or studied. The conceptualization of gender as the primary foundation of battering as a social problem mitigated consideration of culture/ethnicity and other factors as significant in understanding the phenomenon of domestic violence (Kanuha, 1996). Such a conceptualization may have served a purpose for the early battered women's movement. It is easier to gain public sympathy by portraying the battered woman as a White, middle-class, moral, "good" woman who does not know how to fight back and is morally deserving of protection (Loseke, 1992). The abandonment of women from diverse ethnoracial backgrounds in defining the image of battered women, however, limits our understanding of their experiences as well as our ability to provide culturally competent and culturally sensitive interventions for this population. In order to better understand domestic violence and provide effective interventions to stop violence in intimate relationships, it is important to produce additional images of domestic violence that capture the experiences of a broader range of men, women, and children.

The paper presents a review of the literature regarding the experiences of Chinese battered women in North America and provides suggestions for culturally sensitive and competent interventions for them. In addition, the discussion is informed by informal telephone interviews conducted with prominent Chinese or Asian professionals and activists working with Chinese battered women, and documents provided by them. All interviewees are from agencies or shelters providing ethno-specific and bilingual services to Chinese and/or Asian battered women in eight major cities in the United States and Canada (see Table 1). Information provided in the interviews will be referenced using the agencies' initials as indicated on Table 1.

TABLE 1. Personal Communications Conducted Between May 1997 and May 1998.

Agency	Location	Nature
Chinese Family Life Services of Metropolitan Toronto, CFLSMT	Toronto, Ontario, Canada	Ethno-Specific Chinese Family Service Agency
Support Network for Battered Women, SNBW	Santa Clara County, California, US	Mainstream Women's Shelter
New York Asian Women's Center, NYAWC	New York, US	Asian Women's Shelter
Center for the Pacific-Asian Family, CPAF	Los Angeles, California, US	Asian Women's Shelter
Asian American Community Services, AACS	Columbus, Ohio, US	Community Service Agency
Chinese Family Service of Greater Montreal, CFSGM	Montreal, Quebec, Canada	Ethno-Specific Chinese Family Service Agency
Asian Women's Shelter, AWS	San Francisco, California, US	Asian Women's Shelter
United Chinese Community Enrichment Services Society, UCCESS	Vancouver, British Columbia, Canada	Ethno-Specific Chinese Family Service Agency
Department of Social Services of Donaldina Cameron House, DCH	San Francisco, California, US	Ethno-Specific Chinese Family Service Agency
Asian Women Home, Asian Americans for Community Involvement, AACI	Santa Clara County, California, US	Asian Women's Shelter
Chinatown Service Center, CSC	Los Angeles, California, US	Ethno-Specific Chinese Family Service Agency

LITERATURE REVIEW

The Chinese community in North America consists of diverse groups from many different regions who come to stay in this land for a variety of reasons. Almost two-thirds of Chinese in the United States are foreign-born (Huang, 1991). Many of them come to North America for a better future, but some arrive here as refugees. They come from different socioeconomic and educational backgrounds. They all speak Chinese, although they may not be able to communicate among themselves because of the different dialects. They share similar traditional Chinese values about family, although they also express unique ways of thinking because of their different socio-historical contexts. Each group carries its own heritage as well as historical burdens. They are the people from Cambodia, Hong Kong, Malaysia, Mainland China, Laos, Singapore, Taiwan, Vietnam, and other Southeast Asian countries. They are people with many faces.

Prevalence of Spouse Abuse in the Chinese Community

Defining the prevalence of spouse abuse for Chinese in North America is an extremely difficult task. Existing prevalence studies of spouse abuse make few references to race or ethnicity (Kanuha, 1994). Official statistics in both the US and Canada do not include Chinese (or Asians) as a separate category in their analyses. The presence of so many different cultural groups in North America probably makes the task of measuring spouse violence in a culturally sensitive manner for any one group extremely complicated. One study of spouse aggression in Hong Kong indicated a 14% prevalence rate of physical violence between spouses (Tang, 1994). Based on the data from focus group discussions conducted in Seattle, Washington, Chinese women informally estimated that between 20% to 30% of families experienced some form of family violence (Ho, 1990).

Despite the lack of systematic data, professionals and activists working with Chinese battered women in North America unanimously cited the following observations regarding the prevalence of spouse abuse in the Chinese community. First, it is an unfounded myth that spouse abuse does not occur in the Chinese community. Spouse abuse is an ignored, invisible, but significant problem in the Chinese community (Chin, 1994; Lee & Au, 1998; Lum, 1998). There is, however, a problem of underreporting. Chinese battered women also rarely utilize services offered by mainstream women's shelters and other social service agencies because of cultural and/or language barriers–reasons that have been repeatedly cited by many other researchers examining the low utilization rate of social services by Chinese in North America (Sue, Fujino, Hu & Takeuchi, 1991). Second, as suggested by two interviewees of the study who have worked closely with Chinese battered women, there is a trend of increased reporting, and it is closely linked to the increased criminalization of spouse abuse by the legal system and community education efforts (CFLSMT, 1997; DCH, 1997). Third, spouse abuse in the Chinese community happens across all socioeconomic strata regardless of an individual's immigration status. A study conducted by the Chinese Family Life Services of Metropolitan Toronto (Chan, 1989) indicated that 26% of the abusers were either entrepreneurs or professionals; 46% attained post-secondary education, and 24% were university graduates. Regarding the length of residency, 80% of the abusers and 61% of the victims had been in Canada for more than 6 years. The myth that only poor, uneducated, or new immigrants abuse their spouses is not true in the Chinese community. Those who utilize the services provided by women's shelters are, however, predominantly of lower socioeconomic status or are new immigrants who do not have alternative, outside resources (New York Asian Women's Center, 1992; AACI, 1997).

Culture-Specific Influences of Spouse Abuse

Feminist social critics focus on how cultural beliefs about sex roles and the resulting institutional arrangements contribute to and maintain gender inequality and the oppression of women by men (Gondolf, 1988; Martin, 1976). For Chinese, such a dynamic is maintained by cultural beliefs and values around family and gender roles that profoundly influence one's definition of self.

The traditional Chinese self, as rooted in Confucianism, exists primarily in relationship to significant others (Chu, 1985; Ho, 1990). In the past, the self-other relationships among Chinese were built on the traditional collectivity of extended family/kinship networks. Such a collectivity extends even beyond the living relatives to include their ancestors. Thus, a male Chinese would consider himself a son, a brother, a husband, a father, an heir to the family lineage, but hardly *himself*. Likewise, a Chinese woman is a daughter, a sister, a wife, and a mother, but not an independent woman striving for self-actualization. It seems as if outside the relational context of the significant others, there is very little independent self left for the Chinese (Chu, 1985; Triandis, 1995). In order to maintain a collective existence, family harmony, solidarity, loyalty, interdependence, filial piety, chastity, integrity, dignity, and endurance are highly valued (Ho, 1990). In situations involving a clash between individual and family well-being, it is expected that an individual will subjugate his/her well-being for the collective good. As a result of this collective definition of self, an individual's behavior is inseparable from that of the family and, therefore, has consequences not just for himself or herself, but also for the whole family. Shaming the family name and losing face is simply unthinkable (Lee, 1996; Lum, 1998).

Another major characteristic in understanding the Chinese self is that individual self-worth is not measured by what one has personally achieved for *oneself*, but by the extent to which one has lived up to the behavioral expectations of the significant others as defined by predominant cultural ideas. In a family situation, these behavioral expectations are circumscribed by well-defined roles within a hierarchical structure. Power is distributed based on one's age, generation and gender (Chan & Leong, 1994). Based on a patriarchal family structure, Chinese men are legitimate heirs to continue their family lineage and, therefore, are endorsed with a strong sense of importance and entitlement. In the past, the social institutions reinforced such an arrangement by providing men, but not women, with educational and occupational opportunities. With a culturally endowed sense of importance and socially viable means to accumulate resources and wealth, men are naturally given permission to exercise authority over women and children.

At the other end, women internalize values and beliefs about endurance, perseverance, and submission to men as ultimate virtues for any morally good woman. The "three obediences" are widely accepted codes of behavior for morally good women: Before marriage, a woman follows and obeys her father; after marriage, she follows and obeys her husband; after the death of her husband, she follows and obeys her son (Ho, 1990; Lum, 1988). The three obediences establish cultural ideas of unquestionable submission of women to men (Ho, 1990). If the situation demands the shortchanging of individual well-being to fulfill the ideals, the virtues of endurance and perseverance are used to regulate the discomfort involved as exemplified by an old

Chinese saying: "repeated endurance produces precious gold." Such a cultural definition of self as influenced by cultural beliefs around family helps to better understand the responses of Chinese battered women to spouse abuse.

Culture also influences the dynamics of spouse abuse in Chinese couples. In defining who is the abuser, mainstream understanding based on a feminist perspective focuses on male violence against women in intimate relationships. Gender is the fundamental defining concept in woman battering. Because of the patriarchal nature of Chinese families, violence against wives, however, may be instigated by both male and female relatives on the male side, especially from the in-laws (AWS, 1997; Huisman, 1996; Ming-Jyh, Li, Zhang, & Yao, 1994; SNBW, 1997). In Chan's study (1989), 20% of the abused wives lived with in-laws. Among those abused women, 64% were also physically and emotionally abused by the parents of their husband. For all battered women, 39% perceived in-law issues as factors precipitating violence. Even though the data are limited and not representative of all Chinese, such findings did suggest that for Chinese, wife assault may not be confined to male violence against women. Women (especially mothers-in-law) can derive power from their association with the male figures in the family and induce violent acts against other women. Of course, complex family dynamics such as triangulation (Minuchin & Fishman, 1981) are commonly involved in such a situation. Still, such a phenomenon poses new challenges to the predominant conceptualization of gender as the primary foundation of wife battering.

Responses of Chinese Battered Women to Spouse Abuse and Cultural Influences

Chinese battered women face tremendous pressures in trying to break through the abusive cycle within their cultural milieu. As mentioned by most of the interviewees who work closely with Chinese battered women, the first problem is the issue of non-recognition of abuse as a problem. Because Chinese cultural values support male supremacy and dominance over women, male violence against women in the forms of physical, emotional and sexual abuse can be justified differently based on culturally acceptable "reasons." The Chinese Family Service of Greater Montreal conducted a study of Chinese attitudes and beliefs pertaining to domestic violence (Ming-Jyh et al.,

1994). Forty-one percent of male respondents in the Montreal study agreed that "in a Chinese family, if a man beats his wife or girlfriend, a probable reason is to educate her" (Ming-Jyh et al., 1994). Fourteen percent of female respondents were also in agreement with such an assertion. It is, therefore, not surprising that some victims may believe that they deserve the beating, because they have indeed done something wrong. Cultural beliefs offer a gracious "rationale" for the abuser, because his abusive behavior serves to fulfill his duty as the head of the house.

As suggested by the Program Director of Department of Social Services, Donaldina Cameron House, emotional abuse in the form of verbal abuse and financial restraint are accepted; however, sexual abuse is the most grossly underreported form of abuse. In focus group discussions conducted with Chinese women in Seattle, Washington, it was reported that some victims believe marriage was a license for the man to have sex with them. Therefore, they did not feel that they had the right to reject their husbands' sexual wishes (Ho, 1990). As reported by two interviewees who were experienced professionals working with Chinese battered women in San Francisco and Santa Clara County, it was considered a taboo for Chinese women to talk about sex with outsiders. As a result, it was difficult for many Chinese battered women to talk about sexual abuse with their social workers, shelter workers, or doctors (AACI, 1997; DCH, 1997).

Even if the woman recognizes abuse as a problem, it is still difficult for her or the family members to *admit* the occurrence of abuse. First, such an admission will bring shame to the family. Second, such an act may lead to divorce or separation. For many Chinese, marriage is for life. For those Chinese women who have developed a strong collective sense of self, leaving their abusive husbands could be experienced as cutting off herself (and her partner) from a group cultural life that is vitally important (Lum, 1998). As a result, many women and even supportive relatives may go through a massive denial of the abuse. The Executive Director of the Chinese Family Life Services of Metropolitan Toronto reported that many battered women were, in fact, under pressure from the extended family to either cover up or tolerate the abuse (CFLSMT, 1997).

In many circumstances, some women and their families may give a different label to the problem, such as: the man is hot-tempered; he just lost money gambling, or he is frustrated with his work situation. In fact, over half of the female respondents (53%) of the Montreal study (Ming-Jyh et al., 1994) agreed that a probable reason for a man to beat his wife or girlfriend was "he's in a bad mood." In many other situations, these women resort to the traditional virtue of "endurance." In the Toronto study on abused women, the most frequently mentioned coping mechanism was to "endure" (78%). The cultural value of accepting fate may inadvertently lead to an acceptance of violence and remaining silent (Lum, 1998). Giving abuse another label and/or tolerating the abuse, however, prevent the man from taking responsibility for his violent behaviors and finding solutions to the problems.

The dilemma faced by many Chinese battered women has to be understood within a cultural context. For Chinese women influenced by traditional values, leaving the abuser is not just a demonstration of self-assertiveness or saying no to the abuse. Such an act also means exposing family weakness to outsiders, shaming the family name, violating the virtues of perseverance and endurance, and causing divorce or separation to the family. So, instead of developing a "survivor mentality" (that I am a victim of abuse, it is not my fault, and I deserve to be helped) as commonly understood from a feminist perspective, the woman may instead develop an "instigator mentality" (that I am the bad person who brings shame to the family or causes family breakdown because I expose the abuse or leave my husband). As suggested by two interviewees (DCH, 1997; SNBW, 1997), the Chinese community clearly reinforces the "instigator mentality" by viewing the woman as the troublemaker and shifts its sympathy and support from the battered wife to the batterer once the abuse is made known to the police or any outside agencies. Individual suffering is no longer important once the family name and losing face is involved. The Executive Director of the Asian Women's Shelter in San Francisco reported that when a battered woman left the abusive relationship, she also divorced the network of social support offered by her role as a wife (AWS, 1997). Consequently, the more a woman built her life and selfhood around the role of mother and wife, the greater was her sacrifice in not giving in to the abuse. Knowing these cultural issues helps in understanding the passivity, ambivalence, guilty feelings, and shame characteristic of many Chinese women's responses to spouse abuse.

Contextual Factors: Immigration-Related Issues

Mary Dutton (1996) warned against a single vision of the experiences of battered women and argued for a contextual analysis of battered women's experiences that includes the woman's unique individual and social context. In the same manner, it is dangerous as well as a disservice to Chinese battered women to adopt a single vision of their experiences based solely on an understanding of cultural factors. The experience and strategic responses of Chinese battered women are multifaceted and multilayered, influenced by cultural, contextual, and individual factors. While individual factors do not lend themselves to meaningful discussion because of their extreme heterogeneity, one contextual factor of profound influence is a woman's immigration experience in North America.

As suggested by several interviewees who worked with Chinese battered women and/or batterers, many batterers have used immigration status as a "weapon" to psychologically threaten the woman and to keep her in an abusive relationship despite physical, psychological and sexual suffering (CFLSMT, 1997; SNBW, 1997; UCCESS, 1997). Women who do not have permanent residence status in the United States or who are new immigrants belong to the more vulnerable group, because they usually have little social and financial resources, minimal language skills, and little knowledge about North American culture. Many of them are socially isolated and still struggling to understand and adjust to the new environment.

Immigration-related stress may have a negative impact on couple relationships that triggers or exacerbates violent behaviors in intimate relationships. One common phenomenon affecting some couples is spousal role reversal (Song, 1996). Some wives have found employment more easily than their husbands, because they tend to accept lower-paying jobs, for instance, garment work. In addition, it is not uncommon for professional men to lose their status because of unrecognized credentials, working experiences, or limited language skills (Ming-Jyh et al., 1994). In a study conducted by the Chinese Family Life Services of Metropolitan Toronto to understand the phenomena of spouse abuse in the Chinese community, Chan (1989) suggested that underemployment, downward occupational changes, and re-distribution of power in the family were ego shattering realities that directly threatened the concept of manhood and husbandhood of many male immigrants. Drachman and Ryan (1991), in studying immigrant and refugee populations, reported that some men unfortunately resorted to spouse and child abuse, gambling, or chemical abuse in an attempt to regain a sense of power and to reduce their pain. On the other hand, the Program Director of Department of Social Services, Donaldina Cameron House, in San Francisco, suggested that although many abuses might have happened prior to the immigration, immigration-related stress exacerbated the dysfunctional couple dynamics which were, at the core, an issue of dominance and control (DCH, 1997).

Immigration-related experiences also significantly influence a woman's help-seeking responses to her battering experiences. Oftentimes, the seemingly passivity of many Chinese battered women is not just a result of cultural values. Their passivity can be a reaction to their immediate life circumstances in North America. One major issue is social isolation. In the Montreal study (Ming-Jyh et al., 1994), when respondents were asked for the reasons for tolerating domestic violence, one of the most cited reasons regardless of educational level was lacking places from which to seek help because of isolation.

Because of social isolation, many women do not have information about available services. Not having the language abilities, many Chinese women cannot utilize mainstream shelters' services. A counselor at the Support Network for Battered Women, Santa Clara County revealed the following as the most often cited reasons by Chinese battered women for the low utilization of shelter services: language barriers, food choices, cultural dissimilarities, fear of fights among children, and stigma of women's shelters (SNBW, 1997). In the Toronto study (Chan, 1989), only 6 out of 50 abused women who received counseling services used shelter services, and only 2 women were able to adapt to shelter living without much difficulty.

Not able to utilize the services provided by women's shelters is only part of the issue. Davidson and Jenkins (1989), in discussing the socioeconomic oppression experienced by working-class women, mentioned that "a woman might not find that her partner's violence is her first concern nor her worst oppressor" (p. 494). Such a situation is even more true for many Chinese battered women. Equipped with little language skills and no viable means for making a living and supporting their children, many Chinese battered women are "forced" to stay in the abusive relationships for purely economic and survival reasons.

Sometimes, not being able to speak fluent English can become an insurmountable barrier even when the woman actively seeks outside help such as calling the police or going to the emergency room at the hospital. Several interviewees (AACS, 1998; DCH, 1997; SNBW, 1997) mentioned situations in which the police used various members of the household as translators, or even only talked to the batterer to gather information because "he is the only one who speaks English." Language is clearly a formidable barrier to the help-seeking efforts of many immigrant women.

In understanding the experience of Chinese battered women and their strategic responses to their plight, one needs to consider cultural, contextual, and individual factors including couple and/or family dynamics. The faces of Chinese battered women are as varied as the dynamics of spouse abuse. There is no one Chinese version of spouse abuse. The dynamics involved are multifaceted and multilayered. Each battering situation constitutes a unique configuration of the interaction of those factors. Each factor may take on varying importance in an individual's experience. Neglecting any one dimension, however, is likely to result in a biased understanding of the situations of Chinese battered women.

IMPLICATIONS FOR TREATMENT OF SPOUSE ABUSE IN THE CHINESE AMERICAN COMMUNITY

Chinese battered women in North America face tremendous pressure and many obstacles in confronting and escaping abuse; many of these obstacles are pervasive and deep-rooted in cultural values. To fundamentally assist Chinese battered women to combat violence in intimate relationships, a three-tier model of intervention is proposed that targets the individual battered woman, the family system, and the larger community.

Counseling Chinese Battered Women

Similar to working with any battered woman, it is important to assure safety and stabilize clients, explore and validate feelings, listen actively and reflectively, examine coping skills, assist clients to acknowledge the abuse without blaming self, empower clients by exploring options and building on strengths, and help clients to develop a viable plan for the future (Roberts & Burman, 1998; Walker, 1994). If the situation is perceived to be lethal, it is important to develop a safety plan with the woman and provide the needed assistance accordingly. Helping professionals, however, may need to attend to certain specific clinical issues and challenges when working with Chinese battered women.

Assessment

Presence of spouse abuse. Chinese people tend to somaticize psychological or interpersonal problems (Kleinman, 1982: Lee, 1996). Given their cultural values, Chinese battered women might not directly seek help for violence-related problems, but instead have other complaints that are perceived as more socially and psychologically acceptable. Common complaints are somatic problems such as insomnia and headaches (Chan & Leong, 1994), or behavioral problems in children (Lee, 1996). Norton and Manson (1992) noted that for Southeast Asian women dealing with family violence and seeking help at a mental health clinic, *none* presented family violence as an issue in their initial disclosure of problems. It is, therefore, important for helping professionals to consider the possibility of violence in working with Chinese women even when the initial presenting problem is not spousal abuse. Some signals that warrant further exploration may include the client's difficulty in identifying causes of somatic complaints or depressed feelings, and the client's ambivalence in talking about couple relationships despite hints of dissatisfaction.

The intensity of the problems. As a result of the tendency to endure and tolerate abuse in many Chinese battered women, the precipitating event to seeking professional help is likely to be a serious crisis for most clients. The delayed help-seeking behaviors also mean that the problem may tend to be more severe when it comes to the attention of helping professionals (Huang, 1991; Lee, 1996). However, because of the fear of shame and losing face, and the cultural norms of self-reliance and inhibition of emotions, Chinese battered women may outwardly appear to be less distressed and more reserved compared to other battered women in similar situations (Lum, 1998). The discrepancy between the expressed emotionality of the victims and the severity of the abuse is an important factor to consider when working with a Chinese battered woman.

Specific cultural beliefs/practices regarding problem perception and solution finding. Because cultural values influence a person's problem perception, perceived solution, and his or her help-seeking behaviors (Green, 1995; Lee, 1996), it is important to be sensitive to culturally based dynamics in understanding the client's perception of her situation. Some useful areas to explore include: (1) What is the nature of the perceived problem? For instance, the problem of spouse abuse can be perceived as the result of bad fate, not being able to give birth to a male son, unable to be a dutiful wife or daughter-in-law, or bringing bad luck to the family. An interviewee from Asian Women Home, Asian Americans Community Involvement mentioned that some Chinese (e.g., Vietnamese Chinese) tended to accept hitting as a legitimate way to discipline or educate women (AACI, 1997). Next, it is important to determine what are the cultural values that may engender such a perception or contribute to the problem of abuse. (2) What and who are involved in the solution? Who is the expert in resolving the abuse and the related problems? For example, a respectable elder in the family may be considered the best person to resolve the problem of spouse abuse, because the abuser has to listen to his or her advice out of a respect for authority. Based on his experience working with Chinese batterers, the Program Director of Family and Youth Counseling, United Chinese Community Enrichment Services Society said that police were oftentimes perceived as the most effective agent in stopping his clients' abusive behavior because of their fear of the legal consequences of spouse abuse (UCCESS, 1997). It is also important to examine whether the client's perceived solution is in conflict with the legal norms of the society or not. (3) What are the client's perceived strengths and weaknesses in terms of resources including cultural and situational barriers/resources? In many cases, limited language abilities, financial dependency, and limited social support can be powerful situational barriers for the woman to seek help (Lee & Au, 1998; Lum, 1998). (4) Are there values in the client's culture that can be used as a leverage point for clients and therapists to co-construct useful alternative solutions? For example, traditional Chinese culture places great importance on children as someone who will carry on the family lineage. Several interviewees suggested that many Chinese battered women only sought help after they realized the detrimental effect of spouse abuse on their children or when the abusers started hurting their children (AWS, 1997; DCH, 1997).

Immigration-related issues. It is important to make culturally sensitive assessments when working with Chinese battered women who are also immigrants. Congress (1997), based on her experience working with immigrant populations, suggested the following issues to be explored in making an assessment: reasons for immigration, length of stay in North America, legal or nondocumented immigration status, language abilities, contact with cultural and mainstream institutions, social life, values concerning family, relationships, and work. Such information will be helpful for the therapist to have a contexualized understanding of the client's situation. It also provides information regarding resources and strengths of clients that can be utilized or barriers and obstacles that need to be overcome in the helping process.

Joining and Engagement

Because of cultural values of harmony, male superiority, collectivism and obligation, disclosing battering problems to an "outside" helping professional is almost equivalent to shaming the family name or losing face. Clients who have this "insider" versus "outsider" mentality would feel shameful or guilty about seeking outside help and have difficulty talking about the abuse. In addition, many do not have prior experience with therapy. As such, it is of utmost importance to successfully join with the clients early on so that a trustful and therapeutic relationship can be established. In this engagement process, it is important to recognize the client's dilemmas in seeking help, strengthen motivation, respect the culturally embedded mode of social interaction and communication, and impart the structure of help.

Joining with client's dilemmas of seeking help. Before looking at treatment issues or how to stop the abuse, it is important to explicitly recognize the client's dilemmas in seeking help and normalize the emotion of shame or guilt (Huang, 1991; Sue & Sue, 1990). Not assisting a Chinese battered woman to work through her ambivalence and shame regarding seeking outside help may lead to early drop-out from treatment. Moreover, clients will feel they are being understood when the therapist recognizes their cultural dilemmas and validates their feelings of ambivalence rather than insists that they "should not" experience these emotions. Opening the door for the Chinese battered woman to talk about her dilemmas also educates the therapist about the client's culturally embedded perception of her problems. Because of the strong fear of shaming the family name and losing face, issues of confidentiality should be communicated clearly and unambiguously to Chinese clients.

Strengthening motivation. Despite cultural and/or contextual obstacles, the client has made efforts to seek help or accept outside help by either calling the hotline, going to a women's shelter, or receiving assistance from various helping professionals. It is, therefore, very important to reaffirm and strengthen whatever motivating factors are present in the clients. Discovering what made the client decide not to tolerate the situation anymore may be the first step. Besides complimenting the client's ability to seek help despite various obstacles, it is very important to reframe the client's help-seeking behavior as an act congruent with cultural values. For instance, building on the traditional value of family well-being and harmony, seeking cessation of abuse is not a self-oriented effort to protect oneself. Instead, it can be reframed as an *other-oriented* effort to benefit the well-being of the whole family, including the children and/or the abuser (Lum, 1998).

Joining with client's culturally embedded mode of communication. People from different socio-cultural backgrounds will have learned different styles of social interaction and, consequently, will have developed diverse "comfort zones" regarding modes of social interaction and communication. Understanding and pacing the client's familiar language styles is an important part of the joining process (Green, 1995). Because Chinese tend to be more reserved and inhibited about emotions, clients should be given time and space to slowly open up at their own pace and in a way that they feel most comfortable. Lack of direct eye-contact should not be misinterpreted as a symptom of avoidance or anxiety, because it may be a sign of respect (Chung, 1992). Being silent or reserved does not necessarily mean resistance or unwillingness to seek help; it may be just a matter of needing more time to open up oneself. Helping professionals working with Chinese battered women should observe and respect characteristics of both verbal and non-verbal communication in their clients.

Imparting the structure of help. Many Chinese battered women may not have prior experience with women's shelters, therapy, or receiving other forms of treatment. It is important for helping professionals to clearly explain to them the structure of help in order to lessen their anxiety regarding seeking professional help. This is especially important in a women's shelter environment. The Program Director of the Chinese Family Life Services of Metropolitan Toronto mentioned that

Chinese battered women rarely utilized mainstream women's shelters because of cultural and language barriers that posed immense adjustment problems both for the women and/or their children (CFLSMT, 1997). In addition, it is important to educate clients about the purpose and process of therapy/treatment, services available for battered women, and their rights and responsibilities. Because of their unfamiliarity with the service system, helping professionals should take the initiative to find out whether Chinese battered women have any questions about information that has not been covered.

Cultural Value of Pragmatism

Under the influence of Confucianism, Chinese people tend to be pragmatic and instrumental (Ma, 1998). The cultural value of pragmatism for Chinese has significant clinical implications for work with this population. For cultures in which people define a pragmatic, instrumental relationship with helping professionals, it may be quite difficult for them, at least at the engagement stage, to experience "talk therapy" as useful (Lorenzo & Adler, 1984). Concrete actions including case management services (e.g., escort services), financial support, residential services, legal services, support groups and activities, tutoring services for children in shelters, and so forth may be prominent in establishing a positive relationship between the client and the helping professional (Sue & Sue, 1990). It is a way to demonstrate the professional's willingness to help and their competence (Huang, 1991). Such services are also important in view of the usual lack of resources and language skills of many Chinese battered women.

Also, for many Chinese, the goal of seeking treatment is symptom relief, and it is quite common for clients to expect quick assessment and prompt intervention. A recent study of Chinese clients' construction of the roles and functions of family therapists revealed their perception of therapists as teachers/experts who would listen to their difficulties, help them analyze their problems, and provide them alternative ways to solve their problems (Ma, 1998). In view of this pragmatic, problem-solving orientation to help-seeking, it is imperative for treatment to focus on the present and future and to be goal-oriented with clear indicators of progress in order to maintain the client's positive motivation and validate her success in bringing positive changes to her current life situation (Paniagua, 1994).

Empowering Chinese Battered Women

Empowering the battered woman to become a survivor rather than a victim represents one major treatment goal in working with battered women (Walker, 1994). As suggested by the Program Director of the Center for the Pacific-Asian Family, because isolation is a widely used strategy by Chinese male batterers in controlling their spouses, and many Chinese women also lack language skills to access useful information, educating women about their rights and services available to them becomes an important part of the empowering process (CPAF, 1997). It is also important for helping professionals to recognize the cultural dilemma for a Chinese woman in leaving the abusive relationship. Helping professionals need to be careful about "empowering" Chinese battered women by "coaching" them to leave the abusive relationships. Not replicating the dynamics of abuse in which the women were told what to do or what is best for them, several interviewees suggested that it was more helpful to fully respect the women's decisions with regard to their marriages and at the same time provide the required assistance (AACI, 1997; CPAF, 1997). Such a process may take longer and be manifested in the women's repeated struggles of leaving and returning to the abusers. The Chinese battered woman needs to rediscover and reconnect with her needs and resources in her own way and at her own pace in order to experience an empowering process that fosters an internal locus of control and a positive sense of self. Consequently, there is a greater likelihood for them to develop solutions that are appropriate to their needs and viable in their unique cultural milieu. The experiences of several Asian women's shelters validate the positive effects of empowering clients by respecting their culture and supporting self-determination. These empowering efforts have been successful in helping many battered women leave the abusive relationships. For instance, only 30% of Asian women who stayed at the New York Asian Women's Center between 1982-1992 returned to the batterers (New York Asian Women's Center, 1992).

Telephone Therapy: An Alternative

Some agencies have provided "telephone therapy" because of the relative privacy, flexibility, and feeling of anonymity (Shepard, 1987). In telephone therapy, the therapeutic conversation is conducted through using the telephone instead of a face-to-face encounter. Such a form of therapy can be more readily accepted by a Chinese battered woman who otherwise might not seek help, because of the strong fear of losing face both for herself and the family. Further, many Chinese battered women may not have the means of transportation to attend sessions. The Executive Director of the Chinese Family Life Services of Metropolitan Toronto suggested that telephone therapy made it easier, at least at the beginning stage, for helping professionals to reach out to those battered women who might otherwise not be able to utilize the much needed services (CFLSMT, 1997).

Intervention at the Family System Level

Mainstream conceptualizations of services for battered women focus on empowering the individual woman so that she can escape the violence of abuse (Walker, 1994). In many situations, that means leaving the abuser and achieving a violence-free life. Because of the issue of power imbalance in relationships, couple therapy has been cautioned by most feminist therapists (Walker, 1994). However, several interviewees suggested that couple therapy might be an appropriate form of treatment in the Chinese community and was, oftentimes, requested by both Chinese men and women (CSC, 1997; CFLSMT, 1997). Strongly influenced by the ideals of "marriage for life" and family togetherness despite adversities, interviewees from several agencies estimated that between 80% to 90% of those women who sought help from their agency chose to stay in the marriage (CSC, 1997; CFLSMT, 1997; UCCESS, 1997). In such a situation, the best thing for a therapist to do is to advocate for a violence-free relationship. Couple therapy can be a viable choice of treatment when provided under the following conditions: (1) the woman requests couple treatment; (2) there is a cessation of violence in the relationship; and (3) the man is willing to take responsibility for the abuse (CFLSMT, 1997; UCCESS, 1997).

Besides couple therapy, appropriate intervention at the family system level can provide effective and quick solutions in ending violence in marital relationships. Because traditional Chinese culture is a high-context culture (Hall, 1983) in which people pay great attention to the surrounding context of an event to define the appropriateness of one's behaviors, group condemnation of abuse can be instrumental in ending violence in marital relationships if such a behavior is being defined as unacceptable by the larger community. Kibria (1993), in studying the family life of Vietnamese Americans, suggested that social support for battered women and social pressure and stigma placed on the abusers could be effective in stopping marital violence. For instance, conducting family sessions in which other family members, especially the respected members such as the elders, put pressure on the abuser to stop his violent behaviors can be part of an effective solution to the problem of domestic violence.

As a rule of thumb, helping professionals need to consider face-saving techniques when involving the broader family system. Saving face is an important cultural factor in social interaction among Chinese people. Face-saving techniques allow people to make beneficial changes in their habitual behaviors that may have contributed to or maintained the abuse without having to go through the negative emotional experiences associated with losing face which, oftentimes, can lead to defensive behaviors and massive denial of the problem. Ho (1993) warned that the confrontational approach, rather than helping Asian clients, may violate their cultural value of harmony. Face-saving techniques avoid confrontational moves and problem-talk. Instead of focusing on who is responsible for the problem and the history of the problem, the preferred face-saving dialogues assist the couple to identify the time when they can successfully handle their conflict without using violence. In addition, face-saving techniques assist the couple to identify what they can do to contribute to a violence-free relationship and what other family members can do to facilitate the desired change. The focus of face-saving techniques is on identifying, eliciting, reinforcing, expanding, and consolidating the desired change in the couple relationship. It is also important to compliment everyone's motivation and efforts in realizing the solution.

Intervention at the Community Level

The criminalization of spouse abuse, because of its important social control function, is a significant step toward ending violence against women in intimate relationships. All states and provinces in the United States and Canada have passed civil and/or criminal statutes to protect battered women (Roberts, 1996). Grassroots activists and concerned professionals have also set up shelters for battered women and established many other programs and services for victims, offenders, and children (Schechter, 1996). The responses of the criminal justice system and the establishment of various services for battered women have positively affected the Chinese community. A Chinese battered woman has expressed the advantages of being in North America as follows: "Wife beating is really common in China. No laws deal with this problem. . . (In North America) domestic violence is illegal and the social welfare system protects women victims, which, in turn, encourages women to seek help" (Ming-Jyh et al., 1994, p.12). These societal efforts to combat spousal abuse have set a broader social context for assisting Chinese battered women. On the other hand, because of social isolation and/or language barriers experienced by some Chinese women, they may not have access to such information or services. Community education serves an important role in making these services or information available and accessible to the Chinese community in North America.

Community Education

Oftentimes, Chinese battered women do not seek help because they are unaware of available services. Many of them do not even label their suffering as abuse due to lack of knowledge regarding abuse or denial. Thus, effective dissemination of information about spouse abuse and services available to Chinese battered women is the necessary first step in reaching out to this population. Such information, however, has to be disseminated in ways that can reach the Chinese community. Some effective ways that have been used by different agencies include pamphlets, posters, and information brochures printed in Chinese about domestic violence and services offered by an individual organization. These brochures have been displayed and distributed at places that Chinese people frequently visit such as ethnic grocery stores, Chinese language schools, English as a Second Language classes (ESL), ethnic organizations, churches and so forth (AACS, 1998; CFLSMT, 1997; DCH, 1998). In North American cities where there is a sizable Chinese American population, the message is being advertised through ethnic newspapers, radio-broadcasting services, and multicultural television channels (AWS, 1997; CFLSMT, 1997). Chinese battered women have responded to these educational efforts. For instance, the number of spouse abuse cases handled by the Chinese Family Life Services of Metropolitan Toronto has increased from less than 10 cases in 1986 to 118 cases in 1996, 20% of all cases handled by the agency in the same year (CFLSMT, 1997). Similarly, the Domestic Violence Assistance Program at the Cameron House in San Francisco experienced an increase from 80 cases to 300 cases between 1982 to 1997 (DCH, 1997). Both agencies have launched extensive community education programs regarding domestic violence and their services through the media.

Community education to Chinese men serves a very important preventive function. An interviewee from Chinatown Service Center mentioned that some Chinese men believed it was their right and duty to educate and discipline their spouse through corporal punishment. They were ignorant of the legal consequences of wife battering in North America (CSC, 1997). In traditional Chinese society, the government is perceived as an oppressive authoritarian apparatus. The old saying: "never go to court when alive and never go to hell after death" clearly illustrates the fear of government in many Chinese. As suggested by the Program Director of Department of Social Services, Donaldina Cameron House, many Chinese men felt degraded and shamed by the procedure of being body searched when arrested (DCH, 1999). The Program Director of Family and Youth Counseling, United Chinese Community Enrichment Services Society reported that there was not one re-offense in all the male offenders whom he had treated in the past five years. All of them were afraid of the legal penalty (UCCESS, 1997). The mere knowledge of spouse abuse as a criminal act with legal consequences can be an important first step in deterring some Chinese men from using violence toward their spouses.

Chinese culture belongs to a high-context culture (Hall, 1983). In a high context culture, people pay great attention to the surrounding circumstances including social status, history, and social setting to guide their behaviors (Hall, 1983). In a high-context culture, condemnation of spouse abuse by the community will be extremely effective in preventing violence in intimate relationships, because of the social pressure created by the community against spouse abuse. Educating the Chinese community about the detrimental consequences of abuse for an individual and his/her children and the legal consequences involved in abusive incidents will, in the long run, reduce its occurrence and increase community pressure being put on the batterers to stop the abusive behaviors. Such a change in attitude can fundamentally alter the dynamics of abuse in the Chinese community.

Coordination Between Mainstream Service Providers and Ethno-Specific Organizations

Despite efforts initiated and provided by the local Chinese community to serve their people by establishing ethno-specific women's shelters and/or family service agencies, the roles of ethno-specific social services in a multicultural society are always controversial because of the fear of fragmentation of the service delivery system (Lee & Au, 1998). Further, combating spouse abuse involves efforts from a multitude of professionals. Therefore, a more fundamental issue is networking and coordination between ethnic organizations and mainstream service providers in their efforts to provide culturally sensitive and relevant services to Chinese battered women. The mainstream service providers include professionals at the women's shelters, mental health centers, social service agencies, police personnel, and legal professionals. Although they have good intentions for assisting Chinese battered women, these professionals may have difficulty reaching out to the Chinese community as a result of cultural and/or language barriers and lack of knowledge about the ethnic communities. Some effective ways that have been used by ethnic service organizations to build bridges and improve networking and coordination are: providing consultations and/or cultural competence training to mainstream organizations, providing interpreter services for clients who have language difficulties, conducting studies on Chinese battered women (e.g., in Toronto, Montreal), and organizing conferences around issues of Asian/Chinese battered women (e.g., Building bridges: Collaborating toward wellness in Asian communities, Columbus, Ohio, December 4, 1998; Gathering strengths: Coming together to end domestic violence in our Asian and Pacific Islander communities, June 20-21, 1997, San Francisco).

CONCLUSION

Because of both cultural and contextual factors, spouse abuse in the Chinese community is largely an ignored, invisible, but important problem. The experiences of Chinese battered women are both similar to and different from other battered women in North America. They are similar to all other abused women in the sense that they are all victims of male dominance and control. Their battering experience can also be different as a result of the additional burdens imposed by traditional Chinese cultural beliefs and values, their immigration experience, and/or racism in the society. Oftentimes, they are locked in a vicious cycle that makes it extremely difficult for them to escape violence in intimate relationships. As suggested by the Executive Director of the Asian Women's Shelter, besides embattling the traditional values, Chinese battered women have to choose between being exploited by their husbands if they stay in the abusive relationship, or being exploited by the socioeconomic system if they leave the abusive relationship (AWS, 1997).

Being in North America renders Chinese women legal protection from spouse abuse although many Chinese battered women have not been able to benefit from such protection because of cultural and language barriers. To facilitate access to services and combat the problem of spouse abuse, a three-tier model of intervention is being proposed. Spouse abuse is a multifaceted problem that has significance both at the individual, family, and community level. Besides providing culturally sensitive and competent counseling and support services to individual Chinese battered woman, it is important to enlist family support and involvement under appropriate circumstances. Improving access to services requires a two-way effort at the community level. The Chinese community needs to be educated regarding spouse abuse, services for victims, and legal consequences for offenders. At the same time, the mainstream service providers need support and education to provide culturally sensitive, competent, and relevant services.

There is no quick and easy solution to stop violence in intimate relationships. The Asian/Chinese women's shelters and family services agencies have provided a safety net for many first generation Chinese-Americans or Chinese-Canadians. These community-initiated programs work diligently to serve their local ethnic communities despite many constraints. The ultimate well-being of Chinese battered women and their children, however, depends on how well the legal, criminal, and mainstream social service systems coordinate with each other to serve in the best interest of battered women of all colors. Continuous, beneficial dialogues between the ethnic community and the mainstream providers will, ultimately, help to give voices to Chinese battered women.

REFERENCES

AACI (1997). Personal communication, Asian Americans for Community Involvement, May 9, 1997.

AACS (1998). Personal communication, Asian American Community Services, May 16, 1998.

AWS (1997). Personal communication, Asian Women's Shelter, May 12, 1997.

CFLSMT (1997). Personal communication, Chinese Family Life Services of Metropolitan Toronto, May 20, 1997.

Chan, S. L. L. (1989). *Wife assault: The Chinese family life services experience.* Chinese Family Life Services of Metropolitan Toronto.

Chan, S., & Leong, C. W. (1994). Chinese families in transition: Cultural conflicts and adjustment problems. *Journal of Social Distress and the Homeless, 3,* 263-281.

Chin, K. (1994). Out-of-town brides: International marriage and wife abuse among Chinese immigrants. *Journal of Comparative Family Studies, 25,* 53-69.

Chu, G. (1985). The changing concept of self in contemporary China. In A. J. Marsella, G. DeVos & F. L. K. Hsu (Eds.), *Culture and self, Asian and Western perspectives.* New York: Tavistock Publications.

Chung, D. K. (1992). Asian cultural commonalities: A comparison with mainstream American culture. In S. M. Furuto, R. Biswas, D. K. Chung, K. Murase, & F. Ross-Sheiff (Eds.), *Social work practice with Asian Americans.* Newbury Park, CA: Sage.

Congress, E. (1997). The use of culturagrams to assess and empower culturally diverse families. *Families in Society: The Journal of Contemporary Human Services, 75,* 531-540.

CPAF (1997). Personal communication, Center for the Pacific-Asian Family, June 11, 1997.

CSC (1997). Personal communication, Chinatown Service Center, May 22, 1997.

Davidson, B. P., & Jenkins, P. J. (1989). Class diversity in shelter life. *Social Work, 34,* 491-495.

DCH (1997). Personal communication, Donaldina Cameron House, May 14, 21, 1997.

Drachman, D., & Ryan, A. S. (1991). Immigrants and refugees. In A. Gitterman (Ed.), *Handbook of social work practice with vulnerable populations* (pp. 618-646). New York: Columbia University Press.

Dutton, M. A. (1996). Battered women strategic response to violence: The role of context. In J. L. Edleson & Z. C. Eisikovits (Eds.), *Future interventions with battered women and their families.* (pp.105-124). Thousand Oaks, CA: Sage.

Gondolf, E. (1988). *Battered women as survivors.* Lexington, MA: Lexington Books.

Green, J. W. (1995). *Cultural awareness in the human services: A multi-ethnic approach.* Needham Heights, M.A.: Allyn & Bacon.

Hall, E. T. (1983). *The dance of life.* Garden City, NY: Doubleday.

Ho, C. K. (1990). An analysis of domestic violence in Asian American communities: A multicultural approach to counseling. In L. Brown & M. P. P. Roots (Eds.), *Diversity and complexity in feminist therapy* (pp. 129-150). New York: Haworth.

Ho, M. K. (1993). Family therapy with ethnic minorities. Newbury Park, CA: Sage.

Huang, K. (1991). Chinese Americans. In N. Mokuau (Ed.), *Handbook of social services for Asian Americans and Pacific Islanders.* New York: Greenwood Press.

Huisman, K. A. (1996). Wife battering in Asian American communities. *Violence Against Women, 2*, 260-283.

Kanuha, V. (1996). Domestic violence, racism, and the battered women's movement in the United States. In J. L. Edleson & Z. C. Eisikovits (Eds.), *Future interventions with battered women and their families.* (pp.34-50). Thousand Oaks, CA: Sage.

Kanuha, V. (1994). Women of color in battering relationship. In L. Comas-Diaz & B. Greene (Eds.), *Women of color* (pp. 428-454). New York: Guilford.

Kibria, N. (1993). *Family tightrope: The changing lives of Vietnamese Americans.* Princeton, NJ: Princeton University Press.

Kleinman, A. (1982). Neurasthenia and depression: A study of somatization and culture in China. *Culture, Medicine and Psychiatry, 6*, 117-190.

Lee, M. Y. (1996). A constructivist approach to the help-seeking process of clients: A response to cultural diversity. *Clinical Social Work Journal, 24*, 187-202.

Lee, M. Y., & Au, P. (1998). Chinese women in North America: Their experiences and treatment. In A. R. Roberts (Ed.), *Battered women and their families.* (pp.448-482). New York: Springer Publishing Company.

Lorenzo, M. K., & Adler, D. A. (1984). Mental health services for Chinese in a community health center. *Social Casework, 65*, 600-614.

Loseke, D. R. (1992). *The battered women and shelters: The social construction of wife abuse.* Albany: State University of New York Press.

Lum, J. (1988). Battered Asian women. *Rice, 2*, 50-52.

Lum, J. (1998). Family violence. In L. C. Lee, & N. W. S. Zane (Eds.), *Handbook of Asian American psychology* (pp.505-525). Thousand Oaks, CA: Sage.

Ma, J. L. C. (1998). *Cultural construction of the roles and functions of family therapists: The Hong Kong experience.* Paper presented at the Second Pan Asia-Pacific Conference on Mental Health, Beijing, China, October 13-15, 1998.

Martin, D. (1976). *Battered wives.* San Francisco: Glide.

Ming-Jyh, S., Li, N., Zhang, W. M., & Yao, K. (1994). *Research on conjugal violence in Chinese families of Montreal.* Chinese Family Service of Greater Montreal.

Minuchin, S., Fishman, H. C. (1981). *Family therapy techniques.* Cambridge: Harvard University Press.

New York Asian Women's Center (1992). *New York Asian Women's Center, Tenth Anniversary Report 1982-1992.* New York Asian Women's Center.

Norton, I. M., & Manson, S. M. (1992). An association between domestic violence and depression among Southeast Asian refugee women. *Journal of Nervous and Mental Disease, 180*, 729-730.

Paniagua, F. A. (1994). *Assessing and treating culturally diverse clients, A practical guide.* Thousand Oaks, CA: Sage.

Roberts, A. R. (1996). Police responses to battered women: Past, present, and future. In Roberts, A. R. (Ed.), *Helping battered women: New perspectives and remedies.* (pp. 85-95). New York: Oxford University Press.

Roberts, A. R., & Burman, S. (1998). Crisis intervention and cognitive problem-solving therapy with battered women. A national survey and practice model. In A. R.

Roberts (Ed.), *Battered women and their families.* (pp.3-28). New York: Springer Publishing Company.

Schechter, S. (1996). The battered women's movement in the United States, New directions for institutional reform. In J. L. Edleson & Z. C. Eisikovits (Eds.), *Future interventions with battered women and their families.* (pp.53-66). Thousand Oaks, CA: Sage.

Shepard, P. (1987). Telephone therapy: An alternative to isolation. *Clinical Social Work Journal, 15,* 56-65.

SNBW. (1997). Personal communication, Support Network for Battered Women, May 9, 1997.

Song, Y. I. (1996). *Battered women in Korean immigrant families.* New York: Garland.

Sue, S., Fujino, D. C., Hu, L. T., & Takeuchi, D. T. (1991). Community mental health services for ethnic minority groups: A test of the cultural responsiveness hypothesis. *Journal of Consulting and Clinical Psychology, 59,* 533-540.

Sue, D. W., & Sue, D. (1990). *Counseling the culturally different: Theory and practice.* New York: John Wiley.

Tang, C. S. K. (1994). Prevalence of spouse aggression in Hong Kong. *Journal of Family Violence, 9,* 347-356.

Triandis, H. C. (1995). *Individualism and collectivism.* Boulder, CO: Westview.

UCCESS (1997). Personal communication, United Chinese Community Enrichment Services Society, May 13, 1997.

Walker, L. (1994). *Abused women and survivor therapy: A practical guide for the psychotherapist.* Washington, DC: American Psychological Association.

Battered Immigrant Mexican Women's Perspectives Regarding Abuse and Help-Seeking

Martina J. Acevedo

SUMMARY. A qualitative, pilot study employing in-depth ethno-gra-phic interviews was conducted to examine perceptions and attitudes towards abuse and the help-seeking behaviors of a sample of ten bat-tered immigrant Mexican women. Findings indicated that participants' attitudes about seeking help were influenced more by cultural factors (e.g., gender-role expectations, famialism) than by psycho-social stres-sors (e.g., immigrant status, financial dependency). Children's welfare played a salient role in women's decisions about seeking help, both as a deterrent and a motivating factor. Women's attitudes about their own abuse were more tolerant than their attitudes about hypothetical situa-tions involving others. Changes in women's attitudes about abuse re-flected changes only after some type of intervention had taken place. The majority of the women in the sample had misconceptions or were unin-formed about shelters. Suggestions for further research and intervention with this population and a model of internal and external determinants of help-seeking behavior are presented. *[Article copies available for a fee from The Haworth Document Delivery Service: 1-800-342-9678. E-mail address: <getinfo@haworthpressinc.com> Website: <http://www.haworthpressinc.com>]*

KEYWORDS. Battered women, Mexican immigrant women, help-seeking, cultural factors, psycho-social stressors

---

Martina J. Acevedo, MSW, is a doctoral student in the Department of Social Welfare in the School of Public Policy and Social Research at University of Califor-nia, Los Angeles.

[Haworth co-indexing entry note]: "Battered Immigrant Mexican Women's Perspectives Regarding Abuse and Help-Seeking." Acevedo, Martina J. Co-published simultaneously in *Journal of Multicultural Social Work* (The Haworth Press, Inc.) Vol. 8, No. 3/4, 2000, pp. 243-282; and: *Violence: Diverse Populations and Communities* (ed: Diane de Anda, and Rosina M. Becerra) The Haworth Press, Inc., 2000, pp. 243-282. Single or multiple copies of this article are available for a fee from The Haworth Document Delivery Service [1-800-342-9678, 9:00 a.m. - 5:00 p.m. (EST). E-mail address: getinfo@ haworthpressinc.com].

INTRODUCTION

In the late eighties, domestic violence was identified as the greatest public health risk to adult women by the Surgeon General of the United States (U.S. Senate Judiciary Committee, 1992). Domestic violence continues to be the leading cause of injuries to women ages 15-44, more prevalent than muggings, auto accidents and cancer fatalities combined (U.S. Senate Judiciary Committee, 1992). Spousal abuse cuts across all cultural, ethnic, socio-economic, and religious lines (Straus, Gelles, & Steinmetz, 1980; Walker, 1984). Thus, prevention, intervention, and treatment programs for victims of domestic violence that are designed to reflect the needs of battered women from diverse cultural backgrounds are essential (Torres, 1987).

Although spousal abuse is not exclusive to specific social, economic, or cultural groups, various studies have established associations between family violence and low socioeconomic status (Straus, 1990; Kantor et al., 1994), and have concluded that family violence occurs at higher rates in minority families (Gelles & Straus, 1988). Yet, research focused on minority populations is very limited in the area of wife battering (Sorenson & Telles, 1991).

Hispanics are among the largest and fastest growing minority populations in the United States, with Mexican Americans identified as the fastest growing Hispanic subgroup, comprising over sixty percent of Hispanics nationally (Becerra, 1988; De La Torre, 1993). Moreover, the demographic profile of this population suggests that Mexican Americans are of particular concern when considering issues of spousal abuse given specific risk factors that have been associated with the occurrence of wife abuse such as youthfulness, low educational levels, and low income (Gelles, 1972; Cazenave & Straus, 1979; Straus, Gelles, & Steinmetz, 1980; Gelles & Cornell, 1983; Stacey & Shupe, 1983; Straus and Gelles, 1990). Families with these risk factors may have a greater likelihood of experiencing stressful events and have limited resources available to cope with their situations, particularly as compared to families with higher socioeconomic status (Gelles, 1972). However, despite the presence of these risk factors, scholarly investigations of spousal abuse within the Mexican American community are few (Straus & Smith, 1990; Sorenson & Telles, 1991; Torres, 1991; Kantor, Jasinski, & Aldarondo, 1994; Valencia 1996).

LITERATURE REVIEW

Mexican Americans and Spousal Abuse

Straus and Smith (1990) conducted a survey with a nationally representative sample of Hispanics (n = 721) and non-Hispanic Whites (n = 4,052), examining the etiology and incidence rates of family violence. The authors found that one in four married or cohabitating Hispanic couples had physically assaulted their partners during the year of the study, a rate 54 percent higher than non-Hispanic Whites in the sample. However, when structural variables such as age, family income, and urbanicity were held constant between groups, the higher probability rates of marital violence in Hispanics disappeared. Kantor, Jasinski, and Aldarondo (1994), in their examination of incidence rates of marital violence in three major Hispanic subgroups (n = 743) and a non-Hispanic White sample (n = 1025), also found that rates of wife assault among Hispanics were not significantly different from non-Hispanic Whites when variables such as age and economic stressors were held constant.

Sorenson and Telles (1991) examined lifetime prevalence rates of spousal violence in a Los Angeles community survey of U.S.-born Mexican Americans (n = 538), Mexico-born Mexican Americans (n = 705), and U.S.-born non-Hispanic Whites (n = 1149). The study revealed that lifetime prevalence rates were highest for U.S.-born Mexican Americans (30.9%), while rates among Mexico-born Mexican Americans and U.S.-born non-Hispanic Whites reflected no significant differences at 12.8 percent and 21.6 percent, respectively.

Culturally-Relevant Research

Even more limited than the research on incidence and prevalence rates of wife battering is research that addresses cultural issues pertaining to domestic violence in the Mexican American population (Torres, 1991). Some of the more culturally-relevant research in this area specifically identified Mexican Americans within their samples, considered their immigrant status (e.g., Mexico- or U.S.-born), and noted that there were significant differences between these two groups in examining variables related to spousal abuse. Sorenson and Telles (1991) found birthplace to be a significant predictor of spousal abuse, with prevalence rates higher for U.S.-born Mexican Americans. Kantor et al. (1994), found non-Hispanic White families to have significantly higher incidence rates of domestic violence (13.6) than both Mexican American (5.5) and Mexican immigrant (7.7) families.

Other researchers have acknowledged weaknesses in their study designs by having omitted specific culturally-relevant information. For example, Straus and Smith (1990) caution against overgeneralizing their findings inasmuch as the respondents for their phone survey were selected by Hispanic surname, interviews were only offered in English (excluding monolingual Spanish-speaking Hispanics), and respondents were not divided into subgroups, thereby treating Hispanics in the study as one homogeneous group.

Kantor et al.'s (1994) findings revealed substantial heterogeneity among Hispanic subgroups with respect to acculturation level, country of origin, poverty, and cultural norms sanctioning wife abuse. Puerto Ricans were found to culturally approve wife assault at the highest rate followed by Mexican Americans and Cubans. Moreover, actual wife assaults were significantly correlated with cultural beliefs condoning violence towards the wife.

Valencia (1996) sought culturally-specific information in his descriptive analysis of case records of Mexican American women (n = 424) who utilized services at an emergency shelter between 1979 and 1994, including women who were monolingual Spanish-speaking. However, because immigrant status was not available, all subjects were treated homogeneously in the analysis.

An exploratory study of non-Hispanic White and U.S.-born Mexican American women found no significant differences in the manifestation of wife abuse; however, battered Mexican American women were likely to remain in abusive relationships much longer and identified fewer behaviors as abusive. Cultural values associated with family and religion were identified as explanations for whether Mexican American women sought help, the type of help they sought, and whether they stayed in their abusive relationships (Torres, 1987, 1991).

Others have also argued that gender-role expectations, family, and religion contribute to spousal abuse in this community, and some that these aspects of Hispanic culture actually promote spousal abuse (Zambrano, 1985; Martinez-Garcia, 1988). The exact role of culture in this phenomenon, however, is unclear as theoretical and empirical evidence supporting speculation in this direction has been minimally explored (Straus & Smith, 1990; Sorenson & Telles, 1991; Kantor et al., 1994).

Hispanic Culture. Within Hispanic culture, the needs of the family take precedence over the needs of the individual (Becerra, 1988; Flores-Ortiz, 1993; Zambrano, 1985). This value system is often reinforced by Catholicism, the predominant religion among Hispanics, which has long disapproved of and even stigmatized persons who divorce (Zambrano, 1985). Arguably, the Hispanic woman may be reluctant to leave an abusive husband because of her sense of obligation to her family (Zambrano, 1985), and her perception of how "a good Catholic" should behave.

Some researchers have argued that certain aspects of Hispanic culture, when taken to extremes, encourage wife abuse (Martinez-Garcia, 1988). For example, Hispanics tend to adhere to specific roles, particularly in marriage, in which the male is the head-of-household, breadwinner and decision-maker, and the female is self-sacrificing and submissive (Zambrano, 1985; Vargas-Willis, 1987; Becerra, 1988; & Flores-Ortiz, 1993), which may result in greater tolerance of abusive behavior.

If in fact, certain aspects of Hispanic culture encourage wife battering, the rates of spousal abuse among immigrant Mexicans would be expected to be higher than those among Mexican Americans given differences in level of acculturation. However, research indicates that prevalence rates among immigrant Mexicans are actually lower than those among U.S.-born Mexican Americans and comparable to rates among non-Hispanic Whites (Sorenson & Telles, 1991). Sorenson and Telles (1991) speculate that lower rates among immigrant Mexicans can be attributed to family strengths that stem from cultural values regarding family formation and maintenance.

Inconclusive evidence regarding the role of Hispanic culture in spousal abuse in the Mexican American community, in this researcher's opinion, is largely due to the exclusion of relevant cultural factors in research designs. The few large-scale research studies (Sorenson & Telles, 1991; Kantor et al., 1994) that have focused on Mexican Americans and immigrant Mexicans have failed to examine culturally-relevant variables more in-depth when culture was implied as an explanatory factor.

Psycho-Social Stressors. Increased risk of spousal abuse in the immigrant Mexican population has also been related to psycho-social stressors (Vargas-Willis & Cervantes, 1987) such as undocumented status, limited English-speaking ability, feelings of social isolation, and financial difficulties (Vargas-Willis & Cervantes, 1987; Padilla, Cervantes, Maldonado, & Garcia, 1988). Moreover, cultural factors and psycho-social stressors can potentially influence how battered, immigrant Mexican women define spousal abuse (Torres, 1987; Sorenson, 1996). For instance, Torres' (1991) study revealed that at least 92% of the non-Hispanic White women defined all 14 physically abusive behaviors in the study as constituting wife abuse compared to only seven behaviors that were consistently identified as abusive by at least 92% of the Mexican American women in the sample. The development of services and interventions for immigrant Mexican American women requires an in-depth understanding of how they give meaning to the domestic violence in their lives.

PURPOSE OF THE STUDY

The purpose of this research effort was two-fold: (1) to determine the degree to which the identified cultural factors influenced battered, immigrant Mexican women's perceptions and attitudes about spousal abuse and their subsequent help-seeking behavior, and (2) to provide more specific information about immigrant status and related psycho-social stressors and how these factors influenced their help-seeking behavior.

To achieve this purpose, the following three major research questions guided the study: Is there a relationship between the perceptions and attitudes of physical abuse held by battered, immigrant Mexican women and their help-seeking behaviors? Is there a relationship between cultural factors and the perceptions and attitudes about physical abuse held by battered, immigrant Mexican women and their subsequent help-seeking behavior? Is there a relationship between psycho-social stressors and the perceptions and attitudes about physical abuse held by battered, immigrant Mexican women and their subsequent help-seeking behavior?

THEORETICAL FOUNDATION

Social learning theory offers a framework for understanding the role of cultural factors in the perceptions of and responses to abuse of battered immigrant Mexican women. Bandura (1977) views psychological functioning as a constant reciprocal interaction between behavior and the conditions which control behavior. Moreover, social learning theory helps to explain the internal cognitive processes which regulate behavior.

Conditions which determine behavior result from the interplay of environmental and self-generated stimuli (see Figure 1). Environmental stimuli include stimuli which evoke learned and unlearned responses and consequences which maintain behavior and are often the result of social interaction. Self-generated stimuli, on the other hand, are internal processes that serve as a connection between external conditions and a response. These internal processes can occur via verbal messages, imagery, or physiologically. For example, a battered woman may seriously consider leaving her husband after a particularly abusive episode, but decide against leaving when she begins to think about how she will financially provide for herself and her children. Considering these aversive consequences, she decides against leaving. Ultimately, it is not the environment that determined her behavior, but rather her internal verbal and imaginal processes and associations. This type of decision making may also be externally reinforced by others when social interactions reflect cultural rules that dictate that men are the traditional breadwinners and women are wives and mothers. A behavior will always be determined by the value placed on the consequences by the individual.

FIGURE 1. Conceptual Model

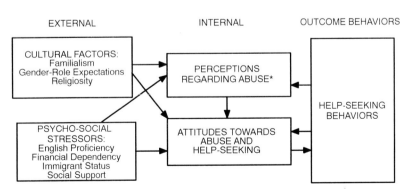

*Internalization of cultural and idiosyncratic factors

Individuals are also able to externally and symbolically reward or punish themselves for their behavior. If an abused woman decides to seek legal assistance and is provided with concrete support, this external positive reinforcement may encourage her to behave similarly in future situations. On the other hand, if a battered woman calls on the police, but no action follows, and her batterer becomes more enraged and abusive because of her help-seeking efforts, in future situations the same woman may not call the police because of the anticipation of punishing consequences.

According to Bandura (1971), the performance or avoidance of responses can either be learned through one's own direct experiences and their reinforcement or by observing someone else's behavior. Through this vicarious learning or modeling process one is able to acquire behavioral responses simply by observing another's behavior. Thereafter, one is able to model that same behavior to obtain the desired reinforcement. For example, if a child is raised in an environment where his/her parents use violence as a regular means for settling disputes, the child may learn to model his/her parents' behavior in similar situations with a partner.

Bandura's theory further proposes that a person's positive behavioral repertoire can be increased by exposing individuals to others whose behavioral responses to similar situations are more positive, particularly when the modeled behavior is rewarded. For example, someone raised in an environment in which violence is a familiar means of daily interaction, may grow up feeling that violence is a normal part of human interaction. Exposing the individual to family models who are rewarded for demonstrating healthier ways of communicating and negotiating differences is one way to change this normalization of violence. However, for the behavior to be performed and maintained, the individual's new behaviors must be positively reinforced.

Social learning theory is primarily concerned with present events because current behavior is the focus, although the past is important to the degree that it provides a learning history and context. One of the theory's basic tenets is that behavior is learned and can be changed by altering the stimulus conditions which control that behavior, whether controlling conditions precede or follow the identified behavior. However, humans have the ability to cognitively influence their perception of the environment, and human behavior is not completely determined by external stimuli. Thus, interventions geared at effectively addressing any population's needs require the incorporation of both an individual's environmental conditions and the cognitions that shape their reality, because it is the client's perceptions about what is deemed valuable that determines their behavior.

METHODOLOGY

Given that appropriate measures have not been designed to capture the variables of interest, this exploratory study conducted as part of an agency program evaluation employed qualitative, in-depth interviews. The open-ended interviews were aimed at capturing the experiences of battered, immigrant Mexican women as a first step in understanding their experiences with spousal abuse from their own perspectives. The ethnographic, pilot data were used in the present study to determine relevant variables to explore in future research with a larger, more representative sample.

Sample Selection

Sample selection took place at a family preservation program in East Los Angeles, serving primarily Latino families identified by the Los Angeles County Department of Children and Family Services for the maltreatment of children, primarily opened due to violence on the male's part. Employing purposive sampling procedures, agency counselors initially identified ten battered, immigrant Mexican women as potential respondents and invited them to participate. Given ethical and safety concerns, all subjects were required to be receiving services at the agency and to be separated from their batterers at the time of the interview. Each participant was also provided with two toll-free, 24-hour domestic violence hotline numbers.

Seven of the interviews were conducted at the agency in a private room; the other three in the subjects' home on their request. All interview sessions were conducted by the author, in the subject's language of preference, and were audio recorded with the participant's awareness. Participants were compensated twenty-five dollars for their time, informed that the tapes were confidential, and would eventually be transcribed and destroyed.

Instrumentation

The interviewer employed a semi-structured interview schedule consisting of open and closed-ended questions that was simultaneously developed in English and Spanish by the researcher who is bilingual and bicultural. English and Spanish versions were provided to agency staff and to a licensed community nurse from Tijuana, Mexico, to assess for vocabulary and question structure appropriateness.

The first section of the interview schedule was comprised of closed-ended questions to obtain basic demographic information about the respondents, their husbands/partners, and their children. In each of the following sections, the researcher attempted not to bias the respondents' answers by first providing each with the opportunity to describe her experiences at length without being prompted regarding specific factors that were of interest to the researcher. Thereafter, the researcher requested information on various factors to assure that specific variables were addressed.

The second section contained open-ended questions that elicited information regarding gender-role expectations, specifically: subjects' core beliefs about men and women's socially appropriate behavior; the socially appropriate treatment of women and men towards each other; the parental roles and responsibilities of men and women; the marital roles and responsibilities of men and women; and the appropriate treatment of spouses/partners towards each other.

The third section employed open-ended questions directed at obtaining participants' own behavior-specific definitions of physical abuse between spouses/partners (e.g., What type of behavior in a man towards his wife/partner would you describe as physically abusive?) Subsequent elaborations were elicited with probes (e.g., silence, repeating the question, reiterating their own comments in question form, asking for elaboration or examples). Thereafter, the researcher provided specific examples of physically abusive behaviors to ascertain subjects' perceptions of the behaviors (e.g., How would you describe the behavior of a man who slaps his wife/partner?).

The fourth section used open-ended questions to uncover attitudes about physically abusive behaviors using the participants' own definitions of physical abuse (e.g., Please tell me what you think about a situation in which a man [*using respondent's own definitions of physical abuse*] his wife/partner? Do you think that a woman should do anything if her husband/partner [*respondent's own definitions of physical abuse*] her?) This inquiry was again followed by questions regarding specific examples of physically abusive behaviors (e.g., Please tell me what you think about a situation in which a man slaps his wife/partner? Do you think that a woman should do anything if her husband/partner slaps her? Do you think that a man should do anything if he slaps his wife/partner?).

The fifth section contained open-ended questions exploring subjects' personal experiences with physical abuse, including a description of male and female behaviors before, during, and after their physically abusive experiences.

In the sixth section, open-ended questions obtained information regarding their specific help-seeking behaviors or lack thereof, the rationale guiding their actions, and the usefulness of the assistance. Ensuing questions identified specific sources of help not mentioned by the subjects and their rationale for not seeking this assistance.

Inquiries were then directed at exploring whether the respondent ever considered specific factors in deciding whether or not to seek help for the physical abuse, including their social support system, cultural factors related to family, religion and gender-role expectations, and psycho-social stressors such as legal status, financial situation, and English-speaking ability.

All ten participant interviews were completed over a six month period, and lasted one hour and forty-four minutes to three hours and forty minutes, with two hours and fifteen minutes being the average length.

Data Analysis

Secondary data analysis[1] was used for purposes of this article. Descriptive statistics were used to analyze the quantitative data. The qualitative data were analyzed utilizing a type of content analysis called "conceptual analysis" (Carley, 1994), in which concepts are defined as "a single idea" (p. 726) whether formulated by one word or an entire phrase and can either be explicit or implicit. Key concepts, as well as phrases or words comparable to those concepts, were delin-

---

1. It is secondary data analysis inasmuch as the data were collected by the agency for a program evaluation, and the source of the data is the written report using anonymous data.

eated and a list created that allowed for like concepts to be identified in the text of the interviews.

FINDINGS

Demographic Profile

Participants' length of time in the United States ranged from three to 21 years, with average length of 13.22 years (see Table 1). Nine of the participants were monolingual Spanish speakers. The other participant was completely bilingual, but preferred to be interviewed in Spanish and reported speaking mostly Spanish in her home.

The sample was evenly divided between those who reported being married, and those who had cohabitated with their partners. The women varied in the length of time they had been separated from their batterers with an average of two years and three months. Overall, women reported having been with their spouses/partners an average of 11.15 years (see Table 1). Half of the women met and joined/married their mates in Mexico before coming to this country.

The modal number of children was four with a maximum of ten and a minimum of three (see Table 1). All minor children were living with their mothers, with the exception of one family.

The women's average age was 34.9 years. Men were on the average five and a half years older than their mates, with an average age of 38.6 and a range of 50 to 33 years of age.

The participants had an average educational attainment of sixth grade (see Table 1). Eight women had been solely educated in Mexico. Their mates had a lower average level of education at 4.14 years, with a high of six years and a low of three years.

While with their spouses/partners, all women identified as home-makers. Some of the women had desired to work; however, their mates prohibited them from looking for a job. Only two of the women indicated that their partners had permanent, full-time jobs during their unions. Five women reported that their partners had temporary part-time jobs, two that their partners had been unemployed, and one woman was not aware of her partner's occupation. Only one woman could actually report an approximate dollar amount when referring to her mate's monthly income, and the total he contributed to the house-

TABLE 1. Participant Characteristics

Length of Time in the U.S.

21 Years	1
19 Years	1
18 Years	1
16 Years	2
12 Years	1
11 Years	1
7 Years	1
6 Years	2
Total	**10**

Marital Status

Married	5
Lived Together	4
Sporadic Living Arrangement	1
Total	**10**

Length of Union with Husband/Partner

27 Years	1
13 Years	2
11 Years	3
6 Years	1
4 Years	2
1 1/2 Years	1
Total	**10**

Length of Separation

72 Months	1
48 Months	2
24 Months	2
18 Months	1
16 Months	1
12 Months	1
11 Months	1
3 Months	1
Total	**10**

Number of Children

Ten	1
Six	2
Four	5
Three	2
Total	**10**

TABLE 1 (continued)

Participant Age

47 Years	1
44 Years	1
38 Years	2
36 Years	1
34 Years	1
30 Years	2
29 Years	1
23 Years	1
Total	**10**

Education

10th Grade U.S.	1
9th Grade Mexico	1
7th Grade U.S.	1
7th Grade Mexico	1
6th Grade Mexico	4
3rd Grade Mexico	1
None	1
Total	**10**

hold. Nine of the women reported not having the slightest idea regarding their mate's financial contribution to supporting the household, much less their income. Of the same nine women, seven revealed that ultimately their mates did not really contribute financially to the family's livelihood in a consistent manner, if at all. The other two participants reported that their mates paid rent and utilities, but never gave them money directly.

At the time of the interview, participants reported a monthly household income average of $1,066.70, with a maximum monthly income of $1,982 and a minimum of $565. This monthly income is relatively low considering that the average number of children per household was five.

Family Background Information

Either the male or the female, or both, in all ten couples had directly experienced or was exposed to abuse in their family of origin. Seven women were physically abused by a family member and/or their mother was physically abused by their father. Eight women reported that their husbands/partners were raised in violent environments. Four women voluntarily disclosed sexual abuse experiences during the course of the interview. Two women felt that their home environment was not abusive.

Half of the women also reported excessive drinking in both their own and/or their mate's family of origin. Eighty percent of the women indicated that their mates drank excessively. Four participants also reported that their batterers were physically abusive only when intoxicated.

Experiences with Domestic Violence

Invariably, women disclosed that the physical abuse in their relationships started as soon as they moved in with their mates. To identify just a few of their experiences, women reported being slapped, having their hair pulled, being hit with objects, being punched in the stomach resulting in hospitalization, being beaten until bleeding occurred, having their heads banged against floors and walls, being choked, being beaten in the face so badly that vision was impaired, and being whipped in the back with a butcher's knife. They were asked to rate each case of physical abuse along a five point scale ranging from very serious to definitely not serious. The majority (n = 7) of participants rated each incident of abuse as serious to very serious.

At least six women reported that they were abused on a regular basis, ranging from daily, to three times a week, to every two to three weeks. Others who initially reported low-frequencies for abusive behaviors or were rather vague about reporting any episodes disclosed a higher frequency in response to interviewer probes.

Perceptions

When asked to provide their own behavior-specific definitions of physical abuse between spouses/partners, six women provided at least one concrete example of physical abuse in their own words, which included immediate or eventual physical contact.

> Well, . . . when [he] strikes you or pulls your hair. . . . Physically, one becomes traumatized with this sort of situation . . . When [a woman] is pushed, socked, or their hair is pulled that is the worse

thing that can happen . . . [Together 19 years/married 11 years, mother of 4, age 47]

Hitting, . . . can [happen] in many ways (Probe) kicking her, socking, slapping. [Together 6 years, mother of 4, age 23]

Three women either provided only nonphysical examples of physical abuse or were unable to provide a response.

Snapping fingers, name calling [Married 11 years, mother of 6, age 30]

Physical abuse? What do you mean? (Reiterated question) I wouldn't know what to tell you. (Reiterated) . . . I'm not going to say what I'm thinking because it will come out there [on recording], and it sounds really awful. (Interviewer assured respondent) [Silence]. [Together 3 years, mother of 3, age 29]

Five of the participants included verbal abuse in their definitions of physical abuse.

. . . physical abuse is when one [husband/partner] is saying things that make [wife/partner] feel bad. For example, you're nothing, you're not worth anything, you're a despicable woman . . . [Together 19 years/ married 11 years, mother of 4, age 47]

Three women also included sexual abuse in their perceptions about physical abuse. Two other women interpreted physical restraint as sexual and physical abuse.

I was sick, and [husband] wanted to have [intimate] relations, and I told him, "No." And he forced me. [Married 11 years, mother of 6, age 30]

It is the worst thing that [husband/partner] could do, physically restrain a woman [sexually] when she wants nothing to do with him . . . [Together 19 years/married 11 years, mother of 4, age 47]

Four women included other behaviors in their definitions of physical abuse such as breaking possessions, threatening with weapons, and "poisoning children's minds" against their mother.

Eight of the women found the actions they had identified as physically abusive at all times. Two other participants mentioned exceptions to their responses.

> Sometimes, in my way of thinking, [women] are at fault. (Probe) He comes home tired from work, and the only thing that he says is, "Stop bothering me." But she continues, and that's why sometimes a man gets to the point of striking. [Together 4 years, mother of 4, age 34]

To ascertain the women's ability to identify physical abuse, the interviewer also provided participants with behavior-specific examples denoting physical abuse, including: slapping, pushing, physically restraining, choking, hitting with a closed hand, hitting with an object, pulling hair, and kicking. In eighty percent of the cases, women identified these behaviors as physically abusive.

All but one of the participants, when specifically questioned, indicated that they considered their own past experiences as abusive. Nevertheless, four of these women reported previously normalizing the physical abuse, and eight respondents relayed tolerating the abuse for a variety of reasons.

> . . . I had problems in my childhood, psychological problems, how my parents were, they lived a life of arguments, blows and violations. I think that does a lot of damage to a person, and more when you get married. You continue to do the same [abuse] . . . Despite their problems, [my mother and father] stayed together until the end . . . I would have liked to have finished my life and my relationship [marriage] the same way. [Together 19 years/ married 11 years, mother of 4, age 47]

> My mother believed/said, "You wanted to leave [the house], God Bless you, I give you my blessings, whether they eat you, kill you, I present you, you gave yourself . . ." I thought that was how life was, and I accepted it however it came. [Married 11 years, mother of 4, age 30]

> I saw [abuse] as normal because it was the relationship I [chose]. I gave him 13 years and he didn't change . . . [In Mexico], [abuse] is normal. No one gets involved because you're [married], no one

interferes . . . [In Mexico] they say [you learn] as a child, that when you are joined with someone, you have to tolerate your [spouse/partner]. [Together 13 years, mother of 4, age 38]

Attitudes

However, women's attitudes about hypothetical occurrences of physical abuse involving someone else elicited an altogether different variation of responses. Half of the sample felt that a woman who was being physically abused should attempt to defend herself by running or by blocking abuse attempts in some way. Two participants indicated that a woman should respond with violence in defense.

Seven women felt that some type of communication should take place between spouses/partners after an abusive episode in an effort to reach a mutual understanding for stopping the abuse. Half of the participants also reported that a woman should inquire as to why husband/partner abused her.

> Well, she shouldn't accept it, but she can't defend herself. The man becomes more furious. In that situation a woman can't do anything anymore. But later, she can talk with husband/partner and let him know that he is not treating her right, and that it is not acceptable. [Married 13 years, mother of 6, age 38]

> She should wait till the situation has calmed down, and then talk with [husband/partner]. Ask him why he [slapped her] . . . come to some sort of an agreement that something has to be done to discontinue the violence. [Married 11 years, mother of 6, age 30]

Two of these women talked as if the woman had caused their husband's/partner's violence or that a woman could prevent the violence by knowing what exactly caused the violent reaction.

> If he slaps her, the husband should tell her why, what was the motive. (Probe) He should talk with her, and [explain] what it was he didn't like. "I don't like it when you do that or I don't like you to say this, or I don't like it when you embarrass me in front of other people." In other words, give an explanation [for his behavior]. [Together 4 years, mother of 4, age 34]

Seven participants also indicated that a woman should call the police. Three of the participants did not mention any kind of police intervention, although two of these women felt a restraining order was a possible course of action.

> Well, if she has [physical] marks, she should call the police . . . one stays quiet [if there are no marks] because one can't say anything because [mate] will deny it. [Married 27 years, mother of 10, age 44]

Half of the sample felt a woman should leave her husband/partner, although two of the women put conditions on the separation.

> Talk with him, come to some sort of an agreement that [abuse] won't happen again or how are we going to remedy the situation. Because if she just leaves, the problem is not solved . . . [Together 19 years/married 11 years, mother of 4, age 47]

> Yes, [she] needs to do something. She needs to separate for good, but if she loves him, she'll tolerate it. [Married 11 years, mother of 4, age 30]

When participants were questioned on actions they felt men should take after they had already abused their wives/partners, half of the women reported that a man should seek out some type of help, usually therapeutic or professional in nature.

> If he continues abuse [after talking], then he needs to ask for help . . . with a social worker, someone who specializes in helping with [abuse], a counselor. [Together 19 years/married 11 years, mother of 4, age 47]

Nine women in the sample indicated that a man should apologize, ask for forgiveness, or "think about" his behavior as well as put and end to the abuse.

> He also needs to talk, "Forgive me. Yesterday I came home upset with a problem, and well . . . Forgive me for what I did." But, [abuse] needs to stop. [Together 19 years/married 11 years, mother of 4, age 47]

[He should] say that he's not going to do it anymore and ask for forgiveness. [Together 6 years, mother of 4, age 23]

Four participants were at a loss as to any actions a man could take after abusing his wife/partner, although ultimately two of these women basically felt that police were the only recourse.

What do you mean? . . . I don't know what he should do [after abuse]. That's a hard question. [Together 4.5 years, mother of 3, age 36]

. . . Like what? What can he do? If he hits [a woman], he can't do anything . . . [Together 3 years, mother of 3, age 29]

Cultural Factors

Familialism and Gender-Role Expectations. Only three of the women reported considering their families of origin and/or extended families in deciding whether to seek help for the physical abuse. Concerns for two of these women centered on their husband's/partner's immediate family. The other seven women indicated that they did not consider their or their spouse's/partner's immediate and/or extended families.

Nine participants reported that the responsibility for their children's welfare was a major factor in deciding to seek help. The one exception indicated that she did not consider the welfare of her children, because she did not feel that her children were being affected by the abusive situation.

I tried to make it work so that [husband] could be with us . . . it didn't work. I worried about damage he could continue to do to the children because he was [very physically and emotionally abusive] with children. I thought I would look for help. Then, I thought, well, he's the father of my children. I'll wait a little longer to see if [husband] changes . . . for children, but he didn't change. [Married 27 years, mother of 10, age 44]

I thought that [the abuse] was wrong, everything that he did to me. And in the future, my children would [repeat the same thing], mistreat their wives because they [experienced it]. They [children] still yell [at each other]. The damage has already been done. [Married 11 years, mother of 4, age 30]

. . . I left him because he slapped my [5 year old] son. That was the main [reason] why I left him. [Together 6 years, mother of 4, age 23]

I only thought about my children . . . One thinks about their children first and what one has to do. [Together 4.5 years, mother of 3, age 36]

Three women reported that they did consider their roles and responsibilities as a wife in deciding whether to seek help, and three women intertwined their marital and maternal roles and responsibilities.

As a wife, I asked for help because I saw that he was not well. It was my obligation as a wife to try to help him. [Married 11 years, mother of 6, age 30]

I didn't want to destroy the little bit of a marriage that I did have . . . As a wife, I looked for a stable relationship for all of my life. [Together 19 years/married 11 years, mother of 4, age 47]

Religion. Eight women in the sample reported that they were Catholic. Four of the participants indicated that they did not consider church or their religion in deciding whether to seek help for the physical abuse, while three other women indicated religion was a factor in their decision process.

Yes, I would ask God for a solution to my problem. Why [was this happening]? It isn't right for a woman to go from one partner to another. That isn't living with God. [Together 19 years/married 11 years, mother of 4, age 47]

Psycho-Social Stressors

Legal Status. Four women reported that they were still undocumented. Two of these women reported concerns about their legal status in previous decisions about seeking help, and their children were a primary element of that consideration.

> Yes, because [husband] would say that [law enforcement] would take me back to Mexico and not give me help because I didn't have papers. I would get scared. Life with him and the abuse was better than my life in Mexico, the better of two hells . . . [Married 11 years, mother of 4, age 30]

> [Partner] didn't want me to fix my papers . . . Sometimes I was scared because I didn't have my papers. If I called for help or we were separated, I might have some problems. He would discourage me from fixing my papers, "What for?" He threatened that he would take the children away from me. [Together 13 years, mother of 4, age 38]

Two other women, presently official residents, reported concerns related to deportation prior to becoming legalized. Only one of these women stated that her partner actually threatened her with deportation. Four other participants, official U.S. residents, relayed that their legal status never came to mind when contemplating help, even prior to their legalization.

English Speaking Abilities. Seven women reported that their English speaking ability was not a consideration in deciding whether to seek help. Respondents indicated that they were confident that someone would be able to communicate with them.

Three women indicated that they did consider their English speaking abilities. However, they all reported that they would still seek assistance.

> Well yes, because [partner] is very smart. I was afraid that if I called for help, because he speaks English well, that they would believe him, like that one time with the police, and I would get scared. But, I was more afraid that they would take my children. That is why I tolerated [abuse]. [Together 13 years, mother of 4, age 38]

Economics. Seven participants also indicated that their financial situations were not considered when deciding whether to seek help for their abusive situations, although, some of these women reported that economic concerns existed.

> No, because I was receiving assistance and he didn't help me at all. I think that if he would have helped me economically, I would

have thought to myself–What am I going to do? But since he didn't help me with anything . . . [Married 11 years, mother of 6, age 30]

Three women reported that their financial situation was a consideration in deciding whether to seek help.

Yes, in that [financial] respect, it was a concern because he worked, and I didn't work at that time. And I used to think to myself–What am I going to do with my daughter? Because at that time, I only had one daughter. In this country, where was I going to go without any money. [Together 19/ married 11 years, mother of 4, age 47]

Well yes, because at the beginning, my children and I depended on him financially. Even if he never gave me money, he paid the rent. [Together 13 years, mother of 4, age 38]

Social Support. Six women related that they did not consider their social support in deciding whether to seek help, primarily because they did not feel like they had social support.

I didn't have support from anyone. I had a brother who wouldn't help because he feared problems with [partner]. I would think about how I didn't have any [social] support even if I wasn't thinking about looking for help. [Together 6 years, mother of 4, age 23]

Three women responded positively to considering their social support in deciding whether to seek help for physical abuse.

Yes, with my sisters because I used to have two sisters [nearby geographically]. I used to have cousins and extended family here, lots. [Together 19/married 11 years, mother of 4, age 47]

Well, [the ones] who are helping me right now are my comadre and my compadre. [Married 27 years, mother of 10, age 44]

Help-Seeking

Women were asked if they ever considered seeking any type of help or assistance following the abusive incidents. Eight of the women indicated that seeking help was simply never considered.

I didn't think. It never really came to mind to look for help. [Together 6 years, mother of 4, age 23]

I didn't know about help [for domestic violence], or that there was help or anything like that. I think that if I would have known before . . . that classes for domestic violence existed, I would have come before all of this happened. [Married 11 years, mother of 6, age 30]

Three other women reported a range of factors that kept them from considering help, including: fear that help would be refused, and they would find themselves alone and helpless and/or unwanted; concerns regarding children and their bond with their father; and a perceived increased risk of danger.

Yes [I would think about seeking help], but I would shut the doors on myself. I would get scared and think "Who would want me?" Without work, what was I going to do? How was I going to support my four children? [Married 11 years, mother of 4, age 30]

No, I didn't think, because I thought that if I asked for help, he was going to kill me or beat me. [Married 27 years, mother of 10, age 44]

Specific Sources of Help

The women were provided information regarding specific sources of help that they may have considered in dealing with the domestic violence in their lives.

Police. Seven participants who called on the police during their physically abusive experiences had mixed opinions about the assistance they received. Four women felt satisfied with the assistance they had received from the police.

[The police helped] by taking [partner] so that he wasn't there anymore. [Together 4.5 years, mother of 3, age 36]

Two women felt that the police did not hold their mates long enough, and they were released too soon to be of any benefit. In fact, two other women reported that when their batterers were released from jail, their situations only became worse.

The police jailed him about three times, but then they would let him go. When he broke the window, he was in jail for a week. He returned to the house 15 days later, slashed all my tires, and broke my car so it didn't work anymore . . . [Together 6 years, mother of 4, age 23]

[The police] would take him but never hold him more than, let's say 24 hours. The next day [the police] would let him out again. [My husband] would return to the house, and [the abuse would continue], and it was worse! . . . because he would [use the fact that I had called] the police [against me]. [Married 11 years/together 19 years, mother of 4, age 47]

One woman's batterer, fluent in English, managed to talk himself out of being at fault when she had called the police.

I showed the police the bumps on my head and my bruised hand. [He] told the police that I had hit him . . . [The police] believed him! I was too out-of-it to defend myself, but [the police] didn't take him. I wanted them to take him out of my house. [Together 13 years, mother of 4, age 38]

Two women reported that, initially, they felt the police had not responded appropriately.

I called [the police], but they didn't show up until days later. [Married 27 years, mother of 10, age 44]

However, these two women eventually got the type of assistance they expected from the police. Consequently, they reported not hesitating to call in the future if they had a need.

Friends. Participants also reported varied opinions about going to friends for help. One woman revealed that she had a very close friend (comadre) that she confided in about the abuse; however, her husband eventually prohibited her from seeing her friend. One other woman also reported having a friend that she could talk to about the abuse. Both of these women felt that just being able to talk about their situations was beneficial to them.

. . . to talk with her [was helpful], to pour out my troubles. I trust [friend] a lot. She knows my whole life. [Together 4.5 years, mother of 3, age 36]

Four of the women reported that although they had friends they could talk to, they would not tell their friends about the abuse.

> I would just talk to her [friend] about the children. I didn't like to talk about my problems. They [problems] were mine and my husband's. [Married 11 years, mother of 6, age 30]

> Well, I always talked to my friend about my problems, but not about [abuse]. I felt bad telling her because my friend seemed to be well [no abuse] with her husband. [Married 13 years, mother of 4, age 38]

Two other women revealed that they had previously gone to friends in an attempt to leave their batterers, but later returned because they felt they inconvenienced their friends.

> One time, I did go to a friend's house, but then I didn't [go] anymore because she [friend] didn't want to get mixed up in any kind of problem. [Together 4.5 years, mother of 3, age 36]

Family/Relatives. Surprisingly, participants differed in their responses to seeking out family help for the physical abuse in their lives, even when support was available. In part, this was due to the fact that women did not feel the assistance family provided was beneficial. Three women reported that they sought out family members for assistance, but received undesirable reactions.

> Sometimes I would talk with my sister, but I didn't like to tell her much because she would scold me right away. She would tell me that it was my fault because I was tolerating it [abuse]. [Married 11 years/together 19 years, mother of 4, age 47]

The two other participants were advised to tolerate the situation when they sought help from family.

> She [mother-in-law] would tell me that I had to tolerate him because he was my husband, and because we were married. "Have patience with him. He will change." [Married 11 years, mother of 6, age 30]

> I have two sisters and a brother [here], and they want the children's father to be with me. And I don't want to have anything to

do with [husband]. They [family] didn't want to help me for anything. [Married 27 years, mother of 10, age 44]

Four participants reported that their family lived too far away. However, these women also felt that if their family had been closer geographically, provided that family was supportive in a desirable fashion, women would have turned to them in times of need. One woman did not turn to her family for support, because she felt the domestic violence was a private matter.

Church/Priest. Eight participants identified as Catholic, and six of the women indicated attending church regularly. Two of these women did not feel comfortable talking with the church priest about their situations.

> No, [I did not consider church or a priest] because I was embarrassed to talk with the Father [Catholic priest] because I hadn't made my [first holy] communion. [Married 11 years, mother of 4, age 30]

However, three women reported seeking out church personnel for aid including help for their mates. A nun and a priest eventually encouraged two of the women to leave their batterers, because their mates were resistant to any assistance or change.

> The Father [priest] would listen to me, and tell me I had to leave him [husband]. [Married 13 years, mother of 6, age 38]

> I talked to the nun [from the children's catechism class] about the problems [abuse] . . . The nun told him that if he wasn't going to treat me well, that it was better for him to leave me. He refused, and the nun recommended a separation. [Together 13 years, mother of 4, age 38]

The third woman attempted to seek help for her husband at two different churches. At one particular church, personnel went as far as paying a home visit in an attempt to help the participant. However, her husband was resistant and exited out the back door before church personnel arrived.

The women felt that the interaction with church personnel was personally beneficial, providing them with some emotional release.

At least I felt listened to. I was able to vent. I wasn't as worried afterwards. It was like therapy. [Married 13 years, mother of 6, age 38]

They gave me a lot of good advice (e.g., treat him like this, talk with him, avoid arguments, try to calm him, try to calm yourself, watch out for the children, don't fight in front of the children) They always gave me very good advice; it helped me a lot. [Married 11 years, mother of 6, age 30]

Moreover, women who reported attending church regularly, but not asking for assistance, and those women who just prayed at home, relayed that prayer alone was beneficial to them.

I would pray to God to help me and not to abandon me and my children. That was all I asked, and it was like my problem was smaller because I had shared it with God. [Married 11 years/together 19 years, mother of 4, age 47]

. . . I've always continued to have great faith. I've always asked God [for help with abuse]. [Married 11 years, mother of 4, age 30]

Counselor. Few women in the study sought professional counseling services. Five women reported that they had never considered going to counseling for the physical abuse. One woman relayed that she would have gone to a counselor if she had had some information. Three other participants indicated having talked with counselors in their attempts to deal with the domestic violence in their lives, but only after they had been referred by someone else. Two of these women had accessed counselors via school personnel where their children were attending. Both women had also sought assistance for their mates. Although, one participant's partner was resistant to the assistance, the other woman's husband had actually accompanied her to the school to see the counselor.

I was going to a clinic for the children's medical needs. I talked to the psychologist there about my headaches from continuous tension with [husband] . . . The doctor referred me because of the severe headaches. I went to the psychologist once a month for six months. He [husband] didn't know I went to the psychologist, but he knew I went to the clinic for the children. [Married 11 years/together 19 years, mother of 4, age 47]

I only talked with the school nurse. I wanted her to help my husband because he would bang his head against the wall every day [to avoid hitting his wife according to the respondent]. I talked to the counselor at school, then I was referred to the school psychologist. But she [psychologist] didn't speak Spanish, so there were three interpreters . . . [Her preference was] that they [the school] call a psychologist to help him . . . that they [school personnel] would have sent us both to school and made us understand that there was help for him and for me, that they could help us so we wouldn't fight so much anymore, for the children, etc. But it wasn't like that. [Married 11 years, mother of 6, age 30]

Shelter. Shelters were not considered an option for dealing with abuse for eight of the women. This was largely due to lack of information regarding shelters. At least four of the participants stated that they did not know what shelters were or that they existed when they were in their violent relationships. One woman, who had been separated from her batterer two years, was still unaware of the existence of shelters at the time of the interview.

Three other participants reported that they were aware of shelters. However, they were uninformed about relevant information regarding shelters (e.g., addresses are not public information), leaving some with fears about their batterers eventually locating them. Four women indicated they would have accessed shelters if they had had more specific information about shelters at the time. Two women felt that the shelter atmosphere would be uncomfortable.

No, [I never considered shelters]. I didn't think that they would allow me to be there with my children. I was afraid that he would be able to find me, because he manages to harass us wherever we go. I was afraid that wherever, if I asked for help or anything, that he would follow me and take my children . . . [Together 13 years, mother of 4, age 38]

No, they [shelters] never really appealed to me. I feel like one cannot be comfortable there. Once, I saw one on television . . .

everyone on top of each other, living together. [Together 3 years, mother of 3, age 29]

No, [never considered shelters] because I didn't want to be in those houses. My sister lived in one of those, and the truth is that I don't like them because it's like you're always being watched. I would feel pressured. My sister liked the shelter, but [her] children couldn't go outside and play. [Married 11 years, mother of 6, age 30]

Two women reported that they had called shelters at some point, but that their interactions with personnel ultimately left them cynical about shelters.

I didn't really think of shelters, because I called once and they never came for me. The lady at the shelter told me to get ready with a suitcase for me and the children that any minute someone would call and come by. No one ever did. My world would just close in on me from so many problems. [Married 11 years/together 19 years, mother of 4, age 47]

Another woman called a shelter and talked with a staff member. However, the only thing the participant remembered was being told that her children could be removed because of the domestic violence. Consequently, she was afraid to ever consider shelters again, fearing loss of her children.

Other Sources of Assistance. Other sources of assistance were used by very few of the women. Although women reported going to the doctor for their children's medical needs, they had never thought about this avenue for dealing with their abuse. However, two women were referred for mental health services after seeking help for medical conditions and another for suicidal ideations.

Only two of the ten women reported that they had turned to a spiritualist (curandero) in their attempts to deal with the physical abuse in their lives. One woman felt that her single visit was somewhat beneficial, and the second that the experience was not helpful and simply an elaborate scheme to make money.

Two other women had sought assistance through Al-Anon; however, their husbands eventually prohibited their participation.

DISCUSSION

The purpose of the study was to explore the role of cultural factors and psycho-social stressors in battered immigrant Mexican women's perceptions regarding abuse; their attitudes about seeking help; and how these perceptions and attitudes affected their actual help-seeking behaviors.

Perceptions of and Attitudes Towards Tolerance of Abuse

All of the women in the sample had tolerated the abuse for many years before leaving the relationship. The findings indicate that the tolerance of the abuse and their hesitancy or willingness to seek help was not due to an inability to perceive their husbands'/partners' behavior as abusive. Eighty percent of the women in the study clearly and consistently identified physically abusive behaviors. Moreover, the ability to identify abusive behaviors did not appear to be affected by cultural factors or psycho-social stressors.

Tolerance of the abuse was related to the women's attitudes towards physical abuse rather than their perceptions. These attitudes appeared to be strongly influenced by cultural factors and minimally affected by psycho-social stressors (e.g., immigrant status and financial dependency). For example, tolerating the abuse reflected cultural beliefs regarding Hispanic gender-role expectations and marriage as a life-long commitment that received social reinforcement from significant others in their environment.

For at least half of the women, their attitudes towards tolerating the abuse were also reflective of childhood exposure to domestic violence as a result of which they learned to "normalize" abuse and to model their mothers' tolerance of the abusive situation. However, in contrast to their own situation, when women were presented with hypothetical abusive situations involving someone else, abusive behavior was not interpreted as normal or tolerable.

Four women reported changes in their internal processes only after receiving some type of assistance for their abuse which helped them recognize that abuse was not normal and tolerable behavior. These women ranged from three months to four years in their period of separation from their batterers. Thus, length of separation did not seem to be related to their attitudinal changes. Women felt that because they had received some type of treatment, whether it was individual or group intervention, their internal processes of normalizing the abuse had been changed and their reaction to abusive behavior was intolerance (see Figure 1).

The majority of the sample identified as Catholic, and reported finding some solace in their religion. All participants appeared to exercise their faith, whether or not they were active in church. However, contrary to what the literature may convey (Zambrano, 1985; Flores-Ortiz, 1993), religious beliefs do not appear to be a major determinant of the women's attitudes towards tolerating abuse in their marriage. Only two respondents stated that religious considerations influenced their attitudes, keeping them from leaving their abusers. Moreover, in two specific instances, Catholic church personnel, a priest and a nun, actually encouraged women to leave their batterers.

Help-Seeking Behavior

The primary factor determining the help-seeking behavior of women in the sample was neither their gender-role expectations regarding their culturally designated behavior as a wife, nor the influence of the external family, but concern for the welfare of their children. It was the children who were specifically and consistently of paramount concern within women's descriptions of their families and their accounts of abuse regardless of the area of questioning. Gender-role expectations regarding maternal responsibility and the importance of family (defined in terms of their children) served as both incentives and barriers to seeking help at various points during their unions. For example, six of the women reported that it was internal processes regarding their children's well-being and/or beliefs about their children needing their father rather than cultural mandates or psycho-social (external) factors that accounted for their staying in their abusive situations. Moreover, women did not see themselves as long suffering martyrs as suggested in the literature (Flores-Ortiz, 1993), but rather, as being strong for their children. Paradoxically, nine of the participants revealed that their concern regarding the well-being of their children was also the main reason for their last separation from their husbands/partners. Ultimately, the possible negative consequences outweighed the perceived benefits to their children having a father figure.

Psycho-social stressors, compared to cultural factors, appeared to figure minimally in respondents' attitudes and their decisions to seek help. A total of four women specifically mentioned that they considered their resident status when making decisions about seeking help. Two of the participants' main concern ultimately revolved around their children and being able to provide for them. Again, it was the perceived consequences affecting their children that were of primary concern.

Given the sample's lack of English proficiency, one might expect this would be a barrier to seeking services for abuse. Although, three women did state that their lack of English-speaking abilities was a concern, they all reported that it was not enough of a deterrent to seeking help. One possible explanation for this finding is that they live in East Los Angeles which is a microcosm of the community from which they originally immigrated, and access to Spanish-speaking personnel in this community is common.

Only three women reported that their lack of financial stability was perceived as an obstacle to seeking help. Four other participants also mentioned financial concerns, but not as barriers to help-seeking. Perhaps this is not surprising given that seventy percent of the sample revealed that their mates contributed almost nothing to the family's livelihood.

Interestingly, for many of these women, financial concerns were rooted in being able to provide for their children. Yet, when these same women had internally processed their abusive situations and decided that the violent environment was more detrimental to their children than a potentially negative financial situation, economics were no longer a concern in the decision to seek help. Central to their decisions was again what they perceived to be in the best interest of their children.

Six of the women perceived their social support systems as geographically and/or emotionally unavailable when they considered reaching out for assistance. This may be the case because all the women were immigrants and their extended family support system may have been outside the country. Ironically, while immigrants may have stronger traditional values regarding familial ties and support, their circumstances make these resources less available to them compared to their American-born cohorts.

Two main categories of reasons discouraged women from seeking help: (1) misconceptions about a variety of factors such as the domestic violence itself, the consequences of seeking help, and specific sources of help; and (2) negative past experiences.

In terms of misconceptions, physical abuse was considered normal and acceptable by the majority of women for reasons previously discussed. Moreover, almost half of the women reported that they believed that domestic violence was a private matter to be dealt with between spouses/partners, and that this treatment of family matters was socially reinforced. At least three of the women specifically mentioned that a woman could literally disappear in Mexico and no one would ask questions or raise a finger.

Anticipation of punishing consequences deterred the women from seeking help. Women had fears about what could potentially happen to them and their families if they attempted to seek help. A number of participants believed that seeking help would somehow result in their losing custody of their children, and that any attempt to seek help would result in failure to escape their situations and a worsening of circumstances. Batterers threatened women with consequences associated with their leaving such as having their children taken away, claiming that they were bad mothers, or deportation. Some of these potential aversive consequences that prohibited their help-seeking behaviors were rooted in actual past experiences, while others were perceived consequences women were simply not willing to risk.

It was not uncommon for women to report that they were unaware that there was help for women in violent relationships. A couple of explanations could be offered for this phenomenon. First of all, battered women, in general, tend to be very isolated with little contact outside their home (Gelles, 1972; Zambrano, 1985). It was not uncommon for women in the study to report that when they had found a friend or family member who was supportive, that their mates had prohibited their continued contact. Second, because of their experiences with abuse in Mexico and lack of help in Mexico for victims of domestic violence, some women assumed a similar lack of attention and scarcity of such services in the United States. These women's learning histories had provided a reality that still existed for them despite the fact that they were in a different country.

Most revealing was the lack of knowledge or misconceptions regarding shelters. Almost half the women were unaware of shelters, and participants who were aware of shelters were uninformed about the secrecy of shelter locations. Thus, women often feared the consequences of their batterers eventually locating them.

Many of the women were discouraged in their help-seeking efforts, because past experiences had demonstrated that certain sources of help were not beneficial. For example, some women turned to the police, shelters, friends, and family members for assistance. However, if the assistance was somehow perceived as ineffective or even punishing based on past experience, women did not continue to seek out their help.

Conceptual Model

The conceptual model (see Figure 1) proposed by the author, was, for the most part, functional in examining the proposed research questions regarding the potential interactions of the major variables. However, some adaptations were required (see Figure 2). For example, cultural factors and psycho-social stressors did not appear to shape women's abilities to define physically abusive behavior in any fashion as may be suggested by the existing literature.

Inasmuch as the findings of this study indicated that attitudes towards abuse and attitudes towards seeking help for the abuse were not necessarily congruent, these two variables were separated in the revised model. For example, although the women's attitudes towards the

FIGURE 2. Revised Conceptual Model

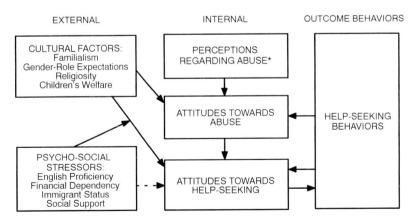

*Internalization of cultural and idiosyncratic factors

abuse reflected a desire for the abuse to cease, their attitudes towards help-seeking varied. While specific cultural factors strongly impelled some of the same women not to seek help, because they felt it was a matter to be dealt with privately or the children needed their father, other women were motivated to seek help because they were concerned for the welfare of their children. Women's attitudes about tolerating abuse and normalizing such behavior were reflective of the internalization of cultural beliefs regarding gender-role expectations and matrimony and exposure to the "normalization" of abuse by parental figures. Because children's welfare was one of the factors that consistently determined women's decisions about help-seeking behaviors regardless of the area of questioning, another revision was made in the original conceptual model, the addition of children's welfare to the list of cultural factors that influenced women's attitudes towards help-seeking. Additionally, when psycho-social stressors influenced help-seeking behaviors, it was the children's welfare that mediated the relationship between psycho-social stressors and attitudes towards seeking help. Psycho-social stressors, in and of themselves, had a minimal impact on the women's attitudes towards help-seeking for the abuse as reflected by the dotted line.

Lastly, actual help-seeking behaviors appeared to impact women's attitudes towards abuse as well as their attitudes towards seeking help. The consequences of their initial help-seeking behaviors were internalized as attitudes towards help-seeking that increased (due to positive consequences) or decreased (due to punishing consequences) their help-seeking behavior. Women's attitudes about help-seeking remained stable until the consequences of new experiences with help-seeking contradicted their originally held attitudes.

IMPLICATIONS

The findings from the study offer a number of implications for practice in dealing with battered, immigrant Mexican women. For example, although women's attitudes towards physical abuse had previously resulted in their normalizing and tolerating abuse, they did not indicate comparable normalization and tolerance when discussing hypothetical situations of physical abuse involving someone else. This indicates that directly focusing on the woman's situation may not be effective in changing her attitudes towards tolerating abuse. Instead, the women may be more receptive to psycho-educational groups in which battered women share and listen to the experiences of others and discuss hypothetical situations and appropriate responses to abuse.

The findings indicate that the women were ultimately open to seeking help regardless of the previous impact of cultural factors and their childhood exposure to violence on their formerly held attitudes about seeking help. The primary driving force was the welfare of their children. This finding has important practice implications for interventions from public service announcements to actual treatment modalities. For example, public service announcements that emphasize the importance of seeking help for domestic violence because of the specific effects that potentially impact the family, particularly the children's overall welfare, rather than the effects of domestic violence to the individual may be more effective in getting battered, immigrant Mexican women to reach out for help.

Given the prominent role that family has in the lives of these women, it becomes important to develop prevention, intervention, and treatment efforts geared at maintaining the family unit when safely possible. A family-oriented focus may increase the likelihood that battered women, such as those represented by this sample, will more readily seek out domestic violence services, especially if such services are seen as linked to the welfare of their children and to maintaining the integrity of the family.

Moreover, when examining participants' help-seeking behaviors, it was common for their efforts to be focused on finding assistance for their husbands/partners in order to preserve their family. A necessary element of assistance to this population is incorporating the batterers into the delivery of services. To minimize their resistance, services designed or modified to include male counterparts in domestic violence groups could be labeled in such a manner that the potential stigma associated with these groups is limited. For example, a couple's group could be designed with the objectives of learning about communication, conflict resolution and anger management. In order to better understand the barriers to seeking help from the batterers' perspectives, further research is needed.

Given that televisions and radios were household appliances that most all respondents reported owning, even if they had no telephone, these avenues of communication may prove to be efficient and effective in disseminating valuable information about family violence to an

isolated population and the community at large. Public service announcements could be delivered in Spanish and aired during hours
when the batterer is likely to be out of the home, for example, during
the middle of the working day.

It is important that education on domestic violence be delivered in a
culturally syntonic fashion that emphasizes the family unit and how
everyone in the family is affected by any type of violence. Accurate
information should also be provided to address women's fears regarding removal of their children. Moreover, public service announcements could also help to educate the broader community about domestic violence and commonly held misconceptions such as the idea that
spousal abuse is a private matter. Community education would also
assist in fostering an environment that is encouraging of help-seeking
behaviors.

Many participants did not know about shelters or had misconceptions about them. Other women recalled negative experiences with
shelter and law enforcement personnel. Thus, complete and accurate
information about sources of assistance should also be disseminated
such as the existence of shelters, their purpose, the secrecy of their
locations, and how to access them. Professional and paraprofessionals
who assist battered women may also need to be educated on assistance
that is perceived as helpful by battered women and be culturally and
linguistically competent to deal with crisis situations.

Community outreach at schools and churches also becomes another
important means for disseminating educational information on family
violence, as parents appear to access these institutions with some
regularity. Several of the women reported accessing these establish-
ments for assistance.

LIMITATIONS

The objective of this study was to begin an in-depth examination of
variables that have been suggested in the literature as contributing to
the occurrence of domestic violence in the Mexican community. Giv-
en the small sample size and its selection, generalizations cannot be
made to any other group. Nevertheless, this pilot study has provided
some important insight regarding battered immigrant Mexican women's
experiences with physical abuse and their help-seeking behaviors. The

ethnographic data have provided an amplification of the factors presented in the literature and indicated points of deviation from proposed models that suggest areas of further research with larger, representative samples.

REFERENCES

Bachman, R., & Saltzman, L. E. (August 1995). *Violence Against Women: Estimates from the Redesigned Survey.* National Institute of Justice, Bureau of Justice Statistics, Special Report.

Bandura, A. (1971). *Social Learning Theory.* Morristown, NJ: General Learning Press.

Bandura, A. (1977). *Social Learning Theory.* Englewood Cliffs, NJ: Prentice-Hall, Inc.

Becerra, R. (1988). The Mexican American Family. In C. H. Mindel, R. W. Habenstein, and R. Wright (Eds.), *Ethnic Families in America: Patterns and Variations* (pp. 141-159). Englewood Cliffs, NJ: Prentice-Hall, Inc.

Bureau of Justice Statistics. (1993). U.S. Department of Justice. Sourcebook of Criminal Justice Statistics NCJ-143496. Washington, DC.

Carley, K. (1994). Content Analysis. In R. E. Asher & J. M. Y. Simpson (Eds.) *The Encyclopedia of Language and Linguistics* (pp.725-730). Pergamon Press Oxford.

De la Torre, A. (1993). Key Issues in Latino Health: Voicing Latina Concerns in the Health Financing Debate. *In Chicana Critical Issues* (pp. 157-168). Berkeley: Third Woman Press.

Flores-Ortiz, Y. (1993). La Mujer y La Violencia: A Culturally Based Model for the Understanding and Treatment of Domestic Violence in Chicana/Latina Communities. *In Chicana Critical Issues* (pp. 167-182). Berkeley: Third Woman Press.

Gayford, J. J. (1983). Battered Wives. In R. J. Gelles & C. P. Cornell (Eds.), *International Perspectives on Family Violence* (pp. 123-137). Lexington, MA: Lexington.

Gelles, R. J. & Cornell, C. P. (Eds.) (1983). *International Perspectives on Family Violence* (1-22). Lexington, MA: Lexington.

Gelles, R. J. (1972). *The Violent Home.* Sage Publications, Inc.

Giachello, A. L. (1997). Latino Women. In M. Bayne-Smith (Ed.), *Race, Gender and Health* (pp. 121-171). Sage Series on Race and Ethnic Relations, Volume 15, Sage Publications, Inc.

Jones, E. G., & Kay, M. (1992). Instrumentation in cross-cultural research. *Nursing Research, 41,* (3):186-188.

Kantor, G. K., Jasinski, J. L., & Aldarondo, E. (1994). Socio-cultural status and incidence of marital violence in Hispanic families. *Violence and Victims, 9,* (3): 207-222.

Lavizzo-Mourey, R. Mackenzie, E. R. (1996). Cultural competence: Essential measurements of quality for managed care organizations. *Annals of Internal Medicine, 124,* (10):919-921.

Levinson, D. (1989). Varieties of family violence. *Family Violence in Cross-Cultural Perspective* (pp.24-38). Newbury Park, CA: Sage Publications.

Martinez-Garcia, T. (1988). Culture and Wife Battering Among Hispanics in New Mexico: *Proceedings of the research conference on violence and homicide in Hispanic communities* (pp. 205-214). Los Angeles: UCLA Publication Services.

Neff, J. A., Holamon, B., & Schulter, T. D. (1995). Spousal Violence among Anglos, Blacks, and Mexican Americans: The role of demographic variables, psychosocial predictors, and alcohol consumption. *Journal of Family Violence, 10*, (1): 1-21.

Padilla, A. M., Cervantes, R. C., Maldonado, M., & Garcia, R. E. (1988). Coping Responses to Psychosocial Stressors Among Mexican and Central American Immigrants. *Journal of Community Psychology*, (16):418-427.

Rogler, L. H., Malgady, R. G., Constantino, G., & Blumenthal, R. (1987). What do culturally sensitive mental health services mean? *American Psychologist, 42*, (6): 565-570.

Sorenson, S. B., & Telles, C. A. (1988). Family Violence in Immigrant and Non-Immigrant Hispanics in Los Angeles. In J. F. Kraus, S. B Sorenson, & P. Juarez (Eds.), *Proceedings of the research conference on violence and homicide in Hispanic communities* (pp. 193-204). Los Angeles: UCLA Publication Services.

Sorenson, S. B., & Telles, C. A. (1991). Self-reports of spousal violence in a Mexican-American and Non-Hispanic White Population. *Violence and Victims, 6*, (1):3-15.

Sorenson, S. B. (1996). Violence against women: Examining ethnic differences and commonalities. *Evaluation Review, 20*, (2):123-145.

Stacey, W. A., & Shupe, A. (1983). *Family Secret* (pp. 26-60). Boston: Beacon Press.

Straus, M. A. & Smith, C. (1990). Violence in Hispanic families in the United States: Incidence rates and structural interpretations. In M. A. Straus, & R. J. Gelles (Eds.), *Physical violence in American families: Risk factors and adaptations to violence in 8,145 families* (pp. 341-367). New Brunswick: Transaction Publishers.

Straus, M. A. (1988). Violence in Hispanic Families in the United States: Some preliminary findings on incidence and etiology. In J. F. Kraus, S. B Sorenson, & P. Juarez (Eds.), *Proceedings of the research conference on violence and homicide in Hispanic communities* (pp. 171-192). Los Angeles: UCLA Publication Services.

Straus, M. A., Gelles, R. J., & Steinmetz, S. K. (1980). *Behind Closed Doors*. New York: Anchor Books.

Torres, S. (1991). A comparison of wife abuse between two cultures: Perceptions, attitudes, nature, and extent. *Issues in Mental Health Nursing.* (12):113-131.

Torres, S. (1987). Hispanic-American battered women: Why consider cultural differences. *Response. 10*, (3):20-21.

Valencia, A. (August/1996). Violence against women in a Mexican-American Community: Peace psychology perspectives. Paper presented at the 104th American Psychological Association Annual Convention in Toronto, Canada.

Vargas-Willis, G. & Cervantes, R. C. (1987). Consideration of psychosocial stress in the treatment of the Latina immigrant. *Hispanic Journal of Behavioral Sciences, 9*, (3):315-329.

Walker, L. E. (1984). *The Battered Woman Syndrome*. New York: Springer Publishing Company.

Zambrano, M. M. (1985). *For the Latina in an Abusive Relationship*. Seattle, WA: Seal Press.

ELDER ABUSE

Tolerance of Elder Abuse and Attitudes Toward Third-Party Intervention Among African American, Korean American, and White Elderly

Ailee Moon
Donna Benton

SUMMARY. Studies have found that professionals and the lay public differ consistently from one another in the ways in which they perceive

Ailee Moon, PhD, is Associate Professor in the Department of Social Welfare, School of Public Policy and Social Research, at the University of California, Los Angeles.

Donna Benton, PhD, is Assistant Research Professor of Andrus Gerontology Center and Alzheimer Disease Research Center at the University of Southern California.

This study was in part funded by the National Center on Elder Abuse and UCLA Academic Senate Research Grant. Part of the study findings reported in this article can also be found in a report titled "Attitudes toward Elder Mistreatment and Reporting: A Multicultural Study," submitted to the National Center on Elder Abuse.

[Haworth co-indexing entry note]: "Tolerance of Elder Abuse and Attitudes Toward Third-Party Intervention Among African American, Korean American, and White Elderly." Moon, Ailee, and Donna Benton. Co-published simultaneously in *Journal of Multicultural Social Work* (The Haworth Press, Inc.) Vol. 8, No. 3/4, 2000, pp. 283-303; and: *Violence: Diverse Populations and Communities* (ed: Diane de Anda, and Rosina M. Becerra) The Haworth Press, Inc., 2000, pp. 283-303. Single or multiple copies of this article are available for a fee from The Haworth Document Delivery Service [1-800-342-9678, 9:00 a.m. - 5:00 p.m. (EST). E-mail address: getinfo@haworthpressinc.com].

elder abuse. A potential variable that may explain this observed difference is cultural norms among ethnic groups. Using 18 statements, this
study examined similarities and differences among elderly from three
ethnic groups in their tolerance for potential elder abuse, perceptions
regarding perpetrators and the causes of elder abuse, and attitudes toward
third-party intervention and reporting of elder abuse to the authorities.
Results suggest that while African American and White elderly are remarkably similar in their responses to most statements, Korean American
elderly differed significantly from the other two groups in their tolerance
for medical mistreatment, financial exploitation and neglect, perceptions
of causes, and attitudes toward reporting elder abuse. These findings
have implications for understanding potential barriers to preventive outreach efforts, investigation, and intervention in cases of elder abuse in a
culturally diverse community. *[Article copies available for a fee from The
Haworth Document Delivery Service: 1-800-342-9678. E-mail address:
<getinfo@haworthpressinc.com> Website: <http://www.haworthpressinc.com>]*

KEYWORDS. Elder abuse, third party intervention, African American
elderly, Korean American elderly, White elderly

INTRODUCTION

Current research into the definitions and types of elder abuse, the
risk factors associated with elder abuse, and the development of good
assessment tools falls significantly short in its applicability to ethnic
elders. A primary reason for this inadequacy is the generally deficient
understanding, evident in the literature, of how elder abuse is manifested within various ethnic populations. This article presents an approach to improved understanding of this aspect by reporting on a
study of perceptions of elder abuse within three ethnic populations.

Definitions of elder abuse generally reflect a White, middle-class
perspective; these definitions have come to be codified in the laws and
policies on the topic (Hudson & Carlson, 1999). Additionally, elder
abuse definitions have generally been based upon professional judgment, whereas the inclusion of the "lay person's" perceptions of elder
abuse has only recently come under scholarly investigation (Chang &
Moon, 1997; Gebotys, O'Connor, & Meair, 1992; Hudson, 1994;
Hudson & Carlson, 1994, 1999; Moon & Williams, 1993). A consistent
finding in these studies is that there are differences between professional and public definitions of elder abuse. The factors that contribute to
these observed differences are the subject of ongoing research.

REVIEW OF THE LITERATURE

Practitioners and researchers have come to recognize that ethnicity determines the way in which elder abuse is manifested, reported, and perceived (Anetzberger, Korbin & Tomita, 1996; Moon, Tomita, Talamantes, Brown, Sanchez, Benton, Sanchez, & Kim, 1998; Nerenburg, 1997). However, research examining perceptions of elder abuse among various ethnic groups is sparse (Moon & Williams, 1993: Tatara, 1999).

A study conducted by Moon and Williams (1993) contributed toward understanding of how various ethnic groups may differ in their perceptions of elder abuse and in help-seeking patterns. In this study, African American, Korean American, and White elderly women were presented with thirteen scenarios to measure their perceptions of elder abuse and help-seeking patterns. Korean immigrant elderly were found to be significantly less sensitive to, or more tolerant of, potentially abusive situations presented in case scenarios, in comparison with White and African American elderly. In addition, differences in perception emerged as a strong predictor of help-seeking behavior by respondents.

Anetzberger, Korbin and Tomita (1996) compared European American, African American, Puerto Rican, and Japanese American focus group participants' responses to hypothetical situations of conflict. One major difference among these populations was their perception of the "worst things that a family member can do to an elderly person." For European American respondents, psychological neglect was the top choice, whereas Japanese American respondents listed psychological abuse as the worst thing. Notably, only African American respondents listed exploitation as a negative behavior toward elderly persons. In addition, for given hypothetical situations, Puerto Rican respondents were most likely to label a situation as elder mistreatment, without qualifications, and European American and Japanese American respondents were the least likely to label a situation as elder mistreatment. African American respondents tended to stress the importance of the context of a given situation for understanding and labeling it as elder mistreatment. The authors concluded that the results suggested that what constitutes elder mistreatment does vary across ethnic groups, and that more research is needed to understand the implications of these differences. Additionally, they pointed out the discrepancy between what lay people consider a major type of abuse, psychological abuse and neglect, and what is emphasized in the literature and policies, physical abuse.

Tomita (1999) looked at domestic violence (including elder abuse) among Japanese American elderly using in-depth interviews from focus groups. Although incidents of abuse were reported to interviewers, for many, defining behavior that was harmful to them as "abusive" was not common. The interviews highlighted that, within this population, elderly females may not perceive themselves as being abused because of culturally-based behaviors and norms. For researchers, it is important to know that these norms may be overlooked in studies using standard definitions or may be misunderstood as acceptance of abuse in studies of perception.

A study by Chang and Moon (1997) indicates that the obverse may be the case. Specifically, the researchers found that eight of forty-six elder abuse examples offered by Korean immigrant elderly respondents were culturally specific types of elder abuse. These included adult children's refusal to live with elderly parents, placing elderly parents in a nursing home, and a daughter-in-law not showing respect toward parents-in-law, all of which can be better understood as abuse in the context of Korean cultural norms of family relationships and filial piety. This finding suggests that employing a uniform professional or statutory definition of elder abuse across all cultures and ethnic groups without attending to the cultural and subjective aspects of a given situation may result in missing incidents of elder abuse and neglect.

The African American population may be more likely to perceive situations as abusive when compared to other ethnic groups. Moon and Williams (1993) found that a higher percentage of African American respondents rated scenarios as abusive compared to Korean and White respondents. Similarly, Hudson and Carlson (1999) found that the African American sample was more likely to perceive situations as abusive in comparison with White or American Indian samples. Finally, Anetzberger, Korbin and Tomita (1996) found that African American respondents, in comparison with American Indian, Japanese, and Hispanic respondents, were more likely to recognize the most commonly defined forms of abuse and were the only group to consider financial exploitation as a form of elder mistreatment.

Research examining abuse issues within the Hispanic population is made difficult by language barriers and by variations within diverse sub-populations. As with the Japanese population, research suggests that behaviors that may be perceived or defined as abusive by the dominant culture are not similarly defined by Latino respondents (Sanchez, 1999). Moreover, the study highlighted differences among the Mexican American respondents. In the study, Mexican American participants were asked to define elder mistreatment and what they might do if they thought someone was being mistreated. The study found that there was a need to develop a culturally defined category of abuse for this population, specifically, "denial of shelter." This was the most frequently cited type of abuse, followed by neglect, financial abuse, and physical abuse.

The review of the literature reveals some common aspects in studies looking at perceptions of abuse. First, these studies highlight that there are considerable differences in the way ethnic groups define and identify elder abuse. Second, culturally-based perceptions and behavior of the elderly, their families, and perpetrators should be taken into consideration in determining culturally appropriate and effective plans for intervention and prevention of elder abuse. Finally, more research is needed to help explain specific cultural and non-cultural factors that contribute to the similarities and differences in perceptions and behavior between and within different ethnic groups.

Expanding on the early work by Moon and Williams (1993), the purpose of this study was to examine tolerance for potential elder abuse, perceptions regarding perpetrators and the causes of elder abuse, and attitudes toward third-party intervention and reporting of elder abuse to the authorities among three ethnic elderly groups, African American, Korean American, and White elderly.

METHODS

Sample

The study sample consists of 100 African American, 95 Korean American, and 90 White elders age 60 or older living in Los Angeles County, California in 1997. Purposive and convenience sampling methods were employed to recruit study participants. To reduce sampling bias inherent in such nonprobability sampling methods, a number of sampling sites, including supermarkets, senior citizen centers, drug stores, barber shops, beauty salons, churches, and senior citizen housing sites, were used to recruit study participants. Further, to minimize the potential systematic sampling bias among the three groups, similar types of sampling sites were utilized to recruit study participants. Respondents were offered $10.00 for participating in the study as partial compensation for their time and also to minimize the refusal rate. The response rate was 97% for the African American, 92% for Korean American, and 87% for White samples.

Table 1 presents the demographic and socioeconomic characteristics of the three elderly groups in the study. Approximately two-thirds of respondents were female, ranging from 62.1% for Korean American to 68% for African American respondents. The average age was 70.5 years of age for African American, 73.3 for Korean American, and 74.3 for White respondents. Most African American and White elderly were born in the U.S. (97% and 90%, respectively), whereas all Korean American elderly were born outside the U.S., mostly in Korea. For the Korean American respondents, the average number of years of residence in the U.S. was 13.6 years, reflecting that most of them came to the country as immigrants in their 50's and early 60's, likely with the intent to join their adult children.

Table 1 also shows that African American and White respondents were similar in their marital status, living arrangement, number of children, and housing arrangement, whereas the Korean American respondents were significantly different from the two groups. Specifically, the majority of Korean American elderly (58.9%) were currently married, while about one-third of the members of the other groups were married (33% for African American and 30.3% for White elderly). The group difference in marital status is in part reflected in the living arrangement. While the majority of African American and White elderly were living alone (60% and 57.8%, respectively), only about one-third of Korean American elderly (33.7%) were living alone. Furthermore, less than one-third of African American (32%) and White respondents (30%), compared to more than one half of Korean American respondents (51.6%), were living in government subsidized senior housing projects. Moreover, the Korean American group, on average, had a significantly higher number of children (4) than those in the African American (2.3) and White (1.9) groups.

Significant differences among the three groups in the self-rated health status, educational level, and income are also indicated in Table 1.

TABLE 1. Characteristics of African American, Korean American, and White Elderly Respondents

Demographic characteristics	African American % (n = 100)	Korean American % (n = 95)	White % (n = 90)	χ^2 or F-value
Gender				
Female	68.0	62.1	65.9	
Male	32.0	37.9	34.3	0.7[a]
Age (Mean)	(70.5)	(73.3)	(74.3)	7.4[b]***
60-64 years old	22.2	8.4	10.0	
65-69 years old	26.3	21.1	16.7	
70-74 years old	23.2	29.5	23.3	
75 years old or older	28.3	41.1	50.0	16.7[a]*
Born in the U.S.				
Yes	97.0	0.0	90.0	
No	3.0	100.0	10.0	291.8[a]***
Marital status				
Never married	9.0	0.0	7.9	
Married	33.0	58.9	30.3	
Separated/Widowed/Divorced	58.0	41.1	61.8	23.9[a]***
Living arrangement				
Living alone	60.0	33.7	57.8	
Living with someone	40.0	66.3	42.2	16.2[a]***
The number of living children (Mean)	2.3	4.0	1.9	32.1[b]***
Housing arrangement				
Own house	42.0	9.5	43.3	
Rented house	16.0	14.7	5.6	
Government subsidized senior apt.	32.0	51.6	30.0	
Others	10.0	24.2	21.2	40.1[a]***
Self-rated health status				
Very good	15.0	6.3	27.8	
Good	43.0	24.2	41.0	
Fair	34.0	34.7	20.0	
Poor	4.0	25.3	10.0	
Very poor	4.0	9.5	1.1	47.9[a]***
Years of formal education completed (Mean)	12.4	7.9	12.5	38.2[b]***
Total monthly income				
Under $599	13.8	44.1	7.5	
$600-$1,199	55.3	49.5	43.8	
$1,200-$1,799	14.9	4.3	23.8	
$1,800 or more	16.0	2.2	25.0	60.1[a]***

* $p < .05$; ** $p < .01$; *** $p < .001$
[a] Chi-square statistics; [b] F value obtained from Oneway ANOVA

Specifically, 34.8% of Korean American elderly, compared to the significantly lower 8% of African American and 11.1% of White elderly rated their health status as poor or very poor. Also, the average number of years of formal education was the lowest for Korean American respondents (7.9 years), compared to their African American (12.4 years) and White (12.5 years) counterparts. Finally, the economic status of the respondents, measured by before-tax monthly income from all sources, varied substantially among the three groups, with the Korean American respondents being the poorest. Approximately 94% of the Korean American sample, compared to 69.1% of the African American and 51.3% of the White samples, reported monthly incomes of less than $1,200.

The 1990 Census data suggest that the substantial differences among the three sample groups reflect, to a large extent, the true differences in their respective elderly populations rather than sampling biases (U.S. Bureau of Census, 1990). Moreover, a recent comparative study based on a much larger sample and using a probability sampling method conducted on the Korean American and White elderly in the same study area revealed similar group differences in their demographic and socioeconomic characteristics (Moon, Lubben, & Villa, 1998).

Data Collection

Data were collected in 1997 in face-to-face interviews conducted by trained graduate students of the same ethnic backgrounds as the respondents using a structured questionnaire. The questionnaire was translated into Korean using a back translation method. All interviews with Korean American respondents were conducted in Korean since this was the preference indicated by all of the Korean American elders.

Respondents' tolerance of potential elder abuse was measured using ten short statements, which aimed to cover various dimensions of elder abuse or mistreatment, including physical, verbal, psychological and medical mistreatment, neglect, and financial exploitation. Four statements were used to measure respondents' perceptions of the perpetrator and the cause of elder abuse, and an additional four statements were adopted as measures of attitudes toward a third-party intervention and reporting of elder abuse to the authorities, such as the police and social service agencies. Interviewers read each of the 18 statements of elder abuse related situations to the respondents slowly, and repeatedly if necessary, until the respondents indicated a clear under-standing of the situation. The respondents were then asked whether they agreed or disagreed with the statement.

FINDINGS

Tolerance of Elder Abuse

Table 2 presents findings regarding the respondents' tolerance of potential elder abuse or mistreatment, as measured by ten statements covering various types of elder mistreatment. Nearly all respondents, ranging from 96.8% of the Korean American respondents to 98.9% of the White respondents, disapproved of the most obvious form of physical abuse, that is, hitting the elderly spouse (Item 1). Regarding an adult child caregiver who ties down a physically or mentally im-paired parent in bed (Item 2), however, some respondents were willing to tolerate it and/or to consider whether or not the circumstance in which the elderly parent was constrained in bed was justifiable in order to determine the acceptability of the behavior. Specifically, 9.5% of the Korean American, 5.6% of the White, and 2% of the African American respondents indicated their approval of the caregiver's be-havior in this item. Although over two-thirds of African American elderly (69%) and three-quarters of the other groups (78.9% of Korean American and 77.8% of White elderly) expressed their disapproval of such behavior, a considerable percentage of respondents were uncer-tain about their positions and were willing to approve or disapprove of the behavior depending on the situation. The percentage of "don't know or depends" responses ranged from a low of 11.6% (Korean American) to a high of 29% (African American). The group differ-ences, nevertheless, were not statistically significant.

It is also evident that a considerable number of respondents, espe-cially Korean American and African American, were willing to toler-ate medical mistreatment of elderly people. Specifically, regarding the statement, "when adult children feel too much stress in caring for their elderly parents, it is okay to calm the parents with medication," 21.1% of Korean American and 14% of African American elders, compared to only 5.6% of White elders, agreed. The differences among the three groups were statistically significant. In addition, a substantial percent-age of respondents indicated that whether to agree or disagree with the

TABLE 2. Respondents' Tolerance of Potential Elder Abuse by Ethnicity[a]

Items	African American (n = 100)		Korean American (n = 95)		White (n = 90)		χ^2 [b]
	Agree (%)	Disagree (%)	Agree (%)	Disagree (%)	Agree (%)	Disagree (%)	
1. Among elderly couples, occasional hitting of the other person is okay. (physical)	1.0	98.0	3.2	96.8	1.1	98.9	1.6
2. It is okay for an adult child caregiver to tie down a physically or mentally impaired parent in bed. (physical)	2.0	69.0	9.5	78.9	5.6	77.8	3.7
3. When adult children feel too much stress in caring for their elderly parents, it is okay to calm the parents with medication. (medical)	14.0	59.0	21.1	67.4	5.6	73.3	7.9*
4. It is okay for adult children to yell occasionally at their elderly parents. (verbal)	3.0	92.0	8.4	87.4	30.0	65.6	32.9***
5. Being ignored, excluded, or isolated by family members is as hurtful as being physically abused. (psychological)	94.0	4.0	89.5	6.3	93.3	3.3	1.1
6. It is okay for an adult child to use his/her elderly parents money for himself/herself. (financial)	2.0	78.0	45.3	37.9	2.2	76.7	85.5***
7. When adult children borrow money from their parents, it is okay not to pay it back, even if the parents ask for the money. (financial)	1.0	97.0	37.9	50.5	3.3	88.9	74.2***
8. It is okay for an adult child caring for bedridden elderly parents to leave them alone occasionally for a few hours. (neglect)	16.0	64.0	37.9	29.5	25.6	60.0	21.7***
9. When elderly parents choose to stop taking care of themselves and their health gets worse, adult children should do something about it. (neglect)	98.0	1.0	92.6	5.3	96.7	1.1	4.7
10. When elderly parents continue to reject food, it is okay for adult children to force them to eat. (neglect or physical)	9.0	75.0	35.8	60.0	10.0	80.0	25.4***

*$p < .05$; **$p < .01$; ***$p < .001$

[a] The percentages in the table are based on a total "n." However, since percentages are reported only for "Agree" and "Disagree," they may not add to 100% due to the exclusion of "Don't know" and "Depends" responses.

[b] Chi-square statistics were calculated based on "Agree" and "Disagree" responses.

statement depends on the situation. The percentage of "don't know or depends" ranged from 11.5% for Korean Americans to 21.1% for White and 27% for African American respondents.

Table 2 further shows that White elderly respondents were significantly more likely to tolerate verbal abuse than the other groups. Specifically, 30% of the White sample agreed that it is okay for adult children, on occasion, to yell at their elderly parents, while only 3% of the African American and 8.4% of the Korean American samples agreed. Most respondents, however, agreed that psychological abuse in the form of ignoring, excluding, or isolating elderly persons from family members is as hurtful as physical abuse. The percentage ranged from 89.5% for Korean American respondents to 94% for African American respondents.

Regarding the respondents' tolerance of potential financial exploitation, the findings suggest that while African American and White elderly hold similar views, Korean American elderly tend to differ significantly from both groups. With respect to a general, non-situation-specific statement involving the use of elderly parent's money by an adult child (Item 6), only 2% of African American and 2.2% White respondents, compared to 45.3% of Korean American respondents, agreed that it is okay for an adult child to use his or her elderly parent's money for himself or herself. Although a considerable percentage of respondents indicated "don't know or depends," ranging from 16.8% (Korean American) to 21.1% (White), this finding clearly suggests that Korean American elderly were far more likely to approve the unconditional use of elderly parents' money. A similar pattern of tolerance for potential financial exploitation prevails among the three groups regarding adult children's refusal to reimburse their elderly parents, even if the parents ask for the money (Item 7). In this regard, over one-third of the Korean American sample (37.9%), compared to 1% of the African American and 3.3% of the White samples, agreed that it is okay for the adult children not to reimburse their elderly parents. In fact, much of the statistically significant group differences found in the two statements about potential financial exploitation were attributed to this relatively high level of tolerance reported by Korean American respondents.

A significant group difference was observed in the respondents' perception concerning whether an adult child, caring for bedridden elderly parents, can occasionally leave them alone for a few hours. As shown in the table, the majority of African American and White respondents (64% and 60%, respectively) disapproved even of the caregiver's occasionally leaving bedridden parents alone for a few hours, while less than one-third (29.5%) of Korean American respondents disapproved of it. It is also of interest that a considerable percentage of respondents indicated that their approval or disapproval of occasional neglect of bedridden parents depends on the health condition of parents and whether or not the caregiver's reason for leaving them alone can be justified. The percentage of respondents indicating "don't know or depends" ranged from 14.4% of White to 32.6% of Korean American elders. Most respondents, however, including the Korean American, agreed that adult children should do something when elderly parents choose to stop taking care of themselves and their health gets worse (Item 9).

Nevertheless, regarding a specific situation of passive neglect which involves elderly parents who continue to reject food, the majority of respondents did not believe that adult children should force the elderly parents to eat. They indicated, rather, that the children must find a better way to deal with the situation, including other efforts to convince the parents to eat and seeking professional help. The percentage of disapproval ranged from a low of 60% for Korean American respondents to a high of 80% for White respondents. The findings also indicate that Korean American elderly, nonetheless, were at least three times more likely to approve the adult children's decision to force their parents to eat in comparison with the other two groups (35.8% versus 9% of African American and 10% of White elderly).

Overall, the findings suggest that there exist considerable differences in the three ethnic groups' sensitivity to or tolerance of various forms of elder mistreatment. In fact, the group difference was statistically significant with respect to six of the ten statements. More specifically, the difference found in four of the six cases (Items 6, 7, 8, and 10) was largely attributed to the significantly different views held by the Korean American group, whereas the White group was significantly different from the other groups regarding the verbal abuse statement (Item 4).

Perceptions of Perpetrators and Causes of Elder Abuse

Turning to the respondents' perceptions of the perpetrators and causes of elder abuse, Table 3 shows that although the majority in the

TABLE 3. Respondents' Perceptions of Perpetrators and Causes of Elder Abuse by Ethnicity[a]

Items	African American (n = 100)		Korean American (n = 95)		White (n = 90)		χ^2 [b]
	Agree (%)	Disagree (%)	Agree (%)	Disagree (%)	Agree (%)	Disagree (%)	
1. Elder abuse is committed mostly by mentally ill persons or substance abusers.	37.0	36.0	58.1	28.0	24.4	53.3	19.3***
2. Elder abuse is committed mostly by family member.	67.0	20.0	65.3	16.8	61.1	22.2	0.8
3. Many elderly people are badly treated because they did something wrong to deserve it.	5.0	85.0	43.2	40.0	3.3	86.7	76.6***
4. Elderly parents who abused their children deserve abuse from their grown-up children.	4.0	93.0	30.5	62.1	7.8	90.0	35.3***

* $p < .05$; ** $p < .01$; *** $p < .001$
[a] The percentages in the table are based on a total "n." However, since percentages are reported only for "Agree" and "Disagree" responses, they may not add to 100% due to the exclusion of "Don't know" and "Depends" responses.
[b] Chi-square statistics were calculated based on "Agree" and "Disagree" responses.

Korean American sample (58.1%) perceived that elder abuse is committed mostly by mentally ill persons or substance abusers, a significantly lower percentage within the African American (37%) and White (24.4%) samples held the same view. Approximately two-thirds of the total sample, ranging from 61.1% of White to 67% of African American respondents, nevertheless, believed that elder abuse is committed mostly by family members.

The findings regarding the respondents' perceptions about causes of elder abuse indicate that African American and White elderly tend to hold similar views, whereas Korean American elderly exhibit a significantly different perception. Specifically, 43.2% of the Korean American, compared with only 5% of the African American and 3.3% of the White cohorts, agreed that many elderly people are treated poorly because they did something wrong, or otherwise deserve it. Similarly, almost one-third of Korean American respondents (30.5%), compared to 4% of the African American and 7.8% of the White respondents, agreed that elderly parents who abused their children when they were young, deserve abuse from their grown-up children. The finding that a substantial number of Korean American respondents tended to blame the victim for causing or deserving the abuse seems to reflect an overall higher level of tolerance of elder abuse, when compared to the other groups.

Attitudes Toward a Third-Party Intervention and Reporting of Elder Abuse

Table 4 presents findings on the respondents' attitudes toward a third-party intervention and toward the reporting of elder abuse to the authorities, such as to the police and social service agencies. Although the majority of respondents supported a third-party intervention and reporting of elder abuse incidents to the authorities, a considerable percentage of respondents, especially Korean American, did not. Spe-

TABLE 4. Respondents' Attitudes Toward Third-Party Intervention and Toward Reporting of Elder Abuse by Ethnicity[a]

Items	African American (n = 100)		Korean American (n = 95)		White (n = 90)		χ^2 [b]
	Agree (%)	Disagree (%)	Agree (%)	Disagree (%)	Agree (%)	Disagree (%)	
1. When an elderly person is abused or neglected by a family member, persons outside the family should not get involved.	21.0	71.0	38.9	53.7	13.3	80.0	17.9***
2. When a neighbor knows that an elderly person is being abused or neglected by a family member, the neighbor should not report it to such authorities as social service agencies and the police.	2.0	95.0	25.3	68.4	3.3	94.4	37.5***
3. When a neighbor suspects that an elderly person is being abused or neglected by a family member, the neighbor should not report it to such authorities as social service agencies and the police until s/he is absolutely sure about it.	57.0	38.0	64.2	31.6	58.9	36.7	1.1
4. Reporting elder abuse to such authorities as social service agencies and the police will destroy the abusers' lives.	9.0	73.0	49.5	37.9	10.0	68.9	54.3***

* $p < .05$; ** $p < .01$; *** $p < .001$
[a] The percentages in the table are based on a total "n." However, since percentages are reported only for "Agree" and "Disagree" responses, they may not add to 100% due to the exclusion of "Don't know" and "Depends" responses.
[b] Chi-square statistics were calculated based on "Agree" and "Disagree" responses.

cifically, 21% of African American, 13.3% of White, and a significantly higher 38.9% of Korean American respondents reported that persons outside the family should not become involved when an elderly person is abused or neglected by a family member. If the third-party intervention included reporting the elder abuse incident to authorities such as the police and social service agencies, considerably greater percentages of all three groups seemed to support third-party intervention by the appropriate authorities. In fact, only 2% of the African American and 3.3% of the White respondents held the view that when a neighbor knows that an elderly person is being abused or neglected by a family member, that person should not report it to authorities such as social service agencies or the police. A significantly higher percentage of the Korean American sample (25.3%), however, did disapprove of the idea of reporting elder abuse to the authorities.

In contrast to the above findings, Table 4 illustrates that when elder abuse is only suspected, but unconfirmed, the majority of all three groups, ranging from 57% (African American) to 64.2% (Korean American), believed that one should not report the suspected elder abuse to the authorities until he or she is absolutely sure about it. Finally, there exists a significant difference between Korean Americans and the other groups in their perceptions of the consequences for elder abusers who are reported to the authorities. Specifically, almost one half of the Korean American sample (49.5%), as opposed to only 9% of the African American and 10% of the White samples, believed that reporting elder abusers to the authorities will destroy the abusers' lives. Concerning this last point, it is also notable that a considerable percentage of respondents reported being uncertain, ranging from 12.6% (Korean American) to 18% (African American) and 21.1% (White).

Overall, the findings in Table 4 suggest that, in general, African American and White elderly, as opposed to Korean American elderly, tend to hold similar and relatively positive attitudes toward a third-party intervention, including the reporting of elder abuse to the authorities, and the consequences of reporting on elder abusers. Moreover, the finding that about one-half of the Korean American respondents perceived that reporting elder abusers to the authorities would destroy their lives may in part explain why a substantial number opposed the idea of reporting elder abuse to the authorities.

DISCUSSION

It must be pointed out that due to the limitations of sample size and potential selection bias, the results of this study may not be generalizable to all members of the groups studied. Also, it should be kept in mind that the responses provided may not represent how people might respond to actual situations of elder abuse. The statements used were only brief descriptions and did not take into account factors such as the severity of abuse or the detailed circumstances which might have led to the events presented. Nevertheless, this study suggests that it is important to consider ethnicity and culture when investigating the social problem of elder abuse and neglect.

In general, African American and White elderly were more likely to have similar responses to statements when compared with Korean American elderly. A possible explanation of this pattern is the fact that the vast majority of African American and White elderly studied were born in the U.S. and, therefore, shared a common native culture, whereas all of the Korean American elderly in the study were immigrants. When looking at items related to tolerance of potential elder abuse, African American respondents were less tolerant of most types of abuse with the exception of medical mistreatment, a finding that is consistent with an earlier study by Moon and Williams (1993). This seems to express the belief on the part of the elderly in this population that abuse, through overuse of calming medication, is less harmful overall than allowing the caregiver to become overly stressed. Future investigators might study the underlying contributors to this response. It may be, for example, that responses may vary depending upon the availability of support networks than provide opportunities for respite care. Furthermore, African American respondents were slightly less tolerant than White respondents of involving non-family members in cases of potential abuse. This response may reflect a cultural value of family-centered problem solving, possible feelings of shame about the situation, and/or, a history of societal discrimination experienced by African Americans in American society (Hall, 1999).

For the White elderly respondents, there was evidence of a significantly higher tolerance for, or lower sensitivity to, verbal abuse. Considering the fact that verbal abuse can lead to more serious types of psychological or physical abuse, this willingness by White elderly to tolerate or accept verbal abuse raises a concern. On the other hand, in cases of elder abuse, White respondents tend to hold the most positive attitudes toward intervention by persons outside of the family as well as toward imposition of consequences for perpetrators.

Among the three groups studied, Korean American elderly were found to be the least sensitive to, or most tolerant of, elder abuse, especially for cases of financial exploitation. The remarkably high level of tolerance toward potential financial exploitation is perhaps related to the long-standing Korean norm of transferring parents' wealth and property to children, particularly to the oldest son, when the parents retire or become elderly. For both parents and children, this tradition, which still prevails within both Korean and Korean American families, has created a sense of co-ownership and of children's entitlement to parents' wealth and property. When abused, this tradition promotes both children's dependence upon and exploitation of their elderly parents along with the neglect of responsibility for their parents' financial well-being (Chang & Moon, 1997).

It is also evident that Korean American respondents were significantly more likely than respondents in the other groups to blame the victims for the occurrence of elder abuse. For example, the finding that about 43% agreed that many elderly people are treated poorly because they did something wrong poses a serious barrier to elder abuse prevention and intervention in the Korean American community. Another finding that almost one-third of Korean American respondents agreed that elderly parents who abused their children deserve abuse from their grown-up children suggests a potential for increased tolerance of abuse among this group. In fact, a recent survey of Korean Americans' perceptions about domestic violence revealed a similar finding in that approximately one-third of 580 respondents held the same perception that victims somehow cause domestic violence (Moon, 1999). The finding regarding the "victim blaming" aspect of elder abuse suggests that the Korean American community needs to discover more effective methods for challenging and changing the belief systems among some members of the population.

Furthermore, the Korean American elderly respondents held significantly more negative attitudes toward involvement of persons outside the family in elder abuse incidents, as well as toward reporting of such incidents to the authorities and the consequences for perpetrators. This finding, combined with their perception of the causes of elder abuse, suggests a strong reluctance among Korean American elders to reveal abuse problems to others or to seek professional help, thereby making it difficult to prevent or intervene in cases of abuse. Their unwillingness to report elder abuse to the authorities and a tendency to blame the victims, combined with a reluctance to seek outside help, places Korean American elderly at a very high risk.

IMPLICATIONS

A number of implications can be drawn from these findings. Some elderly may be at greater risk for elder abuse primarily due to their perception of what constitutes abuse, their willingness to tolerate abuse, and their reluctance to report suspected, or even known, elder abuse incidents to the authorities. In fact, the finding that the majority of respondents from all three groups studied believed that incidents of elder abuse should not be reported to the authorities until they are absolutely sure that abuse has occurred, deserves attention. Public education efforts need to emphasize the importance of reporting suspected, rather than only confirmed, elder abuse for the purpose of early intervention and to ensure the well-being of potential victims of elder abuse.

Second, the finding that a considerable number of all three groups responded "don't know or depends" regarding several potentially abusive or neglectful situations involving adult children as caregivers and the elderly parents as care recipients, illustrates the importance of understanding when and under what circumstances the caregiver's behavior can be considered abusive. For example, in the case of an adult child caregiver who ties down a physically or mentally impaired parent in bed, some respondents with "don't know or depends" seemed to try to balance the safety of the elderly person with the physical discomfort and the feeling of shame associated with being tied in bed. This finding suggests that in determining the intervention plan, practitioners need to consider the circumstances that led to the potentially abusive behavior along with the elder's perceptions of the problem and potential solutions to the problem, as this is likely to influence the success of the intervention plan.

In the above situation, for example, the practitioner needs to consider whether the caregiver left her/his elderly parent alone in order to attend to an unexpected emergency (e.g., injury of the caregiver's child at school), whether the caregiver attempted to find someone to care for the elder while s/he was gone, and whether the reason why s/he had to tie the elder in bed was explained to and understood by the elder. If so, the appropriate intervention by the practitioner would be to work with the caregiver to develop a support network to call upon for assistance in caring for the elder in case of emergency. Also, this finding demonstrates the need for public outreach efforts to educate the elderly population and the caregivers about better alternatives and community resources available to help them. Indeed, it is only when no better alternatives are perceived to exist that potentially abusive situations are justified as inevitable.

Third, the ethnic differences found among the three groups in their tolerance for potential elder abuse, perceptions regarding the causes of elder abuse, and attitudes toward third-party intervention suggest that an ethnic-specific approach to public outreach and educational efforts may be more effective than a more general approach in increasing the awareness and understanding of elder abuse issues pertinent to each ethnic community. For example, it would be useful to focus more attention on verbal abuse issues in White communities than in African American and Korean American communities. For the Korean American population, on the other hand, it would be more useful to address the consequences of victim blaming practices and explain how third-party intervention, including reporting of elder abuse to the authorities, can help stop the suffering of victims of elder abuse. This will need to be framed in the appropriate cultural context, for example, as a method for restoring harmony within the family. Furthermore, alternative sources of help may need to be provided that are not perceived as having the potential to "destroy" the abuser's life, in order to overcome the reluctance of this population to report abuse.

Fourth, the findings regarding the greater tolerance for potential elder abuse by Korean American elderly, and more negative attitudes toward reporting elder abuse to the authorities, seem to suggest that public educational outreach efforts for prevention of and intervention in elder abuse should target recent immigrant populations who are not familiar with the American legal and social service systems related to elder abuse. This is especially true for those immigrants who come from countries where no elder abuse laws exist, where elder abuse is defined or perceived differently, and where no formal, supportive resources are available to assist the victims of elder abuse.

Fifth, there appear to be some areas in which there is a direct conflict between cultural beliefs and practices and legal and professional definitions of abuse, as in the case of shared resources versus financial exploitation of Korean elderly. Resolution of the inherent conflict of these perspectives will require creative, culturally sensitive, problem solving.

Finally, there is a need for future research to identify specific cultural and non-cultural factors that explain how these contribute to the similarities and differences among various groups of the elderly and non-elderly populations in the perceptions and behaviors relating to issues of elder abuse. These data, in turn, can be used to inform the modification of existing intervention strategies or the development of culture-specific interventions for the different populations. How culturally appropriate these interventions are ultimately depends upon their effectiveness as demonstrated by the evaluation of outcomes for each population.

REFERENCES

Anetzberger, G., Korbin, J., & Tomita, S. (1996). Defining elder mistreatment in four ethnic groups across two generations. *Journal of Cross-Cultural Gerontology*, 11, 187-212.

Chang, J. & Moon, A. (1997). Korean American elderly's knowledge and perceptions of elder abuse: A qualitative analysis of cultural factors. *Journal of Multicultural Social Work*, 6(1-2), 139-155.

Gebotys, R.J., O'Connor, D., & Meair, K.J. (1992). Public perceptions of elder physical mistreatment. *Journal of Elder Abuse & Neglect*, 4(1/2), 151-171.

Griffin. L. W. & Williams, O.J. (1992). Abuse among African-American elderly. *Journal of Family Violence*, 7(1), 19-35.

Hall, J.M. (1999). Abuse of black elders in Rhode Island. In Toshio Tatara (ed) *Understanding elder abuse in minority populations*. Ann Arbor, MI: Braun-Brumfield. 13-25.

Hudson, M. (1994). Elder abuse: Its meaning to middle-aged and older adults, Part II: Pilot results. *Journal of Elder Abuse & Neglect*, 6(1), 55-81.

Hudson, M. & Carlson, J.R. (1994). Elder abuse: Its meaning to middle-aged and older adults, Part I: Instrument development. *Journal of Elder Abuse & Neglect*, 6(1), 29-54.

_____ (1999). Elder Abuse: Its meaning to Whites, African Americans, and Native Americans. In Toshio Tatara (ed) *Understanding elder abuse in minority populations*. Ann Arbor, MI: Braun-Brumfield. 187-204.

Moon, A. (1999). *Evaluation Report on Korean Community Empowerment Project.* Report submitted to California Department of Health Services, Maternal and Child Health Branch, Domestic Violence Section.

Moon, A., Lubben, J. E. & Villa, V. (1998). Awareness and utilization of community long-term care services by elderly Korean and non-Hispanic White Americans. *The Gerontologist*, 38, 309-316.

Moon, A. & Williams, O. (1993). Perceptions of elder abuse and help-seeking patterns among African American, White American, and Korean American elderly women. *The Gerontologist*, 33, 386-395.

Moon, A., Tomita, S., Talamantes, M., Brown, C., Sanchez, Y., Benton, D., Sanchez, C., & Kim, S. (1998). *Attitudes Toward Elder Mistreatment and Reporting: A Multicultural Study*. Report submitted to National Center on Elder Abuse.

Nerenburg, L. (1999). Culturally specific outreach in elder abuse. In Toshio Tatara (ed) *Understanding elder abuse in minority populations*. Ann Arbor, MI: Braun-Brumfield. 205-220.

Sanchez, C. (1999). Elder mistreatment in Mexican American communities: The Nevada and Michigan experiences. In Toshio Tatara (ed) *Understanding elder abuse in minority populations*. Ann Arbor, MI: Braun-Brumfield. 67-77.

Tatara, T. (1999). *Understanding elder abuse in minority populations*. Ann Arbor, MI: Braun-Brumfield.

U.S. Bureau of the Census (1990). Poverty in the United States: Current Population Survey Reports. 1990. Washington D.C.: Government Printing Office.

Elder Mistreatment:
Practice Modifications
to Accommodate Cultural Differences

Susan K. Tomita

SUMMARY. New information on elder mistreatment and conflict management among certain ethnic groups has necessitated changes in the practice arena. Clinical approaches depend on the victims' ability to identify themselves as victims, their degree of collective self, preferred conflict management techniques, and ability to identify their own power resources. Practice considerations and modifications include looking for subtle behaviors indicative of psychological abuse and neglect, using words that are culturally familiar and acceptable, and educating elders and their families about how other families relate and solve problems. Other interventions involve the use of the third party for cathartic displacement, and based on a temporal model of the exchange process, creating a power balance by maximizing the victims' potential power while minimizing the perpetrators' potential power. *[Article copies available for a fee from The Haworth Document Delivery Service: 1-800-342-9678. E-mail address: <getinfo@ haworthpressinc.com> Website: <http://www.haworthpressinc.com>]*

KEYWORDS. Counseling, culture, elder abuse, ethnic group, minority

INTRODUCTION

Not enough is known about the manifestations, conditions, circumstances, and consequences of elder mistreatment among various ethnic

Susan K. Tomita, PhD, is Associate Director of Social Work, Harborview Medical Center and Clinical Associate Professor, School of Social Work, University of Washington.

[Haworth co-indexing entry note]: "Elder Mistreatment: Practice Modifications to Accommodate Cultural Differences." Tomita, Susan K. Co-published simultaneously in *Journal of Multicultural Social Work* (The Haworth Press, Inc.) Vol. 8, No. 3/4, 2000, pp. 305-326; and: *Violence: Diverse Populations and Communities* (ed: Diane de Anda, and Rosina M. Becerra) The Haworth Press, Inc., 2000, pp. 305-326. Single or multiple copies of this article are available for a fee from The Haworth Document Delivery Service [1-800-342-9678, 9:00 a.m. - 5:00 p.m. (EST). E-mail address: getinfo@haworthpressinc.com].

groups, and correspondingly, the literature on clinical interventions for these groups is extremely limited. Based on reported data, the majority of elder abuse victims are White (National Center on Elder Abuse, 1997), with a small percentage of the reported victims representing other ethnic groups. However, preliminary data emanating from studies of elder mistreatment among specific sub-population groups have indicated that it may be as prevalent in those groups as within the White population (Brown, 1989; Chang & Moon, 1997; Kaneko & Yamada, 1990; Tomita, 1998a, 1998b).

The main objective of this paper is to answer the question of how recent data on ethnic groups might change our concept of mistreatment and our practice in elder mistreatment situations. The paper first provides a review of the available information on elder mistreatment among ethnic groups, then describes some cultural differences in conflict management. Given these differences, current practice methods of handling mistreatment cases are inadequate unless modifications are made. Suggestions are provided for approaching potential victims, and a temporal model of the exchange process is presented in which cultural norms are identified as important factors, and the victims are identified as powerful. It is impossible to consider all of the cultural differences for all groups. Moreover, the suggestions presented are based on the limited information obtained thus far. They are meant to serve as a general guide for clinicians in different types of agencies and to help create an awareness that differences in approach are necessary when treating elders from different cultural groups if interventions are to be accepted and effective. Because elders and families vary in degrees of acculturation and types of mistreatment situations, the suggested approaches may require additional adaptation among and within the various ethnic groups.

EMERGING CULTURAL ISSUES
IN ELDER MISTREATMENT

Underreporting and underdetection of elder mistreatment among specific groups may be due to several reasons. So far, a good deal of the research on elder mistreatment has utilized instruments such as the Straus Conflict Tactics Scale (Straus, 1979) to quantify mistreatment in categories such as chronic verbal aggression and severe violence. However, abusive behaviors that are subtle or culturally specific will not fall into these commonly known categories and, therefore, will not be reported. In Japan, Kaneko and Yamada (1990) found that the most common forms of mistreatment among mothers-in-law and daughters-in-law were not speaking to each other, saying disagreeable things, and ignoring the other person. In one study of Korean Americans, some of the interviewees felt that a lack of respect for the elder and not being allowed to live with the grown child constituted mistreatment, given the strong Korean cultural norms against such behaviors. In addition, abuse was perceived only within the context of family relations, particularly the parent-child relationship (Chang & Moon, 1997).

Victims may not realize that mistreatment acts committed against them are reportable. In another study involving Korean Americans, on average they were reported to be less sensitive to or more tolerant of abusive situations than both African American and White respondents (Moon & Williams, 1993). When presented with 13 scenarios of elder mistreatment, only 50% of the Korean American respondents perceived them to be abusive compared to 73% of the African American and 67% of the White respondents. In response to one scenario, in which the son threw a frying pan at the mother for the third time after the mother burnt some food, only 60% of the Korean American sample perceived the incident to be abusive compared to 100% of the African American and 97% of the White respondents.

In addition, help-seeking behaviors vary among the different groups. In one study, African American elders were more likely to seek legal recourse against their abusive adult offspring than were White elders (Korbin, Anetzberger, Thomassen & Austin, 1991). Moon and Williams (1993) found that Korean American elders were least likely to seek help had they been the victims in the 13 scenarios of elder mistreatment that were presented to them. Only 36% would seek help while 63% of African American and 62% of White elders would seek help. In a study on attitudes toward elder mistreatment and reporting among eight ethnic groups, Hispanic American elderly in New Mexico (51%) and Korean American elderly (38%) agreed that non-family members should not get involved in elder mistreatment situations, whereas among six other ethnic groups (African American, Japanese American, American Indian, Non-Hispanic White, Puerto Rican, and Texas Hispanic American) a much smaller percentage, ranging from 13% to 26%, felt that outsiders should not be involved (National Center on Elder Abuse, 1998).

Degree of interdependence may affect the elderly's perception of mistreatment. Brown (1989) and John (1988) note that, generally speaking, American Indian families are more interdependent than mainstream White American families. The latter tend to be more independent and see themselves as relying mainly on spouses and immediate family members. American Indian elders feel that it is their privilege and duty to help the less fortunate in their extended family. This was confirmed in a survey on elder mistreatment among elders of the Oljato Chapter of the Navajo (Brown, 1989). The respondents whose money went to other family members indicated that they had voluntarily shared their money, but the younger American Indian practitioners on the reservation perceived the elders as victims of exploitation.

Another reason for the underreporting of elder mistreatment among non-White groups is that while elderly respondents have considered psychological abuse and neglect to be the worst forms of elder mistreatment (Anetzberger, Korbin & Tomita, 1996; National Center on Elder Abuse, 1998), professionals may not be sensitized to their manifestations and, therefore, may be less likely to intervene with them. Current assessments of potential victims do not include inquiries, for example, about being isolated and being forced to eat alone for extended periods of time.

VARIATION IN CONFLICT MANAGEMENT

In order to recognize culturally specific forms of abuse and to consider appropriate forms of intervention, conflict management techniques in which the abuse occurs must also be understood. While most of the interventions mentioned in the previous section are applicable to most clients, it is important not to presume that all victims are capable of expressing themselves verbally and that they think in terms of seeking a solution. Levinson (1989) and Koch, Sodergren and Campbell (1976) note that societies utilize more than one form of conflict resolution including direct violence, verbal aggression, and nonviolence. The latter may include dyadic and triadic conflict management. In dyadic conflict management a third party is not involved, whereas in triadic conflict management, either a mediator or an adjudicator is involved. As one example of nonviolent means, Levinson notes that the Javanese handle quarrels by not speaking to each other (*satru*) for days, years, or indefinitely (Levinson, 1989).

Relatedly, Lebra (1984) provides a continuum of reactions to conflict to show that conflict resolution is only one of many ways of dealing with conflict. On this continuum, which consists of avoidance, repression, displacement, management and resolution, Lebra places the Japanese closer to the conflict avoidance end (see Figure 1).

In a study on conflict management techniques among Japanese Americans, Tomita found that behaviors were governed primarily by group loyalty. The community's or family's needs were placed before an individual's needs. Conditions under which conflict situations occurred included the cultural norm of male dominance, and the operation of dual and multiple selves, that is, presenting to outsiders only the non-suffering aspect of the self while hiding the victimization. In general, a consequence of placing others before the self was a quiet maneuvering and promoting of harmony through accommodation (Tomita, 1998b). Similarly, Boehnlein, Leung and Kinzie (1997) note that among Cambodian American families, the prevailing style of communication is an avoidance of intergenerational conflict, which can contribute to ongoing anxiety for both parents and children. The same dynamic also applies to East Indian American families (Prathikanti, 1997).

In the Tomita study (1998a), the Japanese American respondents used silence and verbal asymmetry, a non-interruptive, non-competitive, non-reciprocal communication style, to prevent the escalation of conflict that often occurs as a result of verbal sparring. Triadic management was also used to promote community harmony. Some confided in a trusted friend or relative for cathartic displacement in lieu of a face-to-face direct communication, and others used a third party to turn a conflictual situation into a more peaceful co-existence, and not necessarily to obtain a resolution. In addition to cathartic displacement, triadic management took the form of a third party who intervened. It was advantageous for third party involvement to be con-

FIGURE 1. Continuum of Reactions to Conflict

```
                                                      Resolution
                                         Management
                           Displacement
              Repression
  Avoidance
```

Source: Lebra, 1984

ducted without too much interaction and talk, because doing so protected the weaker dyad member from further blame and victimization. At times the intervener was a neutral party who could convey touchy messages and search out one person's feelings on behalf of the other. Without direct negative interactions, the relationship could concentrate on its positive aspects, maximizing group stability. This triadic management process differs from the Western expectation of an encounter followed by a resolution of varying duration.

In addition to triadic management, the victim or target of aggression used self-removal to feel better and to alleviate the conflict without calling attention to oneself. This method was the most frequently discussed conflict avoidance or reducing strategy in the study. Self-removal encompasses many tactics, varying in duration and degree of severity. On a continuum, the interviewees mentioned staying away from the source of aggression for a few hours, leaving the home for a few hours, leaving the home overnight, leaving the home for weeks or months, moving out of the home, and placing oneself in a nursing home.

The second solitary method that minimized the chances of a direct confrontation or conflict escalation was through *gaman* or endurance; the individuals kept their aggressive and angry feelings to themselves. Also, the elder victims blamed themselves for the grown child's or relative's misdeeds, since they share a collective self. Feeling responsible for the mistreatment acts, they felt that it was necessary to endure the consequences of failed parenting.

Like the Japanese American and the Javanese elderly, Carson (1995) notes that many American Indian elders are nonconfrontive and non-interventive in others' lives. Some of the basic tenets to which most tribal groups subscribe are a strong spiritual orientation to life, living in harmony with nature, family and tribal interdependence and support, community responsibility, commitment to the welfare of others, and group participation and cooperation over individual achievement. This dependency and interdependency common among generations, when combined with limited resources, creates a greater potential for conflict, related elder mistreatment, and the toleration of such behaviors.

In summary, among some ethnic groups, elder mistreatment victims are under-identified because the mistreatment may manifest itself differently, often with subtle, non-verbal behaviors. Current measurement tools and assessment techniques clearly do not capture all forms of elder mistreatment, especially in ethnic sub-populations. Some elders do not realize that they are victims of mistreatment and, as a result, do not inform others of the mistreatment. Help-seeking behaviors differ among different ethnic groups; some feel that non-family members should not become involved with elder mistreatment situations while others are more likely to seek help from specific agencies such as law enforcement. Furthermore, conflict management techniques vary considerably among ethnic groups, with some victims feeling more comfortable with conflict avoidance instead of conflict resolution techniques. The next section provides an informational framework on practice methods before suggestions for their modifications are provided.

CURRENT PRACTICE

Given the various emerging issues among the different ethnic groups, how do they impact current practice? Current practice consists of case finding, reporting, assessment, crisis intervention, short-term treatment, and on-going monitoring. Within the past ten years, due to increased training among home health, social services, and health care professionals, more cases of mistreatment are recognized and reported to regulatory agencies (National Center on Elder Abuse, 1997). In the case-finding phase, commonly used questions to detect cases of elder mistreatment include such direct questions as, "Have you ever been shoved, shaken or hit, tied to a chair, locked in a room or locked out of a house?" "Have you signed papers for reasons that were not clear to you?" Questions that deal with psychological abuse and subtle forms of mistreatment have not always been included in core curricula and are not commonly asked.

In the investigation phase, situations in which the elderly's physical safety or property are perceived as being in immediate jeopardy receive the highest priority. Crisis intervention may take the form of legal, law enforcement, medical, and home health agencies collaborating to maximize the patients' safety and to protect assets targeted by exploiters. Usually, once the investigation is conducted and the mistreatment is substantiated or unsubstantiated, cases are referred to different units within the agency or to other agencies for service delivery and ongoing monitoring. Often, investigators have an average of one to three contacts with all of the involved parties, then must move on to other cases.

Generally, treatment consists of short-term counseling within a conflict resolution framework. Within one visit or several sessions, health care and other professionals may provide the following interventions: help clients express and manage their feelings, inject a dose of reality to the clients' situation, help clients develop foresight, tap the elders' strengths to counter the mistreatment, use the "teachable moment" to inject information, and create environmental changes (Quinn & Tomita, 1997). Neutralization techniques commonly used by victims and perpetrators to deny or mitigate the mistreatment and responsibility for the mistreatment can be countered with specific statements if professionals are trained to listen for these denial statements (Sykes & Matza, 1957; Matza, 1964; Minor, 1980, 1981; Tomita, 1990).

While these current practice methods are applicable to a good deal of elder mistreatment cases, some modifications are in order when practicing among groups that are less familiar to practitioners. With a greater awareness that among different groups, responses to mistreatment may vary from doing nothing and staying away from the source of conflict to active resolution of the problem, current practice and intervention techniques must vary along this continuum as well.

PRACTICE CONSIDERATIONS AND MODIFICATIONS

Modifications in the Assessment Process

Within the context of elder mistreatment, culturally available conflict management techniques are utilized by some victims to maximize belonging and acceptance and to minimize exclusion and rejection. Some elders who have a strong sense of "groupness" promote the group's objectives often at the expense of their own needs. Their help-seeking behaviors will depend on their commitment to the group, whether it be family or community. Victims who subscribe to cultural norms that support the accommodation of others and discourage individuality are less likely to complain or discuss the mistreatment with others. Sometimes, elders will admit to being mistreated to others only when there is a certainty that the families and the perpetrators will not be affected negatively by revealing the mistreatment. As a result, tasks in the assessment phase are:

1. Explore the elder's degree of collective self or commitment to the perpetrator.
2. Explore the cultural context of elder mistreatment.
3. Assess the likelihood of outside intervention.
4. Look for subtle behaviors that are indicative of psychological abuse and neglect.

For example, with regard to assessing the elder's degree of collective self, having uncovered the mistreatment, practitioners may ask elders what portion of their pension is shared with other family members and how they feel about sharing such resources regularly. In exploring the cultural context of elder mistreatment, Sanchez notes that some Hispanics believe elder mistreatment is an issue of *la familia* and should be dealt only within that context to prevent bringing *vergüenza* (shame) to families. These families believe that only on rare occasions or when someone's life is in danger should outside agencies or organizations be involved (Sanchez, 1998). Similarly, Japanese American elders possessing a strong sense of collective self versus an independent self will not allow agency practitioners into the family circle due to the *haji* (shame) that everyone, not only elders, will experience if they reveal the abuse. For example, should the elderly members report the mistreatment, other family members may deny the mistreatment outright and privately chastise the elderly for being selfish or inconsiderate.

Lee (1997) reports that many Asian Americans do not comprehend the importance of the assessment process which includes taking a history and asking multiple questions that do not seem related to their presenting problems. Also, since verbal expression of emotion to outsiders is not customary, clinicians should not expect clear answers to the questions asked. Instead of sequential questioning, Lee suggests the use of photographs and albums, sharing of stories, paintings, songs, and philosophical discussions in order to elicit necessary information. For example, noticing framed photographs on the wall, practitioners may inquire about the people in them and their relationship to the elderly family members. This approach involves a major shift for typically focused and task-oriented practitioners.

Behavioral Cues

During discussions that are not necessarily focused on the mistreatment, behaviors that cue practitioners that the elders' commitment to the family and perpetrators may override their desire for outside help are: changing the subject when the issue of mistreatment is broached, silence and smiling when the victims sense that they are jeopardizing the shielding of the perpetrator, making vague statements such as, "Well . . . ., uh . . . ." (then silence) instead of making an absolute statement, shifting focus of the eyes, and pretending not to understand the direct question about mistreatment. This verbal asymmetry and indirect communication style may result in mistakenly labeling clients as resistant or in denial (Sue, 1990).

Practitioner's Choice of Words

The term "abuse" is not a familiar term and may even be unacceptable in translation to elders, especially for elders who do not use English as a first language. One suggestion is to use culturally acceptable terms in the assessment. For example, "sacrifice" or "suffering" and related terms are used by many Asians as they recount historical experiences, perhaps because it is the first of Buddhism's Four Noble Truths that life is full of suffering. After the initial stage of establishing a relationship, approach clients with, "Tell me about your work experiences." Clients will vary in what they report, and with encouragement ("You must have worked very hard . . . you must have suffered, sacrificing your own happiness . . . ") will most likely relate how their own needs were denied for the sake of others. When elders make preliminary statements, practitioners may explore suffering in a more narrow context: "With your grandchildren. . . . children. . . . how much do you do for them?" An opportunity may arise to ask a crucial question, "Are they good to you?" Elders may mention tension or even conflict and mistreatment if they believe that relatives have violated the norm of filial piety or reciprocity. Chang and Moon (1997) note that for first generation Korean Americans, mistreatment is perceived to occur only within the family and not by non-family members, so it is important to listen carefully to what is being said or left unsaid about the elders' relationships with their children.

Psychological Abuse and Neglect

Incidents of elder mistreatment will most likely be uncovered informally when elders are less defensive and more free to talk about themselves. In more relaxed settings, more time is available to pursue the possibility of psychological abuse and neglect. Currently, it is unclear if manifestations of psychological abuse and neglect are similar among different cultural groups. In one preliminary study of Korean American elderly (Chang & Moon, 1997), some incidents of psychological abuse reported by the respondents were: repeatedly treating elders disrespectfully or improperly, not using language that denotes respect, refusing to eat or talk with elders who are living in the same house, making demeaning remarks about the elder, taking elders for granted as baby-sitters, and talking back to them (Chang & Moon, 1997). "Do your children treat you with respect?" may be answered with, "My daughter-in-law acts as if I don't exist in the room; when she talks to me her voice is harsh–she has been this way for years." "Do you get enough to eat at night?" may be answered with, "They tell me, 'You really don't need that second helping of rice, do you?'" "With whom do you usually eat your dinner?" may be answered with, "They bring my food to my room and they eat without me in the dining room. They say nothing and I say nothing." As with other questions that assess the severity and lethality of the situation, practitioners should obtain specific examples of psychological abuse and find out how often they occur.

MODIFICATIONS IN THE INTERVENTION PHASE

Reality Orientation:
The Practitioner as Outsider

Practitioners representing an agency are automatically considered to be outsiders, even if they are of the same ethnic background. It is only natural that elders and their families would be on their best behavior if a visit or interview were imposed on them. However, for elders, coming in contact with others perceived to be outsiders may also be advantageous. Practitioners provide an *etic* (majority group) perspective to which elders and their families may not have much exposure. The intervention period can be an opportunity for practitioners to educate elders and families about how other families relate and solve problems.

One main function of practitioners is to provide an outsider's perspective by relabeling behaviors which elders may not realize are abusive. For example, in the case of an elder who had a frying pan repeatedly thrown at her by a son, practitioners might state:

> "If that happened to me, I would be frightened."

> "I am wondering if you believe that kind of behavior is wrong."

> "Are you aware that others may consider you to be a victim of abuse?"

Making tentative, non-accusatory statements preserves the elders' dignity and at the same time helps them realize that outside their immediate family, the abusive behavior is unacceptable and elders for the most part are not treated the way they have been. A psychoeducational approach, explaining client rights and abuse reporting laws may help elders realize that they have some community backing outside the family. A similar approach may be used with abusers, stating when the opportunity arises, "Are you aware that others may find your behavior to be abusive?" At the same time, to gain the *emic* (specific ethnic group) perspective, practitioners may inquire, "Is this (behavior) considered to be normal in your culture? What would others in your community say about this incident if they knew about it?" These statements may help aggressors think twice before engaging in their usual behavior.

Use of a Third Party

Be the third party. The addition of another person to the abuser-abused dyad changes its dynamics. Within some ethnic groups, practitioners are able to fulfill the role of the helpful, authoritative third party that has no allegiance either to victims or perpetrators. In order to do this, practitioners must be aware of the powerful nature of this role. Clients who are used to the norm of third party involvement will respond comfortably to authority figures who present to the entire family an expectation of cooperation and participation in the assessment (Ja & Yuen, 1997). This means making a shift from taking a client self-determination approach in the initial contact to providing structure and guidelines for the entire family in the interviews.

Partner with a third party. In some cases, partnering with a third party already established in the community will create access that might otherwise be impossible. Often indigenous healers, religious leaders including monks and priests, and community leaders or brokers make themselves available to agency practitioners if they consider their objectives to be worthy. These community members can serve as messengers, co-assessors, or be the ones to implement and monitor the subsequent treatment. This allows victims to maintain their traditional role and standing in the community while third party members become the enforcers of regulations. Generally speaking, older victims may not be as likely as younger women to confide about mistreatment to an unknown person (Cook-Daniels, 1997). In those instances, older women who are advocates may be the best representatives to contact victims and to follow up with regular phone calls to build trust.

Use the third party for cathartic displacement. As stated earlier, problem-solving techniques differ among groups. For example, in-depth comparison studies of people in Japan and in the U.S. (Hayashi & Kuroda, 1997) indicate that the Japanese ask themselves, "How can I adjust to this situation?" while Americans ask themselves, "How can I select or create a different situation?" According to Hayashi and Kuroda, Americans view the world in dichotomies and the individual as the prominent societal unit. In contrast, the Japanese are non-absolutists who pay attention to the entire social context rather than just to the individual (contextualism vs. individualism). The values of the Japanese American participants in these studies were found to be closer to the Japanese in Japan than other comparison groups in such areas as subscribing to an ambiguous communication style and a diffuse self.

Applying this information to the mistreatment context, when the collective self takes precedence over the individual self, victims may first use cathartic displacement to adjust to the situation. Elderly victims may want someone with whom to vent, but may never agree to problem-solving counseling due to their unfamiliarity with such a process. The preliminary ethnic group studies mentioned earlier (Chang & Moon, 1997; Moon & Williams, 1993; Tomita, 1998a, 1998b) suggest that many elders do not subscribe to an unfamiliar context presented by outsiders and have never thought in terms of seeking a solution or resolution. A suggestion of regular counseling sessions may not be met positively, but an offer of spending time to be heard with no expectation of change may be accepted. This means promoting increased verbal expression on the part of elders, encouraging them to discuss incidents of suffering and sacrifice without judgment by nodding and injecting comments and minimal verbal responses.

A common error on the part of practitioners is to misperceive clients as incapable of gaining insight or working on a solution for the presenting problems. Practitioners may be feeling frustrated by a lack of "progress" in the counseling. On the other hand, elders may have a totally different feeling, specifically, that they are able to discuss freely the difficult home situation without judgment, thus preparing themselves to endure the problems after the catharsis and maintain their place in the family without the risk of ostracism. Since it is difficult to be available as partners in the displacement process indefinitely, practitioners may want to spend some time finding another resource, usually trusted friends or relatives who are somewhat removed from the conflict situation and with whom victims can continue the displacement.

Development of Foresight: Behavioral Rehearsal

Victims who attempt to "make do" versus trying to find ways of changing their situation will remain in the abusive situation. For them, self-protective activities that will not jeopardize the positions of others may be preferred.

Review previous reactions in conflict situations. A standard of practice with domestic violence victims is to do safety planning and provide information on resources to be better prepared for the next conflict situation. However, handing victims a list of referrals or instructions on obtaining a restraining order may not make the victim safer. Instead, first assess how the victims have reacted in previous situations. It is possible for practitioners to experience some incongruity upon hearing victims say, "I did nothing . . . there is no solution," or, "It was my fate to suffer," or stare blankly at practitioners, not understanding a question that assumes victims feel empowered to take action.

Self removal: Future options that are familiar and culturally acceptable. Conflict avoidance tactics as mentioned by Tomita (1998a) seem to be commonly used by victims in some ethnic groups, perhaps because verbal adeptness is unnecessary, the risk of harm is low, and it is unnecessary for less powerful victims to come in contact with perpetrators in order to feel better. Self removal, including leaving the room or home for a few hours, weeks, months or permanently, has probably crossed the victims' minds or already been tried. It is also a method of gaining strength and control, manifesting self-reliance, and dignity preservation. Seeking help from relatives such as a brother or sister as opposed to the spouse's family is also a common option. A non-blaming, neutral question to ask is, "Where can you go until you feel better or safer?"

Creating a Power Balance

Exchange theory has provided a context in which the relationship of power and elder mistreatment can be understood, but some modifications of its ideas are necessary to include the role of cultural norms. In exchange theory, basic principles are that people tend to maximize their rewards and minimize or avoid their costs or punishments, and people's power is equivalent to others' dependency (Blau, 1964; Cook, 1987; Cook & Emerson, 1978; Emerson, 1972a, 1972b; Homans, 1974). Also, commitment as a constraint on the use of power may explain why victims remain in abusive relationships: to the extent that commitments form, the exploration of alternatives is curtailed, and power use varies inversely with commitment (Cook & Emerson, 1978). If elders are attached and committed strongly to perpetrators, they will be less likely to use their power resources, such as calling the police when they are attacked or withholding money from perpetrators.

In this paper, for better applicability to some groups in which the collective versus the individual self predominates, the term obligation may be a more appropriate word than commitment. While commitment implies choice and free will, obligation recognizes cultural constraints and community factors that limit choices and the use of available strategies. Due to their socialization, many victims do not understand the concept of choice (Masaki & Wong, 1997).

Instead of focusing on power and dependency alone, a temporal model of the exchange process is proposed, and is represented in Figure 2 below. This model is based on the literature on negative outcomes of the exchange process (Lind, 1986; Molm, 1987a, 1987b; Molm & Wiggins, 1979), an aspect of exchange theory not applied to the field of elder mistreatment thus far. This literature is important in the study of elder mistreatment mainly because it provides a frame-

FIGURE 2. A Temporal Model of Power Use

Non-Structural Factors Affecting the Use of Power Resources
Cultural Norms: e.g., male dominance, collective self, obligation
Behavioral Skills/Influence: e.g., cognitive function, self-control

Potential Power ------------------------> **Actual Power**
Examples: *Examples:*
  Mother's money, housing, self-removal,   **Reward Power**
    family support   Mother provides housing & money

  Son's mobility, strength, affection,   Son provides companionship &
    & companionship   attention

                              Punishment Power
                              Mother reports abuse to agency

                              Son inflicts pain, threatens shame

Negotiation Affecting the Use of Power Resources
Exchange own resource for other's resource
Use reward to avoid punishment by other
Use punishment to counter other's punishment

Time 1   **Time 2**

work in which both elders and perpetrators are perceived as potentially powerful, in contrast to some elder mistreatment literature that depicts elders as powerless and perpetrators as those who strike out due to their dependency on elders for resources.

In this model, a time period is added prior to the exchange in which such culturally supported behaviors as elders sharing money are identified as potential power sources. Resources and positions that give a person control over another may not be used between two time periods due to nonstructural factors that intervene, such as cultural norms, history of the relationship, and the degree of collective self. Also, individual differences in such areas as self control (Gottfredson & Hirschi, 1990) and behavioral skills (Patterson, 1980, 1982) are recognized as important factors and included in the model.

Without intervention, the abusers' combination of sparingly used punishment and reward power may make them more powerful than the victims. Reward power in the form of affection and companionship helps to neutralize the abusers' high cost of using punishment power or threats and abuse. Punishment power is likely to be used under certain structural conditions such as when victims are unlikely to retaliate, when victims are unlikely to withdraw totally from the exchange, and when it is likely to produce results faster than withholding rewards.

Maximize the victim's and culture's potential power. Using Figure 2 as a reference, the main tasks of practitioners are to help victims grasp the fact that they too are powerful, and to minimize the perpetrators' power, which sometimes is actualized in the form of abuse. Both victims and perpetrators possess potential power, but some victims who are used to sharing their resources are not aware that they possess this power. It is unused due to such norms as group obligation, placing the group above the self, and a lack of awareness that resources may be exchanged or negotiated. For elders, common sources of potential power are housing, which many perpetrators need and a monthly income from Social Security retirement and Supplemental Security Income funds or a pension. Another source of elders' power are alliances created in supportive environments such as senior centers which elders are able to attend regularly and where they may feel comfortable discussing intergenerational issues. Protective services and law enforcement agencies also provide empowerment against perpetrators.

Some elders may be reluctant to consider resources as theirs alone. However, practitioners can help victims realize their power by asking such questions as, "What do your family members depend on from you?" " What are you contributing to your family?" Eventually they may understand that these resources as well as self removal are powerful tools of negotiation. To further assess the power imbalance, ask, "How much are you willing to put up with in order to belong? How much are you willing to put up with in order not to be excluded from your family?" Some elders may assume that they are obligated to share their resources, and fear being excluded if they refuse to turn over their monthly checks. However, others may hear for the first time from the practitioner that they do not have to share their home and pension check with threatening relatives.

One power enhancing tactic is to create a different context of elders' collective self, one that squeezes out abusers by soliciting others to link up with elders. Elders may not realize that some friends and relatives are staying away from them, feeling helpless and assuming that elders prefer the company of perpetrators. Pursuing their awareness with, "What do the rest of your family or your friends think about what is going on," elders may say that no one knows about the suffering they are going through since they have been keeping it a secret. A crucial intervention statement may be, "They might already know about your problems but are waiting for you to let them in on it–I wonder what they would say if you involved them. They may be staying away from you because they can't stand to watch you suffer or because you seem to them to have chosen to remain in this situation."

Power-enhancing counseling entails tapping cultural strengths in addition to elders' individual strengths. Mistreatment may be minimized by using the cultural strengths that have helped the families cope historically under difficult conditions. Where there is an emphasis on community and tribal interdependence and support, group participation and cooperation, and extended family, Carson (1995) notes, ". . . the collective liability for a family member's actions helps protect family members and regulate individual behavior by providing expected standards of behavior (i.e., by establishing a collective conscience and consciousness) and emphasizing individual responsibility for one's actions and how these reflect on the family and tribe" (p. 31).

Cultural norms such as interdependency and an obligation to help others who comprise the collective self can be mobilized to help both victims and perpetrators. When elders cite family loyalty as a reason not to make attempts to stop the mistreatment, through reframing, practitioners and family members may emphasize the elders' obligation to admit to the mistreatment in order to obtain help for the perpetrators and to stop participating in the perpetuation of a tense atmosphere that is deleterious to all family members.

Minimize the perpetrator's potential power. The potential power of perpetrators includes physical strength and mobility and displays of affection and attention toward the victims, all of which may be used to foster an emotional or physical dependency on them. Some methods of curtailing behaviors are making their actions as public as possible through intermittent drop-in visits to the elders' home and by letting the perpetrators know that everyone in the family and community are aware of their behavior and that they are being watched. This notice may be done indirectly by letting a mutual acquaintance "leak" to perpetrators that "everyone knows" about their behavior. Third party "watchdogs" must be prepared to provide a show of force against perpetrators when elders are immobilized by cultural constraints and be ready to contact outside agencies if the community and family constraints are not strong enough to stop the mistreatment.

SUMMARY

New information on mistreatment and conflict within certain ethnic groups has necessitated changes in the practice arena. Some elders are not aware that they are victims of mistreatment when the mistreatment is culturally syntonic. They also do not realize that help is available within the community and from outside agencies. The challenge for practitioners is to develop an understanding of the cultural context in which the victim-abuser dyad exists. Instead of sequential questions, the assessment process may consist of indirect discussions while the mistreatment is uncovered, and the victims' usual conflict management techniques are explored.

Intervening in cases of elder mistreatment is always challenging; this challenge can be made vastly more complex in certain circumstances wherein cultural norms affect the victims' perception of the mistreatment process and the practitioners' intentions. New information from the few studies conducted so far among specific groups warn practitioners that their approach depends on the victims' preferred conflict management techniques, their degree of collective self, ability to identify themselves as victims, and ability to identify their own power resources. This paper reminds us that in certain groups conflict resolution is an ideal and not the usual method of conflict management. Given this, it is incumbent upon practitioners to think of ways to increase the victims' safety without confronting perpetrators directly, and to use community resources, third party helpers, and self removal as interventions that are compatible with the victims' coping style.

REFERENCES

Anetzberger, G. J., Korbin, J. E., Tomita, S. K. (1995). Defining elder mistreatment in four ethnic groups across two generations. *Journal of Cross-Cultural Gerontology, 11*, 187-212.

Blau, P. (1964). *Exchange and power in social life*. NY: John Wiley and Sons.

Boehnlein, J., Leung, P., & Kinzie, J. (1997). Cambodian American families. In E. Lee (Ed.). *Working with Asian Americans: A guide for clinicians* (pp. 37-45). NY: Guilford Press.

Brown, A. (1989). A survey on elder abuse at one Native American tribe. *Journal of Elder Abuse & Neglect, 1*(2), 17-37.

Carson, D. (1995). American Indian elder abuse: Risk and protective factors among the oldest Americans. *Journal of Elder Abuse & Neglect, 7*(1), 17-39.

Chang, J., & Moon, A. (1997). Korean American elderly's knowledge and perceptions of elder abuse: A qualitative analysis of cultural factors. *Journal of Multicultural Social Work 6*(1/2), 139-154.

Cook, K. (Ed.). (1987). *Social exchange theory*. Beverly Hills, CA: Sage.

Cook, K., & Emerson, R. (1978). Power, equity, commitment in exchange networks. *American Sociological Review, 43*(5), 721-739.

Cook-Daniels, Loree (1997, May). From the frontlines: Older battered women. (Available from Wordbridges, 49 Canterbury Circle, Vallejo, CA 94591).

Emerson, R. (1972a). Exchange theory, Part I: A sociological basis for social exchange. In J. Berger, M. Zelditch, & B. Anderson (Eds.), *Sociological theories in progress, Vol. 2* (pp. 38-57). Boston: Houghton Mifflin.

Emerson, R. (1972b). Exchange theory, Part II: A sociological basis for social exchange. In. J. Berger, M. Zelditch, & B. Anderson (Eds.), *Sociological theories in progress, Vol. 2* (pp. 58-87). Boston: Houghton Mifflin.

Gottfredson, M. & Hirschi, T. (1990). *A general theory of crime*. Stanford, CA: Stanford University Press.

Hayashi, C. & Kuroda, Y. (1997). *Japanese culture in comparative perspective*. Westport, CT: Praeger.

Homans, G. (1974). *Social behavior*. New York: Harcourt Brace Jovanovich.

Ja, D. & Yuen, F. (1997). Substance abuse treatment among Asian Americans. In E. Lee (Ed.). *Working with Asian Americans: A guide for clinicians* (pp. 3-36). NY: Guilford Press.

John, R. (1988). The Native American family. In C. Mindel, R. Habenstein, & R. Wright, Jr. (Eds.), *Ethnic families in America* (pp. 325-363). New York: Elsevier.

Kaneko, Y., & Yamada, Y. (1990). Wives and mothers-in-law: Potential for family conflict in post-war Japan. *Journal of Elder Abuse & Neglect, 2*(1/2), 87-99.

Koch, K., Sodergren, J., & Campbell, S. (1976). Political and psychological correlates of conflict management: A cross-cultural study. *Law & Society Review, 10*, 443-466.

Korbin, J., Anetzberger, G., Thomassen, R., & Austin, C. (1991). Abused elders who seek legal recourse against their adult offspring: Findings from an exploratory study. *Journal of Elder Abuse & Neglect, 3*(3), 1-18.

Lebra, T. (1984). Nonconfrontational strategies for management of interpersonal conflicts. In E. Krauss, T. Rohlen, & P. Steinhoff (Eds.), *Conflict in Japan* (pp. 41-59). Honolulu, HI: University of Hawaii Press.

Lee, E. (1997). Overview: The assessment and treatment of Asian American families. In E. Lee (Ed.), *Working with Asian Americans: A guide for clinicians*. (pp. 3-36). NY: Guilford Press.

Levinson, D. (1989) *Family violence in cross-cultural perspective.* Newbury Pk., CA: Sage.

Lind, J. L. (1986). Exchange processes in history: Integrating the micro and macro levels of analysis. *Sociological Quarterly, 28*(2), 223-246.

Masaki, B. & Wong, L. (1997). Domestic violence in the Asian community. In E. Lee (Ed.), *Working with Asian Americans: A guide for clinicians* (pp. 439-451). NY: Guilford Press.

Matza, D. (1964). *Delinquency and drift.* NY: John Wiley & Sons.

Minor, W. (1980). The neutralization of criminal offense. *Criminology, 18*(1), 103-120.

Minor, W. (1981). Techniques of neutralization: A reconceptualization and empirical examination. *Journal of Research in Crime & Delinquency*, July, 295-318.

Molm, L. D. (1987a). Linking power structure and power use. In K. S. Cook (Ed.), *Social exchange theory* (pp. 101-129). Beverly Hills: Sage.

Molm, L. D. (1987b). Power-dependence theory: Power processes and negative outcomes. *Advances in Group Processes, 4*, 171-198.

Molm, L. D. & Wiggins, J. (1979). A behavioral analysis of the dynamics of social exchange in the dyad. *Social Forces, 57*(4), 1157-1180.

Moon, A. & Williams, O. (1993). Perceptions of elder abuse and help-seeking patterns among African-American, Caucasian-American, and Korean-American elderly women. *Gerontologist, 33*(3), 386-395.

National Center on Elder Abuse (1997). *Understanding the nature and extent of elder abuse in domestic settings: An NCEA summary sheet.* Washington, DC: Author.

National Center on Elder Abuse (1998). *Attitudes toward elder mistreatment and reporting: A multicultural study.* Washington, DC: Author.

Patterson, G. (1980). Children who steal. In T. Hirschi & M. Gottfredson (Eds), *Understanding crime: Current theory and research* (pp. 73-90). Beverly Hills, CA: Sage.

Patterson, G. (1982). *Coercive family process.* Eugene, OR: Castalia Publishing Co.

Prathikanti, S. (1997). East Indian American families. In E. Lee (Ed.), *Working with Asian Americans: A guide for clinicians* (pp. 79-100). NY: Guilford Press.

Quinn, M.J. & Tomita, S. (1997). *Elder abuse & neglect: Causes, diagnosis & intervention Strategies*, (2nd ed.). NY: Springer.

Sanchez, Y. (1998). Elder abuse in Mexican American communities: Issues and challenges. In T. Tatara (Ed.), *Understanding elder abuse among minority populations* (pp. 67-77). Washington, DC: Taylor & Francis.

Straus, M. (1979). Measuring intrafamily conflict and violence: The Conflict Tactics Scale. *Journal of Marriage and the Family, 41*, 75-88.

Sue, D. (1990). Culture-specific strategies in counseling: A conceptual framework. *Professional Psychology: Research and Practice, 21*(6), 424-433.

Sykes, G. & Matza, D. (1957). Techniques of neutralization: A theory of delinquency. *American Sociological Review, 22*, 664-670.

Tomita, S. (1998a). The consequences of belonging: Conflict management techniques among Japanese Americans. *Journal of Elder Abuse & Neglect, 9*(3), 41-68.

Tomita, S. (1998b). Conditions for mistreatment among the Japanese: An exploratory study. In T. Tatara (Ed.). *Understanding elder abuse among minority populations* (pp. 119-139). Washington, DC: Taylor & Francis.

Willer, D. & Anderson, B. (1981). *Networks, exchange, and coercion: The elementary theory and its applications.* New York: Elsevier North Holland, Inc.

Index

Academic outcomes
    in Black youth urban gangs,
        76,78,80-81
    in Khmer refugee adolescents,
        30t,31-37
    violence exposure as predictor of,
        17-19,33-34
    interventions for, 39-40
Acculturation
    elder abuse and, 306
    of Latino populations,
        135-136,140-141,247
    sexual assault model of,
        145-147
    of Vietnamese refugees,
        162-165,182,186
Add Health Survey
    family variables in,
        56-57,56t,62-64
    literature review for, 49-51
    methodology for
        analysis, 54
        dependent measures, 52
        independent measures, 53-54
        procedural, 52
        sampling, 51-52
    purpose of, 47-49,51
    results of, 57-59,57t-58t
        family characteristics,
            56-57,56t, 62-64
        injured someone,
            57t-58t,59,60t,61
        physical fights, 57t-58t,59,60t
        pulled knife/gun, 57t-58t,60t,61
        shot/stabbed someone,
            57t-58t,60t,61-62
        socio-demographics,
            54-56,55t,64-65

    violent behavior,
        57-59,57t-58t,60t
Adolescent violence
    during courtship. See Dating
        violence
    ecological model of,
        47,50-51,62-68
    examples of, 4,32
    family characteristics in
        discussion on, 62-64
        implications of, 67-68
        literature review for, 49-51
        models of, 47-51
        race/ethnicity versus,
            47,51-56,57t-58t,60t,65-68
        socio-demographics of,
            47-51,53-56,55t, 64-66
        study methodology for, 51-54
        study results on, 56-62,56t
    as gang activity, 73,87-88,91
    individual factors in, 49-51
    intervention programs for,
        50-51,67-68
    in Khmer refugees, 3,15-40
    predictors of, 49,50
        family as, 47-51,55t-58t,
            57-64,60t,67-68
        race/ethnicity as, 47,51-56,
            57t-58t,60t,65-68
    research strategies for, 3,47-48
    risk factors for, 48-49
    sexual. See Sexual assault
    socio-demographics of
        discussion on, 64-68
        measures of, 53-54
        models of, 47-51
        survey results of,
            54-56,55t,64-65
    statistics on, 1-2,18,48

theories of, 49-51
urban correlations of, 3,9,18-22.
    See also Urban gangs
Wave 1 analysis of. *See* Add
    Health Survey
African Americans
    adolescent violence in, 2. *See also*
        Add Health Survey
    child abuse by, 196
    elder abuse by, 12,285-286,298,
        301,307
        Los Angeles study of. *See* Elder
            abuse study
    sexual assault by, 5-6,134,138,144
    spousal abuse by, 8-9
    urban gang socialization of,
        4,71-95
Afro-Caribbeans
    lineage of, 75n
    urban gang socialization of, 71-95
Age, as violence factor, 51-52,54-56,
        55t,64-65
Aggressive behaviors
    as adolescent response to trauma,
        19-20
    as child discipline, 173,175t,177
    in dating violence, 110-117,124
    in Khmer refugee adolescents,
        30t,31-32,36-38
    predictors of
        family as, 50-51,55t-58t,57-64,
            60t,67-68
        race/ethnicity as, 47,51-56,
            57t-58t,60t,65-68
        socio-demographic, 47-51,
            53-56,55t,64-68
    redirection of, gangs as vehicle for,
        87,91
Aging-out, of gangs, 88,92-93
Alcohol abuse. *See* Substance abuse
Alternative activities, as child
        discipline, 173,175t
Alternative skill-training structure
    as urban gang function, 91-93
    for urban gangs, 94-95
American Indians

elder abuse by, 286,307-308,310
sexual assault by, 5,134
Amnesia, dissociative, from child
        abuse, 205
Anger. *See* Aggressive behaviors
Anti-establishment beliefs, of gangs,
        73-75,80
Antisocial behavior
    adolescent examples of, 4,32
    as adolescent response to trauma,
        19-20
    Multisystemic Therapy for,
        207-208
    predictors of, 38,50
    as urban gang culture, 73-75,89
Anxiety
    from child abuse, 194-195,
        200-205,201t
    in Khmer refugee adolescents,
        30-31,30t,35-38
    from prolonged violence, 18,20-21
    from sexual assault, 143-144
    of Vietnamese refugees,
        162,174-176,174t,181
Asian Americans
    adolescent violence by. *See* Add
        Health Survey
    child abuse by, 7-8. *See also*
        Vietnamese child abuse
    elder abuse by. *See* Korean
        Americans
    help-seeking behavior by, 104,123,
        166-167,183,219,229
    patriarchal culture of, 103-105,107,
        162-163,221
    sexual assault by, 134
    women abuse by, 9-10,103-105,107.
        See also Chinese battered
        women
Attention-deficit disorder, from child
        abuse, 195
Attitude Toward Women Scale,
        109,115
Attitudes
    about elder abuse interventions,
        296-297,296t,299,301,312

of Mexican battered women,
260-262,273-274,277-278
regarding abuse reporting. *See*
Reporting
societal. *See* Social attitudes
toward dating violence, 108
Authority relationships
in Asian cultures, 103-105,107,122
mistrust of, 178-179,181,183-185
reporting abuse to. *See* Reporting
Autonomy, in Latino culture, 141
Avoidance, as coping mechanism
with elder abuse, 308-311,309f,
318-319
with sexual assault, 138-139

Bandura's model, of social learning,
249f, 250-251
Basic English Skills Test (BEST),
168,169,171
Battered women. *See* Spouse/partner
abuse; *specific ethnic group*
Battered Women's Movement, 216
Behavior problems. *See* Behavioral
outcomes
Behavioral norms
in dating expectations,
5-6,104-107,138-139
in spousal abuse, 10-11,220-221
Behavioral outcomes
of child abuse, 195,199,201-205,
201t,203t
of Khmer refugee adolescents,
30t,31-38
of prolonged violence, 17-22
of sexual assault, 143-144
of spousal abuse, 227
violence exposure as predictor of,
33-34
Behavioral rehearsal, in elder abuse
treatment, 318-319
Behavioral responses, in social
learning theory,
249-251,249f
spousal abuse and, 277-278,277f

Beliefs
in gender behavior. *See* Gender
roles; Sex roles
insidious trauma impact on, 145
restructuring of. *See* Cognitive
behavioral therapy
as societal norms. *See* Behavioral
norms
BEST. *See* Basic English Skills Test
Biculturalism, of Latina sexual
assault, 139,145-147
treatment approaches for, 151-154
Black population
in London. *See* Afro-Caribbeans
in U.S. *See* African Americans
Black urban gangs, study of
findings of
gang formation factors, 80-82
major issues of focus groups,
79,79t
socio-demographic, 76-79,78t
visible gangs, 79-80
functional findings and discussion
of, 82-83,88
as alternative training structure,
91-93
income source, 86-87,91
redirection of anger/aggression,
87,91
security, 86,90-91
self-esteem/self-image,
84,89-90
social activities, 85,90
social group identity, 83,88-89
social status, 84,89
social structure, 85,90
social support, 85-86,90
surrogate family, 83-84,89,93-94
as transitional structure, 93-94
implications of, 94-95
literature review for, 71-75
methodology for, 75-76
data analysis, 77-79,78t
measures, 76
sampling, 76-77
Blame

in elder abuse, 295-296,295t,
299,310
in sexual assault, 135-136,
138-139,141-142
treatment approaches to,
146,150,152-153
for spousal abuse, 222-223
British National Survey of Health and
Development, 50

Cambridge-Somerville Youth Study,
63
CAPI. *See* Child Abuse Potential
Inventory;
Computer-assisted Personal
Interview
CASI. *See* Computer-assisted
Self-Interview
Cathartic displacement, for elder
abuse, 317-318
CBCL. *See* Child Behavior Checklist
CBT. *See* Cognitive behavioral
therapy
CDC. *See* Child Dissociative
Checklist
CDI. *See* Children's Depression
Inventory
Center for Epidemiologic Studies
Depression Scale for
Children (CES-DC), 24
Ceremonial rape, 137
Child abuse
cultural context of, 7-8
help-seeking behavior for,
166-167,183
with spousal abuse, 228,238,
262-263,274-275,278
intervention programs for, 183-184,
183t,186,206-208
by Latinos. *See* Latina/Latino child
abuse
prevalence of, 163-165,193-194,196
psychological impact of, 194-195,
200-206,201t,203t

research strategies for,
182-186,208-210
sexual *versus* physical, 194-198
by Vietnamese refugees. *See*
Vietnamese child abuse
Child Abuse Potential Inventory
(CAPI), of Vietnamese
refugees, 167,169,173,174t
faked-responses in, 173,175-176,
180-182
other measurements with,
174-176,174t,181
Child Behavior Checklist (CBCL)
Latino study results of,
201-205,201t,203
utility of, 8,199,207
Child Dissociative Checklist (CDC),
200,201t,202-206
Child maltreatment. *See also* Child
abuse
prevalence of, 194,196
scope of, 196
Child-rearing practices
cultural context of, 7-8
as predictor of adolescent violence,
50-51
Children's Depression Inventory
(CDI)
Latino study results of,
201-202,201t,203t,205
utility of, 199-200
Chinese Americans
child abuse by, 228,238
dating violence of, 5-6,101-124
demographics of, 218-219
family relationships of, 219-221
women abuse by, 103-105,107. *See
also* Chinese battered
women
Chinese battered women
assessment of
cultural perception and
resolution, 228,238
immigration-related issues, 229
problem intensity, 227
somatic complaints, 227

community interventions for
  criminalization,
    219,234-236,238
  education, 235-236,238
  organizational coordination,
    237-238
counseling of
  assessment for, 227-229
  educational, 219,231,232
  empowering, 232
  goals of, 226-227
  joining and engagement,
    229-231
  pragmatism in, 231
  via telephone, 232-233
culture-specific influences of,
  219-222,228,238
family system interventions for,
  233-234
immigration-related issues of,
  224-226,229
intervention programs for
  community focus of,
    226,234-237
  family system focus of,
    226,233-234
  individual woman focus of,
    226-233
  three-tier model of,
    215-216,226,238
language issues of, 224-226,
  228-229,231-232,235
literature review of, 218-226
overview of, 9-10,216-217,217t,
  237-238
prevalence of, 218-219
reporting to authorities, 218-219,
  228-231,234-236,238
social support issues of,
  223-225,232,234
socio-demographics of,
  218-219,224-225
women's responses,
  220-223,227,229
Church affiliations, spousal abuse and,
  247,263,269-270,274,280

Civil rights organizations, Black youth
  gangs and, 76-77
Co-morbid disorders, with
  post-traumatic stress
  disorder, 18-22
Cognitive behavioral therapy (CBT)
  for child abuse, 208
  as rape crisis intervention, 151-153
Collective identity
  elder abuse and, 312-313,317,319,
    323
  spousal abuse and, 219-223
College students, dating violence by.
  See Dating violence study
Commitment, as elder abuse issue,
  319-323,320f
Communication, therapeutic. *See*
  Therapeutic relationships
Community groups, in Black youth
  gang study, 76-77,94
Community interventions, for spousal
  abuse
  criminalization, 219,234-236,238
  education, 235-236,238,279-280
  organizational coordination,
    237-238,280
Community outreach. *See also*
  Women's shelters
  for elder abuse, 301-302
  for spousal abuse,
    235-238,279-280
Community violence. *See* Adolescent
  violence; Gangs and gang
  activity
Compounded community trauma,
  20,21
Computer-assisted Personal Interview
  (CAPI), 52
Computer-assisted Self-Interview
  (CASI), 52
Confidentiality, spousal abuse and,
  230,232-233
Conflict management
  in elder abuse, 300,308-312,309f
  cultural modifications for,
    312-323

in spousal abuse, 228,231-234,279
Conflict Tactics Scale (CTS)
   in child abuse, 167-168,179-181,182
   in dating violence, 108-109,118,121
   in elder abuse, 306
Contextual Justification of Dating
      Violence Scale, 108
Control issues
   in elder abuse, 319-323,320f
   in spousal abuse, 220-221,224-225,
      232,250
Coping mechanisms
   adolescent, per perceived social
      support, 17,22,39-40
   with elder abuse, 308-311,309f,
      318-319
   with sexual assaults, 119,133,
      138-139,143,145,147
      in children, 194-195,200-206,
         201t,203t
   with spousal abuse
      of Chinese women,
         220-221,223,227
      of Mexican immigrants,
         247,273-274,278
Corporal punishment
   child abuse as,
      163-164,169,179-181
   cultural context of, 7-8,169,
      179-180
   spousal abuse as, 236
Counseling techniques
   for elder abuse, 300-302,308-312,
      309f
      cultural modifications of,
         312-323
   for rape treatment, 142,149-150
   for spousal abuse
      of Chinese women, 226-233
      of Mexican immigrants,
         261,270-271,278-280
Couple therapy, for spousal abuse,
      233,279
Courtship. *See* Dating behavior
Criminal justice system

Black youth gangs and,
   76,79,81-82
spousal abuse and, 234-235,237
Criminalization, of spousal abuse,
   219,234-236,238
Crisis intervention
   for elder abuse, 311-312
   for rape treatment, 150,153-154
CTS. *See* Conflict Tactics Scale
Cultural competence training, for
      spousal abuse treatment,
      216,226-238
Cultural context. *See* Socio-cultural
      context
Culture, definition of, 136
Curanderos, 272

Data analysis methods. *See* Statistical
      analysis programs; *specific*
      study
Data collection methods, 2,23,25-26,52.
      See also specific study
Date rape, 6-7,119-120,139
Dating behavior, gender roles in,
   5-6,101-104,138-139
Dating violence. *See also* Sexual
      assault
   in college students. *See* Dating
      violence study
   contextual justification of,
      106-108,111,111t,113-118,
      114t-115t
   cultural perceptions of,
      5-6,101-107,122-124
   definitions of,
      111,111t,113-117,115t
   intervention programs for,
      104,122-124
   per gender, 4-5,102,107,118,120
   prevalence of, 4-5,102
   psychological *versus* physical,
      110-117,124
   types of, 4,105-107,115-116
Dating violence study, of college
      students

findings and discussion of
Chinese American's experiences,
112-113,113t,118
Chinese American's perceptions,
110-112,111t-112t
contextual justifications of,
111,111t,113-118,114t-115t
cultural relationships of
perceptions/experiences,
113-115,114t,119
definitions,
111,111t,113-117,115t
gender role beliefs and
perceptions/experiences,
115-116,115t,119-120
socio-demographics,
109-110,110t
White student's experiences,
112-113 113t, 118
introduction to, 101-104
limitations of, 120-122
literature review for
Asian culture perspectives,
104-105
gender role beliefs, 107
perceptions and definitions,
105-107
methodology for, 108-109,120
practice implications of, 122-124
research implications of, 120-122
Deference, as gender role belief,
105,107,112,117-118
Definitions of Dating Violence Scale,
108
Defloration rituals, 137
Demographics
Census Bureau predictions on, 103
study considerations of. *See*
Socio-demographics; *specific
study*
Denial, of spousal abuse. *See*
Normalization
Dependency issues
in elder abuse, 319-323,320f
in spousal abuse, 222-225,228
Depression, clinical

from child abuse, 194-195,
199-202,201t,203t,205
from community violence, 18-22
in foreign refugees, 3,17-22,30-31,
30t,33-38,162
as rape sequelae, 143-144
Developmental problems
as adolescent response to trauma,
20-21
family as predictor of, 50-51
Discipline methods
physical, as child abuse,
163-164,169,177,179-182
of Vietnamese refugees,
163-164,169,173,175t
per children *versus* parents,
176-177
Discussion. *See* Talking
Displacement, for elder abuse,
309,309f,317-318
Dissociative disorders
from child abuse, 200,201t,
202-206,203t
scope of, 205
Divorce, spousal abuse and,
222-223,261
Domestic violence. *See*
Spouse/partner abuse
Dress
as sexuality factor, 138
as urban gang identity, 80,89
Drug abuse. *See* Substance abuse
Drug dealing, by urban gangs,
79t,80,91-92

Early childhood, interventions
programs for, 50-51,68
Early starter model, of aggressive
behavior, 51
Ecological model, of adolescent
violence, 47,50-51,62-68
Economics and economic mobility.
See Socioeconomic status
Education, as spousal abuse, 222,228
Educational intervention

for elder abuse, 300-302,312,318
for spousal abuse
     community, 235-238,279-280
     group, 279-280
     individual, 219,231-232
Educational status
     in Black youth gang study,
          76,78,80-81
     spousal abuse and,
          218-219,244,254, 256t
Ego strength, of Vietnamese refugees,
     174-175,174t
Elder abuse
     blame for, 295-296,295t,299
     coping mechanisms for,
          308-311,309f,318-319
     cross-sectional study of. *See* Elder
          abuse study
     definitions/perceptions of
          cultural context of, 12,285-287,
               300-302,305-308
          professional *versus* public,
               283-287
     exchange theory of, 319-323,320f
     family relationships and, 286,295,
          295t,298
     help-seeking behavior for, 285,294,
          299-300,307,311
     intervention programs for. *See*
          Elder abuse treatment
     prevalence of, 11, 306
     psychological *versus* physical,
          285-287,298
     reporting to authorities, 296-297,
          296t,301,306-307
     risk factors for, 12, 300
     safety planning for, 291,293-294,
          300,318,321
     as social issue, 11-12,287
     types of, 285-287,291-294,298-299
Elder abuse study
     definitions for, 284
     family *versus* non-family in,
          286,295,295t,298-299
     findings and discussion of
          causes of abuse, 294-296,295t

perceptions of perpetrators,
     294-296,295t
reporting attitudes,
     296-297,296t,301
socio-demographic,
     288,289t,290
third-party intervention attitudes,
     296-297,296t,299,301
tolerance of abuse,
     291,292t,293-294,298,301
language considerations with,
     286-287,290
limitations of, 298
literature review for, 285-287
methodology for
     data collection, 290-291
     sampling, 287-290,289t,298
practice implications of,
     300-302,323
research implications of, 302
Elder abuse treatment
     assessment process for
          behavioral cues in, 313-314
          of psychological abuse, 314-315
          tasks of, 312-313
          word choices for, 314
     conflict management variations of,
          308-311,309f
     cultural issues of, 301-302,305-308
     cultural modifications of
          assessment process, 312-315
          intervention phase, 315-323
     current practices, 311-312,323
     dyadic techniques,
          308-309,309f,323
     intervention phase modifications
          for
          behavioral rehearsal as, 318-319
          power balance, 316-318
          reality orientation as, 315-316
          third party usage options,
               316-318,322
     overview of, 12-13,300-302,323
     solitary techniques, 309f,310
     third-party (triadic)

attitudes about,
296-297,296t,299,301,312
techniques for,
308-312,316-318,322
Elder mistreatment. *See also* Elder
abuse
intervention programs for. *See*
Elder abuse treatment
scope of, 285-287
tolerance of, 291,292t,293-294,
298,301
Emotional distress. *See* Anxiety
Employment status. *See*
Socioeconomic status
Empowerment, for Chinese battered
women, 232,233
Endurance
of elder abuse, 310
of spousal abuse
by Chinese women,
220-221,223,227
by Mexican immigrants,
247,273-274,278
Entrepreneurial skills, as urban gang
function, 92
Environmental stimuli, in social
learning theory,
249-251,249f
Erikson's developmental stages
gang membership and, 92-93
in Western *versus* Asian culture,
163
Ethnic groups. *See also* Racial groups;
Socio-cultural context;
specific group
adolescent violence per,
47,51-56,57t-58t,60t,65-68
child abuse in, 7-8
dating violence in, 5-6
elder abuse per,
12,284-287,305-306
interventions per,
301-302,305-308
as gang formation factor, 4,73-74
as research direction, 1,3
sexual assault per, 6-7,132-137

spouse/partner abuse per, 8-9
statistical limitations of, 2-3
violence model of, 4
European Americans. *See* White
Americans
Exchange rape, 137
Exchange theory. *See* Social exchange
theory
Extramarital affairs. *See* Sexual
infidelity

Facilitators, ethnic *versus* non-ethnic,
185
Familismo, of Latino culture,
139-142,146,153-154
Family cohesion
as adolescent violence factor,
47,50,53,56-57,59-61,63
in Asian cultures,
103-105,107,219-220
Chinese spousal abuse and,
219-220,222-223,229-230
interventions for, 233-234
elder abuse and
conflict management of,
309,312-313,316
exchange theory of,
319-323,320f
gang formation and, 73-74
Family crisis intervention. *See* Crisis
intervention; Family therapy
Family relationships
adolescent violence and, 47, 50,
53, 63-64. *See also*
Adolescent violence
of battered women
Chinese, 219-220,222-223,
229-230,233-234
Mexican, 256-257,262-263,
268-269,275,279
child abuse and, 198,207-208
in Chinese culture, 219-221
elder abuse and,
286,295,295t,298,307

in Latino culture,
139-142,146,246-248
surrogate. *See* Surrogate families
of Vietnamese refugees, 162-163
disintegration of, 186-187
strains on, 163-165,173-175,
173t,174t,182
Family structure. *See* Family
relationships
Family therapy
for child abuse, 207-208
for elder abuse, 300-302,306-311
cultural modifications for,
312-323
for rape treatment, 150,153-154
for spousal abuse,
233-234,279-280
Family violence. *See* Child abuse;
Elder abuse; Spouse/partner
abuse
Fear. *See* Anxiety
Femininity, 107,122,141
Feminist views
on dating violence, 103,107
on sexual assault, 132,137-138,
140-141,147
treatment applications of,
150-151
on spousal abuse, 216,219,221,233
Filial piety, 163,214,220,286
Financial exploitation, as elder abuse,
292t,293,299
Financial restraint, as spousal abuse,
222,228,238
Forgiveness, for spousal abuse,
261-262

Gangs and gang activity
aging-out of, 88,92-93
antisocial behavior of, 73-75,80,89
of Black youths. *See* Black urban
gangs
formation model of, 73-75,80-82
illegal scope of, 79t,80,91-92

interventions programs for, 94-95
of Khmer refugee adolescents, 32
prevalence of, 72
rehabilitation dynamics of, 92-94
socio-cultural functions of,
4,71-75,82-95
violence feature of, 73,87-88,91
Gangsta image, of urban gangs, 80
Gender
as adolescent violence factor,
51-52,54-56,55t,64-65,67
dating violence per,
4-5,102,107,118,120
Gender roles
in dating behavior,
5-6,101-107,119-120,122
college student study on,
108-124
violence justification per,
115-116,115t
definitions of, 107,122
patriarchal, 103-105,221
in sexual assault,
7,132,135-141,147
spousal abuse and,
106,117,119-120
Chinese, 216,219,221
Mexican, 246,262-263
Genital contact, as sexual assault,
137,151
Genital penetration, in child abuse,
196
Government systems
as gang formation factor,
73-75,80-82
in gang rehabilitation programs,
92-94
Grade point average (GPA)
in Khmer refugee adolescents,
16,30t,31-37
violence exposure as predictor of,
33-34
Group identity, as urban gang
function, 83,88-89

Harmony
  in Asian cultures,
      103-105,107,122-123,220
  elder abuse treatment and, 301,309
  spousal abuse and,
      220,229,230,234
Harvard Trauma Questionnaire
      (HTQ), 23
Health care personnel, abuse detection
      by, 226-227,270-272
Help-seeking behavior
  in Asian culture, 104,123,166-167,
      183,219,225,229
  for child abuse, 166-167,183
      with spousal abuse, 228,238,
      262-263,274-275,278
  cultural influences on, 10-11
  for elder abuse,
      285,294,299-300,307,311
  in Latino culture, 140,147-148
  for sexual violence,
      104,123,140,147-148
  for spousal abuse
      Chinese, 218-219,222-223,
      225,227,229-230,235
      Mexican immigrants, 245-246,
      248,253,265-272,274-278
Hembrismo, in Latino culture,
      141,147
Hierarchical relationships, in Asian
      cultures, 103-105,107,122
Hispanics. *See* Latinas and Latinos
Hitting
  as child discipline,
      173,175t,177,179
  as elder abuse, 291,292t
  as spousal abuse, 257-260
Hollingshead Four Factor Index of
      Social Status, 199
Honor, as Vietnamese value, 162-163
Hostility. *See* Aggressive behaviors
Household characteristics. *See*
      Socio-demographics
Housing, elder abuse and,
      286-288,289t,321

HTQ. *See* Harvard Trauma
      Questionnaire
Humiliation. *See also* Shame
  as male violence justification,
      106-107,117,122

Immigration-related issues, of spousal
      abuse
  Chinese, 224-226,229
  Mexican, 245-248,263-264
Income. *See* Socioeconomic status
India, child abuse in, 168,180-181
Individuality
  in adolescent violence, 49-51,62
  as Western cultural notion, 105
Infidelity. *See* Sexual infidelity
Insidious trauma, 145
Instigator mentality, of spousal abuse,
      223
Institutional systems
  Black youth gangs and, 76-77
  as gang formation factor,
      73-75,80-82
Intergenerational conflict,
      ethnic/racial, 74,93,163,309
Internalization
  of rape myths, 138-139,141,146
  in social learning theory,
      249-251,249f
  spousal abuse and,
      277-278,277f
Interpersonal threat, of sexual assault,
      144-145
Intervention programs
  for adolescent violence,
      50-51,67-68
  for child abuse, 183-184,183t,
      186,206-210
  for crises. *See* Crisis intervention
  for dating violence, 104,122-124
  for early childhood, 50-51,68
  for elder abuse. *See* Elder abuse
      treatment
  for gangs and gang activity, 94-95

for sexual assault,
132-133,140,142,145-154
for spousal abuse, 10-11
of Chinese women, 215-216,
219,226-238,233-234
of Mexican immigrants,
261,270-271,278-280
women's shelters as,
225,230-232,234-235,237-238,
271-272
utilization of. *See* Help-seeking
behavior
Interviews
for adolescent violence,
25-26,52,75-78
for child abuse,
166-167,169,178-181,185
for dating violence,
120-121,134-135
for elder abuse, 290-291,316
focus group
for child abuse, 185
for dating violence studies,
120-121
for elder abuse, 285-286
for spousal abuse, 218,222
individual face-to-face
for adolescent violence survey,
25-26,52
for Black youth gang study,
75-78
for child abuse, 180-181,185
for elder abuse, 290-291
for sexual assault, 134-135
semi-structured
for child abuse,
166-167,169,178-179
for spousal abuse, 252-253
for spousal abuse,
217,217t,218,222,252-253
telephone, for spousal abuse,
217,217t
Intimacy *versus* isolation, in gang
membership, 92-93

Intimate violence. *See* Dating
violence; Spouse/partner
abuse

Japanese Americans, elder abuse by,
285-286,307
Javanese, elder abuse by, 308,310
Justification, of abuse. *See*
Normalization; Self-blame
Juvenile crime
in Black youth gang study,
76,79,81-82
research on. *See* Adolescent
violence
scope of, 48-49

Khmer refugee adolescents, survey
study of
aggressive behaviors of,
30t,31-32,36-38
findings of
academic well-being,
16,30t,31-37
behavioral well-being,
30t,31-38
mental health disorders,
30-31,30t,33,35-38
predictive correlations, 33-35
social support perceptions,
30t,32-35,37
socio-demographic, 26-27
violence exposures,
27-29,28t-30t
language considerations of,
26-27,34,37
literature review for, 17-22
associated psychosocial
sequelae, 18-22
perceived social support, 22
violence exposure rates, 17-18
mental health findings of
clinical depression,
3,17-22,30-31,30t,33,35-38

emotional distress results,
30-31,30t,35-38
post-traumatic stress disorder in,
3,17-21,30-31,30t,33,35-38
methodology of
data analysis, 26
data collection, 25-26
instrumentation, 23-25
sampling, 22-23
overview of, 3,15-17
practice implications of, 39-40
research implications of, 39-40
Kinship, adolescent violence and,
53,64
Korean Americans
elder abuse by,
285-287,298-302,307
Los Angeles study of. *See* Elder
abuse study
family relationships of, 286

LA-ECA. *See* Los Angeles
Epidemiologic Catchment
Area
LA PTSD Index. *See* Los Angeles
Posttraumatic Stress Index
Language
in child abuse studies, 166,168,
182,184,198,202,205
as ethnic generational conflict, 74
in Khmer refugee survey,
26-27,34,37
as refugee resettlement issue,
161-163,187
as research consideration,
135,166,168,182,198
as spousal abuse issue
Chinese, 224-226,228-229,
231-232,235
Mexican, 246,264,275
as urban gang identity, 89
Late starter model, of aggressive
behavior, 51
Latina/Latino child abuse,
psychological study of

findings and discussion of
anxiety, 201-205,201t
behavior problems,
201-205,201t
clinical significance of,
202-203,203t
comparative
between caretaker, parent,
and child, 204-205
with non-Latinos, 205-206
depression, 201-202,201t,205
dissociation, 201t,202-206
socio-demographic,
197-199,198t
indications for, 193-194
language considerations for,
198,202,205,208,209
literature review for, 194-196
methodology for
data analysis, 200,206
instrumentation, 198-200
sampling, 197-198,198t,
208-209
practice implications of, 206-208
purpose of, 8,196-197
research implications of, 207-210
Latina sexual assault
bicultural model of,
139-141,145-147
treatment approaches for,
151-154
characteristics of, 135
cultural variables of, 136
familism as, 141-142
gender roles as, 139-141
rape and, 136-139
socioeconomic status as,
142-143
transcending strategies for,
149-154
intervention programs for
accessibility and acceptability
of, 148
bicultural model for,
145-147,151-154

gender sensitive services,
140,142,147-149
NIMH model for, 148-149
specific services, 149-154
underutilization factors of,
140,147-148
overview of, 7,131-133,154
prevalence of, 133-136
sequelae of
security trauma as, 144-145
symptomatic responses as,
143-144
Latinas and Latinos
acculturation levels of,
135-136,140-141
sexual assault model per,
145-147,151-154
adolescent violence in. *See* Add
Health Survey
child abuse in, 8,194-196
interventions for, 206-210
psychological study on. *See*
Latina/Latino child abuse
demographics of, 244
elder abuse by, 285-287,307
familism in, 141-142,146,153-154
help-seeking behavior of,
140,147-148,245-246
matriarchal culture of,
139-142,147,153
sexual assault in. *See* Latina sexual
assault
social support for,
139-142,146,153-154
socioeconomic status of, 132-133,
136,141-143,198,199,254
spousal abuse in, 9,11. *See also*
Mexican battered women
therapeutic relationships with,
151-154
Leadership skills, as urban gang
function, 92
Learning, behavioral, social theory of,
248-251,249f
spousal abuse and, 277-278,277f
Linguistic factors. *See* Language

London, England, ethnic gang study
in, 71-95
Loneliness, of Vietnamese refugees,
172,174-175,174t,181
Los Angeles, ethnic gang study in,
71-95
Los Angeles Epidemiologic
Catchment Area (LA-ECA),
sexual assault data from,
134,135,143,145,147
Los Angeles Posttraumatic Stress
Index (LA PTSD Index), 24
Loss of face. *See* Humiliation; Saving
face
Loyalty
as Chinese value, 220-221
in elder conflict management,
309,312-313
as gender role belief,
105-107,112,117-118,121
as Vietnamese value, 162-163

Male domination
in Asian cultures,
103-105,107,122,219-221
spousal abuse as, 219,221,229,247
through rape, 132-133,137
violent forms of,
104-105,118,132,219
Marianismo, in Latino culture,
140-141,147,153
Marital abuse. *See* Spouse/partner
abuse
Marital rape, 137,151
Marital separation, with spousal
abuse, 222-223,261
Masculinity, 107,122
Matriarchal culture, of Latino
populations,
139-142,147,153
Media, for spousal abuse education,
235-236,279-280
Medical mistreatment, as elder abuse,
291,292t,293,298
Men of color, as rapists, 5-6,134

Mental health
    child abuse and, 8,194-197,
        200-207,201t,203t
    cultural perspectives of, 104
    elder abuse and, 295,295t
    perceived social support and, 17,22
    post-traumatic stress disorder
        comorbidities, 18-22
    prolonged violence and, 17,20-22
    of refugees, 160,162-165
    sexual assault and,
        7,119,133,138-139,143-145
        of children, 194-195
        interventions for,
            140,142,145-154
    spousal abuse and,
        225,257,270-272
    violence exposure as predictor of,
        33-34
Mental health services. *See*
        Intervention programs
Mexican-Americans
    child abuse by,
        196,262-263,274-275,278
    elder abuse by, 287
    sexual assault by,
        7,134-135,138,146,257-258
    spousal abuse by, 9,245
        in immigrants. *See* Mexican
        battered women
    urban gangs of, 73-74
Mexican battered women, study of
    church affiliations of,
        247,263,269-270,274,280
    counseling for,
        261,270-271,278-280
    cultural context of,
        245-248,262-263,273-275
    findings and discussion of
        on attitudes,
            260-262,273-274,277-278
        on conceptual model,
            277-278,277f
        cultural factors,
            262-263,273-275

family abuse background,
        256-257
    help-seeking, 265-266,274-278
    help sources, 266-272
    on perceptions,
        257-260,273-274
    personal abuse experiences,
        257,276
    police intervention,
        260-262,266-267
    psycho-social stressors,
        263-265,273-275,278
    socio-demographic,
        254,255t-256t,256,275
help-seeking behavior by, 245-246,
        248,253,265-272,274-278
immigration-related issues of,
        245-248,263-264
language issues of, 246,264,275
limitations of, 280-281
literature review for, 245-248
methodology for
    data analysis, 253-254
    instrumentation, 251-253
    sampling, 251
practice implications of, 278-280
psycho-social stressors in,
        247-248,263-265,273-275,278
purpose of, 244,248
reporting to authorities,
        260-262,266-267
social learning theory in,
        248-251,249f,277-278,277f
social support for, 265,267-272,275
women's shelters for, 271-272,280
Minority demographics. *See also*
        specific minority
Census Bureau predictions on, 103
Minority models. *See also specific*
        minority group
    of child abuse, 7-8,161,163-165
    of dating violence, 103,118-119
    of elder abuse, 12,285-287,305-308
    of gang socialization, 71-74,80-82
    of sexual assault, 133-136
    of spousal abuse, 9-10

Modeling processes, in social learning
 theory, 249f,250-251
 spousal abuse and, 277-278,277f
Mood disorders
 as adolescent response to trauma,
  21-22
 from child abuse, 195
Moore's model, of gang formation,
  73-75,80-81,88
Motivation therapy, for Chinese
  battered women,
  230-231,234
Multisystemic Therapy (MST), for
  child abuse, 207-208
Music, as urban gang identity, 80,89

Nagging, as violence justification,
  112,117-118,121
National Center for the Prevention and
  Control of Rape (NCPCR),
  148
National Family Violence Resurvey
  (1985), 9
National Institute of Mental Health
  (NIMH), rape crisis program
  of, 148-149
National Study of Adolescent Health,
  4
 Wave 1. *See* Add Health Survey
National Survey of Families and
  Households, 8
National Youth Survey, 64-65
Neglect. *See* Physical neglect;
  Psychological neglect
Neutralization technique, for elder
  abuse, 312
Non-physical abuse, of spouse,
  258-259
Non-verbal abuse, of elders
 conflict avoidance as,
  308-311,309f
 neglect as, 285-286,292t,293,
  299,307
Normalization, of spousal abuse
 Chinese, 220-223,227

Mexican, 247,273-274,276,278
Normative rape, 137

Obedience
 as Chinese value, 220-221
 as gender role,
  105,107,112,117-118,121
 as Vietnamese value, 162-163
Obligation issues
 in elder abuse, 319-323,320f
 in spousal abuse, 247
Orthogonal Cultural Identification
  Scale (OCIS), 25
Overseas violence
 as adolescent outcome predictor,
  33-35
 Khmer refugee adolescents
  response to
  literature review of, 16-22
  survey results, 28,28t,30t,37-39

Parental control, adolescent violence
  and, 47,50,53-56,64
Parenting skills
 child abuse and, 207
 disciplinary. *See* Discipline
 elder abuse and,
  295-296,295t,299,310
Partner abuse. *See* Spouse/partner
  abuse
Patriarchal culture, of Asian
  populations,
  103-105,107,162-163,221
Peers, adolescent violence and,
  38,47,50,62,67
Penetration. *See* Genital penetration
Perceived Social Support from Family
  (PSS-Fa), 25,33
Perceived Social Support from Friends
  (PSS-Fr), 25,33
Perceptions
 of battered women,
  228,238,257-260,273-274
 of dating violence

by Chinese Americans,
110-116,111t-112t,114t,
119-120
by college students,
5-6,101-108,122-124
of elder abuse
cultural context of,
12,285-287,300-302,305-308
of perpetrators, 294-296,295t
professional *versus* public,
283-287
of social support, by Khmer
refugees, 25,30t,32-33
Perceptions of and Attitudes Toward
Dating Violence
Questionnaire, 108
Perpetration, statistical influences on,
2-3,5
Perseverance, in Chinese spousal
abuse, 220-221
Personal rights, as Western cultural
notion, 105
Personal Risk Behaviors Scale
(PRBS), 24
Personal security. *See* Security
Personalismo, in Latino culture,
152,207
Personality disorders, from child
abuse, 203,205
Physical abuse
of children, 194-197
cultural context of, 7-8
in dating violence, 110-117,124
of elders, 285-287,291,292t,
293,298,307
psychological consequences of,
195
with sexual assault, 144
of spouses,
252-253,256-260,273,276
Physical constraint, as elder abuse,
291,292t,300-301
Physical discipline, as child abuse,
163-164,177,179-182

Physical neglect, as elder abuse,
285-286,292t,293-294,
300-301
Picture vocabulary test, in adolescent
survey, 52
Police intervention, for spousal abuse,
226,237,260-262,266-267
Political activities, urban gang
involvement in, 92-94
Post-Traumatic Stress Disorder
(PTSD)
from child abuse, 195,205,208
comorbid disorders with, 18-22
in foreign refugees, 162
in Khmer refugee adolescents,
3,17-21,30-31,30t,33,35-38
from prolonged violence, 18-21
Potential power, in elder abuse,
320f,321-323
Power
as elder abuse issue, 319-323,320f
as spousal abuse issue, 219-221,
224-225,229,232,247
types of, 320-321
Power balance, in elder abuse
treatment, 319-323,320f
Pragmatism, for Chinese battered
women, 228,231
PRBS. *See* Personal Risk Behaviors
Scale
Prevalence rates
cross-cultural comparisons of, 1
per violence. *See specific abuse or
group*
Prevention programs
for adolescent violence, 3
for spousal abuse, 236
Privacy, as Vietnamese value,
163,178-179,184,187
Privilege sanctions, as child
discipline, 173,175t,176
Problem resolution. *See also* Conflict
management
in elder abuse, 300,308-311,309f
in spousal abuse, 228,231-234

Problems with people. *See*
    Relationship problems
Protective services
    for elder abuse, 300-302,318,321
    for spousal abuse,
        260-262,266-267
PSS-Fa. *See* Perceived Social Support
    from Family
PSS-Fr. *See* Perceived Social Support
    from Friends
Psycho-social stressors
    of Mexican battered women,
        247-248,263-265,273-275,278
    with refugee adjustments,
        160,162-165
Psychological abuse
    in dating violence, 110-117,124
    in elder abuse,
        285-287,298,314-315
    with sexual assault, 143-145
Psychological neglect, as elder abuse,
        285-286,292t,293,299,307
    assessment of, 314-315
Psychological outcomes. *See* Mental
        health
PTSD. *See* Post-Traumatic Stress
        Disorder
Public policy, information sources for,
        1-3
Punishment power
    in elder abuse, 320f,321
    in spousal abuse, 276-277
Punitive rape, 137
Pushing, as spousal abuse, 257-259

Questionnaires
    for adolescent violence, 52
    for child abuse,
        166,199-200,204-205
    for dating violence,
        108-109,115,118,121
    for elder abuse, 290-291

Racial discrimination. *See* Racism
Racial groups. *See also* Socio-cultural
        context; *specific group*
    adolescent violence per,
        47,51-56,57t-58t,60t,65-68
    dating violence in, 5
    elder abuse per, 12,285-287
    sexual assault per, 6-7,132-136
    spousal abuse per, 8-10
    statistical limitations of, 2-3
    urban gang socialization of,
        4,71-95
Racial marginality, urban. *See* Gangs
        and gang activity
Racism
    as gang formation factor,
        74-75,80-82,93
    in sexual assault, 141,146-147
        as reporting deterrent, 134,147
Rape
    ethnographic types of,
        137-139,150-151
    as regulated, 132,137
    as violence. *See* Sexual assault
Rape crisis intervention
    cognitive behavioral therapy as,
        151-153
    counseling as, 142,149-150
    family focus of, 150
    feminist and ethnic psychologies,
        150-151
    for Latino culture,
        140,142,145-154
    NIMH model program for, 148-149
    research focus of, 132-133
Rape myths
    ethnographic assessment of,
        137-139
    internalization of, 138-139,141,146
    in Latino culture,
        132-133,135-136,139,146
        transcending strategies for,
        149-154
Rape survivors
    coping factors of, 119,133,138,
        139,143,145,147

security trauma dimensions in, 144-145
symptomatic responses of, 143-144
Rastafarian identity, of urban gangs, 80,89
RCMAS. *See* Revised Children's Manifest Anxiety Scale
Reality orientation
in elder abuse treatment, 315-316
insidious trauma impact on, 145
Refugee Resettlement Program, 161-162,187
Refugees
conflict resolution among, 181-182
Khmer. *See* Khmer refugee adolescents
language issues of, 161-162,163,187
psycho-social adjustments for, 160,162-165
resettlement programs for, 161-162,187
Southeast Asia. *See* Vietnamese refugees
trauma experiences of, 3,16-18,160-163
Regulated rape, 132,137
Rehabilitation, of ethnic gangs, 92-94
Reinforcement, in social learning theory, 249f,250-251
Relationship problems, of Vietnamese refugees, 174,174t,176
Religion, spousal abuse and, 247,263,269-270,274,280
Reporting
of elder abuse, 296-297,296t,301,306-307
of sexual assaults, 133-136,147
of spousal abuse
by Chinese women, 218-219, 228-231,234-236,238
by Mexican immigrants, 260-262,266-267
in surveys. *See* Self-reports
Repression, of elder abuse, 309,309f
Research strategies, 1,3

for adolescent violence, 3,47-48
for child abuse, 182-186,207-210
for dating violence, 120-122
for elder abuse, 302
language considerations in, 135,166,168,182,198
for refugee adolescents, 39-40
for sexual assault, 132-135
Resettlement program, for foreign refugees, 161-162,187
Respeto, in Latino culture, 152
Restraining orders
for elder abuse, 318
for spousal abuse, 261
Revised Children's Manifest Anxiety Scale (RCMAS), 200,201-205,201t,203t
Reward power, in elder abuse, 320-321,320f
Rewards, in social learning theory, 249f,250-251
Rigidity levels, of Vietnamese refugees, 174,174t,176,181
Risky behaviors. *See also specific behavior*
adolescent examples of, 4,32

Sacrificing
elder abuse *versus,* 314,318
spousal abuse *versus,* 223,247
Safety planning
for elder abuse, 291,293-294,300,318,321
for spousal abuse, 226,251. *See also* Women's shelters
Sampling methods. *See also specific study*
variations in, 4,5,120
Satru. *See* Silence
Saving face
as male violence justification, 106-107,117,122
spousal abuse and, 220-223,227,229,234
by Vietnamese refugees, 187

SCECV. *See* Survey of Children's
    Exposure to Community
    Violence
School systems
    as predictor of adolescent violence,
        47,50-51
    social support role of, 39-40
    spousal abuse education through,
        270-272,280
Security
    sexual assault trauma to, 144-145
    as urban gang function, 86,90-91
Self-actualization. *See* Self-identity
Self-assertiveness, spousal abuse and,
        223,230
Self-blame
    for elder abuse,
        295-296,295t,299,310
    in sexual assault,
        135-136,138-139,141-142
        treatment approaches to,
            146,150,152-153
    for spousal abuse, 222-223,260
Self-care, as sexual assault therapy,
        152-154
Self-defense
    against spousal abuse, 260-261
    as violence justification, 106,118
Self-disclosure
    of child abuse, 199-200,206,208
    for establishing trust, 183-185
Self-esteem/self-image
    Latina sexual assault and,
        133,140-141,146,151
    as urban gang function, 84,89-90
Self-generated stimuli, in social
        learning theory,
        249-251,249f
Self-identity
    Asian culture inhibition of,
        162-163,219-220
    collective *versus* individual,
        219-223,312-313,317,319,323
    elder abuse and,
        312-313,317,319,323

exchange theory of,
        319-323,320f
    spousal abuse and, 219-223
    as urban gang function, 83,88-89
Self-removal, with elder abuse,
        310,318-319
Self-reports
    on adolescent violence, 2,52
    on child abuse, 199-200,206,208
    on dating violence, 108-109
SES. *See* Socioeconomic status
Sex roles
    rape myth internalization and,
        138-139,141
    as rape reporting deterrent,
        135-136
    spousal abuse and, 219,222-223
Sexual abuse
    of children, 194-195,197-198,203
    ethnographic survey of, 136-139
    of spouse, 222,257-258
Sexual assault
    coping mechanisms for,
        119,133,138-139,145,147
    in children,
        194-195,200-206,201t,203t
    during courting. *See* Dating
        violence
    cultural context of,
        6-7,124,131-133,135-136
    ethnographic types of,
        136-139,150-151
    fear of, as oppression, 132-133
    feminist views on,
        132,137-138,140-141,147
    gender role beliefs and,
        7,117,119-120,132,136-142,
        147
    help-seeking behavior for,
        104,123,140,147-148
    intervention programs for,
        140,142,145-154
    in Latino culture. *See* Latina sexual
        assault
    prevalence of, 6,132-136

reporting inconsistencies with,
133-136,147
research on
confounding variables in, 135
strategies for, 134-135
sequelae of, 119,138,144-145
Sexual dysfunction, as rape sequelae,
143-144
Sexual Experiences Survey, 134
Sexual infidelity, as violence
justification,
106,107,112,117
Sexual rituals, 137
Sexual violence. *See* Dating violence;
Sexual assault
Sexuality beliefs. *See* Sex roles
Shame. *See also* Humiliation
as cultural notion, 105,300,313
with elder abuse, 300, 313
with sexual assault, 139
with spousal abuse,
222-223,227,229
Silence, elder abuse and, 307-309
Skill-training structures, for urban
gangs, 91-95
Social activities, as urban gang
function, 85,90
Social attitudes
behavioral link to, 106
on gender. *See* Gender roles; Sex
roles
Social class. *See* Socioeconomic
status
Social exchange theory
of dating violence, 104,119
in elder abuse treatment,
306,320-323,320f
principles of, 319-320,320f
Social harmony. *See* Harmony
Social identity, as urban gang
function, 83,88-89
Social isolation
of Chinese battered women,
223-225,232
intimacy *versus*, in gang
membership, 92-93

Social learning theory, in spousal
abuse, 248-251,249f,
277-278,277f
Social marginality, urban. *See* Gangs
and gang activity
Social mobility
of Asian college students, 120
gangs as vehicle for,
74,84,86-87,89,91-95
Social services. *See* Intervention
programs
Social structure, as urban gang
function, 85,90-94
Social support
elder abuse and, 321-323
of Latino populations,
139-142,146,153-154
perceived
adolescent coping per,
17,22,39-40
of Khmer refugee adolescents,
30t, 32-35,37
measurement tools for, 25
schools' role in, 39-40
spousal abuse and
Chinese, 223-225,232,234
Mexican, 265,267-272,275
as urban gang function, 85-86,90
for Vietnamese refugees, 162-165,
168,170t,171-172,186-187
Socialization factors
in adolescent violence,
4,47,49-51,62-68
in Asian cultures, 103-105,107
of Black youth, 4,71-75,82-95
Socio-cultural context. *See also* Ethnic
groups; Racial groups
of child abuse,
7-8,161-165,186-187
of child-rearing practices, 7-8
of corporal punishment,
7-8,169,179-180
of dating violence, 5-6,101-108,
111,111t,113-118,114t-115t,
122-124

of elder abuse,
  12,285-287,300-302,305-308
of help-seeking behavior, 10-11
of physical abuse, 7-8
as research direction, 1,3
of sexual assault,
  6-7,131-133,135-139
of spousal abuse, 8-11,103-107,117
  Chinese, 216,219-221,236,244
  Mexican immigrants,
    245-248,262-263,273-275
of therapeutic relationships,
  149-154
of urban gang formation,
  4,71-75,82-95
of Vietnamese refugee adjustment,
  160,162,168,178-179,182-187
Socio-demographics
of adolescent violence,
  47-51,53-56,55t,64-68
in Black youth gang study,
  76-79,78t
of Chinese battered women,
  218-219,224-225
in dating violence study,
  109-110,110t
in elder abuse study, 288,289t,290
of Khmer refugee adolescents,
  26-27
in Latino child abuse study,
  197-199,198t
of Mexican battered women,
  254,255t-256t,256,275
of Vietnamese child abuse,
  160-161,165,169,170t,171,
  177-178
Socioeconomic status (SES)
of Black youth, 73-75,76,78,80-81
  gangs as vehicle for,
    84,86-87,89,91-95
elder abuse and, 292t,293,299,321
of Latinas, sexual assault and,
  132-133,136,141-143,146-147
spousal abuse and,
  218-219,224-225,244,264-265

of Vietnamese refugees,
  161-165,168
Somatic outcomes, of spousal abuse,
  227,270-272
Southeast Asian refugees. See
  Vietnamese refugees
Spanking. See Hitting
Speaking. See Talking
Spiritual threat, of sexual assault,
  144-145
Spiritualists, 272
Spousal role reversal, as abuse factor,
  224-225
Spouse/partner abuse
in Asian cultures,
  103-105,107,217t,218
blame for, 222-223
by Chinese Americans, 215-238
coping mechanisms for
  of Chinese women,
    220-221,223,227
  of Mexican immigrants,
    247,273-274,278
cultural context of,
  8-11,103-107,117
  Chinese, 216,219-221,236,244
  Mexican,
    245-248,262-263,273-275
gender roles and, 106,117,119-120,
  219,221,246,262
help-seeking behavior for
  with child abuse,
    228,238,262-263,274-275,278
  by Chinese women, 218-219,
    222-223,225,227,229-230,235
  by Mexican immigrants,
    245-246,248,253,265-272,
    274-278
intervention programs for, 10-11
  Chinese, 215-216,226-238
  Mexican, 261,270-271,278-280
language issues of,
  224-232,235,246,264,275
as male domination,
  219,221,229,247
by Mexican immigrants, 243-281

police intervention
  for,260-262,266-267
prevalence of, 8-9,216,244-245
reporting to authorities
  by Chinese women,
    218-219,228-231,234-236,238
  by Mexican immigrants,
    260-262,266-267
safety planning for, 225,226,
    230-232,234-235,237-238
shame with, 222-223,227,229
social learning theory in,
    248-251,249f,277-278,277f
theories of, 10-11,106
women's shelters for, 225,230-232,
    234-235,237-238,271-272
Statistical analysis programs
  SPSS, in trauma response analysis,
    26
  SUDAAN, in adolescent violence
    survey, 54
Statistics
  limitations of, 2
  sources of, 2-3,4,5
Status rape, 137
Stereotypic generalizations, sources
  of, 1
Stimuli, in social learning theory,
  249-251,249f
Submission, in Chinese spousal abuse,
  220-221
Substance abuse
  elder abuse and, 295,295t
  spousal abuse and,
    225,257,270-272
  violence association with,
    3,19,50,67
Suffering
  elder abuse *versus*, 314,318,322
  spousal abuse *versus*, 223
Support networks. *See* Social support
Surrogate families
  in foreign refugee communities,
    163
  as urban gang function,
    83-84,89,93-94

Survey of Children's Exposure to
  Community Violence
  (SCECV), 23
Survivor mentality, of spousal abuse,
  223,232
Symbols, as urban gang identity, 79,89

Talking
  as child discipline,
    173,175t,176-177,179
  elder abuse and, 307,308-310. *See
    also* Verbal abuse
Telephone counseling, of Chinese
  battered women, 232-233
Theft rape, 137
Therapeutic relationships
  with Asian refugees, 183-184,183t
  with Chinese battered
    women,22-233
  with Latino populations,
    151-154,206-208
  socio-cultural context of, 149-154
  triadic, in conflict management,
    308-311
  Western *versus* ethnic values in,
    149-150,309-310
Third-party interventions
  for elder abuse. *See* Elder abuse
    treatment
  for spousal abuse,
    226-233,260-262,266-267,
    270-271,278-280
Thought stopping, as child abuse
  therapy, 208
Threats, as child discipline,
  173,175t,177
Toleration, as coping mechanism. *See*
  Endurance
Transactional model, of adolescent
  violence, 47,49-51,62-68
Transitional socioeconomic structure,
  for urban gangs, 93-94
Trauma
  adolescent rationalization of, 19-20
  insidious, 145

mental health effects of, 18-19. *See also* Depression; Post-Traumatic Stress Disorder

prolonged, outcomes of, 17-22

refugees' experience with. *See* Overseas violence; U.S. violence

sexual assault dimensions of, 143-145

Trauma Symptom Check List for Children, 207

Triangulation, as spousal abuse issue, 221

Trust, as Vietnamese research issue, 178-179,181,183-184

Turf wars, of urban gangs, 80,86,90

Unhappiness, of Vietnamese refugees, 174,174t,176,181

Urban gangs

ethnic study of. *See* Black urban gangs

socio-cultural context of, 4,71-75,82-95

Urban violence

adolescent response to, 3,9,18-22

marginally-based. *See* Gangs and gang activity

U.S. Census Bureau

minority demographic predictions of, 103

poverty thresholds of, 171,178

U.S. Refugee Act (1980), 161-162,187

U.S. violence

as adolescent outcome predictor, 33-35

Khmer refugee adolescents response to

literature review of, 17-22

survey results, 28,29t-30t,37-39

sexual assault culture in, 132

Verbal abuse

of elders, 291,292t,293-294,298,301

of spouse, 222,258

Victim-blame

in elder abuse, 295-296,295t,299

in sexual assault, 138-139,141-142

treatment approaches to, 146,150,152-153

Victimization

dating violence and, 107,115,119

in elder abuse, 295-296,295t,299,309

sexual. *See* Sexual abuse; Sexual assault

statistical influences on, 2-3,5

Vietnamese child abuse, pilot project on

demographics of, 160

findings and discussion of

adjustment to U.S., 168,172,173t,178-179

comparative

between children and parents, 176-177,180

between studies, 179-182

discipline methods, 169,173, 175t,176-177,179-180

English proficiency, 168,171,178

potential for child abuse, 169,173,174t,179-182

reasons for leaving Vietnam, 172,172t,178

socio-demographic, 168-169,170t,171,177-178

support network, 168,170t-171t,171-172

language considerations for, 166,168,182,184

methodology for

data collection, 169

instrumentation, 166-168,184-186

operationalization of variables,
   168-169
sampling, 165-166
overview of, 7-8
practice implications of,
   183-184,183t,186
research implications of, 182-186
resettlement significance to,
   161-165,186-187
Vietnamese refugees
acculturation of, 162-165,182,186
child abuse among, 7-8,163-165
   intervention programs for,
      183-184,183t,186
   pilot study on. *See* Vietnamese
      child abuse
children of, 163,165
demographics of, 160-161,165,
   169,170t,171,177-178
discipline methods of,
   163-164,169,173,175t
   per children *versus* parents,
      176-177
family structure of, 162-163,165
   disintegration of, 186-187
   strains on, 163-165,173-176,
      173t,174t,182
psycho-social adjustment of,
   160,162,168,178-179,182-187
   anxiety as,
      162,174-176,174t,181
   ego strength, 174-175,174t
   loneliness as,
      172,174-175,174t,181
   rigidity levels, 174,174t,176,181
   unhappiness, 174,174t,176,181
research strategies for, 182-186
resettlement of, 161-162,186-187
socioeconomic status of,
   161-165,168
support networks for, 162-165,
   168,170t,171-172,186-187
Violence
in communities. *See* Adolescent
   violence; Urban violence
foreign. *See* Overseas violence

in the home. *See* Child abuse; Elder
   abuse; Spouse/partner abuse
national. *See* U.S. violence
sexual. *See* Dating violence;
   Sexual assault
in youth. *See* Adolescent violence

War traumas
adolescent response to,
   18-19,20-22,37-39
in Khmer refugees, 3,15-40
in Vietnamese refugees, 160-163
West Indians, urban gang socialization
   of, 71-95
White Americans
adolescent violence in, 2. *See also*
   Add Health Survey
child abuse by, 196
dating violence of, 5-6,101-124
elder abuse by,
   12,285-287,298,301,306-307
   Los Angeles study of. *See* Elder
      abuse study
sexual assault by,
   6-7,132,138,139,144,146
spousal abuse by, 9
Wife battering
cultural context of,
   10-11,104,105,117
per ethnic group. *See* Chinese
   battered women; Mexican
   battered women
Women of color, sexual assault of,
   132-134,136,138-139,145.
   See also Latina sexual assault
Women's shelters
ethno-specific, 237-238
grassroots efforts for, 234-235
utilization factors of
   Chinese women, 225,230-232
   Mexican immigrants,
      271-272,280

Youth violence. *See* Adolescent
   violence